Robert
Murray

The Split
Australian
Labor
in the
Fifties

Cheshire

SBN 7015 0504 4
© Robert Murray 1970
First published 1970
Printed in Australia for
F. W. Cheshire Publishing Pty Ltd
346 St Kilda Road, Melbourne
142 Victoria Road, Marrickville, NSW
at The Griffin Press, Adelaide
Registered in Australia
for transmission by post as a book.

Acknowledgments

Information for *The Split* came from many sources. The daily press provided a basic, continuing background to work from and also the only records in existence of many events. I worked principally from the Melbourne *Age* and *Sydney Morning Herald*, but also consulted the files of other newspapers selectively, particularly for reports of important events. I read the files from the first copies until the end of the period of *News Weekly* and *The Catholic Worker* and, more selectively, the files of various communist, Labor, left and Catholic publications.

The conference and executive minutes and other records of the Victorian Branch of the ALP until 1955, which are in the possession of the Democratic Labor Party office in Melbourne, were the source of much previously unpublished material. I am indebted to the DLP officers for making them available freely and often. I am also indebted to the officers of the Victorian Trades Hall Council for making their records available to me. I used the official published reports of all the ALP Federal conferences from 1951 until 1957 and Mr E. G. Whitlam's staff helped me obtain them. Father Paul Duffy's thesis, 'Catholic Judgments on the ALP Dispute', was another source of otherwise unpublished material and I am grateful for his permission to draw on it. The election results are mostly from *A Handbook of Australian Government and Politics, 1890-1964*, by Colin A. Hughes and B. D. Graham.

There were few other consolidated sources of material, but Leicester Webb's *Communism and Democracy in Australia* was useful in writing the chapter on the *Communist Party Dissolution Bill* and Clem Lack's *Three Decades of Queensland Politics* was an important source for the chapter on the Queensland split. References to these and other books consulted are contained in footnotes and the bibliography. The quotations from Parliamentary speeches are nearly all from the appropriate *Hansard*, which I read comprehensively.

My own recollection of events was very much through the eyes of fascinated youth, but I think it helped me understand the emotional feeling of the time and heightened my interest.

The Split is essentially based on other people's recollections, however. I interviewed or had more informal conversations with dozens of people and visited all states in the search for information. I was able to 'cross check' most points by consulting people who saw them from differing

positions. Almost everybody I asked was willing to help supply information and some also helped me with a variety of documents and records; I
am most grateful to them all. I interviewed most of them between 1964
and 1968, when passions had cooled somewhat, but memories were only
beginning to fade. Some helped further by reading the manuscript. I
am sure that a history of these events based entirely on written records
would be less accurate and full than one supplemented by comprehensive
interviews.

A portrait of a political party in trouble is never likely to be attractive.
Since this story is mainly about the Labor Party, I have mentioned the
other parties only in passing. I did not think it necessary to point out in
the text, to give a spurious 'balance', that the other parties and the
employer and business organisations also have their unattractive aspects.

R.M.

Melbourne, July 1970

Contents

Part
One

Chapter One
A Party for the People

In the autumn of 1954, hundreds of thousands of eager and confident Australians looked forward to the election of the Australian Labor Party as the National Government. The party had spent five and a half years in Opposition.

The Liberal and Country Party coalition government led by Robert Menzies had presided over the worst inflationary period in Australian memory, after a promise in 1949 to 'put value back into the pound'. In 1952, the first of the post-war recessions, though brief, had produced noticeable unemployment for the first time since 1940. Development of social services for the weak and the struggling had stagnated. In the name of a free market economy, several publicly owned enterprises had been sold back to private enterprise.

State elections and public opinion polls over the two previous years had shown that the political 'pendulum' was swinging back to Labor, the party of social welfare, economic planning and public enterprise. Labor had gone out of office in December 1949, with the votes of only 46·9 per cent of electors behind it. However, at the depth of the 1952 recession, the polls were showing well over 50 per cent of voters favouring Labor. Though the tide had started running out again by 1954, slightly more than 50 per cent were still for Labor.

The Labor Party which went apparently united and confident to the polls on 29 May 1954 received 50·03 per cent of the votes; but small differences in a handful of electorates prevented it from winning a majority of seats. A year later, the party was torn by the greatest split in its turbulent history.

In one sense, the Labor Party was a victim of a changing nation. In the early 1950's, Australia was at a critical stage of transition from the semi-colonial and predominantly agricultural society of the first half of the twentieth century to the more independent, industrialised and complex society that emerged after about 1955.

When the Chifley Labor Government was defeated at the end of 1949, the great immigration program had barely started, the motor and chemical industries were in their infancy. The cities of Australia and their sprawls of suburban hinterland had changed little in appearance since the 1930's. The great depression was only fifteen years away in time, the Second World War a mere four years. Both these historic visitations still crushed on the spirit of the people and, despite official rhetoric to the contrary, foreboding rather than optimism coloured feelings about the future.

The change brought by the five years 1949-54 was astonishing. The shortages and strikes of the post-war years had ended and a broad industrial base had developed. Australia had absorbed, with no apparent difficulty, half a million migrants from half a hundred countries since the war. The first of the 'stop-go' recessions had passed, despite its electoral impact on the Menzies Government, without causing mass unemployment on the scale of the inter-war years and without growing into a depression. The Korean War had remained short and 'limited'. Confidence that man could reasonably look forward to a world without global wars alternating with economic catastrophe had returned. Vast new rings of post-war houses surrounded every city and glassy skyscrapers were beginning to rise in the city centres. The problems of the 'affluent society' were too new and too little understood to cause concern.

Between the defeats of 1949 and 1954, Labor had held the heady but unjustified belief that it was the 'natural government' of Australia. With more justification, it felt that its administration from 1941 to 1949 had solved, or at least mitigated, the greatest problems of pre-war Australia, and had laid the foundations of the new prosperity which was depriving it of power. The party's mood predominantly was of hunger for a return to office combined with pique against an electorate which kept it out; of nostalgia for the golden 1940's and unwillingness to understand the 1950's. One can guess at many reasons for Labor's failure to win national office in the 1950's, but it rarely looked like a party at home with the era.

The human failings of nostalgia and pique were reinforced by sixty years of history as a party which despised intellectuality and doctrines and believed supremely in the efficacy of a feeling in the pit of the stomach for social reform. Yet it is doubtful if Labor was ever as free of doctrines as it liked to think, or as doctrinaire foreign observers often portrayed it. Its characteristic refutation of doctrine was in itself a doctrine of great importance; but there was also a Marxist fringe from the start, and the writings of European, American and (very occasionally) Australian radicals had an erratic but continuing effect. What is truer is that, reflecting the fledgling and recently pioneer society from which it was derived, Labor did not understand doctrines. The occasional penetration of new ideas, mostly from the left but occasionally from the right, was apt to have a more damaging effect than it deserved because of the hollowness at the centre. Labor had to rely on inertia and commonsense, both of which it had in abundance, more than a well-established body of practical ideas to protect it from the pacifism and revolutionary ardour of the First World War era and from the often hysterical patriotism on the right—but it suffered gravely in doing so. Though here the Australian Labor Party was not alone, it had no answer to the Great Depression and suffered again from the pedlars of quack remedies. Hardly had the splits of the 1930's healed, when the party was once again beset by ideologies which were again an expression of the yearnings of the time, but with which it was little equipped to cope.

Australian Labor's style was overwhelmingly rhetorical and emotional. It was a party for the people, of words and passion, not careful thought, of conformity in the name of unity rather than original ideas. Unlike the few best-ordered of the world's electorally successful social democratic parties, it had little ability to absorb intellectuality into the social forces driving it.

The great split of 1954-57 was about power and personalities rather than ideology, but it was nevertheless ideology which formed the tense background against which this most complex and damaging of Australian schisms opened. Where ideas were discussed, they tended to become weapons in faction fights—in a political tradition that spread far beyond Australian Labor.

Despite the superficial unity, attained after a period of division and proclaimed on all sides, the Australian Labor Party which Dr Herbert Vere Evatt led to the polls in the autumn of 1954 contained many deep and threatening internal contradictions and suppressed personal animosities. In one view, there was nothing new about this; Labor had always been a coalition of forces and both warm and embittered human emotions came more naturally to it than to the cooler conservative parties. What this view missed, however, was the complexity and depth of the forces working divisively in the party.

Australian Labor was one of the oldest of the world's social democratic parties, and the first to win office. Its formation in the 1890's had been rushed, an emergency response to deteriorating economic conditions. It was envisaged simply as a political arm of the organised Trade Union Movements long established in the six colonies. This was an obvious and convenient form of organisation, and when Federation came in 1901 Labor organised loosely for national issues with an Interstate Political Labor Conference and Executive.

Though the proportions varied from state to state and from time to time, the trade unions usually sent of the order of two thirds of the delegates to the annual or triennial state conferences, the supreme bodies of each state. The branch membership, perhaps 70,000 or so in the mid-1950's, sent the minority of delegates. This arrangement gave the parliamentarians and branch rank and file a low status, compared to most political parties; but it did accurately reflect the enthusiasm felt for Labor, the party of equality and a 'fair go', by a far wider population than the branch faithful. Labor was the only Australian party that regularly received more than 50 per cent of the vote.

The form of organisation meant that the roots of the Australian Labor Party lay in the Trades Halls of the six state capital cities. Although in theory ultimate power lay with the hundreds of thousands of members of unions affiliated with political Labor, the real power lay with the bureaucracies of the Trades Halls. Most typically, the successful Trades Hall bureaucrats were self-made men with all the vices of the self-made of

their era: proud, often autocratic, defensive against those of more fortunate origins, fearful of a return to their own origins, almost irrationally
hating the merest suggestion of interference. A rare humanitarian spirit, of
love of service and justice, existed side by side with some thoroughly unpleasant examples of human nature at work. Colouring the whole mixture
was more than the Trade Union Movement deserved of narrow, short-
sighted thinking, muddled work and incompetence.

More often than not, the Trades Halls were riven into feuding factions
by deep social forces. Most typically, the divisions were between the practical men, the pragmatic union traditionalists who tended to be manipulated by events, and the zealots and ideologues, manipulated by Marxism
and other set ideologies. But while these were common basic forces, many
more mundane issues and rivalries complicated, aggravated and often
overlay them.

The demands of the industrial wing of Labor were usually so pressing
and so concerned with daily life that they took precedence over the
concerns of the political wing. Often this would be expressed by the comparative apathy of most industrialists towards political Labor; then the
pendulum would swing and the political wing, as the alternative Trades
Hall power base, would be swept into the affairs of the industrial wing.

These conflicts between the political and industrial wings were a recurring pattern in Australian Labor, especially in the bigger states, from the
start. They tended to flow into and exaggerate and distort the conflicts,
natural to any party, in the political wing itself. The complexity of the
Labor power structure, covering so many interests and so apt to touch
off power struggles, had a stultifying effect in that it discouraged change
and individuality. By the early 1950's, it had caused three disastrous splits
in sixty years, and the memory of these reinforced the instinct for stifling
conformity. In 1954, the greatest of all these splits was building up
throughout the maze of ALP centres of power.

The Federal Parliamentary Labor Party which Dr Evatt led to defeat on
29 May 1954 appeared, in contrast with the organisational 'machine' of
the party, to be reasonably united. It could be broadly described, in retrospect, as comprising three factions: left, centre and right. At the time,
however, these were hardly apparent. There were often disagreements and
groupings in the Caucus, but these were largely ephemeral, based on passing issues and personalities. Evatt's leadership was not much admired by
any section, but all accepted it as the best available.

The left wing of the Parliamentary Party at that time, in as far as it
could be distinguished, was made up predominantly of men whose political style was derived from the militant, bombastic left of the 1920's and
1930's which had developed mainly in New South Wales and got its
style from men like the depression-era State Premier, J. T. Lang. Its most
influential figure in Caucus in 1954 was Edward John Ward, a harsh, vain,
but curiously attractive man whose gift for demagogic oratory earned him
a reputation as the 'Firebrand of East Sydney', the title of the biography

that appeared after he died in 1963. Most other left-wingers in the Caucus followed the same style, and a 'style' it was rather than a coherent set of ideas: bombast against the rich, the employers and the imperialists, bombast in favour of the poor and downtrodden, bombast in Caucus meetings against the established leadership of the Labor Movement. Its scale of values, it seemed, often saw little difference between nationalising banks and refusing to wear a dinner suit.

Rhetorical and empty as this style seemed to a new generation, it had a natural place in the Labor Movement of the middle years of the century, expressing the militant, resentful feeling of many an Australian working man. Ward and some of his followers were also, in their way, men of exceptional ability; Ward was one of Chifley's best administrators. Off stage, many were surprised to find him a far more moderate, responsible figure than they expected.

Along with this form of left, a second left could be seen emerging to take its place in the Labor Movement; this was cooler and less class-conscious in style, more influenced by Marxism and a passing sympathy for communist societies, romantic about the possibilities for revolution in the emerging countries of Asia, Africa and Latin America rather than a class war at home. In 1954, however, it had few representatives in the Parliament.

About 60 per cent of the Caucus members were Catholics, the result of a long, ideologically untidy but socially logical semi-alliance between the most socialist of Australia's main parties and the Church most doctrinally opposed to socialism. The relationship had had its tensions, but Labor had long learned to live with it. Catholics of varying degrees of attachment were found in all sections of the party—Ward, the left leader, was a Catholic; but the most distinctively Catholic section could be termed the right wing. These men were the more conventional Catholics, mainly of Irish ancestry and accepting Catholic conventional wisdom. In a party where above half the rank and file were Catholics, their home bases usually lay with people of similar disposition. Particularly at this time, after the Eastern European persecutions, the Korean War and a bitter fight in the Australian unions, they were bound together by a detestation of communism. At the same time, most had a concern for social reform that enabled them to work without misgivings in the same party as the two left groups.

The two best known, though hardly most typical, men of the right were two extraordinary Victorians, John Michael Mullens and Standish Michael Keon. Their uniqueness lay in their use of the flamboyant, oratorical styles of the left to present the concerns of the right.

Jack Mullens, born in Ballarat in 1896 and representing the industrial Footscray district through his electorate of Gellibrand, was a large, genial, urbane but furiously bigoted man given to florid eloquence and anti-communist zeal. He was very much the Irish Catholic politician, never more at home than when he was earning support on the Church steps after Sunday Mass. He appealed most to an older Labor generation. In April 1949, shortly before he entered Federal Parliament, Mullens told the Footscray Rotary Club of the need to ban the Communist Party. 'The crawlers [i.e., the Chifley Government] in Canberra are doing nothing about it,' he said. 'I am extremely disgusted to have to say that men who are supposed to govern have jumped into their funkholes and refused to govern.'

Stan Keon was a more complex man than Mullens, but was possessed of an equally colourful tongue. Born in Tasmania in 1915 but a product of the inner Melbourne district of Richmond, famed for its rough and tumble politics, he showed both flair and courage early in local Labor affairs. He built up a personal, Catholic-based 'machine' which beat the corrupt machine supported by the financier, John Wren, to enter the State Parliament as MLA for Richmond in 1946. In 1949, he beat the local 'old guard' again to win endorsement for the seat of Yarra, left vacant when the former Labor Prime Minister, J. H. Scullin, retired. Some thought then that Keon had the makings of a future Prime Minister.

His appeal on the bigger stage was somewhat less, however. 'We have one chap coming in from Victoria,' Chifley wrote to a Canadian friend after his Government's defeat, 'who is not a great orator, but has more capacity to disturb the House than any speaker I know. His name is Keon, a former member of the Victorian Parliament, and whenever he spoke there, there were always two or three members thrown out.'[1]

Keon was mentally quick and incisive, but perhaps lacked the deep common sense desirable in a political leader. Ambitious, passionate in his beliefs, sometimes intemperate but never dull, he came (inaccurately) to epitomise the Catholic, rightist group expelled from the ALP in 1955.

Though the names Keon and Mullens were to become almost synonymous with this group, they were untypical of the Parliamentary right of the time. Typified more by Cyril Chambers from South Australia, Tom Burke from Western Australia and Tom Andrews from Victoria, the right-wingers were mostly moderate, conventional men, indistinguishable from their colleagues on most issues.

The men in the centre were more the conventional social democrats who, more than the others, would have been at home in other left of centre parties. There were non-Catholics like the ex-journalist Alan Fraser from Eden-Monaro in New South Wales; the barrister from Sydney, Gough Whitlam, who was to become leader; and less conventional Catholics, like the Party's General Secretary, Pat Kennelly. Evatt, himself a non-Catholic, was essentially a man of the centre as was his Deputy, Arthur Calwell, a Catholic.

The principle underlying issue divisively at work in this Caucus was foreign affairs, until the 1950's a fringe issue in Labor policy and even then building up only faintly on the horizon. In the first half-century of its existence, Labor had been in favour of 'White Australia' and a less dependent attitude towards Imperial Britain. Yet even the warmth of its nationalism contained a trap of interpretation, sprung with such deadliness

[1] Quoted by L. F. Crisp in *Ben Chifley: A Biography*, Longmans, Melbourne, 1961, p. 383

in the Conscription split of 1916. In the 1930's, Labor was generally in favour of good things—of being resolutely anti-fascist, pro-disarmament and somewhat pacifist. At the outbreak of the Second World War, the Federal Parliamentary Labor Party adopted a resolution against involvement, soon to be reversed and followed by a period of notably skilful wartime government. After the war, basking in the reflected grandeur of Evatt's foundation Presidency of the United Nations, Labor developed a simple, cosy doctrine of 'support for the United Nations'.

The characteristic feature of all these attitudes was that foreign policy could be dismissed with one or two emotionally pleasing generalisations. The rest of the world was far away and few Australians had visited it recently, if at all. The exceptions to this generalisation were the two world wars, and in a country short on history the wars inspired a complex of legends. 'No conscription for overseas service', a policy of dubious ancestry, became a symbol of Labor's superior humanity; while the legend of the dashing, independent 'digger' under fighting Labor governments became to a broader spectrum an equally important symbol of Australia's nationhood. In the late forties, the combination of righteous anti-militarism and pride in the wartime achievements of John Curtin's Labor Government made the party almost schizophrenic.

The victory of the Chinese Communist Party in 1949, coming at the end of a program of communist victories in Eastern Europe and at the same time as the British, French and Dutch were preparing to leave their Asian colonies, brought a new era in foreign policy to Australia. For the conservative parties there were easy answers: communist parties, not only totalitarian but socialist as well, were clearly evil; the British Navy and the imperial link had been the basis of Australia's defence and foreign policies until the Second World War and now the American Alliance (obtained by Curtin, not entirely with the blessings of the conservative parties) complemented it. The doctrine of reliance on 'great and powerful friends' came easily and naturally to the parties and government led by Robert Menzies.

The problems were as difficult for Labor as they were easy for the conservatives. A distaste for imperialism, for great powers and for authoritarian military régimes such as that of General Chiang Kai Shek in Nationalist China was as much part of the feeling in the gut of a Labor man who cared about the outside world as something like the reverse was for a conservative. The ALP was avowedly anti-communist and often militantly so. Its attitude was reinforced by the great industrial battle of the late forties and early fifties against communists in the unions. Yet in a world view it had to rely heavily on the totalitarian (a difficult concept for free Australians to grasp) rather than the socialist nature of communist régimes in forming a hostile opinion.

While these were the objective problems of the party in facing the power of Asian communism, their impact on individuals differed greatly. At one extreme, there was a feeling that violent revolutions and sharp social changes—irrespective of whether or not they were communist—were the answer to Asia's problems. Many of those who thought like this were themselves considerably influenced by Marxism or communist associations in the unions. At the other, predominantly Catholic extreme, there was abhorrence and fear of a force which had recently rampaged through largely Catholic Eastern Europe.

The men facing these issues in Caucus were mostly middle-aged and elderly, products of the isolation of pre-war Australia and of Labor's instinctive isolationism. They would have ridiculed any suggestion that the party could split over foreign affairs. But increasingly, on all sides, they were being influenced by views developed by small groups of intellectuals outside Parliament, propagated by conversation and talks and, more often, in small magazines and newspapers. As was not unusual in Australia at the time, such views were often ill-formed and rarely subject to critical analysis; but they had a sense of their time and, in the end, a profound impact on men unaccustomed to working with abstract ideas.

The leader of this last united Labor Caucus, Herbert Vere Evatt, would have had a turbulent career in any society. In the provincial, easy-going, but occasionally passionate Australia in which he worked he was a clumsy colossus, bigger than the age he bestrode, yet terribly affected by it.

Evatt was born in April 1894, the son of a storekeeper at East Maitland, New South Wales. His mother was widowed early and brought her four sons to Sydney where she and they struggled to get the boys' talents the education they deserved. Bert Evatt had an outstanding scholastic career, almost matched by the sporting prowess of his bull-like frame, and he became a lecturer in law. He entered New South Wales State politics in the late 1920's, standing against an endorsed Labor candidate in Balmain in 1928— a controversial incident that led to lasting suspicion of his political reliability in his home state. Through the Scullin Labor government he was appointed to the High Court bench in 1930, at the age of thirty-six— extraordinarily young for that distinguished tribunal. The originality and grasp of his judgments, nevertheless, were regarded by many as showing close to genius in the law. He combined his legal career with solid achievements in writing history, most notably *Australian Labor Leader*, a biography of the expelled First World War Labor Premier of New South Wales, W. A. Holman.[2]

Burning through Evatt since his university days had been the feeling of being a man apart, destined to lead his people to greatness. He stepped down from the High Court bench in 1940 to win for Labor the difficult seat of Barton; he became a senior Minister and subsequently Deputy Prime Minister in the Labor governments of 1941-49. In 1946, he became the first President of the United Nations Assembly. He was elected Leader of the Party in 1951, on Chifley's death.

Evatt was one of the most familiar of public figures to Australians in the years of his greatness and early decline—a bespectacled, pudgy-faced man of middle height and hugely strong frame, dressed always in dark

[2] H. V. Evatt, *Australian Labor Leader: The Story of W. A. Holman and the Labor Movement*, Angus and Robertson, Sydney, 1940

blue, three-piece suit and downturned grey hat. He had rumpled white hair and a flat, harsh voice strangely out of character with his reputation as a writer, jurist and world statesman. To those who knew him more closely, he could be a warm and generous but never completely trusted friend, prone to hectoring and arguing and an extraordinary suspicion. Morbidly egocentric, he combined extremes of naïveté and labyrinthine cunning, astounding feats of honesty and dishonesty, simple trust and near paranoid suspicion, impulsive generosity and wounding rudeness.

Intellectually, Evatt was above all a lawyer and often seemed to lose his sureness of touch in other fields. He was the type of a mental athlete able speedily to assess masses of complex information, yet, outside the law, often lacking speculative qualities and insight. He would read Roman literature in the original Latin and had a strong cultural sense; but he was equally happy with simpler hobbies, watching Rugby League or cricket at the Sydney Cricket Ground, playing from *Hymns Ancient and Modern* on the piano of his home overlooking the entrance to Middle Harbour.

In 1954, two figures in the wings exerted an influence on the Caucus Evatt led. One, immensely powerful, was the legend and memory of Chifley, which took superhuman shape as the symbol of the golden past. As a financial thinker and administrator, Chifley had earned a place at the top of Labor history even before his Prime Ministry. As Prime Minister he inspired both respect and, among those who disagreed with him politically, fierce animosity. Though he had a rare ability to attract personal affection, in the eighteen months between his defeat and his death he had increasingly become prone to the pique and prejudice which were the reverse side of his nature. It is doubtful if he understood the new world into which his party was heading after 1949.

Waiting, still dimly perceived, in the opposite wing was Bartholomew Augustine Michael Santamaria, then only thirty-nine years old, lay member of Catholic Action and a persuasive Catholic intellectual with the capacity to articulate extraordinarily lucid thought.

Santamaria, born in Brunswick, Melbourne, in 1915, had studied law at the University of Melbourne. His intense, perhaps romantic interest in political ideas led him to the group of young Catholic intellectuals who founded the *Catholic Worker* in 1936 to press for reconstruction of Australian society in line with their understanding of Catholic social principles. In 1937 he became Assistant Director of the newly formed National Secretariat of Catholic Action, the base from which his subsequent power grew. Leading a network of laymen known as The Movement in support of the ALP fight against communism in the unions, he had built up a potentially powerful pressure group for right wing foreign policies. His influence was still slight and the issues to which he drew attention were secondary in party affairs, but events were soon to conspire and throw him to centre stage.

On 5 October 1954, four months after the election that cost him the coveted Prime Ministership and after a series of outbursts before the

Petrov Espionage Commission, Evatt issued one of the most extraordinary press statements ever issued by a political leader. Discussing over three pages the defeat of Labor, he said:

One factor told heavily against us, namely the attitude of a small minority group of Labor members, located particularly in Victoria, which had since 1949 become increasingly disloyal to the Labor Movement and Labor Leadership.

Adopting methods which strikingly resemble both Communist and Fascist infiltration of larger groups, some of these groups have created an almost intolerable situation—calculated to deflect the Labor Movement from established Labor objectives and ideals.

The statement went on to say that these activities were part of a plan to help the Menzies Government 'initiate in Australia some of the un-British and un-Australian methods of the totalitarian state.' Evatt continued:

It seems certain that the activities of this group are largely directed from outside the Labor Movement. The Melbourne *News Weekly* appears to act as their organ . . . having in view the absolute necessity for real, and not sham, unity within the movement, I am bringing this matter before the next meeting of the Federal Executive with a view to appropriate action being taken by the Federal Labor Conference in January.

Evatt's statement was directed principally at Keon, Mullens and Santamaria. Evatt made good his threat and though the Federal Conference was postponed for two months (until March 1955) it saw the culmination of the division which had been working in the Labor Movement since before 1949.

Chapter Two
The Rise of the
'Groupers'

Between 1935 and 1945, when the threat from the Nazi and Facist powers took up most of the world's attention, the Communist Party directed a massive campaign to penetrate the Australian Trade Union Movement, and for a few years was almost able to control it. If the traditional Labor Movement had not fought back, its double strategy of arbitration for the unions and social reform through politics would have been impossible to continue. Direct action designed to produce revolution through the unions would have taken its place and liberal democracy in Australia could even have been in danger. But the fight back against communist influence contained dangers: it carried the seeds of the long decline of the Australian Labor Party after 1949.

The Australian Communist Party, which until the mid-1960's closely followed the Soviet Union 'line' for world parties, had a 'zig zag' policy towards the ALP and the organised Labor Movement, alternating between violent hostility towards the established leadership and attempts to under-play the fundamental differences and more gently influence the 'reformist' unions and political party in a revolutionary direction.

In the early twenties, the communists had wished to join the ALP, but by the depression years a decade later they were vehemently denouncing it as 'social fascist'. Against no section were the diatribes harsher than against the once favoured 'left social fascists', identified with the New South Wales Premier J. T. Lang and alleged to be 'using the language of socialism for a capitalist purpose'.

After the Nazis won power in Germany in 1933, however, the Kremlin directed a policy of seeking the 'popular front' with other labour and left organisations, to combat fascism. By 1934, the former violent tone of the communist press in Australia—and it is difficult to imagine journalism more violent in tone—had receded and the following year unsuccessful attempts to form the united front were being indignantly recorded. ALP policy was to reject the communist overtures—hardly surprisingly since neither communist nor fascists had much support.

The failure of the first united front offensive against all sections of the ALP was followed by the promotion of 'front' organisations, in which ALP members, Communist Party members and others sympathetic were asked to participate as individuals. The best known was the Council Against War and Fascism. By the late 1930's ALP proscription of such fronts resulted in communists seeking to join local ALP branches, while concealing their Communist membership. The result was dissension and suspicion in ALP branches, expulsions of suspect members and refusal to admit others. Many left-wingers protested and even resigned because, they alleged, of 'Catholic control' of the ALP.

The third and only really successful communist line of offensive at this time was in the trade unions. In the mid-1930's, most unionists either had the sharpest memories of the depression, or were still suffering from it. Many right-wing union leaders had been unable to cope with the unprecedented difficulties of the depression years; others, under no serious challenge for many years, were simply lazy and incompetent. The communists partly built up and partly rode a wave of militant unionism, which made spectacular advances in the late 1930's and early 1940's as workers gave expression to their bitterness or allowed the communists to exploit their apathy about union affairs.

The two biggest communist successes were the election of Ernest Thornton as General (National) Secretary of the Federated Ironworkers' Association and James Healy as General Secertary of the Waterside Workers' Federation, both in 1937. By 1940, communist-led militants were within a relatively few votes of controlling the citadels of power in the Trade Union Movement, the capital city Trades Halls and the Australian Council of Trade Unions, and they actually gained control of the Brisbane Trades and Labor Council. The main activity was in the industrial wing, but there were also attempts to influence the ALP. In 1940, the communist-led left unions backed Don McSween, a well known ALP left-winger, on a 'reform' platform for the job of Assistant Secretary of the Victorian Branch against P. J. Kennelly. McSween came within a few votes of winning. About the same time, concealed communists and their supporters dominated the Hughes-Evans factional party, which was able to control the New South Wales branch for a short time until its success with a 'Hands Off Russia' motion precipitated Federal intervention in Sydney.

Organised attempts to stop the communist advance started as early as 1938, with small, informal, Catholic-dominated groups organising against communist factions in the Boilermakers' Society and Australian Railways Union in Melbourne. The Newport Railway Workshops, traditionally a militant centre, was the scene of much of this activity, and by 1939 anti-communists were publishing the *Rail Worker*.

In the emergency conditions of wartime, stronger anti-communist organisation was soon coming from three main sources. The first, most exotic and best known of these was the Catholic Social Studies Movement, led by B. A. Santamaria and best known simply as 'The Movement'. It was formed in 1942, following small scale efforts, several months of discussions at the Catholic Action Office in Melbourne and an approach to the Archbishop of Melbourne, Dr Daniel Mannix. The Deputy Leader of the State Parliamentary Labor Party, H. M. Cremean, who had considerable personal experience of fighting the communists at the Trades Hall and in his local district, especially pressed for The Movement to be established.

The job of leading it went to Santamaria, who was twenty-seven years old when the much discussed organisation finally set to work.

The Movement in these years was an informal lay organisation, allowed by the Archbishop to use the machinery of the Church. Groups of eight to ten laymen, where possible trade union members, were organised in each parish. They compiled lists of the Catholic trade union members of their parish, by trade, and set out to encourage them to attend meetings of their unions and vote at union elections. A newspaper, *Freedom*, started publication on 25 September 1943. Wishing to avoid the charge of being 'negative' anti-communists as well as following an established inclination, The Movement leaders spread the message in the organisation of Catholic social principles, one of the main interests of the National Secretariat of Catholic Action.

The Movement worked mainly with the Secretary of the Melbourne Trades Hall Council, J. V. Stout, a Protestant and Labor traditionalist. In 1942, Stout had a bare majority in the Trades Hall Council and communists, working quietly in the 'gallant ally' period of sympathy for embattled Russia, were penetrating the pro-Stout unions. Most of the industrial organisation of The Movement was done by its Secretary, Norman Lauritz, who had become a full-time employee in November 1942. Each Monday Lauritz would meet with Stout. At these meetings and in telephone calls, Stout would inform Lauritz of union meetings at which his 'friends' would be welcome.

At the insistence of Stout, who feared the propagandist use communists would make of a link with 'Catholic Action', the whole operation was kept confidential. Using the parish groups and their lists as the basis of organisation, and often the cars of sympathisers for transport in those less affluent times, Lauritz would arrange for Catholic unionists to attend the meetings in force and block communist attempts at takeover or lesser penetration. The Munition Workers', Storemen and Packers', Shop Assistants' and Cold Storage were among unions where The Movement fought communist influence.

Towards the end of the war, a second informal anti-communist organisation developed at the Melbourne Trades Hall itself. Among the founders were D. Lovegrove of the Fibrous Plasterers' Union (a dedicated anti-communist since his expulsion from the Communist Party in 1933), the Assistant Secretary of the Trades Hall Council, M. C. 'Mick' Jordan, and Gil Hayes, State Secretary of the Boot Trades Union. The Boot Trades Union office, strategically placed near the Council Chamber, became the organising centre, with the Treasurer of the Union, J. A. Little, and another official, F. Carmody, also active.

Younger union officials, some Movement members and men from the swelling ranks of disillusioned, embittered ex-Marxists joined up with the group centred round the Boot Trades, which formed the nucleus of an attacking anti-communist force on the floor of the Trades Hall Council. A smaller group of Trotskyists, concerned at the advance of 'Stalinism', also became active at the Trades Hall about the same time.

Stout had the 'numbers' on the Council floor and The Movement could provide transport to make sure delegates attended Council meetings for vital votes. The job of the Boot Trades group and the Trotskyists was to make sure Stout could use his numbers. The communists were trained to a loud, violent style of oratory and in the use of technical points to upset a meeting. The Boot Trades group developed the art of attacking the communists with their own game, shouting, talking and tactically tricking them down on the floor of the Council Chamber. Healthy lungs, a loud voice and free flow of oratory—never in really short supply in the Labor Movement—were much in demand by the 'caucus' meetings in the Boot Trades office.

A third source of anti-communist organisation was the Curtin Labor Government, in office from 1941 and by the middle years of the war concerned at communist direct action in support of a 'Second Front now', against Allied policy, to relieve Russia in Europe. The Government began to encourage ALP unionists to organise; it freed some men from the services and got experienced industrial men to watch some of the communists. One result of the government's policy was the provision of a newsprint allotment to *Freedom*, organised by the Minister for Information, Arthur Calwell.[1] David Woodhouse, a young member of the Civil Construction Corps in the Northern Territory, who came from a Melbourne ALP family, was quietly switched over to organising against the communist strikes in the Territory. Later, he was freed from the corps and started anti-communist organisation in the building trades in Victoria.

Stout, like a good union bureaucrat, was in touch with all this activity and coordinated it, but encouraged the various streams to stay apart. Each developed its own character: The Movement, earnest, quiet and rather middle class; the Lovegrove-Boot Trades group, aggressive and strident; a growing number of ex-servicemen seeking a better world, but not the communist way.

In Sydney, the communist advance had been only a little less militant than in Melbourne and informal anti-communist organisation also developed there. The Reverend Dr P. J. 'Paddy' Ryan, a flamboyant Catholic publicist, had made useful contacts in the course of anti-communist lectures and debates. But the main organisation was from the Sydney Trades Hall where the Trades and Labour Council, under the secretaryship of R. King, was narrowly holding off the communists.

With the approaching end of the war in Europe, and removal of a short-term ban on the Party, communist militancy increased dramatically by the start of 1945 and the 'numbers' for the ACTU biennial Conference, to be held in June, were in grave doubt.

Officials and close supporters of the Sydney Trades and Labor Council, concerned not only for their view of the world but their jobs, were desperate. The solution hit on was to galvanise the political wing of the Labor movement and the name of the ALP in a fight back against the communists. The Assistant Secretary, James Dennis Kenny, took over the organisation,

---

[1] The communist press also got a newsprint allotment about this time, when the ban on it was lifted.

and the 1945 Conference of the New South Wales branch of the ALP agreed to form ALP organs in industry. These were to combat the communists by putting the ALP viewpoint to the workers and by organising to get ALP-backed rather than communist candidates elected. In the ensuing twelve months they were organised as the ALP Industrial Groups, with the warm blessing of the political wing. Their patron, Kenny, born in Sydney in 1906 and a product of the Glassworkers' Union, was a warm, superb industrial wheeler dealer who organised wide support for them. The Groups were formed on a Commission from the ALP Central Executive and their first secretary was Harry Jensen, a member of the Electrical Trades Union and later Lord Mayor of Sydney.

The Groups spread to Victoria the following year.

The Victorian Easter Conference of the ALP of 1946 was confronted with fifteen motions on its agenda, all from suburban branches, calling for the setting up of ALP groups, cells, bodies and other organisations in industry. The decision taken was to lead to the virtual destruction of the Party in the state in less than a decade.

The Agenda Committee selected Item 316 of the agenda for debate by the Conference. This item came from the East Melbourne branch and read:

That the Executive be directed to immediately organise officially recognised ALP Groups in factories and shops for the purpose of advocating Labor policy and combatting the Anti-Labor propaganda of the Liberal and Communist parties in the factories.

The motion was moved by J. L. Cousland, a disillusioned former militant from the Tramways Union, and seconded by E. W. Peters, a former Party President and later an MP.

After a long debate, with the left unions bitterly opposing the motion and the various anti-communist streams as aggressively supporting it, a statutory majority (of the total number of credentialled delegates) adopted the historic resolution.

The left-wing unions had an obvious motive in strongly opposing establishment of the Groups. Some were under direct communist influence. Others, led by men who despised the traditional industrial right as 'tame cat' and not sufficiently militant or socialist, relied on an alliance with the communist side to strengthen their numbers at the ALP Conference, while the communists relied on them at Trades Hall Council meetings.

However, some of the moderate industrial section and supporters of the ALP Executive also either opposed establishment of the Groups or pressed for them to be propagandist only. This was partly the reaction of men whose influence depended on balancing the industrial right against the political wing or the left; for success for the Groups would inevitably mean a boost for the industrial right on the one hand and more power for the political wing over the unions on the other. Union officials, engrossed in their jobs and often without formal training, were hypersensitive to the possibility of being voted out of office.

To implement the Conference decision, the Victorian Central Executive appointed an Industrial Committee from among its members to control the Groups. Lovegrove, who became Assistant Secretary of the ALP shortly afterwards, was President of the Committee, and G. F. Piera was appointed Groups organiser. Broadby, Peters, F. J. Riley (State Secretary of the Manufacturing Grocers' Union), A. M. Fraser, MLC, W. Quirk, MLA, T. W. Brennan (a lawyer and later MLC), J. J. Roberts and J. V. Barry (later a Supreme Court Judge), formed the Committee membership. It was a fair cross-section of the then 'establishment' of the Labor Party in Victoria, rather than of the new anti-communist streams growing up.

The Committee's report to the 1947 Conference said sixteen ALP Industrial Groups had been formed in the following unions and work sites: Railways, Shop Assistants, Watersiders, Postal Workers, Boilermakers, Carpenters, Clerks, Electrical Trades, Munitions, Essendon Aerodrome, Moorabbin Housing Estate, Moulders, Tramways, Abbotsford Brewery, Building Industry, Ballarat Railways.

Bitter and complicated debates took place over the Groups at the 1947 and 1948 Conferences, with the left demanding that they be disbanded and the right wing of the Conference—by now including growing numbers of dedicated anti-communists—pressing for stronger backing for them. By 1949, the Groups were established, successful and accepted by much of the Party and there was little debate on them at Conference for some years.

The Groups in Victoria differed considerably in their level of activity and the complexion of their membership. Some had quick success against relatively weak and over-stretched communist forces and either died away or were absorbed into the union 'establishment'. A few declined without success. In others, including some of the biggest unions, a long, bitterly contested fight finally dislodged the communists in the much more anti-communist climate of Australian public opinion of the early 1950's.

Membership of the Groups was typically about 25-50 in Victoria, all ALP members. Each Group had the right to select its members, so as to keep out nuisances or the dreaded 'comm. stooge' who would reveal its strategy, and to meet privately, provided it reported regularly to the ALP Executive. The architect and inspiration of the Groups was Lovegrove, the ex-communist, who developed much of their strategy.

Group members often modelled their style on the aggressive, fighting ways of the old Boot Trades group and this was particularly true of their leaders. Many of the Group members were ex-communists or men who had fought with the communists, perhaps originally over minor issues, on the job. Others were ALP loyalists, often Catholics. Interviews by the author with Group and Movement officials suggest that about 30 per cent of the Group members were also in The Movement, while 60 per cent or so would have been at least nominally Catholics: i.e., about the same proportion as Catholics in the ALP generally. The proportions varied considerably, however, with individual Groups and at different times.

The Movement continued to work with Stout, providing an additional anti-communist force, until the early 1950's. But in 1945, following a near-victory for the communists in the ACTU, it had expanded to a national organisation. It added the extra function of providing a support force of workers to get out the Catholic vote for the ALP Industrial Groups. This threw it into increasingly close liaison with them.

By 1950, the 'Groupers', as the ALP Industrial Group members and their supporters became known, were a powerful force both in the ALP and in the unions. Men elected to union office on Industrial Group 'tickets' tended to be brash and aggressive, typically younger and more able than the traditional unionists, either right or left. The fight against the communists had been hard-fought and bitter—though there was sometimes surprising personal respect on both sides—and the Groupers were militantly anti-communist. Often there was a streak of fanaticism or larri· kinism. But at their best the Groupers also felt a sense of mission about their union work and about the possibilities of social welfare for their members through the political wing. Not for them the rhetorical, musty 'socialism' of the older generation, but a hard and pragmatic search for practical benefits. Some were influenced by the economic decentralism of Catholic social theorists and The Movement. Most were conscious of the faults of union leadership that had opened the way to communist penetration a decade earlier and determined that they would be different.

The Groups raised much of their own finance through raffles, subscriptions and donations, but much bigger sums were needed for the long struggles in the major unions, such as the Railways and Ironworkers'. The Victorian Central Executive of the ALP loaned them several sums of £100 or so, mainly after Group influence on the Executive strengthened in 1950, but over the eight years of Group operation this would hardly have totalled more than £1000. Much of this was repaid in affiliation fees, as unions expelled from the ALP in 1943 for backing communist candidates in the General Elections reaffiliated under Group control. The Move· ment often helped pay the Groups' printing bills, and Group members knew The Movement could often get its hands on a 'special' amount in an emergency. Although it was always a close secret, some Groups also certainly obtained large sums from employers—who considered they were 'buying industrial peace' in the strike-prone post-war years. They may also have got money from American government officials, who often seemed to be on hand to help anti-communist causes.

In Victoria, the successful Groups in the big unions formed a 'big five'. There were:

The Federated Clerks' Union: This developed from a wartime Trotskyist group, but became one of the most active vehicles for promoting Movement policy by the early fifties. The Secretary of the Group was J. P. Maynes, a Movement organiser, who became General President of the FCU; E. W. Peters was President of the Group. The communist controllers of the union were not considered particularly efficient. The Group claimed irregularities in the 1947 and 1949 union elections, including the burning of 3,000 ballot papers in 1949. It then sought and won a court-controlled ballot in 1950, by 2,500 votes to 1,100.

The Australian Railways Union: This was the biggest and most political Victorian union, with a scattered membership of about 20,000. The Industrial Group organisation was fairly loose and up to 300 people worked in the Group at the peak of its activity. It relied heavily on Movement machinery for organisation and help. The Secretary of the Group, F. R. Scully (later MLA for Richmond), was in The Movement, but Movement men probably were not much more than 20 per cent of the active membership. J. W. (Jim) Neill, the Group candidate who became President of the union in 1950 and Secretary—to beat the 'unbeatable' communist J. J. Brown—was a former left-winger and Catholic.

The Building Trades: David Woodhouse began organising in the Building Workers' Industrial Union on his return from the Northern Territory and he became secretary of the first Group. The Group was defeated in 1948, on what it claimed with accuracy was a crooked ballot. It worked with the Timber Merchants' Association to have the BWIU deregistered by the Arbitration Court, for having placed a 'black ban' on employers who would not pay above the Court's minimum award wage. The Group then successfully organised, with Movement help, a breakaway union called the Amalgamated Society of Carpenters and Joiners, after an earlier union merged into the BWIU. The existence of rival unions in the same trade was opposed to ACTU policy and formation of the ASC & J upset many conventional unionists.

The Federated Ironworkers' Association: The Victorian Group was formed at the end of 1947, after ironworkers had lost a lot of pay in the communist organised 'engineers' strike', which lasted seven months. The Group membership was hardly more than a dozen and, although not especially Catholic in complexion, had to rely heavily on The Movement for its background organisation. A Group ticket, with R. Lundberg as Secretary, was successful in the 1950 election.

The Waterside Workers' Federation: Members of the staff of the Chifley and Curtin Minister for Labour, E. J. Holloway, who represented Melbourne Ports, promoted this Group, formed to combat the influence of Healy, the General Secretary in Sydney, on the Melbourne waterfront. Its most prominent members included J. Cummins, who was Melbourne district president for many years, and V. C. (Gus) Alford, a member of Moral Rearmament converted to Catholicism some years later. The communists tried to portray the Group as run by 'MRA boss's men', but Alford was a popular man of notable intelligence. The first Grouper Secretary of the Melbourne branch was H. A. Clarke, who was gaoled for two years in 1954 for misappropriating £1,200 in union funds. Healy initiated the prosecution, apparently to extract the propaganda potential, but it created wide bitterness. Traditional union practice was never to 'cry copper' in such cases, unhappily not unknown in the disorderly world of union bookkeeping. A communist, C. Young, got the job in the ensuing election.

Other Groups in Victoria were active for years in the Amalgamated Postal Workers' Union, the Amalgamated Engineering Union (where it had a different name and more independence for tactical reasons), the Electrical Trades', the Vehicle Builders', Builders' Laborers', Boilermakers' and Plumbers' unions.

In New South Wales, the Groups admitted non-members of the ALP who were not members of other political parties. This allowed a larger membership than in Victoria and more activity in workshops. About thirty different ALP Industrial Groups operated in the state at various times, with complexions and styles broadly similar to those in Victoria. Many disbanded after early successes against the communists or patent lack of success, and by 1949 the Group organisation was dwindling. Its two great successes of the early 1950's were in two of the largest and most nationally significant unions, the Miners' Federation and the Ironworkers—the keys to Australian heavy industry.

In the winter of 1949, the communist leaders of the Miners' Federation organised a seventy-five day strike, which had minimal industrial content. This was difficult to see as other than an attempt by the Communist Party to 'stand over' the Chifley Government in a key industry, to demonstrate crudely the advantage of direct action over arbitration and Labor Government. In what was a fairly traumatic experience for the Labor Movement, Evatt as Attorney-General 'froze' union funds, Chifley ordered troops into the mines and the New South Wales branch of the Railways Union carried 'black' coal. The strike collapsed, amidst bitterness and heavy wage losses for the miners, and they elected most of the well-organised Grouper tickets at the next union elections, with G. Neilly as Secretary.

The Federated Ironworkers' Association was the biggest and wealthiest union in New South Wales, firmly under communist rule headed by the charismatic secretary, Thornton. Its wealth financed much communist industrial activity. For years the main opposition to Thornton had come from a small group, originally Trotskyist in inspiration, in the individualist Balmain branch. Its driving force became Lawrence Elwyn Short, born to an intensely socialist waterside workers' home at Rockhampton in 1915. Short joined the Communist Youth League briefly during the depression and then for some years was a Trotskyist. By the war years, he had joined the ALP and, like many ex-Marxists, was strongly anti-communist. The Balmain group fought alone for many years, but eventually took the initiative in forming an ALP Industrial Group in the union in 1949. By then, rank and file feeling was rising against the increasingly dogmatic, arrogant and strike-prone communist control. Memories of the depression had previously inclined much of the membership to the militants. By 1949, too, there was a strong post-war European migrant influx into the iron and steel industry.

In 1949 Short ran with a team for National Secretary, and challenged the ballot in the Arbitration Court when he was defeated. After a long hearing, the Court found that the ballot had been falsified and in 1950 it declared Short elected. He was National Secretary in an intensely hostile office until 1952, when a highly organised Industrial Group team captured the union throughout Australia.

The Movement was an important part of the elaborate organisation that secured this victory, but only part. Other metal trades unions, the Australian Workers' Union, the Group members and the candidates themselves all added to the successful team work. Several members of the Group who became officials were in The Movement, but most were not even Catholics. Short had a flair for publicity and attracted the support of several press men on a personal basis. He read widely and was keenly interested in ideas. The 'image' that developed was of a man more interested in making the best of capitalism than dedicated to socialism, attracted by many features of American unionism and quite different in style from the old-time socialist. Many older unionists resented him and in some ways he was the archetypal—if there could be such a man—Grouper. He was a key part of the 'image' of the Industrial Groups.

In Queensland, the Labor-in-Politics Convention of 1947, in Townsville, voted to establish the Industrial Groups in Queensland. The Group Committee, at the height of its activity, comprised R. J. J. Bukowski, the State President of the Australian Workers' Union, T. Rasey, MLA and M. Brosnan, MLA. Membership was open, as in New South Wales.

As Chairman of the Committee throughout the effective life of the Groups, Bukowski, a man with a violent, almost physical hatred of communists, became a most influential figure. For many years, he had a close partnership with The Movement Industrial Organiser, William Thornton. The Movement did not have the manpower in most of Queensland to canvass on the scale of Victoria, or even New South Wales, but it provided an intelligence network for discovering potential Group members and a workforce for addressing envelopes, providing transport and the like. Bukowski's relationship with the Groups and Movement remained personal; he would not use the AWU machinery in Group affairs.

Unions won from the communists included the Waterside Workers' Federation, the Meat Workers'—an economically vital union in Queensland—Clerks', and Ironworkers'. The Groups made limited impression on left strength in the metal and transport unions and could not dislodge communist control of the Brisbane Trades Hall office. However, with strong local Movement backing, they won control of the Rockhampton Trades Hall.

The South Australian branch of the ALP established Industrial Groups in 1946. Although there was little direct communist influence in the state and no strong communist industrial leaders, South Australia was ripe—without the Groups as a counter-force—for communist expansion through unions they controlled federally.

The Groups operated in unions such as the Ironworkers', Watersiders' and Railways, scene of wider conflicts.

South Australia, however, had become the home of a 'cosy' arrangement, where factionalism was slight and all sides wished 'not to rock the boat'. The Groups represented a potential alternative power centre to the tightly-knit Adelaide Labor 'establishment', whose dominant figure was the left-wing MP Clyde Cameron. The 1951 South Australian Conference, largely through the influence of Cameron and interstate opponents of the Groups, voted to disband them. Communist power was then fast declining, but the decision came as the sprawling battle for the Ironworkers—for which South Australia was the second biggest state—reached its climax. Group supporters throughout Australia bitterly resented the decision.

Attempts were made in the late 1940's to have the Groups accepted in Western Australia and Tasmania, to give them national organisation, but communist strength and potential in those two states was slight and the ALP Conferences rejected formation of the Groups.

Group supporters never had the strength on the ALP Federal Conference to get approval for a federal organisation. The difficulty of three and four separate state organisations cooperating in federal elections led in mid-1952 to the formation of an Interstate Group Liaison Committee. Its Secretary was Maynes, Chairman, J. Kane (then newly elected Assistant Secretary of the New South Wales Branch of the ALP) and Vice-Chairman, Short.

Were the Groups really necessary? In later years, when anti-communism became less fashionable, it was often argued that the Groups had been a noxious and destructive growth, menacing the good order of the Labor Movement, if not semi-fascist in inspiration.

Observers could argue about the details, but they could hardly deny that communism was a daunting force in Australia between 1935 and 1950. The control of the Brisbane and many provincial Trades Halls by dedicated Stalin communists, and their ability to wield 'numbers' only slightly fewer than those of the controlling faction in Melbourne and Sydney, are simple, recorded facts.

The communists were brilliant industrial showmen and often—but certainly not always—union leaders of more than average ability. But they left little doubt in their heyday that they sought to control the machinery of Australian unionism, smash the arbitration and 'reformist' political system and at least work for violent revolution. They got many small gains, in minor conditions, that more timid men might not have got, though in wages comparative performances are difficult to assess and rarely agreed upon. What successes they had were at a heavy cost in wages and production as the result of spectacular post-war strikes.

Often it seemed in the late 1940's that half of Australia was on strike half the time. Official figures show that days lost through strikes were around three times as high in the post-war years as after 1955; but these do not indicate 'go slow' and other variants of the simple strike. Strikes were also common in the disturbed years after the First World War, but the distinguishing feature of the strikes after 1945 was their barely disguised political motivation and the neatness with which they fitted a world communist pattern. At first, depression-scarred workers often seemed to welcome them, but the landslides to the Groups showed that by 1950 the communists had gone too far.

The communists reached their zenith at the ACTU Congress of June 1945 in Sydney. With left supporters, they had a majority of about ninety. Mainly non-communist officials chosen by them were elected to the non-permanent posts. The left also obtained a vital decision, against agitated opposition from the traditionalists, to make all future decisions binding on all member organisations. The result would have been to reverse the traditional character of the ACTU as a loose confederation of state-based organisations, plus federal unions. Whatever the ideal value of a more unitary arrangement, the proposal adopted in 1945 would have made the ACTU a much stronger potential weapon of communist purpose.

In the event, the election of office bearers was challenged on technical grounds and delayed until the 1947 Congress. The Melbourne, Sydney and Hobart Trades Halls rejected the proposals for reorganisation, after violent debates. As under the Constitution they had to be ratified by state branches, this effectively killed the proposals. By 1947, the successes of the Groups and The Movement had given the traditionalists control once again. By 1951 a slender majority had become 'comfortable'.

Apart from their revolutionary purpose and industrial record, another controversial aspect of the communist penetration of Australian unionism was the totalitarian, zealously ideological climate that surrounded it. The communists rigged ballots (if the findings of half a dozen Australian judges are to be believed) ; they shamelessly smeared their opponents and ran ruthless 'wars of nerves' against them; they lied; they were often physically violent; they revered Stalin and the Soviet Union. Some of their allies were men of socialist passion, genuinely despising the traditionalists of unionism, but they also recruited men who were little more than 'stooges' and thugs, ever ready to obey, to employ verbal and physical violence. A warped idealism often motivated this behaviour, in the tradition that the 'end justifies the means'; but it raised the question of whether such behaviour was good enough for the Australian Labor Movement.

Most of the opposition to the Groups was based purely on their effect on power distribution in the Labor Movement: if a man was, or felt potentially, threatened by them, he objected. This applied both to those who were frightened of the Group organisation, and those who disliked the brash newcomers it threw up. Though arguments were often given a theoretical disguise, usually the real concern was power.

Nevertheless, there were genuine objections to the Groups on other grounds. Though it is difficult to see what else they could have done, 'deals' with employers were obviously likely to cause offence. The communists and other opponents portrayed them as a wing of 'Catholic Action' so often and so vigorously throughout their life, that it would probably not have mattered much whether or not they had the more subtle links they in fact did have with The Movement. Nevertheless, the existence of these links and the appearance of dedicated Catholic anti-communists caused some upsets.

The records show the Groups, in their role as union controllers at ALP Conferences, to have been a relatively unpolitical force, however; except in the Clerks' Union, under the dedicated Maynes, they may have been 5 or 10 per cent as 'political' in their control of unions as their predecessors. Perhaps the Groups' most controversial cause within the Labor Movement was court-controlled ballots. They had from the start sought legislation empowering the Arbitration Court to conduct union ballots, on rank and file demand. It seemed the only way to circumvent communist ballot rigging, and the communist press hysterically opposed the ballots. A more moderate section of union opinion was also opposed, claiming such a system would open the way to Government interference in the Labor Movement and cause much extra keeping of records.

The Chifley Government compromised with the 'Chifley legislation', which provided for court ballots where malpractices had been proved or where the union management sought them. The Groupers claimed malpractices were often hard to prove and that communist managements would, of course, never seek a court ballot. In 1951, the 'Menzies legislation', allowing court ballots on a petition of, with some variations, 500 members of the union involved, was passed. The Groupers welcomed this and used it, though by then the weaker and more vulnerable communist managements had fallen. Used many times over the ensuing years, and not only by Groupers, the 'Menzies legislation' soon ceased to be very controversial.

From time to time 'unity tickets' were issued in union elections, in which ALP members linked their names in a team with communists on the 'how to vote' card. This was against the rules and led to automatic expulsion, but it nevertheless caused resentment.

As well as strictly enforcing the rules on unity tickets, the Grouper-dominated Executives were also strict about ALP members associating with communists on the Peace Council, which they claimed was a communist 'front'. There were some expulsions over this, and generally a good deal of left wing resentment against the Groupers for it.

The rule in union elections was that members of the Industrial Group could not stand against candidates endorsed by the Group, but ALP members not belonging to the Group could, except where the union was not affiliated to the ALP; it was argued that members of the ALP should not upset an election that could bring the union back to the ALP. There were complaints from time to time that this rule interfered with the rights of union members.

Issues of power and pride apart, however, the remarkable thing about the decade of ALP Industrial Groups is the smoothness of the operation and its comparative lack of controversy among the majority of union leaders and members. In the political wing, the discord might have been expected to be even less. But it was in that wing that the issues of power and pride were most felt, with disastrous consequences.

Chapter Three
The Industrial Groups
as a Political Force
1945-53

In a party beset by personal and ideological rivalries, the creation of the Industrial Groups and commitment of the Party as a whole to a war against communism caused an internal upheaval. The Groups created new centres of power and new issues, with bitter factional strife as the result.

The course the ALP took in the Industrial Group era was deeply embedded in its history. The conscription split of 1916-17 had devastating effects, from which the Party never fully recovered. It broke up the old moderate, predominantly secular political wing and led in the 1920's to greater influence than previously by the industrial wing of the Labor Movement, particularly the Australian Workers' Union. These were not particularly memorable years for Labor. The party was mostly out of office and bereft of ideas after the period of vigorous reform in the previous decade. Too often an empty socialist rhetoric and wild promises at election time became Labor's public style, with bitter, not always scrupulous, wrangling in the background. Corrupting alliances with liquor, gambling, marginal manufacturing, leasehold grazing and other forms of fringe capital were forged in the struggle for enough money to run a party. There were a number of spectacular scandals, most notably in the Sydney City Council.

Gradually the political wing was rebuilt, but where the old pre-split political wing of Labor had been predominantly Protestant or secular, often with a non-conformist, puritan strand, the new political wing was increasingly dominated by Catholics. An informal semi-alliance between the ALP and the Catholic Church had been developing since well before the First World War. Most Catholics were of Irish descent and were either manual workers or more recently and less securely arrived in the middle class than those whose forebears had brought the middle class from Britain. It was natural that Irish Catholics would be attracted to the more radical and reforming and less imperialist of Australia's two main political groupings. This movement of Catholics into the ALP got a tremendous impetus from the split, which on the one hand increased the attractions of the ALP (at the time of the Irish 'troubles') to Catholics and on the other weakened the more secular elements. Before 1914, less than 25 per cent of Labor Parliamentarians were Catholics; but between the wars the proportion rose to around 50 per cent and by 1954 it reached a peak of about 60 per cent.

Irish Australians appeared, like their counterparts in the United States Democratic Party, to have an uncommon flair for left-of-centre politics. A degree of cohesion as a community helped increase their numbers; everybody in a district tended to know everybody else and it was natural for a politically minded youngster to be drawn to the ALP, the party of the Catholic community. From about 1920-60 Irish-Australian Catholics were notably socially mobile, as those with the appropriate means and talents entered the professional and business classes. In the early 1930's, a lay Catholic intelligentsia emerged for the first time for many years and was drawn towards the ALP.

The problem of the 1920's had been for Catholics to adjust the traditional views of the Church on socialism to working in an avowedly socialist party (if in practice a party of pragmatic social reform) along with secular socialists. In theory, this was overcome by a concensus that the Party was essentially one of social reform and that its socialism was non-Marxist and acceptable to Catholic principles. Many Catholics became enthusiasts for a rhetorical form of socialism. But in practice, the solution was for both sides to concentrate on day to day issues and internal politicking. The politics of ideology and the grand design for society declined and gave way to the age of the 'wheeler-dealer'. The post-depression generation of intellectuals was largely lost to the pragmatic, anti-intellectual ALP. Instead, they sought cures for a sick society in Marxism or Catholic Distributism.

While the wheeling and dealing discouraged intellectuals and ideas and had its unsavoury aspects, it did pay off with the election in the 1940's of Labor governments in the Commonwealth and several states that produced some of the best administration Australia has known. The mid-1940's was the golden age for the wheeler-dealers of the political wing, but like most golden ages it also contained the seeds of decline.

The most typical of the wheeler-dealers, indeed their very personification, was Patrick John Kennelly, born in Northcote, Melbourne, in 1900, who began working as a clerk in the ALP office in Melbourne soon after the First World War. In 1940 he beat off a challenge by the left and a section of the industrial wing and became Assistant Secretary of the Victorian Branch. He had been elected a Member of the Legislative Council for Melbourne West in 1938, became Federal Secretary in 1946 and reached the peak of his power in 1948, when he became Victorian Secretary as well.

A man with a colourful stammer and mordant wit, which he learned to use with dramatic effect, 'Pat' was essentially a machine politician. His overriding goal was to win every election, from a local pre-selection or a vote on the Executive to the supreme aim of getting Labor governments elected. His philosophy was to get and use 'the numbers'. He delighted in the exercise of his talent for backstage organisation, in use of the power his skills brought him and in his reputation as 'the kingmaker'. He could be ruthless, cynical, blunt, autocratic and vindictive, but also charming, honourable, sentimental, passionately dedicated to social reform and fervently loyal to his parliamentary leaders, Ben Chifley and John Cain.

He was equally strong in his likes and dislikes. As early as the 1920's and 1930's, under the ageing Victorian and Federal Secretary, Dan McNamara, Kennelly had built up personal strength not only through his friendship with the leading parliamentarians, but by becoming a 'go-between' to the financier and sports promoter John Wren, and to J. J. Liston, of the Liquor Trades Defence League. Both helped keep a struggling party financially alive. With A. A. Calwell, another of the Melbourne wheeler-dealer generation but more a parliamentarian than Kennelly, he became by the time of Chifley's Government the principle collector of the unofficial fund used to finance election campaigns.

This background made Kennelly supremely powerful in Victoria in the late 1940's. Experienced control of the ALP office gave him tremendous influence in the unprecedentedly big round of pre-selection contests for endorsement of parliamentary candidates that took place in those years. There were so many because the Federal Parliament was increased from 74 Representatives and 36 Senators to 123 and 60 respectively from the 1949 election. In Victoria alone, the number of Representatives seats increased from 20 to 33. The opportunities opened were further increased when many members of the State Parliament sought endorsement for Federal seats, thus leaving their own vacant. Kennelly sought to dominate this round of pre-selections and ensure wins for his private selections as 'horse for the course'. He had some successes and some failures.

At the same time, Kennelly had dominant influence over the ALP Central Executive, balanced between the various sections in the Party so no one group could control it, and with Calwell and Cain allied to him. A master of the backstairs intrigue, the well-placed rumour and press 'leak', he was an antipodean version of the Irish Tammany politician at his most attractive and best. As Federal Secretary—then an office of theoretically minor importance in a party that was intensely confederalist in organisation—he was only a little less influential in Australia as a whole.

The studied accumulation of great power over two decades had made many enemies for Kennelly, however. He made innumerable ones over the pre-selections of the late 1940's, among those who felt themselves 'outs' at the Trades Hall, those who opposed the wheeling and dealing with Wren, the liquor trade and the like. This opposition had shown up as early as the sponsorship of the left-winger Don McSween against him in 1940, but for many years the industrial wing was using all its spare energy in the anti-communist fight. Victories in this fight about the same time as Kennelly became State Secretary cleared the ground for a new industrial attempt to control the ALP.

The leader of the Melbourne industrialists was James Victor Stout, born in Port Melbourne in 1885 and Secretary of the Trades Hall Council since 1939. A proud, prickly man, moralistic and autocratic, 'Vic' Stout had much of the turn of the century puritan in his make-up. His personality could hardly have been better designed to clash with that of the equally proud and autocratic Kennelly.

Kennelly's experience had made him deeply conscious of the character of the Party as a coalition of Catholic, left and moderate industrial elements. His personal inclination towards the political wing, his concern for the precious left-Catholic balance and his consciousness of the role of this balance in his own personal power made him oppose the Industrial Groups from the start. He believed the Groups would become intolerable pressure groups within the party, deflecting it from its true role in fighting political—as distinct from union—elections and upsetting the well tried balance of power. Knowing Stout, The Movement and other backers of the Groups only too well, he realised the threat they posed to him personally as more unions were won over to the industrial right. He gave Group members and supporters the impression that he was doing everything possible in the ALP office to thwart and frustrate them.

The clash between the Groupers and Stout on one side and Kennelly on the other was part of a wider conflict, as the industrial wing re-emerged from the fight for survival to demand a greater share of political power. Union leaders claimed that Chifley ministers were getting too far away from the unions and the people. Much of their complaint was based on relatively minor incidents, which they felt represented ministerial arrogance; but there was also disapproval of some political acts of the government and of the organisational side of the political wing, the 'machine'. They were also disturbed by stories of corruption in the 1945-47 state government and on the Melbourne City Council. At the same time, much of the older Catholic political right was antagonistic to Kennelly, as a result of factions in the 1945-47 Cain Labor Government, the preselection troubles and to a minor extent his attitude to the Industrial Groups.

The first test came at the 1948 Easter Conference in Melbourne. It was the peak of the Cold War—only a few weeks after Czechoslovakia fell to the communists—and the peak of the battle in the Australian unions. The Trades Hall Council was practically under siege. There had been a long, bitter fight over handling of strikes, culminating later in the year in the circulation of violently anti-Stout literature and the suspension of eight unions from the Council. The following year the suspended unions tried to physically force their way into the Council, to be repulsed by organised counter-violence. That was the industrial climate of the late 1940's.

In 1948 most communists believed they had capitalism near its doom—and many of their opponents feared they might be right. Often with a warped idealism, the communists were hysterically unscrupulous in trying to fend off those they believed to be the tools of capitalism in its last days. They subjected the Industrial Groupers to violence, smears and a persistent war of nerves. The wife of a Group activist might be telephoned while her husband was out on union work and told he was with yet another mistress; Eureka Youth League members would create disturbances outside the home of another absent Grouper. On all sides the atmosphere was bitter and emotional. Men felt they were fighting not only for jobs and power, but for the very soul of the Australian Labor Movement.

The Industrial Groupers, fervently believing in their cause, were dismayed and bitter at the support the communists got from sections of the ALP left, inside and outside the unions; quite apart from the patronage the communists were able to exercise through their strength in the unions, there was the widespread claim that the communists made the best union leaders and the lingering pro-Russian feeling from the 'gallant ally' days.

The strongest supporters of the Industrial Groups decided to make the 1948 Conference a confrontation with those in the ALP who were sympathetic to the communists and critical or unenthusiastic about the work of the Groups. It was to become famous in ALP lore as the 'red-baiters' picnic' Conference. The violent verbal engagements of each Thursday night at the Trades Hall Council inevitably flowed over to the annual ALP Conference, where many of the same people were present. But this year it had a heightened ferocity. Lovegrove, 'Mick' Jordan, Stout's Assistant Secretary, Keon, Frank Scully, Secretary of the Railways Industrial Group, M. J. 'Jock' Travers of the Vehicle Builders' Group, Jack Little of the Boot Trades and others used every opportunity to launch vitriolic attacks— and language in the Labor Movement can be very vitriolic—on the communists and all who supported or condoned them. In a memorable climactic moment, Lovegrove denounced the legal firm of Slater and Gordon, in which W. Slater, a prominent state parliamentarian, was a partner, as a 'kindergarten for communism'.

The 'old guard' of the political wing sensed the passion and zeal of the new force that was building up, as Group supporters, backed by loudly cheering squads of Movement men and other Groupers, demanded active work for the Groups by parliamentarians, support for them from the ALP office and discipline for ALP members who worked industrially with the communists. Those who questioned the mood of the militant right were often shouted down. Then at the Sunday afternoon high point of the Conference, A. A. Calwell, Minister for Immigration, Central Executive member of twenty years standing and the most prominent of the thirties generation, rose and made a placatory speech in which he criticised in passing those who, he said, had an 'obsession' about communism. That night Keon rose and attacked his senior and political mentor, with all the forceful eloquence he could command, for not understanding the nature of the fight. It was a signal that the character of the ALP was changing, as it did every few years, and that the Groupers had arrived as a distinctive force.

The new Industrial Group force was itself a coalition of several lesser forces: the traditional industrial right around Stout, the younger Trades Hall Groupers who had developed from the Boot Trades nucleus, The Movement, younger, mainly Catholic parliamentarians such as Keon, who sought new power lines and modernisation of the Party's ideals, Group members themselves and people who had fallen out with Kennelly, Calwell and others of the 'old guard' for a variety of reasons.

The upsurge against the political wing was pursued relentlessly again in 1949, when pro-Group unionists demanded at a pre-Conference meeting at the Trades Hall that some politicians be dropped to make way for their own men. Kennelly had been under attack for months—for inadequate support for the Groups, for his power of the purse in holding party funds, for his toleration of the Wren interests, for the number of jobs he was holding. The 1947, 1948 and 1949 Conference agendas contained many motions calling for the 'one man, one job' principle to be enforced. In 1947, when he became Acting State Secretary, Kennelly had been a State Minister for Public Works as well.

Calwell and J. J. Dedman, Minister for Post-war Reconstruction and a rigidly Presbyterian Scottish socialist, were the first marked down to go. Lovegrove visited Calwell and warned him that the numbers would be against him at Conference, and for the first time in two decades the name of A. A. Calwell was missing from the Central Executive nominations. Dedman made a less dignified exit; he nominated for the Executive and missed election by four votes. New faces on the Executive included Keon, Little, H. O. 'Brahma' Davis of the Australian Workers' Union and Arthur Kyle of the Storemen and Packers' Union. Kennelly found it increasingly difficult to work with his Executive as it moved to the right. After defeats on several issues, and with prospects of the Federal Secretary's job being enlarged with Chifley's support, he resigned at the end of 1949. Lovegrove became Acting Secretary.

The new right completed its defeat of the old broad centre the following year. Lovegrove was confirmed as Secretary. Frank McManus, a vice-President and senior Movement man, defeated Kennelly's choice, the Country Organiser since 1947, J. M. Tripovich, for the job of Assistant Secretary and radio commentator.

Francis Patrick Vincent McManus, born in Melbourne in 1905, and ALP member since 1925, had been a high school teacher and more recently director of the Catholic Adult Education Association, which had an office near that of The Movement. Both he and Lovegrove went in with the full backing of the traditional industrial right, of the THC and the two Australian Council of Trade Unions officers most concerned with the ALP, the retiring President and newly elected MHR for Bendigo, Percy Clarey, and Reginald Broadby, the Assistant Secretary. There had been rumblings that McManus's election was due to the machinations of Catholic Action, but he had the backing of Clarey, Stout and others as much because they wanted a talented, university-educated administrator as out of a desire to cultivate The Movement.

Stout defeated Calwell for one of the two positions as Federal Executive delegate, in what the Melbourne *Herald* described as a 'bombshell'. The first candidate from an Industrial Group union, Bert Clarke of the Waterside Workers' Federation, replaced Davis on the Executive. This was mainly because of Davis's difficult personality and clashes with others during his year on the Executive, but, first, it showed that the Groupers could now succeed without the AWU and second, made a powerful enemy.

Denis 'Dinny' Lovegrove, the man the upheavals of the past two years had brought to the organisational head of the ALP in Victoria, was to prove as tempestuous and controversial a Secretary as his predecessor. Born in Fitzroy, Melbourne, in 1904, Lovegrove had been trained as a plasterer and rose rapidly through the Labor Movement in his union in the late 1930's. But in 1930 he had joined the resurgent Communist Party and, suffering grievous economic distress himself, had become quickly prominent and a leader of the militant unemployed; under the party name of Jackson, he had been known as a violent, eloquent young hater of the 'social fascists' leading the orthodox Labor Movement. In 1933 the Communist Party had swung all over the world to a more conciliatory attitude towards social democrats. In Australia, a breed of cooler, more devious 'apparatchiks', who were to retain office for a generation, took over from the violent young innocents of the early depression. There were many expulsions, one of whom was Lovegrove. He was expelled for writing a critical document which, allegedly, 'denied the leading role of the Party', and he was brutally bashed.

By the late 1930's, Lovegrove, like many ex-communists, had developed a searing hatred of his former association. He became one of the first to raise the alarm over communist penetration of the unions, as he saw communists he knew—sometimes disguising their membership—moving in and taking over or manipulating indirectly, according to the Leninist plan. He addressed small groups at the Trades Hall and gave public talks. A listener at one of his lectures was the young Santamaria.[1] Lovegrove's high intelligence, energy and trained understanding of political ideas brought him rapid progress in the conventional industrial right. By 1938, the revolutionary of only five years earlier was President of the Trades Hall Council. By 1947, when McNamara retired, he was Assistant Secretary of the Victorian ALP, under Kennelly as acting Secretary.

Lovegrove's ability and political understanding brought him admiration and success in the general, but too often his highly strung, emotional, overcritical nature made him unpopular in the particular. He was tactless, often intolerant, a good hater and had a flair for making enemies as well as friends.

Under Lovegrove's secretaryship, the ALP came close to its zenith in Victoria. It won the state election in 1952 and was backed by excellent organisation. Between 1949 and 1954, communist influence in the unions was almost destroyed. The combination of Lovegrove's erratic brilliance and the more solid, better educated talents of McManus as a political administrator brought one of the best administrations, for the price, any Australian party had known.

The honeymoon of the new, Grouper-dominated political wing with the industrial right hardly lasted three months beyond the Easter 1950 consummation of the marriage.

In June 1950 a familiar crisis developed in Victorian state politics. The Country Party, which had been in a coalition government with the Liberals under T. T. Hollway as Premier, split. One section joined the Liberal Party, which changed its name to Liberal and Country Party. Together, Labor and the remaining section of the Country Party had sufficient votes to defeat the Hollway Government in the Legislative Assembly.

On 21 June, the ALP Central Executive met urgently and Cain outlined proposals from the Country Party. In return for Labor support, he said, a

[1] B. A. Santamaria, *The Price of Freedom*, Campion Press, Melbourne, 1964, p. 26

Country Party minority government would introduce a number of reforms in superannuation, workers' compensation, industrial law, weights and measures and the mental hospital system. It would nationalise gas distribution, then in the hands of small, inefficient private enterprise companies. Most important of all, it would introduce universal franchise for the Legislative Council, voting for which was then confined to property holders and matriculants who bothered to enrol.

Cain appears to have had reservations about this course, but it was urged by W. P. Barry, the right-wing leader in the State Parliamentary Party, who was not an Executive member. Archie Fraser, MLC, the Caucus right representative on the Executive, supported Cain in pressing for the deal with the Country Party. Stout read a motion from a meeting of ALP trade union officers:

This meeting of ALP trade union officers views with mistrust the offers made to the Labor Party by the Country Party, as being impossible of being carried out, and regards the complete independence of the Labor Party in the State Parliament as vital to the development of the ALP and service of its members.

Stout and Jordan then said they would have to consider withdrawing from the Executive if the Country Party proposals were accepted. Cain expressed his regret that these views had not been expressed earlier in the affair.

Broadby, who was President of the ALP that year, then moved that Labor support a Country Party government, provided it agree to implement a sweeping, fifteen-point program of domestic reform. McManus seconded the motion and it received the support of Fraser, Clarke, and others in debate. Stout opposed it and withdrew from the meeting. Fred Riley of the Manufacturing Grocers' Union, Little and Keon also opposed it, and eventually Lovegrove too, because of the threatened resignations. When the meeting resumed after lunch, Stout and Jordan were both absent. The motion was adopted by fifteen votes to eight. On 27 June, the Central Executive accepted the resignations of Stout and Jordan. The bitterness and argument caused by this split of opinion was remembered for many years. Stout never forgave the ALP.

The background was that Labor had supported an earlier Country Party Government with A. A. (later Sir Albert) Dunstan as Premier, from 1935 to 1943. Supporters of this had argued that it was a way of keeping the Liberals out and exercising some influence over the Government, but many union leaders bitterly resented the liaison. They considered the Dunstan Government anti-union and worse in all ways than any conceivable United Australia Party (as the Liberals were then known) government. It was significant that opponents of a new liaison with the Country Party were nearly all from state union backgrounds. Support came mainly from the political wing and the ACTU leaders, who did not deal with state governments. A further point was that Stout had developed a close friendship with Hollway, the Liberal Premier to be deposed, and considered him an infinitely better friend of union members than McDonald, the Country Party Leader whom Labor proposed to make Premier. The break between the Liberal and Country parties had been caused partly by the Country

Party insistence on an anti-strike Essential Services Act, which the unions considered severely anti-union.

The breach was repaired the following year, when Stout and Jordan rejoined the ALP Executive. In the meantime, Stout had in small ways retaliated against the ALP and Lovegrove was rather prone to comment that he was a silly old fool. These remarks got back to Stout and, only too conscious of his advancing age and lack of any life outside the Trades Hall, he became resentful of Lovegrove, the man he had made Secretary.

About the same time, a further, benign breach with the industrial right came when Clarey resigned as President of the ACTU to pursue his career as Member of the House of Representatives for Bendigo. In the new situation of deflated communist strength, his successor, Albert Monk, preferred a policy of playing the middle of the Trade Union Movement off against the wings. He stayed apart from Victorian ALP affairs and left Broadby to represent the ACTU there.

While the breach with Stout was still being repaired, a new series of issues arose in 1950 and 1951 to drive the sides further apart. The Menzies Government elected at the end of 1949 introduced penal clauses into the Arbitration Act, giving the Arbitration Court the right to ban specific strikes. It brought down legislation to ban the Communist Party and prevent 'declared' communists from holding union office. It also greatly widened the powers of the Arbitration Registrar to hold secret ballots in unions. The ACTU opposed the Government on all these measures and, after some hesitation, the Trades Hall Council did too. The Movement supported all of them. The ALP was divided and timorous, and under pressure from some Groupers to support the government.

These issues had passed by the end of 1951, but in 1952 a further issue arose to deepen the rift between the Victorian ALP Executive and Stout. In the early days of broadcasting, the Labor Movement had successfully applied for a licence to run a broadcasting station. The licence was placed in the hands of trustees—one of whom was Stout—and leased as station 3KZ to the commercial firm of Val Morgan and Sons, as the Industrial Printing and Publicity Co Ltd, the Labor company, could not raise the capital to run the station itself. In New South Wales, however, the Labor Movement had successfully run two stations, 2KY in Sydney and 2KD in Newcastle. Both became sources of handsome profits, as did 3KZ.

In the early 1950's, the Sydney Trades and Labor Council officers suggested in informal discussions that when the 3KZ lease again came up for renewal, the ALP and THC, the IPP controllers, could take it over. This would make possible network arrangements between the Labor stations and improve their financial strength. The ALP Conference supported this when the lease came up for renewal in 1952, but Stout, one of the few remaining trustees, was bitterly opposed. He claimed the Labor Movement in Victoria could not successfully run a radio station, and became suspicious that it might become a vehicle for ALP office views. This led to a protracted, often violent series of rows and at a heated meeting of the THC on 29 May Lovegrove declared that 90 per cent of a report by Stout on the situation was incorrect. Stout claimed that the ALP's inability to run mass media was indicated by its newspaper, *Labor Call*, losing £12,000 a year, and by a threatened libel action against McManus for saying in his nightly 3KZ news commentary that the Gallup Poll was a fraud. Stout won on this occasion, but the row continued in a series of complex manoeuvres and was still going when the ALP split in 1955. It flowed over into a struggle between the various forces for control of the Industrial Printing and Publishing Co, the Trades Hall printing and publishing house which published the mustily socialist, quaintly bellicose *Labor Call* until it ceased publication in 1953.

The series of Industrial Group victories in big unions from 1950 on had, in the meantime, radically altered the distribution of power in the Trades Hall Council. The once mighty left wing had declined to a rump and the remaining communists were less active in debate. The Industrial Groups and their allies were able to command about a third of the vote on the Council, and as the breach with the traditional industrial right widened they became a distinctive force. The Groupers began to caucus before meetings of the Trades Hall Council at which contentious issues were to be discussed. Some of their meetings were at the Catholic Action office, where Movement officials gave talks on foreign policy. The Groupers felt Stout had used them and The Movement to get himself out of trouble and was now dumping them. Stout became deeply suspicious of the organised force around him.

The Groupers first appeared as a significant force federally at the Nineteenth Federal Conference of the ALP, held at the Hotel Kingston, Canberra, in March 1951. The Conference was predominantly 'old guard', but representatives of the more aggressive industrial right and a few Groupers constituted a substantial challenge. The Victorian delegates were Calwell, Clarey, Stout, Lovegrove, Monk and Peters. Some of the men round Chifley did not welcome the new aggressiveness from the right, which was being felt in Sydney almost as strongly as in Melbourne, and in other states as well.

Typical of the men under pressure was the Federal President, J. A. Ferguson, Chifley's faithful lieutenant, with Kennelly. Born in Glen Innes in 1903, John Alexander 'Jacky' Ferguson had been a communist in the depression and subsequently came up in the centre of the ALP through the Railways Union. An intelligent, dapper, personable man, with a little of the doctrinaire leftist still in him, Ferguson had originally been a Group supporter; but like Kennelly and Chifley, he had become strongly opposed as they gathered strength.

As State President for several years, Ferguson was the dominating figure of the New South Wales branch in the later Chifley years. A rival force built up in an alliance of the Trades and Labor Council officers and the smaller unions supporting them, the Industrial Groups and The Movement. Partly it was a simple power struggle, of 'ins' and 'outs', small versus big unions, the TLC versus the ALP. It was partly over inadequate support by the Ferguson forces for the Groups after 1949, partly rightists and pragmatists objecting to Ferguson's mild leftism, which they regarded as pretentious, partly a feeling that Ferguson was vain and autocratic and ought to step down. There was a serious clash of personalities between Ferguson and the right leaders, J. Shortell and W. Colbourne, another Chifley favourite.

Ferguson felt he was fighting for the retention of a socialist, militant spirit that was slipping away in the heat of the industrial battle. He disliked the attempted influence in the right of The Movement and United States Labor officials.

Ferguson and the much more aggrieved Kennelly turned the 1951 Federal Conference into a calculated snub to the Groupers and their allies. Conference rejected a motion that the Industrial Groups be placed on a federal basis, and even an amendment to put on record the Conference's appreciation of the 'splendid work performed by the Groups'. Refusing to blame only communists for the continuing bout of strikes, it adopted a motion that 'legitimate industrial disputation was taking place', partly as a result of the Federal Government's failure to control inflation. And it said that 'certain political influences were at work, both from the extreme left and the extreme right, which materially assisted in the creation of the present industrial situation.'

In his Presidential address, Ferguson said there was

unfortunately evidence of weakening belief in the Labor Party. It was revealed in the actions of a few who would repudiate vital political principles and lower the Movement to the level of a Party without an effective policy. It seems that too many of our people are encouraged to believe that hatred of communism is the only condition of good membership, the test of which is true belief in Labor principles as a whole.

Ferguson had made several oblique attacks on Grouper attitudes about this time, and the result was a series of excited attacks on him in *News Weekly*, culminating later in the year in the banning of this magazine by the Federal Executive.

The Conference saw a lengthy revision of ALP policy on socialisation, inevitably the usual compromise between a pragmatic, reformist purpose and socialist language. It was nevertheless an emotional and vital issue at the time, as 'socialist regimentation' had been one of the chief sticks the Liberals used to beat Chifley. Since 1921, the party policy had been, with a bewildering succession of wordy qualifications, 'socialisation of the means of production, distribution and exchange'. There was never a cohesive, intelligent body of opinion at work for nationalisation of industry on the grand scale. The party's policy in practice was extension of public ownership and control of industry where practicable, sensible and likely to achieve some purpose. It remained so, whether the so-called 'left' or 'right' controlled the machine. But there was a widespread love of socialist rhetoric in the Labor Movement and attempts to re-write the socialisation plank always found jealous opposition. It was not so much that those who wished to retain the plank untarnished wanted to nationalise big business—the Australian Constitution forbade that anyway—as that they opposed people being against it. Younger and less ideological people tended to be in favour of extensive re-writing of the platform, to a more precise and meaningful form. Because so many of these in the early 1950's were Catholics, because the issue fitted to some extent the lines of a deeper power struggle and because *News Weekly* was so vehemently for change, the whole debate took on an unhealthy sectarian flavour it did not warrant. It had not been a live issue for Catholics in the ALP since the 1920's.

The 1951 Conference also saw, in a small way, The Movement as a more aggressive force than previously. Motions from the Victorian Executive before the Conference called for co-operatives of all types, encouragement of working proprietorship, a more doctrinaire limitation on nationalisation, land settlement, and individual endowments for students at non-state schools. Recognisable to any reader of *News Weekly*, these were Movement items brought before the Victorian Executive by Keon at the request of Santamaria. The significance of this move was limited, however, as a Victorian Executive member had the right by custom to have his motions for Federal Conference agenda accepted automatically. At the Federal Conference, they got short shrift from the committees which handled the agenda items, mainly with the claim that they were covered in some way by existing policy.

This was a predictable fate for them first time up, but the presence of them at all marked a more aggressive Movement policy from about 1950 onwards. Partly it was inspired by the potential power coming its way as the Grouper faction, of which it was a valued segment, gathered national strength; partly by pressure from the membership for their understanding of Catholic social policy to be implemented. There also seems to have been a feeling that in the late 1940's senior politicians used The Movement up, with few thanks for unpaid or underpaid and certainly under-rewarded work. By 1950 Santamaria was thirty-five and less inclined to have his organisation regarded simply as a collective messenger boy for the grown-ups. From then on there was ample illustration that Santamaria wished to use The Movement to influence politics.

While generally a rebuff for the Groupers, the Conference did see major changes on State Aid, which Catholics had for many years not pressed. The Movement's role here was minor, however. The successful motion, 'That financial aid be granted for the purpose of assisting all forms of education', came from Western Australia and was adopted on the motion of Kim Beazley, MHR. Lovegrove seconded it.

The snub at Canberra was the signal that the Groupers would have to strengthen their organisation. This became more urgent when Clyde Cameron successfully organised for the South Australian Conference to disband the Groups in that state in the middle of 1951. In Queensland, by contrast, the Group organisation was expanding in its alliance with the AWU. The weak spot was New South Wales.

By the start of 1952, the Groupers gained two immensely powerful, if uncertain, allies, who were to catapult them to the top of the machine for two pyrrhic years.

The first of these was Evatt, who became Leader when Chifley died in the middle of 1951. Kennelly had backed Evatt's rival for the leadership, Calwell, in the vital election for Deputy Leader a few weeks before Chifley died. The anti-intellectual, intuitive Kennelly, with his long ties with Calwell and adoration of Chifley was totally incompatible with Evatt. Ferguson, with the traditional mistrust and dislike of much of the New South Wales Party for Evatt, was equally hostile. Realising this only too well, Evatt formed an alliance with the Groupers after the difficulties of the Communist Bill referendum were over. He threw the prestige and organising power of his office behind them.

Although virtually a political necessity, this alliance was not only a stratagem. Evatt, who often seemed to flourish in Melbourne, appears to have been attracted to Lovegrove and McManus as more intelligent, literate, efficient and perhaps honest than more typical ALP administrators. He also had an occasional but old friendship with Archbishop Mannix.

The second potentially disastrous ally for the Groupers was 'big Tom' Dougherty of the AWU, who had some scores to settle and brought the right to power in Sydney in mid-1952.

In the meantime, growing strength had emboldened the Groupers to gamble on getting rid of their arch enemy, Kennelly, as Federal Secretary. He and his friends were villifying them all around the party, they felt, exaggerating and distorting their links with The Movement and Catholic Action. In particular, they blamed him for intriguing against them with Chifley. They feared he would try to use his command of the Federal machinery to outlaw the Industrial Groups, thus breaking the *raison d'être* of their faction. They did not have the Federal strength to get him before he got them, but in Victoria they did.

Most of Kennelly's salary now came as a Member of the Legislative Council in Victoria. There had been speculation for years, particularly in the late 1940's, that he might enter federal politics, and as a result ambitious eyes began to feast on the potential Council vacancy. Then in 1950 he stirred up opposition, already there, in the South and Port Melbourne district by backing F. Crean against the Grouper's choice, V. C. Alford, for the seat of Melbourne Ports, which E. J. Holloway was vacating. This and other incidents set off a fierce feud with the locally powerful family of S. Corrigan, MLA, whom Kennelly also had opposed for pre-selection. This complemented the forces of J. M. Mullens and The Movement, which were strong west of the Yarra in the Footscray district.

Gradually the notion evolved that Kennelly should be opposed at the preselection ballot for the seat, due early in 1952. If he lost his Legislative Council salary, he would have to get a job somewhere else. It would be difficult for him to continue as Federal Secretary and even more difficult for him to stir up trouble.

By the spring of 1951, extensive organisation was on throughout the Melbourne West Province. The ALP officers, the THC, The Movement, the

Corrigan and Mullens machines all joined in. The two opposition candidates were J. D. Cummins, Grouper Melbourne President of the Waterside Workers' Federation, who was well known in Port Melbourne, and A. J. 'Bert' Bailey of the Amalgamated Engineering Union anti-communist group, who came from Footscray. Bailey was in The Movement. They agreed verbally to exchange preferences, thus drawing strength from the two halves of the Province away from Kennelly.

Pre-selections at that time in Victoria, Western Australia and Queensland were by a secret, voluntary ballot of members of unions affiliated to the ALP and of local branches. They had some of the features of an American 'primary', but faced much greater apathy among the unionist voters. The key to pre-selection was to organise support amongst union members and encourage them to vote. Under the rules, unions had to make lists of their members available to all candidates, or none. Advertising, 'how to vote' cards and the use of cars to take voters to the polls were all banned. Despite these precautions, few pre-selection ballots were without their controversies and spirited animosities. If, as happened rarely, a sitting member—especially a very prominent one—was defeated, the bitterness spiralled enormously.

Tragedy struck suddenly at the height of the battle for Melbourne West. On 18 December 1951 Kennelly's younger son Neil, aged thirteen, was killed when he was thrown from the back of a truck while on a trip with friends to pick up a Christmas tree. Neil's twin brother had died some years earlier and the blow distressed Kennelly, an emotional and affectionate man, terribly. For some weeks he paid little attention to his pre-selection troubles.

Intense personal and factional opposition to Kennelly, coupled with the ambitions of the other contenders, meant that the fight was still on. On 1 March 1952, the ballot was held and Bailey defeated Kennelly by 1,335 votes to 1,058.

Kennelly's distress and rage at defeat while he was still grief-stricken was never likely to be forgotten by those who experienced it. He swore vengeance, and the differences in the party intensified more than ever. Kennelly immediately sought selection for a Senate vacancy coming up at the 1953 Senate election. This time the Groupers, somewhat chastened and probably with an element of compassion for his double sorrow, did not organise so hard and Kennelly easily defeated J. J. Roberts, the ALP Treasurer. He became a Senator the following year and remained Federal Secretary.

In retrospect, the 'rolling' of Kennelly seems foolhardy, vindictive and certainly against party traditions, but it indicates the intense feelings of the time. Men backing the Industrial Groups felt they were fighting for the soul of the Labor Movement. They looked on Kennelly as a 'fixer' who would compromise with the communists or anybody else to get his way; they were almost obsessive about him. Conscious of the need to constantly encourage men putting several nights a month, if not a week, into politics, they were infuriated by the insults of the Kennelly-Ferguson faction.

Encouraged by the run of successes, the Groups and especially The Movement were developing a spirit of intolerant, almost evangelical zeal. And Kennelly's own energy and love of power had made many bitter enemies for him, not the least of them Stout and Lovegrove.

While this was the factional background, the evolution of the decision to 'roll' is obscure. It appears to have, if not started, at least reached significant proportions in South Melbourne and spread into the Western part of the Province from there. Whether or not it originated with The Movement, as Kennelly later claimed, it certainly had Movement support. Knowledge of unionists' voting preferences obtained from Movement work provided a base for Bailey's vote. The officers of the ALP and the Trades Hall Council also appear to have been sympathetic. Kennelly had not been a hard electoral worker and had not cultivated ALP branches in the way less highly placed politicians did, particularly in the Western part of the electorate. This and his personal tragedy limited the amount of organising he could do. It is not clear whether the backers of the move really expected to defeat Kennelly—or whether they had originally only meant to frighten him.

Bailey told the author he had been approached by a number of ALP members—two at least of whom stayed in the ALP after the split—to stand against Kennelly. He said he agreed to do so both as a trial run for future endorsement in the Footscray district and as a protest against Kennelly's attitude to the Groups. He said he had not expected to win the pre-selection. After Kennelly's son was killed, he said, he considered withdrawing but decided not to for two reasons: earlier experience working for Mullens had indicated that candidates for pre-selection who withdrew during a contest found it difficult to maintain their support for future attempts; and he had also been warned earlier about the pressure that would be applied on him to withdraw.

Whatever the real origins and motives of the affair, its consequences were incalculable.

Its effect on the party was magnified by the defeat in a pre-selection ballot the same day of the veteran W. J. Beckett by the Mayor of Richmond, Maurice Sheehy, who had the support of the Keon-Scully forces. Beckett, then 82, was a benign, gentlemanly figure who nevertheless had been regarded as a leading 'Wren man' in Parliament. Cain had also been opposed for pre-selection for the first time in 27 years, at least in part the result of a personal, local dispute. He easily defeated his right-wing opponent, L. Purcell, by 583 votes to 225, but the incident produced indignation and suspicion.

The defeat of Kennelly was followed quickly by change in New South Wales.

Tom Nicholson Pierce Dougherty, born at Bollon in Western Queensland in 1902, was an AWU Leader in the traditional mould—physically huge, not very subtle, ambitious, egocentric, autocratic and proud, yet with deep and genuine belief in the cause of social justice and reform.

He came to Sydney to be General Secretary of the union in 1944, and brought with him a desire to strengthen the influence of the AWU in the political wing, and to be a star himself on the Sydney political stage. With nearly 200,000 members throughout Australia, the AWU could just about control the balance of power in the ALP, and certainly it did in the four smaller states.

The traditional industrial right had always been suspicious of the AWU, a relic of the 'one big union' theories. It competed with smaller unions in many parts of Australia for members. The traditionalists considered it inept, ignorant and suffering from a form of collective megalomania. In Sydney, Dougherty's ambitions were scorned, and by nobody more plainly than Ferguson. Dougherty had sought nomination for the New South Wales Legislative Council, a part-time chamber to which members were nominated by the whole Parliament, but was refused.

In the internal politics of 1951, the previous distrust between the traditional right and the AWU was overcome. The AWU coalesced with these, the Industrial Groups and The Movement in an anti-Ferguson front. Using their collective weight to span the state, they organised for suitable changes in some union and State Electoral Council delegations and for support for their faction in others. There had been a significant feeling that the Ferguson administration was tired and that a change was needed. There had also been complaints that the Ferguson Executive was not vigorous enough in tackling widespread corruption on the Sydney City and some other councils and to a limited extent in the state parliament and government. There were some spectacular scandals at that time.

In the autumn, Ferguson was offered, and accepted, a government job as Chairman of the Milk Board. He withdrew from politics and took on the challenge to reform Sydney's chaotic milk supply—successfully, but ironically, with a conservative policy of high-priced milk.

Dougherty signalled a strategy at the AWU Conference in the summer, when he called for abolition of the Legislative Council. A campaign by the AWU and its flamboyant newspaper, *The Worker*, against the Council followed.

When the Conference opened in June, Dougherty moved that the Legislative Council be abolished. Although a popular idea with the rank and file, this was, as expected, defeated; but then an apparently 'compromising' motion that Members of the Council be classed as Parliamentarians and banned from the ALP Executive was adopted. Its implications were tremendous. Parliamentarians had not been allowed to sit as general members of the New South Wales Executive since the days of the conscription split. They had been confined to a stipulated number, elected by the State Caucus and New South Wales Federal members. The new rule effectively barred eight members of the outgoing Executive from re-election. There was a series of bitter clashes on the floor of Conference between the AWU-Grouper faction and the Fergusonites, but it was clear that the coup was successful. Ferguson's political wing supporters were out, while pro-Groupers flowed into the vacant places on the Executive and took control.

New South Wales Labor politics had completed a circle since 1927, when the supporters of J. T. Lang had ousted a tired and corrupt AWU-dominated administration. In 1940, the originators of what evolved into the Chifley-Ferguson machine won control from the Langites and now in 1952 the AWU was back with the balance of power and its uncomfortable bedfellows.

The takeover was completed in December when the Executive sacked the pro-Ferguson State Secretary, Ernest Wright, on the motion of Dougherty. The claim was that there had been maladministration, with suspicious over-ordering of stationery. The dismissal was controversial and made many enemies for the Groupers. Charles Anderson, the Assistant Secretary, was appointed Secretary. J. T. Kane was appointed Assistant Secretary and Industrial Groups organiser. Anderson, Kane, the new State President, W. R. Colbourne, and Jim Kenny, the Assistant Secretary of the TLC, were all Catholics close to The Movement. There was alarm in some quarters that 'Catholic Action' had captured control of the New South Wales branch.

The new régime in New South Wales and continuing victories for the Groups in unions in Victoria and Queensland brought a radically altered line-up to the Twentieth Federal Conference held in Adelaide in January 1953. There were now two sharply defined, bitterly opposed and well matched factions. The New South Wales delegation comprised Dougherty, Colbourne, Kenny, Shortell, R. A. King (the TLC Secretary), and H. J. Blackburn of Lithgow. The Victorians were Lovegrove, McManus, Peters, Stout, Clarey and Fred Riley. The changed disposition of the AWU and accession to the Premiership of Vincent Gair in early 1952, on the death of E. A. Hanlon, made for a more pro-Grouper delegation from Queensland. Pressures emanating from the AWU and, to a small extent, The Movement, gave a more right-wing slant to the Western Australian and Tasmanian delegations as well. South Australia was solidly for Kennelly. The Federal President was Eric Reece, a Tasmanian Minister and former AWU official, who was nevertheless a friend of Kennelly. On the face of it, the Groupers may have had 'the numbers', but they did not have Kennelly's tactical skill.

Despite the background clashes, there was not much open division at the Conference. Much of it was taken up with a long series of routine proposals for domestic reform, designed for the 1953 and 1954 elections. They included £600 marriage loans and a referendum to confer full industrial powers on the Commonwealth. In foreign affairs, some Victorian and New South Wales delegates strongly but unsuccessfully opposed a motion that Britain should be in the ANZUS Pact because of her commitments in Malaya and Borneo. The Movement at that time was discouraging belief in Britain's defence potential for Australia, fostering instead the policy of close ties with the United States in the region. A long preamble on the purpose of the ALP, prepared by Beazley, was adopted unanimously.

An indication of future differences was shown when a motion from South Australia, very much under Cameron's influence, 'warning private enterprise that the ALP will pursue a policy of socialisation', was overwhelmingly rejected. It nevertheless showed a stronger hard-line left tendency in part of the party than was evident in 1951, when Senator Morrow of Tasmania was a lone far left nationaliser.

What was potentially the most divisive issue arose on 21 January, with two motions from the Queensland branch on Industrial Groups. One attacked South Australia for withdrawing support from the Groups and the second declared the 'financial and moral' support of the ALP for them. A third motion from Queensland called for withdrawal of the 1951 ban on *News Weekly*, in the spirit of free speech.

Kennelly and his supporters feared that if the Groupers successfully got the Queensland motions through the evenly divided Conference, they would then push their plan for a formal Federal basis for the Groups, possibly try to write them into the Party Constitution and even move against him. Kennelly successfully manoeuvred to cut across this possibility with an innocuous motion:

That as communism is accepted as an enemy of the working class movement, Conference congratulates all sections working within the Labor Movement in the persistent fight against communism. Conference commends to all State branches the necessity for full . . . support to any section working within the ALP and/or the trade union movement, consistent with the principles, rules and platform of the ALP for the complete elimination of communist influence.

This was moved by the Queensland Treasurer, E. J. Walsh, a friend of Kennelly.

With the passing of this, the other, more divisive motions were abandoned. The pro-Kennelly, anti-Grouper forces, coming to be known somewhat inaccurately as the 'left-wing' of Federal Conference and Federal Executive, had won the significant victories. But the factional rivalry and personal animosity were stronger than ever. It seemed inevitable that the struggle for national control of the party machine would go on, at least until the next Conference, set for Hobart in January 1955.

Chapter Four
The Movement and
'Catholic Action'

The National Secretariat of Catholic Action was formed in Melbourne in late 1937, to put on a more permanent and official basis a form of lay Catholic activity that had been developing for several years. In the early 1930's, young Catholic intellectuals in Melbourne and Sydney had formed Campion Societies, for discussing and advocating Catholic social teaching. By 1936, the stronger Melbourne Campion groups were publishing the monthly *Catholic Worker*, following publications with similar titles in the United States, Britain and Europe. The editor, until 1940, was B. A. Santamaria. Kevin Wallace was named as proprietor in the early years, and the business manager was Frank Keating.

The inspiration of the Campion Society and the *Catholic Worker* was the Distributist tradition, which had attracted great interest in Britain after the First World War. Its best known publicists were the Catholic writers G. K. Chesterton and Hilaire Belloc. The central idea of Distributism was that capitalism was a distortion of human society that had resulted from the Reformation. The natural, 'organic' form of human society, which had reached its flowering in thirteenth century Europe, was the small individual owner of property, peasants or craftsmen organised in co-operative guilds. Distributists argued that property should be returned to the people, instead of being concentrated in either large accretions of capital held by a few owners or vested in the state.

Early issues of the *Catholic Worker* carried the slogan, 'Property for the Proletariat', and under the editorship of the enthusiastic young Santamaria it flamboyantly attacked both capitalists and communists. Calls for a social 'revolution' were common and the paper supported nationalisation of enterprises such as the Broken Hill Proprietary Company Ltd, the steel monopoly, as an interim step to Distributist control by the workers. The paper's heroes were the corporatist Catholic states led by Salazar in Portugal and Dollfuss in Austria, and it fervently supported Franco when he emerged at the head of the Spanish 'Loyalists' six months after the paper started publication. Santamaria himself had had a passing interest in Mussolini as a youth, but he was also a reader of Lenin. The paper was strongly against Hitler, but references to 'Prussian militarism' suggested a partially religious reason for this antipathy.

Often an infatuation with communism showed in the paper. It was run by an undisclosed 'Central Committee', it talked incessantly of 'revolution', 'capitalism', 'exploitation' and 'the workers' and often seemed to feel itself in competition with the communists for the soul of the Australian worker. It revelled in the few attacks from conservative and business interests that came its way.

Santamaria was appointed Assistant Director of the National Secretariat when the bishops agreed to its formation in 1937; the Director was F. K. Maher. Santamaria became Director in 1940, on the resignation of Maher. Over the five or six years from 1937, several specialist organisations were established, under the overall control of the Secretariat (Maher, Santamaria and two clergy) and an Episcopal Committee on Catholic Action. The National Catholic Workers' Movement was intended for workers over twenty-five, but was never really successful. The Young Christian Workers' Movement was for younger workers and was successful, but its controllers could not personally work with Santamaria. The National Catholic Girls' Movement was for teenage girls and the Young Catholic Students' Movement operated in secondary schools. The National Catholic Rural Movement was for farmers and the Secretary from its formation in 1943 was Santamaria.

'Catholic Action' was a concept that developed in Europe from the late nineteenth century, being a general heading to cover a wide variety of social initiatives by laymen. Between the wars, a more formal organisation evolved: lay organisations, given formal charters by the bishops and placed under broad guide-lines, became official organs of 'Catholic Action'. The usual guiding motive was to encourage young adults to keep their faith, while at the same time being banded together in organisations offering a common interest. Catholic Action organisations were enjoined to avoid party politics and it was usually assumed that the organisations would not try to impose firm, specific views about open questions on their members.

Even in Europe, but particularly in Australia, there was an experimental flavour about Catholic Action, with some organisations succeeding, some lapsing for want of interest or a clear-cut task and others again developing embarrassing distortions. In Belgium, an extreme example, the *Jeunesse Ouvrière Chrétienne* (JOC—Christian Working Youth) was an outstandingly successful spiritual and youth movement among young Belgian workers. An arm of *Action Catholique de la Jeunesse Belge* (Catholic Action of Belgian Youth) at the same time developed into the demagogic and eventually fascist *Rex Party* under the demagogue Léon Degrelle and was eventually disowned by the bishops.

By the late 1930's, the National Secretariat of Catholic Action office in Queen Street, Melbourne, became an informal meeting place for young men concerned by communist successes in the unions. The informal organisation around the Newport railway workshops and publication of *The Rail Worker* were early products of such discussion. Herbert Michael Cremean, born in Melbourne in 1900, Deputy Leader of the Victorian Parliamentary Labor Party, encouraged Santamaria and others and put them in touch with Labor leaders at the Trades Hall. The jobs to be done multiplied faster than the organisation available, and in 1941

Cremean and Santamaria visited Archbishop Mannix and asked him to agree to the establishment of a wider organisation.

Cremean introduced Santamaria to Stout at the State Parliament House and The Movement worked closely with him for many years. In these early years, it also worked in the Tramways Union with the anti-communist leader there, Reginald Broadby. Born in Tasmania in 1904, Reginald Broadby was a candidate for the job of Assistant Secretary of the ACTU. Santamaria was also introduced to Percy Clarey, the President of the ACTU. However, on Stout's recommendation, The Movement kept its activities confidential and adopted a policy that the fewer who knew about it, the better. The communists and left had been dubbing their opponents 'Catholic Actionists' and 'Fascists' for years. Stout and other union leaders feared the adverse propaganda the communists would pour upon an open Catholic body organising in the unions.

The controversial secrecy seems hardly to have been an issue at first as The Movement grew from small beginnings at a time of severe newsprint rationing; it might not have had publicity if it sought it. Afterwards, in the judgment of experienced union officials working with it, there was simply never a suitable time to become public.

In the middle of 1942, meetings were held of interested Catholic trade unionists, and of priests from each parish in the Archdiocese. The priests were asked to select groups of unionists and others interested in the Labor Movement, to organise anti-communist activity in each parish. Norman Lauritz, then a wool store clerk, joined the staff as full-time secretary towards the end of 1942. Santamaria in *The Price of Freedom* says the first general gathering of the groups took place on 4 January 1943. A coordinating committee, including Santamaria, Cremean and Lauritz, controlled the work of the parish groups. In 1943 and 1944, the Melbourne organisation developed informal links with the Rev. Dr P. J. Ryan of the Catholic Social Bureau in Sydney, and a small group of Catholic union leaders and interested priests in Broken Hill. Although Dr Ryan's work had been mainly as an anti-communist publicist and speaker in Sydney rather than as an organiser, an embryo National organisation was now under way.

The name Catholic Social Studies Movement was chosen, partly because of Santamaria's interest in Catholic social thinking and his activity in the (Catholic) Post-war Reconstruction Committee and an interdenominational group, never really successful, which held discussions on joint approaches to social questions. The name reflected a desire for a more positive role than just anti-communism, but it was not really appropriate and was hardly ever used. 'The Movement', and even 'The Show' were adopted informally, and these suited the policy of secrecy adopted. The name 'Movement' easily merged into references to the Labor Movement, and reduced the chances of attracting undue attention. From the formation of the National Secretariat in 1937, 'Catholic Action'—a term that often sounded vaguely sinister to non-Catholics—had attracted hysterical attacks from the communists and far left, who portrayed it as near-fascist and involved in a variety of reactionary machinations. And religious sectarian undercurrents had long been a characteristic of the Australian Labor Movement. With this knowledge it would take little imagination to see the propaganda opportunities an organisation such as The Movement would offer its opponents, if it operated openly. The effect would have been largely to nullify its work.

For about ten years, around the time of the First World War, a Catholic Federation had been operating actively—and openly—as a political pressure group for Catholic aims, mainly aid to Church schools. There seemed to be a vague impression abroad that Catholic Action was a semi-underground extension of this work. Certainly, by the 1940's it was common gossip that 'the Catholics' were acting in some mysterious way as a pressure group to Catholicise Australia. This was sometimes seen as a real purpose of the mass migration system initiated, ironically, by Calwell.

Certainly at that time, The Movement and some other Catholic Action offshoots were campaigning for a massive migration program, the result of which would have been greatly to increase the Catholic proportion of Australians. The more modest program adopted was in fact a major cause of the Catholic proportion rising from less than 20 per cent between the wars to about 25 per cent in the 1950's. This was merely getting it back to nineteenth century proportions, however, as the overwhelmingly British nature of migration from 1900 to 1945 had helped reduce Catholic strength. Religion never seems to have been a serious factor in Australian migration policy.

The Movement's weekly newspaper, *Freedom*, launched in September 1943, explained itself as an independent Christian journal, based on twenty points adopted by the interdenominational meetings, which had taken the name of Christian Social Order Movement. In practice, it provided a new journalistic platform for Santamaria, who had broken with the *Catholic Worker* in 1940 after a dispute over control. The name was changed to *News Weekly* in 1946, as part of a policy of giving more urgency and 'punch' to the paper as more newsprint became available.

Distributist social views dominated the paper for many years. But by 1943 much of the youthful revolutionary zeal had gone, though a peculiar dogmatic stridency always characterised Santamaria's popular journalism. The first issue of *Freedom* named the Twenty Points which were to be its policy.

1 Public control of monopolies
2 Public control of credit
3 The Institution of Industrial Councils
4 Assistance to small owners
5 Part ownership of industry for the workers
6 Co-operation in all its aspects—producers, consumers, marketing, insurance and credit
7 The principle of an Adequate Income for all, including a minimum wage that will meet all the needs of the family, allow it to provide for the future, attain to the ownership of property and improve its cultural condition

8 Payment of a marriage bonus and payment of adequate family allowances

9 Wages a first charge in industry, before dividends or profits

10 Equal pay for equal work

11 Possession of Family Homes for all

12 A strong program of regionalism, including spreading of all the conveniences of the city to the country home

13 A national campaign for Family Land Settlement

14 A radical crisis to solve the problem of rural debt

15 Independent Farming as the normal productive policy

16 Co-operation in agriculture

17 A Fair Return for the farm production

18 Self-government of agriculture

19 A National System of education

20 Recognition of religion as the Basis of Education

The main lines of these policies were improved social services, wider distribution of property; a degree of worker control in industry; and extensive land settlement on the basis of small family farms of a semi-subsistence type. The Industrial Councils proposed were envisaged as national, regional and local councils of employers and employees in a particular industry, which would decide wages, conditions, prices, production policies and the like. A society based upon such 'corporations', a modernised form of the mediaeval guild, had long been uppermost in the social thinking of Catholics in the traditionalist wing in Europe, and they formed the basis of organisation in Franco's Spain, Salazar's Portugal, Mussolini's Italy and, for a much shorter time and in a less authoritarian way, Dollfuss' Austria. Pope Pius XI gave the corporative form of society warm approval in his Encyclical *Quadragesimo Anno* in 1931.

Despite the extreme right nature of the European corporative societies, the form itself was neutral and in Australia was mainly advocated on the assumption of a sharp re-distribution of wealth and power back to employees. Corporatism was superseded by a modified form of Distributist ideas in *News Weekly* after the Second World War, but it continued as central to *Catholic Worker* policies until the mid-1950's. After that time, the *Catholic Worker*, ironically, evolved as the organ of liberal Catholicism in Australia. Never at any stage did either journal see corporatism as an alternative to democratic parliamentary government; it was seen rather as an alternative to industrial 'capitalism' and the class struggle.

In the 1940's, foreign policy had little interest for either journal. The romantic admiration for Iberia of the 1930's had gone and the concern about Asia that was to develop in the 1950's was still in the future.

The basic operation of The Movement as it developed after 1943 was to use the parish groups as centres for local anti-communist organisation. The groups prepared lists of Catholic, and sometimes non-Catholic, union members living in their parish, sub-divided according to unions. At the request of Stout and others, The Movement would try to get Catholic union members to attend meetings of their unions, thus providing a counter to communist attempts to influence their policies or election of officers. Apathy was the single strongest characteristic of Australian trade unionism and perhaps the best friend of communist influence. Movement members, not always unionists themselves, took the responsibility for encouraging Catholic unionists to go to vital meetings, of providing cars for them, of encouraging them to vote in elections for officers. The Movement had many early successes, but lost its biggest single early fight—trying to stop the communist leadership of the Ironworkers' Association from merging the Munition Workers' Union into the Ironworkers'. In those days, union meetings were often exceedingly bitter. There was always the risk of a physical fight, while taunts about 'boss's stooges' and 'Catholic Actionists' were so common they were hardly noticed.

The communist victories at the ACTU Congress of June 1945 led to formation of The Movement on an organised, formal basis. The bishops were meeting in Sydney in September, and Santamaria submitted a formal memorandum on the situation in the unions. He asked them to agree to The Movement being established nationally. The bishops, accepting that 'there is no other force in the community which possesses either the determination or the necessary degree of organisation to withstand communism' agreed. They appointed Archbishop (later Cardinal) Gilroy of Sydney, Archbishop Mannix of Melbourne and Bishop J. P. O'Collins of Ballarat to control The Movement. The two archbishops delegated their power to Bishop O'Collins, one of Santamaria's strongest episcopal admirers. The bishops agreed to make limited finance and the use of Church facilities available to The Movement, but it was to remain essentially a lay organisation. From 1945 on, Bishop O'Collins attended most meetings of its National Executive and other meetings as an observer, but the bishops otherwise had little contact with or influence on The Movement.

In the memorandum to the bishops—which covered twenty-nine pages of closely typed foolscap—Santamaria appeared to oscillate between humility at the size of the task, even of intensifying anti-communist feeling among Catholics, and enthusiasm for the possibilities. While the tone was generally moderate, occasionally the memorandum talked of 'controlling' various unions or ALP branches and of numbers of 'reliable Catholics'.

On the question of secrecy, on which he seemed uneasy at times and which he twice sought to modify or reverse, Santamaria said:

It is also essential that nothing should be done which would give the appearance of truth to the charges made by those who use the sectarian weapon. In a way, the existence of Catholic organisations, powerful at least in numbers, hampers all our work—and it must be emphasised again that the work which is going on is not that of simply winning elections, but that of spreading every kind of Catholic idea. The difficulties which we have had to face everywhere through the wearing of the Holy Name badge, to give one instance only, have been very great.

That is why we recommend that in all spheres outside the parish, the work of spreading the Faith should be done by these anonymous groups, welded together as they are in one disciplined organisation, and trained to the minute in both the spiritual and intellectual sense. We feel that openly organised Catholic Action Movements should operate on a parish basis only. The factory and union field should be left to The Movement.

We feel that if this suggestion is not followed, the more powerful the organisations we build, and the more impressive they are from the public viewpoint, the greater and more impassable the bridge between us and the non-Catholics around us.

From the narrower point of view, namely the defeat of communism, the success of our work depends completely on an active alliance with non-Catholics, who, if they do not share our religion, at least share many of its ideals. From their point of view, the alliance has no difficulties so long as they collaborate with individual Catholics, even though they may have good reason to believe that these Catholics are organised. But they have made it perfectly clear that it would be impossible for them to collaborate with an open Catholic organisation.

In a brief reference to the wider community, Santamaria said:

Our sections have been advised that their members should interest themselves in all local affairs, and as a consequence Progress Associations, Community Hospitals and Community Centres in many districts have our representatives on their committees.

Community Centres are being watched with particular interest. In one district, practically the whole of the Provisional Committee is composed of our people. This is, of course, a mistake and is the result of over-organisation. We realise that at the present time at least we should aim only for just sufficient representation to exercise control.

In practice, national organisation meant mainly the establishment of a strong Movement organisation, on Melbourne lines, in Sydney. It was given offices at Cusa House, the main diocesan office building in Elizabeth Street, Sydney, and F. O'Connor was appointed Secretary. In 1948, he was succeeded by Terry Ludeke, later a prominent industrial barrister, and in 1952 by Kevin Davis, a school teacher who had once trained for the Jesuits. For most of the time, Roy Boylan was the industrial organiser.

A strong Movement group also arose in Newcastle, with Frank Rooney, a fitter and turner at the State Dockyard, the most prominent member. There were groups also in the main country towns of New South Wales, especially those with mines, railway workshops or heavy industry.

Dr Ryan, a personally popular man of notable intelligence, but somewhat given to melodrama, was appointed Chaplain for the Sydney Archdiocese. In 1950, Bishop P. F. Lyons, who had been appointed Auxiliary Bishop of Sydney, also became a chaplain and episcopal overseer of The Movement in the Archdiocese. Before the war, Lyons had been private secretary to Archbishop Mannix, and was something of a favourite of Mannix. He had a difficult personality which made him many enemies, however, and in the 1940's a coup in clerical politics got him appointed Bishop of Christchurch, New Zealand. He ran into more trouble there, and was virtually out of a job when given the Sydney appointment. The Movement in Sydney thus came to have a more clerical flavour than in Melbourne.

In Brisbane, Archbishop Duhig had reservations about The Movement and it never had his full support. A small office was established in the Hibernian Insurance Company building in Adelaide Street, with Alex Polgrain as Secretary and William Thornton, a member of the Clerks' Union, industrial officer. Because of the Archbishop's lack of enthusiasm, The Movement did not develop a parish organisation in Brisbane and its membership stayed small. The provincial bishops in Queensland, however, were well disposed, and its organisation was much stronger in the bigger country towns, notably Rockhampton. It was able eventually to pay full time organisers in Rockhampton, a strong Movement centre, and Townsville.

The organisation in South Australia was smaller again, though a full-time organiser was employed for a while. The Movement was almost as strong in the industrial centres of Whyalla, Port Pirie and Port Augusta, as in Adelaide. Representation in Tasmania and Western Australia was never more than token in character.

No count was ever kept of membership of The Movement, but various estimates given to the author range from 5,000 to 10,000 nationally in the best times, the early 1950's. Most estimates would have been nearer 5,000 than 10,000, and before the 1949 coal strike it would have been considerably smaller. About half the membership was in Victoria, mainly in Melbourne, and most of the rest in New South Wales.

The money to pay for The Movement mainly came from private Catholic pockets. Part of an organiser's job was to raise his own salary. In most parishes at some time or other confidential meetings of better off Catholics were called. Santamaria, a Movement official, or often one of a number of articulate, interested priests, would address these meetings and encourage those present to present regular bank order contributions to the 'fight against communism'. There was often a melodramatic air about the meetings, with their confidential nature and oratory about the threat of communism. There was almost certainly money from confidential American Government sources available for anti-communist work in the Australian Labor Movement at this time, and some of this may have gone to The Movement—though no-one is likely to admit it.[1] Movement employees were mostly poorly paid, usually at about the ruling rate for a skilled tradesman. They worked long hours and the organisers travelled around the cities by public transport.

With the formation of ALP Industrial Groups in New South Wales (1945), Victoria (1946) and Queensland and South Australia, the nature

[1] Santamaria strongly denied to the author that The Movement ever received money from any *Government* source.

of The Movement's work changed. From being almost the sole organised force fighting the communists, it developed principally as a service organisation for the Industrial Groups.

Movement members were a minority among Industrial Group members, rarely numbering more than 25 per cent, but they provided a basic national organisation for the Groups to rely upon. The servicing functions of The Movement, which became its principal task, were:

1 Finding members for the Groups, and candidates for union office. The parish groups usually had enough local contact to know of suitable people and either The Movement people locally, or members of the Industrial Group, would then approach them. This function was particularly important in large, complex national unions, such as the Railways, Ironworkers', Miners', Clerks', and Amalgamated Engineering Union, where often several hundred candidates would be needed to nominate for all positions in a national election. It was much more important in unions where the communists were in control of the office than in those where the Industrial Group was in charge, fighting off communist advances.

2 Canvassing Catholic unionists to vote in elections, and encouraging them, as before, to attend vital meetings.

3 Providing cars (usually those owned and driven by Movement men) to carry people to union meetings and to carry Group members in the country.

4 Addressing envelopes containing the Group 'ticket' for union elections. In the AEU, the 'ticket' had to be hand-written and Movement people did this job. The Movement could also organise for girls to do typing jobs for the Groups.

5 Recruiting members for the breakaway Amalgamated Society of Carpenters and Joiners.

6 Assisting the Groups with finance. This was mainly confined to the bigger, more complex unions. The Movement specialised in paying for the printing of propaganda and 'tickets' and often organised the printing as well. The Movement was occasionally able to get access to large sums for special purposes.

7 Miscellaneous other functions, such as obtaining legal advice, sometimes free, from friendly lawyers, making suggestions on organisation and methods, distributing literature and the like.

8 Advocating support for the Industrial Groups inside the ALP.

From the start, until the sudden exposure at the end of 1954, secrecy was remarkably well maintained, though there were some uneasy moments. A bishop returning by train from Sydney after the historic 1945 conference lost a copy of Santamaria's memorandum on the need for stronger organisation. A few months later, in February 1946, it turned up as a communist pamphlet, 'Catholic Action at Work'. The communist editing and presentation made it all seem very sinister. As a result of 'Catholic Action at Work', Santamaria raised the question of whether secrecy should be maintained, but Stout particularly was adamant that it should be continued.

In 1950, extracts from the memorandum appeared again in the scandalous, best-selling novel *Power Without Glory*, by the communist author Frank Hardy. The latter parts of this novel portrayed 'Catholic Action' in an unattractively sinister light.

In 1951, attacks by *News Weekly* on several prominent members of the ALP, over the Communist Party Dissolution Bill and the subsequent referendum, abolition of the Industrial Groups in South Australia and other issues, led to the ALP Federal Executive banning *News Weekly*. The climate leading to such events led Santamaria to another move to end secrecy. He prepared a memorandum outlining a plan for the Movement to be reformed as a series of Church-based 'Civic Committees', a name taken from similar organisations formed in Italy when the communists had a chance of electoral victory in 1948.[2] Unlike The Movement groups, these would have been open to anybody suitable who wished to join. The meetings themselves would not be open to the public, but the existence of the Committees would not have been concealed. A meeting of the bishops[3] in April 1951 rejected this proposal, as did the National Conference of that year. The strongest opposition to 'going public' came from the Sydney hierarchy, and was partly the result of strong opposition from union leaders, fearful of the consequences of malevolent publicity at impending union elections. There was almost always an important, bitterly contested union election going on somewhere in Australia in those years.

While secrecy was remarkably well maintained, anybody who was interested knew there was something going on and that Catholics were involved. There was continual whispering about 'Catholic Action' and meetings in churches. The shrill, sneering, smearing quality of *News Weekly* attracted many critics. The communists, who of course were being deprived of both power and jobs, vigorously promoted hysteria about 'Catholic Action' and its association with the Industrial Groups. Anybody who opposed communists in the Labor Movement could rely on being characterised as a 'Catholic Actionist', even if he was an agnostic freemason.

Parish groups of The Movement usually contained eight to fifteen members, and seem more often to have been nearer eight than fifteen. It was a 'cadre' style operation, with everybody having a job to do. There would be a finance officer, raising money, an industrial officer, to organise canvasses and work for the Groups, a *News Weekly* officer to promote sales of *News Weekly* in the parish (particularly at the Church door on Sunday), and an intelligence officer, watching the local press for signs of communist activity. Meetings were usually monthly and a chaplain, typically the parish curate, would be present for Gospel discussions. Members were asked to join the political party of their choice,

---

[2] Quoted by P. J. Duffy in 'Catholic Attitudes to the ALP Dispute', unpublished MA thesis, University of Melbourne
[3] Ibid.

and perhaps three quarters of them were members of the ALP. They were also asked to be active in their own union.

Membership of The Movement, as of the Communist Party, involved heavy sacrifices of time. As well as attending the monthly parish group meeting, members had to attend their union and ALP branch meetings, perhaps address envelopes in town one night a month, sell *News Weekly*, canvass unionists, collect money, attend training classes and the like. Not surprisingly, there was a large turnover of members and it was often hard to maintain enough members to keep the group efficient.

Membership was confined to fully practising Catholics. It was by invitation only, and the local group had to approve new members. People considered to have unsuitable political sympathies, to be lazy, badly motivated, lacking in common sense, over-talkative or heavy drinkers were usually excluded from consideration.

Parish groups elected delegates to regional conferences—a typical region would be the northern suburbs of Melbourne—and these in turn elected delegates to the controlling National Conference. Larger but less authoritative National Conventions, which anybody could attend, were also held. Between Conferences, control was vested in the National Executive, which was made up of the officers.

Policy was decided by National Conference, either on the basis of motions coming up from the parish groups through regional conferences, or from papers read to the Conference on specific subjects. A number of social policies were adopted in this way, usually either based on modified Distributism, on proposals for streamlining the fight in the unions, or on a tough anti-communist line in foreign policy.

While the structure was theoretically fairly democratic, the atmosphere was more authoritarian. Santamaria's control over staff appointments gave him effective control of the Executive, while the power of the Executive to pick the date for Conferences—which varied to meet circumstances, needs and convenience—and its power to select the speakers and papers to be given gave much central control over the Conference.

Members were supposed to adhere to Movement policy and this gave a measure of ability for it to discipline its members in the ALP and elsewhere. However, apart from the issue of support for the Industrial Groups—which it is hard to imagine any member *not* supporting—distinctive Movement policies arose only on a small number of occasions at the higher levels of the ALP in the last two or three years before the split. The split that developed in New South Wales over very few such issues, and the failure of Movement men to vote *en bloc* on the Victorian Executive suggests very limited ability to discipline the vote.

Did the Movement control the ALP Industrial Groups? As energetic, zealous minorities within Groups, Movement members obviously were influential; but the records show little attempt by Group-controlled unions, other than the Clerks', to put forward distinctive Movement policy. Perhaps a fair conclusion would be that The Movement acted as an effective pressure group in support of status and backing for the Industrial Groups and sharpened their ideological approach to communism—perhaps too often at the cost of members appearing to be haters, like the communists themselves—and gave added strength to the Groups as an ALP faction. Beyond that, its importance was peripheral.

The most important influence on the social thinking of Santamaria and The Movement in the post-war years was Colin Grant Clark, economic advisor to the Queensland Government. Clark, born in 1905 of a Queensland family but brought up in England, was a convert to Catholicism. He was a man of intelligence and vision, but of a rather romantic and doctrinaire nature. He had been unsuccessful as an endorsed Labour candidate for Parliament in 'blue ribbon' Tory seats in the West of England in the 1930's and was Private Secretary to C. Attlee, the British Labour leader. He came to Australia as an economics lecturer in 1938. Like many intellectual English Catholics, Clark was considerably influenced by Distributism and Traditionalism. But as an economist, he realised that in the primitive, dogmatic form in which these ideas were often discussed, they were totally impractical. He applied his original mind to modifying Distributism, to make it applicable to modern conditions.

The post-war years in Australia were characterised by severe inflation and rapid industrialisation. Clark believed that the pace of industrialisation, the inefficiency, in economic terms, of much Australian industry and the system of automatic quarterly adjustments to the basic wage, based on price changes, were the main contributors to inflation.

Instead of industrialisation, he advocated more intensive settlement on the land, with Australia improving its balance of payments by becoming a much greater food producer. This is discussed in more detail in Chapter 8. He also advocated lower tariffs on 'non-essential' industries and strong legislation against restrictive trade practices to combat industrial inefficiency and its contribution to inflation.

He wanted the quarterly basic wage adjustments abolished and instead a productivity index established, with wages fixed according to rises in productivity. This would tend both to counter inflation and to increase productivity. He preferred profit-sharing to over-award payments, as more likely to benefit the lower paid worker.

Clark advocated measures that would produce the fastest possible mechanisation of industry, believing the best way to avoid overwhelming the population in soulless, giant corporations was to cut back the work force through mechanisation. This would lead to a growth in demand for service industries, which were well suited to control by the small proprietor. The result would be a gradual return to the working proprietor ideal of the Distributist society.

He opposed the simpler 'back to the land' Distributist ideas, but instead advocated a modified form of geographic decentralisation: creation by Government action of well planned regional cities of 100,000 to 250,000 people. Cities of this size would be large enough to support viable secondary industry and universities, he argued. They would be far more likely to be successfully established than decentralisation in the form of a retreat to the small town and village, as some Distributists wished.

Mostly under the influence of Clark, the main lines of Movement social policy by the early 1950's developed as:

1 Replacement of quarterly adjustments by the productivity wage system, accompannied by profit sharing, tariff cuts and bans on restrictive trade practices.

2 Strict curtailment by legislative action of the growth of Sydney and Melbourne, and encouragement of smaller regional cities.

3 Emphasis on land settlement rather than rapid industrialisation.

4 Social services designed to encourage big families.

5 A bigger migrant intake, to build up the population, with many of the migrants being settled on the land and a high proportion of them Catholics.

6 Corporative Industrial Councils were still sought, but by the early 1950's the tendency was to emphasise more joint consultation and moderate forms of worker representation in industrial management.

7 The widest possible encouragement of co-operatives, in industry, agriculture and as a means of consumer credit.

8 Intensive irrigation in the Murray River basin, with hydro-electricity generated in the Snowy Mountains scheme to be used exclusively inland, to encourage industrialisation. (However, Clark was not enthusiastic about irrigation.)

By 1949, however, foreign policy had started to take precedence over domestic policy in Movement priorities. In the middle of that year, the Nationalists of Chiang Kai Shek collapsed suddenly in China and by October China was a communist country. In the previous four years, seven European countries had been won for communism, often by the most ruthless tactics under the umbrella of the occupying Russian Army. In Asia, already the Russians had turned their northern half of Korea into a 'satellite' and in French Indo-China the communists had captured the Nationalist Movement and led a civil war against the French. In Malaya, Chinese-led communists had unleashed a guerilla war against the British. A communist uprising had been crushed in Indonesia, but the communists remained a powerful political force and there were doubts about the competence and political sagacity of the Indonesian Nationalists.

In this situation, it was natural that many men involved in a bitter fight against communists in Australia would wonder if the seemingly invincible international force would not soon threaten Australia, isolated beyond an unstable Asia. Santamaria, who as well as being a militant anti-communist also had the politician's instinct for a good issue, soon made the 'threat from the North' into a high priority issue for The Movement. From 1950 onwards, the theme of fund-raising meetings was less concentrated on the unions and more on the threat from Asian communism, under the slogan 'Ten Minutes to Midnight'.

The outbreak of the Korean War in the middle of 1950 intensified this trend in The Movement. Santamaria believed there was a danger that it would spread beyond Korea and engulf the whole of Asia. A note of fear, bordering on hysteria, often showed in *News Weekly* early in the Korean War.

This fear and the whole 'threat from the North' thesis can seem crude and unwarranted in retrospect. Obvious objections were that, even at the height of the Cold War, Stalin and the communist leaders preferred to 'pick off' easily vulnerable weak spots in other countries; and the supply lines of communist forces seeking to invade Australia would have been impossibly long. Also, the Chinese Revolution had marked ideological differences, including emphasis on peasant guerilla war, with that of Russia. A student of communist affairs might have forecast that sooner or later the monolith would break up.

In 1950, however, it would have been a bold man who forecast that the sudden spreading of the communist empire would halt for many years at halfway lines in Vietnam and Korea. And the chances of communist parties capturing Asian Nationalist movements were always rated high. Menzies himself, in the autumn of 1950, had warned that Australia must be ready for war 'in three years'. The Government, however, believed that the danger was of communist expansion in the Middle East, and that war breaking out there might not be contained.

Santamaria's view of Asian relations, which in a more developed way became the principal concern of his middle years, represented something of a pioneering approach to Australian foreign relations. While the Liberals and the Country Party, particularly Menzies, saw events very much in terms of relations with Britain, America and the European colonial powers, and Labor was dominated either by isolationism or by a pacifistic view, The Movement's contribution was a distinctively Australian approach to armed and allied preparedness—a subject European countries had had to concern themselves with for centuries. However, the pages of *News Weekly, Rural Life* and other such publications reveal an extremely cataclysmic approach to Asian relations and most other questions. In Santamaria's world view, it seemed, immense crises always lay immediately ahead. In most years of the early 1950's, his publications warned in end-of-year and new year messages of the crisis lying immediately ahead. 'Red Asiatic Tide May Engulf Australia', warned the main headline in the first issue of *News Weekly* for 1950. The issue of 31 December 1952 spoke of 'Australia's Race Against Time'.

The possibility of war led The Movement in 1950 to reverse its earlier opposition to the ban on the Communist Party, first advocated by the Country Party and taken up by Menzies for the 1949 election. Santamaria's view, shown in both *News Weekly* and in a memorandum quoted by Duffy,[4] was that such a ban would not work, and would end the isolation into which the communists were being driven. It was a view based on the practicality of the situation, not on any concern for civil liberties. The threat of war may have been a convenient excuse for reversing this stand, however. Some Catholics and Industrial Groupers

[4] Ibid.

supported the ban from the start. At least a few Group members saw it as an easy way of defeating the enemy and getting envied jobs for themselves.

To many of its opponents, the influence of 'Catholic Action' seemed enormous and threatening by the early 1950's. Well publicised parliamentarians, such as Keon and Mullens, seemed to be reflecting the 'C.A. line', in their harsh anti-communism, as did the Catholic-dominated Labor Party machines of the eastern states. *News Weekly* was on sale outside the churches of the main cities and many of its attitudes pervaded the official Catholic press. Movement ideas spread in varying degrees through other Catholic Action organisations, through the Church youth, and were eagerly supported by many clergy, teachers and bishops. 'Catholic Action' often seemed to be extremely active and well organised in local Labor Party branches.

Yet much of this influence was an illusion. The circulation of *News Weekly* rarely rose much above 20,000. Many older priests disliked The Movement, sometimes for ideological reasons and more often because it was a nuisance, a competitor for time and money in the parish. The support of most of the metropolitan bishops was conditional on The Movement remaining uncontroversial, as was the support it appeared to get from a few parliamentarians. The leadership of the Young Christian Workers, the strongest of the Catholic Action organisations, feuded with Santamaria for many years.

The Movement had only occasional members on the Victorian ALP Executive until 1950, and from 1950 to 1955 about six to eight members at various times. Of the officers only the Assistant Secretary, Frank McManus, and the Treasurer, Jack Roberts, were members. After 1952, there were about half a dozen Movement men in the Parliamentary Labor Party in Victoria. Federally, Keon, Mullens and Andrews were close to The Movement, but Keon at least of these eventually became one of its most scathing critics.

Actually, very few formal members of The Movement were at all prominent in public life. Many leading Catholics and some non-Catholics in the political wing, the Groups and the unions were close to it, attending and speaking at meetings and encouraging the work. But almost all avoided formal commitment to a quasi-political outside organisation. This was partly because they did not have the time, but there was always the possibility that membership could be embarrassing while there were political advantages to be gained from being informally influential with it.

Movement people tended to be active and zealous by nature and many became office holders in local ALP branches. At Victorian ALP conferences, in the early 1950's, about 25 per cent of delegates were members of the Movement, according to some estimates given to the author. Many went as proxy delegates for uncontroversial unions, whose membership was too apathetic to supply enough delegates. Movement social policy began to appear on ALP Conference agendas, coming mainly from either the Clerks' Union or from a handful of branches in middle class suburbs, until the newly Group-controlled Railways Union put forward the productivity wage in 1954.

All this activity was largely unsuccessful. Only a small proportion of agenda items are ever debated at the main conferences of the Labor Movement; the great majority, passed over by the Agenda Committee, are there mainly in a spirit of 'showing the flag'. Until the Victorian Conference adopted the productivity wage in 1954, Movement policies rarely reached the stage of a Conference decision or debate. The reason was that the Agenda Committee and the officers, inevitably highly selective, considered them too divisive or theoretical, and used their influence to keep them off the floor.

In Sydney, further removed from Santamaria and a less ideological city, The Movement always had a less ideological flavour. Enthusiasm for Distributism was confined to a few individuals and Movement social policy generally was a minor part of the ALP picture. The social policies were less important again in the smaller states, though short-lived vogues for intensive land settlement appeared from time to time.

Proposals for joint consultation, the productivity wage and the like appeared on the agendas for the 1951 and 1953 biennial congresses of the ACTU. They came from the Clerks' Union and the Queensland Service Union. As at Victorian ALP Conferences, they never reached the stage of debate.

Foreign affairs remained a rather academic discussion, apart from the Communist Party Dissolution Bill, because in the post-war decade there was little interest in it among the Labor Movement rank and file. Motions about foreign affairs simply did not appear on Labor Conference agendas before 1953, when it arose at the Adelaide Federal Conference. The tradition was to leave it to the Parliamentary parties. Movement members did on a few occasions bring ideologically worded motions on China, the Japanese Peace Treaty and the like before the Victorian Central Executive of the ALP; but whether passed or not they usually ended up being 'lost' somewhere in the labyrinth of Labor.

The main reason for The Movement's lack of success in influencing ALP policy was simply that people were not interested. The climate of the ALP was overwhelmingly emotional and rhetorical, not ideological. Anti-communism came to it as easily as anti-capitalism, particularly with Catholics, and to this limited extent The Movement was able to influence it. There was no great ideological opposition to Movement social policies; their enemy was tradition, orthodoxy, inertia and apathy. But one strand running through them was that they were against the interests of trade union leaders. Productivity wages, joint consultation and profit sharing would have taken power away from trade union leaders. Decentralisation would have meant they had to travel more—or delegate power. This was probably the main reason why veteran trade union leaders, who knew the weaknesses of their colleagues only too well, kept such issues from coming alive.

It should not be assumed, either, that Movement membership was united in fervent support for its social policies. The policies certainly had the fervent support of many, but others were in The Movement for its anti-communism and to help the ALP. There were two broad streams of attitude: one of highly ideological admirers of Santamaria; the other, represented by men like McManus and Colbourne, strongly anti-communist but otherwise imbued with fairly orthodox ALP attitudes. To some extent the policies represented a political necessity within The Movement. Younger members, particularly, often demanded positive policies and—quite apart from Santamaria's own zeal—they had to be given them if they were to stay interested. There was also the fear of The Movement becoming a purely negative anti-communist organisation.

Why, in view of its comparative lack of success in influencing the ALP, did The Movement become so controversial? It caused two broad groups of difficulties—one arising from its intrinsic nature and probably inevitable, and the other arising from the accident of Santamaria's personality. Since before Santamaria was born, an element of religious sectarianism had bedevilled the ALP. Simple Protestant-Catholic bigotry, or the feud of orange and green, in itself was never a serious problem. It was more that there were two groups of people, more or less evenly matched in numbers, with significant differences in their values, intolerances and emotional responses. A succession of issues arose which tended to play on and exaggerate these differences. Conscription and Ireland versus Britain were the issue of the First World War years. After the war, some Catholics objected to the socialist rhetoric and values then fashionable. Many Catholics, however, were influenced by these themselves; one cause of trouble was the common experience of an interest in materialist socialist theory being accompanied by a dwindling of religious faith. By the late 1930's, Catholic opinion was more militant than non-Catholic—with the socialist issue in the background—in opposing the intensified communist attempts to penetrate the Labor Movement. 'State Aid' to Catholic schools was a perpetually divisive issue.

Catholics in the Labor Movement, typically, were prejudiced against the whole range of the intellectual left, from Fabianism to Marxism in its various forms. They were hypersensitive to any suggestion of anti-Catholicism, and often saw it where it was not intended. They were deeply suspicious of Freemasonry. An intensity and dogmatism often characterised their attitudes.

Non-Catholics were more diverse, varying from active Protestants to agnostics, from doctrinaire socialists to wheeling and dealing social reformers. But very often, whatever their motivation, they all reacted against Catholic intensity on sensitive issues. And there was always in the background the deeply ingrained Protestant instinct that in some vague and mysterious way, Rome was organising in the background.

These inherently divisive attitudes were set against a background in the Australian community of a sort of religious tribalism. Catholics and non-Catholics tended to have a deep-seated mistrust for each other, whatever the surface pleasantries, and to each go their own way. Catholics were usually educated separately, and the two groups did not mix much socially as children. Though inter-marriage was common, it often caused more conflict than harmony.

The sharpness of the division can be exaggerated, though. It varied greatly from district to district, even within the same city, and personal likes and dislikes and vested interests caused many local variations. There were always some Protestants who shared Catholic attitudes, and many Catholics who shared Protestant ones on particular issues. And even among Catholics, the rate of church-going was not especially high in Australian working class districts. The comparatively low rate of religious practice in the cities was an important reason for Santamaria's decentralism. However, religious people often had the zealous temperament that was also attracted to politics and regular church-goers were probably more numerous in the ALP than in the working class community generally.

Factionalism and power struggles were a longstanding characteristic of the ALP, and when there was no better issue at hand they tended to follow the broad religious lines indicated. The factionalism was always aroused most fiercely over pre-selection ballots for endorsement of Labor candidates for public office, even if it was only a local council.

The effect of The Movement was to strengthen and intensify the long existing, more anti-Marxist, predominantly Catholic faction. Movement members themselves joined the ALP and often stayed in it after their two or three years in The Movement. They encouraged their friends and relatives to join. They, and the whole climate surrounding Catholic Action, affected the attitudes of other Catholics. The longstanding tendency to use Church organisations as a recruiting ground for the ALP, and to 'stack' branches for pre-selection and other factional purposes, became exaggerated.

Intensifying activity on the Catholic-dominated side started to concern the others; and the more their concern showed, especially if accompanied by allegations of 'Catholic Action', the more Catholics tended to react. A vicious circle began to spin. The battle in the unions after 1947 heightened the factional feeling yet again. There was often stacking and counter-stacking of local branches to enhance or weaken the status of some person controversial in the union struggles. The Movement brought into ALP branches many young Catholic zealots who seemed to be motivated entirely by religion and hardly at all by grass roots politics. There were veterans who were bewildered by, perhaps, being treated to an enthusiastic lecture by a youth on the sanctity of family or rural life.

There is no evidence that The Movement itself took an organised part in pre-selection ballots; but what Movement men did with their contacts and lists of unionists in their role as ALP members was something else. Santamaria often used his influence to encourage his members to give their support in pre-selections to pro-Group Protestants, to dampen down the sectarian atmosphere created around Industrial Group activity. This occasionally had the ironic effect of arousing anti-Group feeling among Catholics.

In Sydney, where Santamaria's control was less, even more melodrama than in Melbourne surrounded The Movement. It was active in Sydney University for some years, and took on some of the 'cowboys and Indians' flavour of student politics. It had an informal association in the late 1940's with a highly secret anti-communist paramilitary organisation that developed in Sydney for a while. The Sydney hierarchy was concerned about the lurid anti-Catholic publication, *The Rock*, in the late 1940's, and some melodramatic 'raids' by its supporters to 'free slaves' in Catholic laundries. It used The Movement to 'tail' sellers of *The Rock*, and generally to watch *The Rock* activities. Melbourne seems to have looked on *The Rock* as a bad joke (though J. L. Cremean sponsored an unsuccessful bill in the Victorian Parliament to ban it, at the cost of stirring the familiar factional upsurge in the Parliamentary Labor Party). There were several instances in Sydney of Movement people and their friends voting at union meetings, though they were not members of the unions. Movement people were used to collect the registration numbers of cars outside 'Peace Council' meetings in 1950. All this seems to be due in varying degrees to Ryan's instinct for melodrama, divided control and perhaps a little clerical naïveté.

The divisions that wracked local ALP branches flowed naturally into the unions and the ALP conferences. But it is difficult to see how any of this could have been avoided, if the fight against communism in the unions was to be taken seriously. It was unattractive, perhaps, but the price that had to be paid.

News Weekly, with its cocksure stridency, earned many enemies for The Movement. It was addicted to flamboyant, lively attacks on the Parliamentary and industrial leaders of the Labor Movement, and this was a continuing cause of controversy. Those who opposed the Industrial Groups, or favoured a conciliatory line towards communism at home or abroad, quickly came under fire. Calwell, Evatt and even Chifley were attacked for such deviation from the *News Weekly* line, as were the ACTU leaders, Albert Monk and Reginald Broadby, when they tried to balance between right and left.

In the Korean War period, particularly, *News Weekly* was a fervent supporter of General MacArthur and the notion of a virtual preventative war against China. Later it was perhaps the strongest voice in Australia for the 'hard line' in Asian affairs, as laid down by John Foster Dulles. Earlier, it had been fervently for Chiang Kai Shek and 'Free China'; later it was equally fervently for Ngo Dinh Diem, of South Vietnam.

Partly, the stridency of *News Weekly* was deliberate sensationalism, designed to give the paper 'punch' and popular appeal. It needed this if it was to both influence Catholic workers and not be an economic burden straining Movement finances. But, sold outside the Churches as it was, it made enemies.

There were also rumours—denied and unprovable, but unlikely to be entirely unfounded—that The Movement maintained informal links with the Australian Security Intelligence Organisation. ASIO was building up its anti-communist contacts and information strenuously in the first years after the Menzies Government came to power; the Labor Government had been more interested in the far right until soon before it fell.

The Movement attracted much more controversy, when it was finally exposed, because of the melodramatic and malevolent nature of the disclosure and the extent of Santamaria's influence.

Santamaria was by nature a brilliant and eloquent politician, with all the sense of issues, manipulation, personal destiny and love of power that has typified controversial politicians through history. He would have been a senior minister, if not leader, in any government. A mysterious Providence placed him in a curious, emotional and somewhat naïve hothouse atmosphere where he was able to win easily the influence he instinctively sought, at an early age. Of Italian extraction, he was something of an outsider in the mainly Irish Catholic world in which he grew up, but he developed an extraordinary instinct for the prejudices of the Irish-Australian lower middle class. His Catholic faith was of the unquestioning, rarely troubled kind. An easy certainty of being right often seemed to characterise his actions and views. He was something of an autocrat, most at home with his intellectual equals if they agreed with him and shared his clear-cut certainty. Egoism aside, he had many attractive personal qualities, with a gracious charm and little malice, bigotry or hate in his nature. His charm, tact, patience and clarity made him unusually persuasive, both in oratory and private conversation. He could be both a vigorous, readable, popular journalist in *News Weekly* and a competent writer for the more serious press. His writing never had quite the eloquence of his speech to a sympathetic audience, however.

Santamaria's persuasiveness and industry, and his feeling for the instincts of his audience, gave him tremendous influence over a whole generation of students for the priesthood and religious teaching orders, particularly in the Diocese of Melbourne. He cultivated this influential field with great care, and the doctrines implanted in the seminaries eventually began to flow from pulpits and in schoolrooms around Australia. The common practice of transferring religious from state to state helped spread the Santamaria attitudes. He had an almost father and son relationship with the ageing Archbishop Mannix and was greatly admired by most of the provincial bishops.

The offices of the National Secretariat of Catholic Action, which were established for several years in Curtin House, Swanston Street, Melbourne after some changes, spawned an ever-growing number of lay-orientated Catholic organisations. There was a publishing house, education and training organisations and the like, as well as The Movement and the official Catholic Action bodies, all in a loosely related complex. People found it difficult to be other than either for or against as powerful a personality as Bob Santamaria—and most were for.

From 1940 on, the National Secretariat had issued an annual Social Justice pamphlet on Social Justice Sunday, each April. These were widely distributed, mainly written by Santamaria and reflected his ideas. From 1947, they were signed by the bishops and became more 'official'. By 1954, an explanatory note said:

Insofar as these Statements declare PRINCIPLES, Catholics will accept them without discussion . . . the APPLICATION of the principles, as distinct from the principles themselves, does not, of course, seek to close discussion on the matters suggested.

Although Santamaria's influence in the Church decreased away from Victoria, transfers of religious and the Movement and national organisations made it nevertheless considerable. Often recordings of his talks were sent interstate.

By the early 1950's—this is amply documented[4]—Santamaria saw the ALP Industrial Groups as the coming power, and worked hard to influence them. He made friends with not only non-Movement, but non-Catholic Industrial Group leaders, such as Laurie Short and Lloyd Ross. There was often a quick sympathy between the doctrinaire, intelligent and charming Santamaria and the ex-Marxist, not quite comfortable in a changing world and a non-ideological party. He travelled interstate regularly, maintaining and intensifying his widening range of religious and political contacts.

In Melbourne, he lunched each Monday at the Latin Restaurant with Keon, Mullens, McManus, Andrews, Scully and others. Through such friendly contacts, he was often able to influence their attitudes. In 1950, when Keon, Mullens and other new Catholic parliamentarians entered the Federal Parliament, Santamaria after an informal meeting he organised, invited them to use the facilities of his office when it suited. The Movement made its facilities freely available to likely allies.

Santamaria was prone, particularly in the last years before the split, to talk expansively of 'us' and 'we' about the broad Industrial Group faction and its influence in the ALP. Sometimes this gave listeners the impression he was more influential than he was; it was also an impression many enemies of the Groups wanted to have.

There was practically no intellectual tradition in the Catholic Church of Australia at that time to offer any competing viewpoints to that of Santamaria, though there were unconnected pockets of difference and even outright opposition. The result was that Santamaria's intense and ideological views often appeared within and without the Church to be *the* Catholic view. It was this intangible mood that often brought a hostile response of 'Catholic Action'.

For many Catholics—not to mention some Protestants—this aroused difficult questions of Catholic authority and the role of the Church in politics which had hardly been faced before in Australia.

Although the spirit of the Papal Encyclicals was claimed as a basis for The Movement's views, the precise nature of Church authority for them does not seem to have been formulated. However, there was no doubt that many lay and clerical leaders presumed a considerable degree of authority.

The operation of The Movement and some of its associates in the Groups came in fact close at times to resembling a 'mirror image' of the

---

[4] See the 1951 Rural Movement Speech in Part I, Chapter 8; the references to the 'Movement of Ideas' speech in Part II, Chapter 12.

force it was fighting. There was the same dogmatic certainty and rigid ideology, the sense of dedication, conspiracy and counter-conspiracy, the tightly run small organisation trying to manipulate larger ones from inside. The bellicose oratory of many Trades Hall and political Groupers completed the picture.

The Federal Labor Caucus that reassembled in Canberra at the end of summer in 1950 was very different from that which had stood as government of Australia in the elections of 10 December 1949. Labor's share of the vote for the House of Representatives had fallen from 51·3 per cent in 1946 to 46·69 per cent in 1949; but the unusual circumstance of the size of the House having been increased from 74 to 123 for that election meant that there were forty-seven instead of forty-three Labor members in the new House, many new to the Parliament. In accordance with the Constitution, the Senate had been enlarged from thirty-six to sixty members, of whom thirty-four were Labor.

The flood of new members aggravated the shocked, recriminative feeling that was the normal response of the Parliamentary Party to its defeat, apparently unexpected by many of the senior ministers. An American aphorism used in the mid-1960's against former 'New Frontiersmen' critics of the Johnson administration was: 'Power corrupts. Loss of power corrupts absolutely.' It would be too strong to say that defeat corrupted the Chifley Government, but it did create a mood of sourness and stubbornness. The ranks tended to be closed against outsiders, especially in the form of new ideas, while the Party indulged in a little self-pity.

Among the most outstanding of the new members to join Caucus for the Parliament that opened in February 1950 was a group known loosely as 'the Victorians' or 'the Victorian group'. They were notably better educated, on average probably more intelligent, and younger than was usual for Caucus. An even more striking characteristic of the group, however, was that six of the eight were Catholics—T. W. Andrews (Darebin), W. M. Bourke (Fawkner), J. M. Cremean (Hoddle), S. M. Keon (Yarra), J. M. Mullens (Gellibrand) and E. W. Peters (Bourke). The new non-Catholic Victorian men were A. Bird (Batman), and the president of the ACTU, P. J. Clarey (Bendigo). This religious composition of a group bound to be controversial in the post-defeat atmosphere of Caucus was partly fortuitous, but also reflected the high point in the ALP of the rising Catholic middle class.

Caucus as a whole was at that time about 60 per cent Catholic, reflecting fairly accurately the religious division of the ALP branch membership, but much less so the predominantly Protestant or agnostic flavour of organised trade unionism. A common suggestion was that the entry of these men to Parliament was attributable to the machinations of 'Catholic Action', a feeling enhanced by some of the attitudes they took on communism and foreign affairs. The role of The Movement in the pre-selections of the late 1940's was limited, however. The presence of its members and supporters in the Party branches and their knowledge of local union members provided a climate favouring the selection of right-wingers, but many other factors were at work.

Andrews, though friendly with Santamaria, was a conventional Labor man well known and popular in his electorate. Bourke had the backing of Kennelly and the Executive as a 'horse for the course' of Fawkner. He was well known as a liberal Catholic and intellectual, likely to attract both Catholic and middle class intellectual votes in a Division covering Prahran and South Yarra, where both were important. Clarey also backed him, with the support of the Storemen and Packers' Union, which had many members in parts of the electorate.

Mullens had been a member of the State Parliament in the 1930's and 1940's, retiring when his electorate was abolished in a redistribution. In a district with strong sectarian consciouness, he received most of the Catholic support against Hector McIvor (Mullens' successor in Gellibrand), with the support of Protestants and the left and William Divers of the Municipal Employees' Union, the industrial wing man. Peters, the member for Bourke, had been a president of the Victorian branch of the ALP as far back as 1936, a member of the Central Executive since 1931 and President of the Clerks' Union Industrial Group. He had been waiting on his seat for many years and his main rival was the first Industrial Groups organiser, G. Piera.

Keon and Cremean had both been contenders for the Yarra pre-selection, with the retirement of former Prime Minister J. H. Scullin imminent, and they fought bitterly for it. Cremean, whose brother had been Deputy Leader of the State Parliamentary Party, was the selection of the Labor 'establishment' in Richmond and Collingwood. Although the Cremean family themselves were respected and honest, some of their backers in the district were not. Cremean had the support of the local 'machine', influenced by the financier John Wren, and also the support of Scullin.

Keon, who had been elected MLA for Richmond in 1945 and Secretary of the Victorian Public Service Association in 1940, decided to challenge the 'establishment's' choice for the right to succeed Scullin. He used The Movement (with which he was on good terms) and Church youth groups as the base for building up a rival machine of his own. Both sides included many non-Catholics, but the Irish Catholic flavour of both was strong. St John's Church, East Melbourne, became the Keon camp's virtual headquarters, while the Cremean supporters organised at St Ignatius', Richmond. Keon's appeal—he was then in his early thirties— was to youth, to opposition to Communism, Wren, the local councils and the 'old gang'. The ALP Executive, which might normally have unofficially backed Cremean for the sake of harmony, stayed out of the contest because of the obvious rising strength of Keon's support, while Wren and the forces supporting Cremean were declining.

In the event, Cremean withdrew from the pre-selection and instead—now with the backing, in virtual defeat, of a wide section of the party—won pre-selection for the neighbouring and vacated seat of Hoddle. This was a poor consolation prize, however, as population trends indicated that at any future redistribution of seats one must disappear from inner Melbourne. This seemed most likely to be Hoddle, which lay between the Yarra and Bourke electorates to the north of Melbourne. Such a redistribution also seemed likely to remove working class sections from W. M. Bourke's electorate of Fawkner, turning it into a reliable Liberal electorate.

The knowledge of what a redistribution would bring was a constantly divisive factor with 'the Victorians' and this and memories of the struggle in Yarra made Keon, Cremean and Peters all watchful of each other. It also had the effect of tying Keon to his base in The Movement and was a factor in these three all being members of the Central Executive.

The ideological issues thrust into this unsettled Caucus by fortune and the new Menzies Government were much concerned with communism and trade unions and could hardly have been better selected to divide it. The specific measures involved included the Communist Party Dissolution Bill, introduced into Parliament on 27 April 1950; the legislation to provide for compulsory secret ballots in unions and fines for strikes outlawed by the Arbitration Court; the problems raised for Australia by the victory of the Chinese Communist Party in September 1949 and the founding of the Chinese People's Republic on 2 October, and, a few months later, the Korean War.

The first of these issues to be debated in the new House was foreign affairs, following a White Paper on the new Government's views by the new Minister for External Affairs, P. C. Spender. Although both sides then subscribed to the principle of a 'bi-partisan foreign policy', marked differences in emphasis became clear in this debate, as much within the parties as between them.

Perhaps the most outstanding feature of this debate, which took several days in mid March, was a new feeling of competence and urgency about foreign policy discussion, very different from a key foreign policy debate a year earlier when the House debated a statement by the then Minister for External Affairs, Evatt. Then Evatt's rather legalistic interpretation of the role of the United Nations had dominated Labor thinking, while the Liberals and Country Party for the most part seemed barely able to envisage a world without colonial powers. But by the autumn of 1950 the question of Asia and Asian communism had 'arrived'; speeches on both sides showed more thought and research, a greater readiness to understand other points of view and a far greater concern. The quality of this debate was perhaps a false dawn in Australian discussion of foreign affairs, but the attitudes it revealed came to have profound meaning.

Evatt opened for the Opposititon on 16 March. Acknowledging that he agreed in principle with Spender's statement, Evatt predictably said that a basic policy should be that Australian support for the United

Nations 'should not be grudging or qualified. It should be steady and unfaltering. Only if member nations give the organisation such support should it be able to enlarge its area of success, politically and economically.' On the burning Chinese question, he said:

I should think that the whole situation in relation to the recognition of the Chinese Government has to be watched closely from day to day, and I suggest that the Government might consider the desirability of making conditions governing Australian recognition of that Government. Further, recognition of the communist government of China need not carrry with it recognition in respect of Formosa. I see no difficulty at all about such a practical distinction being made. But in the long run recognition may have to take place and some form of provisional recognition might be considered.

P. M. C. Hasluck, later to become Minister for External Affairs and then Governor-General, followed Evatt and emphasised the continuing importance of power politics in world affairs. He said that some apparent UN accomplishments—in Greece and Palestine, for example—represented only a 'superficial smoothness' based on power realities.

Bourke and Mullens were the first of the 'Victorians' to speak. Bourke, in a coolly analytical, intellectual's speech, raised the question of communist expansionism, now blocked in Europe and the Middle East, being redirected by the Kremlin through China into unstable South East Asia. Mullens, in the first of the witty and rather clowning, but notably anti-intellectual, speeches he was to deliver in the next five years, attacked the character of the Department of External Affairs—Evatt's creation:

How can mere academic distinction fit a man for diplomacy? . . . I am almost inordinately suspicious of people named Algernon, Reginald or Percy. I do not think they are very good candidates for high ranking in the diplomatic field . . . I am astonished that the destiny of this land and my children should depend upon such weak reeds.

Mullens concluded that parliamentarians should represent Australia abroad and that Dr Evatt would be his first choice as Australia's representative abroad. But he continued with foreboding:

I remind honourable members that the Churchills and Roosevelts sold Europe down the drain at Yalta and Potsdam . . . we are confronted with a scourge in the form of the subtle expansion of an empire and we must face the fact that that empire, which is the intangible heresy of modern times, is independent of the limitations of geography, speech, national patriotism and pride, may one day engulf this Australia of ours.

Evatt's friend, the former journalist Leslie Haylen from Sydney, was the first to indicate a different strand in Labor thinking. While acknowledging the possibility of communist expansion in South East Asia, he predicted that communism would fail there and turn to anarchy. He emphasised the social aspects of the situation and indicated the stirrings of anti-Westernism in the ALP. 'The revolt in Asia is a rebellion of the peasants,' he said.

> . . . the peasant wants land and the people want food . . . the trouble is that the countries which were our allies in the recent war, particularly the USA, have been dubious about supporting socialist states in the east. . . . The support our allies gave in China went in the wrong direction.

This last comment reflected the corruption and unexpectedly total and sudden collapse of the Nationalist forces in China only a few months before. This seems to have been a traumatic and particularly significant experience for the Chifley Government. Chiang Kai Shek, their wartime ally and perhaps hero, had had feet of clay when confronted with an apparently popular, peasant revolution. A common sentiment in the Labor Movement and the Department of External Affairs was that, had Australian and other Western aid gone instead to the communists, who had apparently captured the mood for change in China, the inevitable communist régime may have been less hostile to the West.

S. M. Keon on 22 March gave a speech that seemed more than most to blend the two strands in Labor thinking. It was without the bombast and exhibitionism of many of his speeches and reflected the qualities that had led some to see him as a future leader.

> If we are to compete against the glow of hope that communism brings to the depressed people of the world, we must help to raise them out of their miserable state. . . . We must not waste time addressing pleas to ourselves and to the European people about protection of our way of life, but we must remember how empty these things are to the teeming millions of the East. . . . Let us call a disarmament conference, if that is desirable, and say how far we are prepared to go. If, as seems almost inevitable, the Soviets will not allow international inspection of armaments etc. if it is not prepared to lower the Iron Curtain to that extent, then it will stand convicted before the free nations of the world as the breaker of world peace.

The climax of the debate, for Labor, came when Chifley spoke as Leader of the Opposition. 'Whatever the distant future may hold for us in the way of dangers in the Pacific, it can never be denied that the real storm centre of the world today is in Europe,' he said, in what history showed to be a combination of blindness and foresight.

> Perhaps, in ten, fifteen or twenty years, some of the dangers we now envisage as threatening Australia from the North will become realities; but if, in the meantime, Europe has gone over to communism, or to some radical ideology foreign to democracy, it will not matter much to Australia whether or not there is in existence a Pacific Pact. . . . The essential thing for the western democracies is to remedy in Europe those evils which have encouraged the growth of communism and which, in the countries behind the Iron Curtain, according to all the evidence, have

produced the police state in various countries. . . . The fact is that communism has developed in Europe because of conservative action—or inaction—in the past.

On China, Chifley said:

. . . I often considered that I should have told the House long ago about the real position in that country. . . . The administration of the Nationalist government was completely corrupt. When I make that statement, I want it to be understood that I am not referring to the Generalissimo himself, but am speaking of the administration of national affairs in China. That administration was so corrupt that the arms which were sent from the United States of America to assist the National government in the war against Japan were sold or given to the communist armies in China. In fact, communism triumphed in China because of the arms which had been sent to that country by the United States of America for the purpose of defending democracy. . . . There can be no question whatever that the only government on the mainland of China today is the so-called People's Government, or the Communist government. . . . Extensive references have been made to the spread of communism in Asia and to the need for a Pacific Pact. I express the opinion that the chance of getting a Pacific Pact on any concrete terms is remote. It is possible to obtain a pact between Australia and New Zealand, and to have some understanding with the United Kingdom, but it is certain that Canada and South Africa will not be parties to a Pacific Pact. The Minister for External Affairs must know that India will not join in any pact while Pandit Nehru and Mr Patel have any influence with the government of that country. Pandit Nehru is the most powerful figure in Asian politics, and indeed in the Asian world. . . . We can rest assured that whatever is done by India will also be done by Pakistan (sic) and, perhaps, by Ceylon. . . .
It is said that communism is responsible for all that has happened in the East, the Far East and the Pacific. Nothing could be further from the truth. . . . It is a grave mistake to attribute to the Communists responsibility for all the disturbances that have taken place in the East. On this point Pandit Nehru said, 'If anybody thinks he can stop the spread of radicalism in Asia by guns, soldiers and ships, he makes the greatest possible mistake.' He also said that the only thing that can save the East from some form of radicalism is an improvement in the economic conditions of the people . . . all these creatures are God's creatures. . . . We cannot give much assistance because we are only a young country but what we can give in the way of technical equipment and educational facilities we should give. By giving it we should render a service to ourselves and humanity.

This speech, and others like it by Chifley at this time, show sentiments that could hardly be further from those expressed by *News Weekly* and large sections of the Catholic press, with their emphasis on the urgency of containing communism after the 'fall' of China. Chifley's views were a projection of orthodox Labor sentiments in the post-war world: concerned with social justice and opposed to exploitation, colonialism and war, reflecting pride in the British Labour Government's granting of independence to India and Pakistan and Chifley's intense admiration for Nehru. Not surprisingly, they tended to become the 'conventional wisdom' in a party deeply traditional and slow to change. Yet one does not need to agree with the opposite *News Weekly* view, to see grave defects and a tendency for Chifley to be looking backwards from 1949 rather than forward.[1] In particular, he greatly underestimated the role of communist parties—his assessment of the Eastern European communist take-overs was incredibly out of balance—and the expansionist nature of the drive then coming from Stalin's Moscow.

His speech irritated some of the 'Victorians' and that evening Keon, in the Parliament hardly a month, rose on the adjournment to publicly criticise the revered leader before an incredulous Party, Parliament and Press Gallery.

Taking issue with a minor point in Chifley's speech, that the Christian churches had not combatted the social injustice of pre-war Central Europe, Keon said:

> The statement has been made that the Christian churches of Europe have failed. Such a proposition made by responsible people at a time like this should be promptly repudiated. Whatever the faults of the Christian church in Europe may have been in the past, today the clergy is putting up with death, torture and imprisonment. We owe it to the memory of men like Cardinal Mindszenty and Archbishop Stepinac when such an allegation is made, to point out that today when other defences have failed, the Christian Church is the only force that is standing firm in the defence of humanity, spiritual rights and freedom. The Christian Church in Europe is the one force that has proved firm and that has been able to stand up against those who would attempt to suppress every spark of freedom and those values which we hold dear. . . . That statement [that the church had failed] does not represent my view and I hope that it does not represent the view of any substantial section of the community.

This brash attack by a boyish newcomer of thirty-five on the ex-Prime Minister was an isolated incident, yet it attracted considerable publicity and comment and has tended to stay fresher in the minds of many who noted it than perhaps more significant incidents. It summarised the sort of ideological cleavage that was just emerging. In a Caucus in which foreign affairs had traditionally been so unimportant, it would have been crazy in 1950 to have forecast a split derived from them; but in view of later developments, Keon's criticism of Chifley, even on a minor point, was of the first importance. Then and afterwards, however, Keon and the other 'Victorians' shared the basic admiration and affection of the Labor Movement for Chifley; the differences were in a spirit of 'more in sorrow than in anger'—aggravated by the Leader's tendency in defeat to revert to dogmatism.

The attack on Chifley was perhaps the most important of various steps which led to Keon acquiring the 'image' of an ascetic, priestly fanatic. His real character was much more complex. As a public speaker he was

---

[1] Chifley was not the only Leader of the Opposition at that time to misunderstand the emerging situation. The speeches of R. G. Menzies, before he became Prime Minister, show little appreciation that the Imperial world was breaking up.

forceful and passionate, happiest on the attack and something of a natural extremist. He could attack the communists violently, with frequent physical allusions to 'punching the comms on the nose' and the like, but the Liberals, and more particularly the Country Party, were as much recipients of his invective. Offstage, though still inclined to think in sharp blacks and whites, he was a more moderate figure, jovial, with an earthy charm, fond of good food and wine, a raconteur and wit. A bachelor, he was well known among Melbourne's stylish diners and enjoyed a wide circle of friends of many different views.

Keon was an intense, extremely ambitious man of penetrating intelligence and rapier wit, dedicated to and consumed by politics. Though he had left school early and suffered in the depression, he was enormously well read and insatiably curious. He could, and did, mix easily with intellectuals of much more formal education, though he had something of the love-hate suspicion of the intelligentsia that characterised many of the most intelligent, imaginative men in the Labor Movement. An uncompromising confidence in the correctness of his somewhat sharp, contrary and suspicious views marred his intellect, however. Keon was only forty when he left politics defeated in 1955. There was no way of knowing whether maturity and the experience of reverses to counter the brashness of his fast rise would have made him into a respected figure in Australian politics.

The generalised treatment of foreign affairs typical of the early months of the Menzies Government was ended by the North Korean invasion of South Korea in June 1950. Though a few on the extreme left protested that the South had in fact first invaded the North, all significant sections of the ALP supported the government in its commitment of troops to support the United Nations 'police action'. As the quickly victorious, American-led UN troops pushed into North Korea towards the Manchurian border, a new ideological issue developed inside the ranks of the Labor Movement, with *News Weekly* taking up its 'warhawk' position on the issue of whether the fight should be taken to China, and the Chifley-led mainstream of the ALP wishing to limit the war to the most modest objectives. The impression of most people the author interviewed was that if any senior Labor parliamentarians had reservations about the official approach, they did not air them. The Korean issue was not debated in the House of Representatives to the extent one might imagine, largely because there was no great difference between the parties and the Opposition did not want to encourage any misgivings in its ranks. The activities of 'peace' organisations and a 'doves' versus 'hawks' debate had some effect in the branches and unions, however, and contributed to the rising spirit of mistrust between extremes of right and left.

Mullens and more particularly Keon, were active members of the House in 1950 and 1951, but their attacks were more against the Liberals than the Communists, and with Keon, the Country Party. If a distinctive feature could be seen separating them from Labor orthodoxy, it was a tendency to be emotional and coercive such as in their attacks on the pro-communist journalist, Wilfred Burchett, who reported from behind the communist lines in Korea, and other Australians who publicly sided with the communist forces. Keon was also caustic on occasions about trade with Russia during the Korean War. On 7 December 1950 he asked the Minister for Trade, John McEwen, whether purchases of Australian wool by Russia had increased in the last few years from £500,000 to £12·5 million. 'For how long will this war profiteering on the part of Australian graziers, who are held in unutterable contempt by all decent Australians because they are prepared, for thirty pieces of silver, to supply . . .' he asked, until checked by the Speaker for exceeding the forms of a Parliamentary question. McEwen replied angrily that he resented the attack and 'if economic sanctions against Russia is the policy of the Opposition, I should expect it to be stated by the Opposition'.

Nearly a year later, on 22 November 1951, there was another incident which indicated the way in which what were essentially differences of emphasis were causing irritation in the Caucus. Mullens used the adjournment debate for an attack, in typically florid language, on the pro-communist journalist Wilfred Burchett and communist author Frank Hardy for their pro-communist writing on the Korean War. He called them 'Australian Haw Haws', traitors, 'Judas-like', 'pro-everything but pro-Australian', and the like. He called for Government action against them.

Shortly afterwards Pollard rose to attack Mullens. Hansard records as follows:

Mr Pollard (Lalor) [12.26 a.m.]: I do not claim to be as good as, or a better Labourite than, the honorable member for Footscray.
Mr Speaker: Order! There is no member for such an electorate in this House.
Mr Pollard: I meant the honorable member for Gellibrand (Mr Mullens). I take this opportunity to dissociate myself from what appears to have been a request to the Government and to this Parliament——
Mr Mullens: The honorable member is defending the 'Coms'.
Mr Pollard: I am not.
Mr Speaker: Order! I ask the honorable member for Lalor to address me.
Mr Mullens: They are two 'Coms', and the honorable member defends them.
Mr Pollard: Obviously the honorable member for Gellibrand is just as competent at making false accusations——
Mr Speaker: Order!
Mr Pollard: Against a member of this Parliament, in the House, as he is to take advantage of parliamentary privilege to attack men who are outside it.
Mr Mullens: Oh, get out! They are a couple of 'Coms', and the honorable member is defending them.
Mr Pollard: I am defending the right of free speech.
Mr Mullens: Free speech for Hardy!
Mr Speaker: Order! I ask the honorable member for Gellibrand to refrain from interjecting.
Mr Pollard: I am defending what the great Churchill and the great Roosevelt were prepared to advocate. They stood for the Four Freedoms, and the Allies fought for those Four Freedoms, which were: Freedom

from fear, freedom from want, freedom of speech, and freedom of worship. I do not want to do the honorable member for Gellibrand an injustice, but it appears to me that he asked the Government to take some action to prevent two men, who are now in foreign lands, from continuing to write and express their opinions about the international situation.

Mr Mullens: That is plain rubbish, and the honorable member knows it.

Mr Speaker: Order!

Mr Pollard: The honorable member for Gellibrand wants to keep out of the country two Australians, and because I say that they should be allowed to re-enter this country and tell the people about what they saw, and what they think——

Mr Speaker: Order! Will the honorable member face the chair, and address me?

Mr Pollard: The honorable member for Gellibrand and I, if he is so disposed, could meet those two men in public debate, and deal with their arguments. After all the British Empire was built up on the struggle for the right of men to express their opinions, however unpalatable those opinions were. For the honorable member for Gellibrand to say that I am defending Communists, as such, is a perversion of the truth, and an unfair attack upon me, and I brand him for what he is—a narrow-minded skunk.

Mr Speaker: Order!

Mr Mullens leaving his seat, and advancing towards the table,

Mr Pollard: He is a man who is prepared to do violence.

Mr Speaker: Order! The honorable member for Gellibrand will resume his seat.

Mr Mullens: Is not the honorable member for Lalor required to withdraw his remark that I am a narrow-minded skunk?

Mr Speaker: That remark was entirely unparliamentary, and I ask the honorable member for Lalor to withdraw it.

Mr Pollard: I withdraw the words to which objection has been made, but I expect the honorable member for Gellibrand to withdraw the statement that I have defended the Communists. . . .

Apart from the tensions imposed on the 1950 Caucus by new members and the bitterness of defeat, there was the complication of Labor still having a majority of four in the Senate; only half the members of that House of six-year terms had had to contest the 1949 election. This meant that there was a constant threat of double dissolution hanging over the Parliament, and naturally both sides were manoeuvring to ensure that any dissolution occurred on strategically favourable terms. The Government's tactic was to force Labor into a corner of principle, where its basic philosophy would clash with public sentiment, while Labor wanted to wait for an issue on which the Government would be unpopular with swinging voters. A common view in the Labor Caucus was that the dissolution should be staved off until the normal triennial elections due in 1952. By then, it was argued, the severe inflation characteristic of the years 1949 to 1953 would have made the Government so unpopular that its defeat would be certain. Labor hoped that the Governor-General, Sir William McKell, its own appointee and former Labor Premier of New South Wales, would not grant a double dissolution in conditions unfavourable to Labor.

The issue on which Menzies eventually forced the dissolution was the apparently minor one of replacing the Governor of the Commonwealth Bank with a Board representing largely private business. This proposal appalled Chifley, who had keen memories of the ultra-conservative financial attitudes of the 'sound money' men of private banking in the depression. He led the resistance to it in Caucus. Though he had majority support and his view prevailed, a substantial section of Caucus, in which 'Victorians' such as W. M. Bourke were prominent, regarded the question as not important enough to risk a double dissolution. Chifley, it is still vividly recalled, was not amused and rather dictatorially closed down the Caucus meeting when he was under attack over it.

At the same time, the Secret Ballot legislation (described in Chapter 2) was before Caucus and again the 'Victorians' and much of the right-wing generally could not support the opposition to it. Their views seem to have been an amalgam of a general belief that such a provision was necessary if communist ballot rigging in the unions was to be overcome, combined with reluctance to risk their newly won seats and pre-selections in an expensive election. They were often sensitive to Catholic opinion in particular on Communist questions.

The Communist Party Dissolution Bill and associated questions were also matters of high public moment at this time, aggravating the other tensions.

As the general election necessitated by the double dissolution of March 1951 approached, something of the atmosphere in Caucus can be imagined from the following report from Frank Chamberlain in the Melbourne *Sun* of 16 March:

Federal Labor Caucus is torn asunder on the eve of a general election. The Leader of the Opposition [Mr Chifley] is hoarse and tired tonight after defeating an attempt by Victorian Labor members to denounce certain features of Labor strategy. Today's Caucus meeting revealed strong support for the Menzies Government proposal for secret ballots in unions, which was described in the meeting as a 'strong counter to communism'. Mr Chifley declared the whole discussion out of order because the Federal Labor Conference had ruled that the Labor Opposition must resist any interference with union affairs. A section of the Party resented this ruling. When the meeting broke up there were cries of, 'Is this another dictatorship?' When the Deputy Leader, Dr Evatt, resumed debate in the House on the Secret Ballot Bill, several Victorian members were absent from the House and there were keen and bitter discussions among groups of Labor members in the lobbies and King's Hall, with criticism of the 'Old Guard NSW Control' of Labor affairs. . . . It is fair and accurate to report that some of the younger members of the Party in doubtful seats are hysterical about the prospects of an election on communism. They blame Mr Chifley and Dr Evatt for failing to direct the strategy of the Party so that an election would be avoided. They are particularly saying that the point of difference on the banking bill is only the establishment of a Commonwealth Bank Board. They point out that the Menzies-Fadden Cabinet has accepted every other aspect of the Chifley banking policy, apart from bank nationalisation. Mr Chifley's own personal hatred of a Bank Board, they claim, has the Party in an untenable position. With communism certain to be a major issue in the Federal Election, high Caucus feeling today sprang from strong religious affiliations, which are increasingly influencing all Labor debates.

The Governor-General, William McKell, granted the double dissolution the following day, 17 March, following the Senate's refusal after twelve months to pass the Banking Bill restoring the Bank Board.

Chifley's last policy speech, delivered in the Empire Theatre in Sydney on 28 March, seems in retrospect curiously tired and uninspired. He offered a ten shillings rise in pensions, home building loans at low interest, a rise of five shillings in endowment for the first child, a referendum on transfer of price control powers to the Commonwealth and 'action within the present laws' against internal communism. Nevertheless, much hard work by Chifley, Evatt, the ACTU leaders and a committee of Federal Conference had gone into it and at the conclusion of this work, according to his biographer, Crisp, '. . . after two weeks of vigorous parliamentary struggle and a week of exhausting election preparations, Chifley looked gaunt and grey. He was taking little notice of the terrible warning of the previous November that he was driving himself too hard.'[2]

Crisp added that the eventual delivery of the policy was 'equal to the best he had ever achieved', adding, 'there can be little doubt that the double dissolution and the ensuing election campaign constituted a death sentence for Chifley, but he pressed on relentlessly.'

Mindful of a barrage of much hardly scrupulous propaganda against Labor eighteen months before, Chifley pressed home the obvious point of Menzies' inability to fulfil his promises to 'put value back into the pound' and to cut public expenditure.

The results, available on the last day of April 1951, showed, however, that there had been little public impact, because the proportions of the vote were little changed from 1949, except that Menzies had won control of the Senate by 32 votes to 28. Minor changes in percentages gave Labor an additional five seats in the House, four of them in rural divisions where the Government's wool income levy, to counter the inflationary effect of wool prices during the Korean War, was an issue.

Foreign affairs were not of major importance in the campaign, although the Government's predictable claim to a superior anti-communist approach may have had some effect. A sidelight that was to have continuing importance was the resignation of the Australian Ambassador to Ceylon, Dr John W. Burton, who returned to Australia in the hope of getting pre-selection as a Labor candidate to protest against the Government's China policy. He was successful in getting pre-selection for the Sydney suburban seat of Lowe, but not in winning it. Burton was even then only thirty-six, and had been appointed Secretary of External Affairs by Dr Evatt (to whom he had been private secretary) in 1947 at the age of thirty-two. He was a doctrinaire left-winger, and at that stage politically insensitive and over-confident after his heady rise to power and subsequent downgrading after six months by the Liberal Government.

2 L. F. Crisp, *Ben Chifley: A Biography*, Longmans, Melbourne, 1961

When the new Caucus met on 11 June Chifley was re-elected leader unopposed. Evatt, with the support of the right and the 'Victorians', retained
his deputy leadership against a challenge from Ward by 53 votes to 26.
An expected bid from Calwell, based in some quarters partly on his
being a good Catholic, did not materialise. J. L. Cremean, a 'Victorian',
stood for election to the Caucus Executive, but was defeated. T. P. Burke,
from Western Australia, also identified loosely with the right, retained
his position on the Executive only narrowly. These votes indicated both
the strength and weaknesses of the right in Caucus at the time.

Chifley's concern at the trends in the Party were indicated in his
last speech, to the New South Wales Conference on 10 June. This has
become something of a political testament and might variously be interpreted as either the wise old leader warning against impending disaster
or the admired and loved but increasingly dogmatic old leader standing
out against new ideas. It has been interpreted both ways.

'We have difficulties within our movement,' Chifley said. 'Some feel
they can best serve their own personal interest or political expediency by
trying to get over as far as possible to the right without becoming
opposed to the Labor Party.' He concluded with the well-remembered
words:

I can only hope that the sincerity which you have shown over the years
in victory and defeat won't be lost; that you will be inspired by the same
things which inspired the pioneers of this movement, and that you will
not be frightened and made to get over to the 'right' because of the
whispered word 'communist'. I could not be called a 'young radical', but
if I think a thing is worth fighting for, no matter what the penalty is,
I will fight for the right and truth and justice will always prevail.

Three days later Chifley died suddenly of a heart seizure in his room at
the Hotel Kurrajong while most of the Parliamentarians were attending
an opening night ball at the House 300 yards away. He was buried with
the full rites of the Catholic Church at Bathurst and the genuine sorrow
of not only the whole Labor Movement but much of the nation as well
put the divisions of the previous fifteen months into perspective.

The Caucus chose Evatt unopposed as his successor, and at this point
the issues in the Parliamentary Party became for a while overwhelmingly
concerned with the Communist Party Dissolution Bill.

A sad and ironic aspect of Chifley's death was that *News Weekly*,
which had been increasingly critical of him, published its strongest attack
on him in the issue dated 13 June, the day of his death, but actually
printed earlier. 'Was Chifley Driving the Final Wedge into the Labor
Movement?' it asked in a comment on his speech to the New South
Wales Conference. 'Although the well-oiled and well-heeled Chifley-
Ferguson machine prevented any open explosion at the New South Wales
State ALP Conference, it was an open secret that there was very strong
resentment among a large number of delegates at the Leader's scarcely
veiled attacks on the effective anti-communist elements in the Labor Party.'
The article was, however, more critical of Ferguson than of Chifley.

Chapter Six
Labor and the
Communist Party
Dissolution Bill

The period of less than two years in which the attempt to ban the Communist Party was a serious issue in Australian politics dramatised the tensions which were building up in the Australian Labor Party. The proposal to ban the Communist Party originated in the Country Party during the period of post-war strikes, and the then Leader of the Opposition, R. G. Menzies, put it forward in his policy speech for the 1949 elections. Labor, in the meantime, repeatedly asserted its opposition to the communists and their ways, but proposed to fight them with the more conventional weapons of existing legislation and ALP Industrial Groups.

Menzies introduced the Communist Party Dissolution Bill into the House of Representatives on 27 April 1950. In his second reading speech he justified the measure—which a year or so earlier he had been reported as opposing—on the grounds of both the recent industrial record of the communists and the danger of an imminent war with Russia. The year 1950 was the high point of Stalinist expansion. A few weeks earlier, Menzies had called an urgent Premiers' Conference on Defence. 'We have not a day more than three years in which to get ready [for possible war with Russia],' he told the Premiers, 'and that time may well be shorter.' He said there was a danger of an explosion in Kashmir and Afghanistan, both bordering the Soviet Union, and that in the previous six months there was 'the clearest evidence of communist world strategy'. He said the technique was to engage democratic forces in places which, though intrinsically significant, had no direct relation to 'those vital theatres of possible war, such as West Europe and the Middle East, where the world's fate will be determined'.

Labor quickly split into three groups in its attitude to the Bill. Much of the left and the centre, led by Chifley, strongly opposed the Bill and wished to use Labor's Senate majority to block it. The second main grouping was on the right wing of Caucus, much of the industrial right and in the State Parliamentary parties. The attitude of this group was that the Bill was undesirable and, more importantly, unlikely to work satisfactorily. 'Why damage yourself to help the Comms?' was its case. It argued that Labor would only lose its Senate majority and chance of a comeback in 1952 if Menzies forced a double dissolution and election on the communist issue. Better, it felt, to let Menzies get into difficulties trying to administer the ban in the two years prior to the election, and in the meantime perhaps see the influence of the Communists weakened.

A third, much smaller grouping, actually supported the Bill. As might be expected, its mouthpiece was *News Weekly*, and it was mainly associated with The Movement. Although as early as 1948 the extreme right South Richmond Branch of the ALP had a motion on the Victorian Conference agenda for a ban on the Communist Party, The Movement opposed the ban until about the time the Bill was introduced into Parliament. It felt that the wartime ban had only served to strengthen the Communist Party, while a new ban would end the isolation into which the party was being driven. The Movement's strong fear of war in 1950, so amply demonstrated in the pages of *News Weekly*, was the critical reason for its switch to supporting the ban, although there also seems to have been a sentiment that it was the decent anti-communist thing to do.

The extent of support for the ban, except among The Movement leadership, is difficult to estimate because it merged into the passive attitude to the Bill outlined above; those who supported the passive approach varied considerably in their degree of opposition to the measure itself. The New South Wales Parliamentary Caucus declared itself in favour of the Bill on 28 April, with the Attorney-General, W. F. Sheahan, stating that such an attitude was necessary because of the Kremlin's plans. The Caucus Chairman, R. Hamilton, said that the decision was unanimous. However, little was heard again of the New South Wales Parliamentary Party's attitude, and it may have been influenced by a coming election. In the Federal Caucus only a handful of members actually supported the Bill. The recollection of several parliamentarians interviewed by the author was that there were 'less than half a dozen' supporters of the ban in principle, but there was a difference of opinion as to who they were. The names suggested showed no clear ideological pattern. The general impression was that there was no consistent or determined support for the ban, but at times a few supported it for a variety of reasons. Keon and Mullens both supported the principle of the ban on the Communist Party in the House of Representatives on 16 May, but with the qualification that a ban alone would not subdue the Communists.

The issue in Caucus, then, became passive or active opposition to the Bill, with Chifley and Evatt throwing their weight behind active opposition. Chifley called both the Federal Executive of the ALP and the Federal Advisory Committee (an informal consulting body representing the Parliamentary Party, the 'machine' and the Australian Council of Trade Unions) to Canberra. The Advisory Committee met and had long discussions with Chifley and Evatt on 1 May and next day the Federal Executive met. It was unofficially reported to have decided that Labor should seek amendments to some parts of the Bill, and the following day Caucus adopted this position by 34 votes to 27. The next day the ACTU Interstate Executive adopted a policy of qualified support, similar to that of Caucus.

Quite apart from the issue of freedom involved, one of the difficulties of trying to ban such a determined organisation as the Communist Party is drafting legislation that is tight enough to prevent loopholes, without at the same time being so onerous as to endanger other freedoms.

The most contentious clause in the Communist Party Dissolution Bill was the 'onus of proof' provision, empowering the Governor-General to 'declare' a person a communist. The Bill provided, among other things, that communists or 'declared' persons could not hold office in an industrial organisation considered by the Governor-General to be vital to the security of Australia, or hold employment with the Commonwealth. A committee of five, including the Solicitor-General, the Secretary of the Department of Defence, the Director-General of Security and two others, was empowered to authorise 'declarations' of individuals, to be proclaimed by the Governor-in-Council. The onus would then be on the 'declared' person to prove that he was not a communist and not 'engaged, or likely to engage, in activities prejudicial to the security and defence of the Commonwealth or to the execution of maintenance of the Constitution or of the laws of the Commonwealth.' The implications of such sweeping legislation for a free society, particularly one with a fairly large 'pink' left, are obvious; yet it is difficult to see how the ban could have been made effective without the 'onus of proof' clause.

The Labor Caucus position of modified concurrence in the Bill was as follows:

It would support the Second Reading, thus agreeing to the Bill in principle.

It would attempt to secure amendment to the onus-of-proof clause.

It would attempt to modify the provision of right of search without warrant.

It would secure the right of appeal to a State Supreme Court as well as the High Court.

This was a compromise between the two views held in Caucus, the unions and the Executive, and it contained difficulties for what had become an intense battle of tactics. Chifley's Second Reading speech on 9 May emphasised the clauses covered by the Caucus motion, and particularly the onus-of-proof provisions, but there could be little doubt of his distaste for the whole concept of the Bill. Using its majority, Labor succeeded in passing amendments to the Bill in the Senate, in accordance with the Caucus resolution, but the Government, predictably, refused to accept them when the Bill was returned to the House of Representatives. On 23 June the House passed a resolution by the Prime Minister that the Bill be set aside.

Parliament adjourned soon afterwards—the Korean War having broken out shortly before—and the Bill was reintroduced the day after it reassembled on 27 September. But during the adjournment there was intensive discussion on the Bill within the Labor Movement. A wide range of union opinion strongly opposed it, regarding it as an intolerable interference with and weapon against trade unionism. The right-wing Melbourne Trades Hall Council, however, voted by 96 to 44 on 24 August in favour of recommending that the ACTU reconsider its opposition to the Bill. This reflected a growing public feeling, perhaps bordering on hysteria, against communism, with the early reverses and confusion of the Korean War, communist-instigated refusal by watersiders to load supply ships for Korea, continuing strikes including protests against the Bill and inflation. Australian Public Opinion polls in July and August showed public opinion to be 80 per cent in favour of the ban though 56 per cent against the onus-of-proof clause. This climate of feeling was not lost on members who had returned to their electorates for the adjournment.

The Prime Minister, in his Second Reading speech on the new, slightly amended Bill said (ominously for the Labor parliamentarians in border-line seats or with slim electioneering funds): 'Let us vote on this matter, let the Senate vote, and let the Australian people then say what they have to say.'

The ALP Federal Executive had met in Canberra on 5 September, but split evenly on the question of a change of attitude, the Victorian, Tasmanian and Queensland delegates favouring a change, if it was necessary to avoid a double dissolution. The Interstate Executive of the ACTU, however, had voted 12 to 3 against any change of policy—not a vote formally binding the ALP but carrying weight in its internal politics. The right-wing Australian Workers' Union, which was then outside the ACTU, favoured allowing the Bill to pass.

Within a month, the pressures weighing on the Parliamentary Party were resolved by a change of attitude in the Western Australian Branch. Caucus was bound by the May decisions, but newspaper accounts left little doubt that the formerly solid majority for the compromise on the onus of proof—there were reported to be only 12 to 18 opposed—had crumbled. Following correspondence between the Western Australian Secretary, F. E. Chamberlain, and the Victorian Executive, already in favour of letting the Bill pass, the Western Australian Executive sought a further meeting of the Federal Executive on the Bill. This was attributed to the influence of the member for Perth, Tom Burke, who was something of a protegé of Chifley and influential with both the right and centre in Caucus.

According to Chifley's biographer, L. F. Crisp[1] (quoting a person in the room at the time), when Burke rang Chifley from Perth to inform him of the decision, Chifley's face 'went white with anguish and shock. "You couldn't have done a worse thing for the Party," he said bitterly, and then, "Oh well, boy, this is the end." '

Crisp continues:

When his visitor [another Labor member] expressed his disgust, Chifley quietly remarked, 'I'll never forget it!' but almost immediately recovered himself and then characteristically urged on the visitor: 'But you've got to see it as it appears to him—a young fellow with a family, fearing annihilation in a "dickie" seat. You've got to see his side of it.' Then on the general issue he remarked bitterly of Burke and the Victorians: 'We could beat them yet by getting the Executive to refer the question to Caucus, but you'd have a first-class split and all those mad buggers would know Caucus couldn't really give a binding decision!'

[1] L. F. Crisp, *Ben Chifley: A Biography*, Longmans, Melbourne, 1961

Crisp then quotes Chifley's own strategic view, as given in a letter to the Victorian Judge J. V. Barry on 8 October: 'My own view is that an election on the Communist Bill by itself would not be a winning ticket for Labor and may even cause the loss of further seats. I have, however, seen a number of elections, purported to be fought on some particular issue, in which the stated reasons for the election were entirely forgotten—or partly so—when the campaign started.' Crisp says Chifley mentioned inflation as the sort of issue which could be used against the Government.

The expected decision of the Federal Executive, instructing Caucus at the last minute—the Bill was then before the Senate—to let it through came on 16 October. Next day, the Leader of the Opposition in the Senate, N. E. McKenna, read the Federal Executive's statement in the Senate and announced that the Opposition would allow the Bill to pass in its existing form.

The wounded, reluctant and ambigious tone of the Federal Executive's 'chicken' resolution is indicated by the following extract:

The Federal Executive asserts that the Menzies Government wishes to avoid responsibility for giving effect to the main purposes of the Bill; to avoid its election pledges in regard to communism and to conceal its abject failure to take effective steps to prevent the great ills that flow from spiralling costs of living.
The Federal Executive has decided that, to test the sincerity of the Menzies Government before the people, and to give the lie to its false and slanderous allegations against the Labor Party, that the Bill should be passed in the form in which it is now before the Senate.

Victoria, Tasmania, Queensland and Western Australia voted for the resolution; New South Wales and South Australia opposed it.

The Communist Party Dissolution Bill had invoked fierce, principled dissension among the more articulate and caring sections of the Australian public. Most newspapers, the governing parties and now the ALP had supported it, but among the liberal intelligentsia, no less than among Labor leaders like Chifley and Evatt, the disappointment was bitter. Labor, it was felt, had sold out its principles to save a few seats and an untimely election. It was natural that those who felt sold out looked round for a scape-goat and there was an obvious one—'Catholic Action'.

Hardly were the Hansard proofs of the day's debate ready, however, when the Communist Party and ten communist-controlled unions announced their intention to challenge the new Act in the courts. They applied to Mr Justice Dixon of the High Court for an injunction to restrain the Commonwealth from putting any part of the Act into operation. The judge refused, but referred key questions in the Act to the High Court. He ordered the Commonwealth not to dispose of any communist property it might seize or to declare any association or persons, pending decision on a case to the High Court.

On 23 October Commonwealth police raided Communist Party head-quarters in Sydney, Melbourne, Perth, Hobart and Darwin, seizing documents and printed material.

On 25 October the divided and shaken Labor Party was rocked once again by the unexpected announcement that Evatt had accepted a brief from the communist-led Waterside Workers' Federation to challenge the Act in the High Court hearing. His grounds would have been reasonable enough normally, that he was accepting a brief as a barrister and was not obliged to share the ideals of his client, but the political effect was to intensify the bitterness and division in the Party.

The case came before the Hight Court on 14 November, with Evatt lead-ing the case against the Commonwealth and a prominent Victorian com-munist, E. A. Laurie, alongside him. Whatever the political difficulties of his action, it was legally successful and six of the seven members of the bench declared the Act invalid; the dissentient was the Chief Justice and former United Australia Party (Liberal) leader, Sir John Latham. To compress a set of seven technical reasons in one sentence, the majority view was that the Court did not accept that the Defence powers of the Commonwealth could be invoked in the current circumstances.

A week after the High Court decision Menzies secured the 1951 Double Dissolution, on the ostensible grounds of the Senate's rejection of the Commonwealth Bank Bill—though one must suspect that the future of the anti-Communist measure played a part in his strategy.

In the event, communism was invoked in the election only in a general way. Labor gained seats, but within a month Chifley, the most prestigious opponent of the measure, was dead and Evatt was Leader.

With Labor under a new leader, the Government decided to force the issue to a Referendum, the only practical way in which the powers it needed to ban the Communist Party could be obtained.

Menzies introduced the Constitution Alteration (Powers to Deal with Communists and Communism) Bill on 5 July 1951, and a newly defeated Labor Party was once again faced with a problem: if it opposed the Bill, it would have to follow through to probable defeat in a referendum and risk troubles in the Party in the process.

Before Caucus had a chance to determine its attitude, the Federal Execu-tive, led by such old Chifleyites as the Federal President, Ferguson, and Federal Secretary, Kennelly, moved into Canberra, and on 5 July—the day the new Bill was brought down—instructed the Parliamentary Party 8-4 to oppose it. Victoria and Western Australia voted against the resolution, but in the meantime Queensland and Tasmania had changed.

Passage of the Constitution Alteration Bill through the now Liberal-controlled Senate and Labor's opposition to it there meant a Referendum, with Labor morally bound to urge a 'No' vote.

The Referendum campaign which ran from 17 August to 22 September was a tribute to the conviction and will of Herbert Vere Evatt. In a Party demoralised by defeat, division and the recent death of a revered leader, he and a small group of supporters alone seem to have had the dedication and courage to oppose what was more clearly becoming—as the Korean

War dwindled in intensity and the Industrial Group victories in the unions continued—a potential blot on the Australian statute books. Evatt did not appear often in his career in the role of a hero. On most social issues he was an opportunist interested principally in power; but on issues affecting his great loves, the law, civil liberties, the standing of his country, he could be adamant. This is born out time and again in his career, though in the early spring of 1951 he had the added incentive of establishing his authority and acceptance as Leader in most difficult circumstances.

The tone of his campaigning, however, did him less credit than the courage and tenacity. His campaign speeches and the official 'Vote No' pamphlet seemed to have been cynically designed to confuse the issue, with wild allegations of an incipient police state and even warnings that the powers sought by Menzies—for the Commonwealth to legislate on communists and communism—could be used to advance communism. The alarmism of Evatt's approach was 'tit for tat' however; a similar alarmism had been typical of Menzies' campaign in the 1949 election campaign, and in the whole lead-up to and execution of the anti-Communist measures in 1949-51.

The Australian Public Opinion Poll published on 23 August showed the odds Evatt campaigned against: some 73 per cent of Australians would vote 'Yes' (compared, however, with 80 per cent in June and in 1950); 17 per cent would vote 'No' (compared with 12); and 10 per cent were undecided (previously 8).

Yet with amazing vigor and tenacity, in one month's campaigning, Evatt, dragging his Party behind, was able to turn potential defeat into victory.

The results, clear by the late evening of 22 September, showed that the Referendum had been defeated. The first progress count, at 9.20 p.m., showed 53·18 per cent of votes for 'No'. This was the peak, and the 'No' vote declined over the subsequent hours and days to the hairbreadth's majority of 50·48 per cent, but the Referendum was still defeated and the pro-Labor vote was higher than that obtained under Chifley three months earlier—49·07 per cent of votes cast. The percentage 'No' vote was highest in New South Wales (52·79 per cent) but only slightly lower (51·36 per cent) in the right-wing Labor state of Victoria. It was lowest (44·57 per cent) in the less liberal and more 'threat from the North' conscious Queensland.

It was often claimed during the troubles over the Communist Party Dissolution Bill that the lack of a firm Labor line was due to the machinations of 'Catholic Action'. Over a period this was often implied, though rarely stated expressly, in daily Press reports reflecting Caucus and lobby 'leaks'. From reading and personal contacts, ALP Branch members and the general public often formed a similar impression.

The truth is more mundane. It is certainly true that The Movement and *News Weekly* supported both the original Dissolution Bill and the

Referendum for Commonwealth powers on communism. It is less certain that this campaign, which at times reached a very strident level, had much effect.

The original break on the Dissolution Bill came in Western Australia, the state in which The Movement was least powerful and where the Industrial Groups never existed. The man most influential in securing the Western Australian *volte face*, Tom Burke, was a fairly conventional Labor man popular with all sides. In Caucus there was no consistent or significant support for the ban as such, as distinct from ambivalent tactics towards it, and the occasional expressions of dissent in state parties were not followed up.

The case for 'Catholic Action' influence must rest with the record of the Victorian Branch, and the official records of the Branch make one cautious of assigning a major role to The Movement, or 'Catholic Action'. Nevertheless, Movement opinion was probably important in Victoria, and to a lesser extent in other states, but rather indirectly as a power to be reckoned with and affecting the overall climate of the Party.

At the Victorian Central Executive meeting of 2 June 1950, J. V. Stout (Secretary of the Trades Hall Council) reported on the Federal Executive meeting of the previous month; and E. W. Peters, with J. L. Cremean seconding, moved:

That this Executive, believing that the question of onus-of-proof, which is the last remaining amendment proposed by the Federal Parliamentary Labor Party not yet disposed of, is not a sufficiently vital issue on which a double dissolution of Federal Parliament should be forced, resolves:
1 That the question of making the final decision on amendments to this Bill should be left to the Federal Parliamentary Labor Party;
2 That in order to give effect to this resolution, a postal ballot of members of the Federal Executive be held;
3 That the Victorian members of the Federal Executive be instructed to vote for such resolution in the telegraph ballot.

A. M. Fraser and J. M. Sheehan opposed the motion and F. McManus and D. Lovegrove supported it. R. R. Broadby of the ACTU opposed the motion and moved an amendment widening it, that decisions as to amendments be left to the Federal Parliamentary Labor Party. J. A. Little seconded the amendment. M. C. Jordan, Assistant Secretary of the Trades Hall Council, and S. M. Keon supported the motion, F. J. Riley supported the amendment.

The issue arose again with the second bill, at the meeting of 25 August. The Executive voted to ask the Federal Executive to rule against a double dissolution on the question of onus-of-proof. The ACTU representatives, P. J. Clarey and R. R. Broadby, together with Senator Sheehan, opposed the motion, while the Movement men, McManus and D. Devlin, a recent addition to the Executive, supported it. The motion had been moved by Lovegrove and seconded by J. A. Little, and was carried 14-6.

On 16 February 1951, the Executive considered a letter from the Coburg Branch of the ALP, where The Movement was strong, attacking Evatt's role in taking the WWF brief before the High Court.

Peters moved and Keon (who had attacked Evatt passionately on the issue in Caucus) seconded, that 'In the opinion of this Executive it is most undesirable for any member of the Labor Party who is also a member of the legal profession, to appear in law cases of a political or semi-political character on behalf of members of political parties other than the Labor Party'.

A. M. Fraser, a lawyer, opposed the motion on the grounds that it was too wide, though he agreed that Evatt's action was politically unwise. D. Lovegrove and F. McManus then moved an amendment, 'That this Executive protests against the action of the Deputy Leader of the Federal Parliamentary Labor Party in appearing for communist union officials in the Federal Arbitration Court and believes such action damaging to the Labor Party and should not be permitted'. This was carried unanimously, and the Easter Conference shortly afterwards endorsed it.

Another incident in Victoria about this time was when the Melbourne *Argus* industrial correspondent, Jack O'Sullivan, who was close to Kennelly, reported in the *Argus* of 15, 16 and 18 September that 'right wing' Victorian Federal members were meeting to make a statement on the Communist Party Dissolution Bill. With full publicity in the *Argus*, Kennelly reported on this to Chifley; but the Executive Officers and later the full Executive vehemently denied that any such meeting took place. It condemned both the *Argus* for publishing the report and Kennelly for accepting it without checking. Whether because of the *Argus* report or for some other reason, no statement was ever issued.

A further series of incidents came during the Referendum campaign, though the Victorian Executive backed Evatt as it was bound to. It secured a majority of the Victorian vote for his point of view, and the president, R. Hoban, chaired the opening meeting and pledged his own support for the 'Vote No' cause.

The main incident at the opening meeting of the campaign was the absence from Evatt's meeting of Keon and Mullens, an absence forecast in the press. These two had not been especially active in supporting the ban on the Communist Party, but both they and the strong right wing Catholic, the former Minister for the Army, Cyril Chambers, had been absent from the Chamber when the vote was taken on the Bill to amend the Constitution, and thus make way for the Referendum.

On 7 September, several newspapers quoted Ferguson, the Federal President, as announcing that the North Richmond Branch, of which Keon was a member, had censured him for not attending the opening campaign meeting. This report brought a public rebuke to Ferguson from Lovegrove, the Victorian Secretary, followed on 14 September by a rebuke from the full Executive, on the recommendation of the Executive Officers; the Executive claimed that the report was false and was made outside the Party rules. The North Richmond Branch met again and declared its confidence in Keon.

The incident conveys something of the climate of the times, but may have been exaggerated by personal dislike between the two ex-communists, Lovegrove and Ferguson. An aspect of the bout with implications for the future was that the State Parliamentary Leader, J. Cain, and Stout were unsuccessful in putting an amendment on the Executive against further publicity being given to the incident.

Yet another incident indicating the strains in the Victorian branch came on 13 September, when an advertisement in the Melbourne *Age* announced that the newly returned Burton would be principal speaker at a 'No' rally in the Caulfield Town Hall. The Central Executive banned this meeting, under a rule forbidding interstate Labor speakers from appearing at Victorian Labor meetings without the approval of both their own and the Victorian Executive—a rule believed to have been introduced originally to keep E. J. Ward out of Victoria following controversy about election meetings he addressed in 1949.

A slanging match developed in the press between Burton, who claimed that a 'small clique' really supporting the Referendum, had kept him out, and Lovegrove, who said Burton had been invited by Jim Hill, a recent arrival from New South Wales, former high official in External Affairs and brother of the Communist Party Secretary, Ted Hill—another bitter enemy of Lovegrove, from his communist days.

A drawn-out controversy followed, in which the Executive suspended the Caulfield Branch. Hill claimed that the Branch had authorised the invitation to Burton, but the Branch Secretary, N. Hendrickson, a son of Senator A. Hendrickson, said Hill had asked three times to invite Burton, but that the Branch had shelved the matter. Hill questioned the minutes, but on 18 June 1952 a meeting of the Disputes Committee found Hill and eight other members of the branch guilty of unworthy conduct. They were excluded from the Party. The branch was subsequently re-formed and eventually most of those expelled were readmitted to the ALP.

Yet another incident in this vein came when the Toorak Branch, which, despite, or perhaps because of, its salubrious surroundings was left wing dominated, criticised the attitude to the campaign of W. M. Bourke, its local member, with press publicity on 24 September—two days after the voting. The branch, whose members included the left-wing parliamentarians-to-be S. H. Cohen and J. F. Cairns, ceased holding meetings shortly afterwards. In the absence of the secretary and on the recommendation of Lovegrove the Executive suspended the branch—an unusually rigorous action in a party where lapsed branches were common enough. The actual motion to suspend it was moved by J. J. Roberts, Treasurer, and seconded by J. L. Cremean. Supporters of the Executive's action claim that the Toorak minute book showed only one motion in eight months— that opposing the Dissolution Bill. They said the branch would not work for Bourke in the 1951 election.

The details given above show that the attitudes of the Victorian Branch, in as far as they were distinctive during the controversies over the anti-communist legislation, had the support of a wide right-wing opinion, in which The Movement was not unduly important. However, the stridency of *News Weekly* and its vituperative attacks on Evatt, Ferguson, McKenna, Pollard, Ward and others most actively associated with opposition to the legislation, helped fan anti-Movement feeling in a wide section of the ALP, already strained by the right-left tensions surrounding the legislation.

A finale to the period came on 19 November, when the Federal Executive, in a case of the bitten biting back, proscribed *News Weekly*, with Ferguson leading the attack on it. The press reported Ferguson as saying that the paper 'attempted to present its news in a manner suggesting it had Labor sympathies, while at the same time it was attacking Labor leaders and Labor principle and was seeking to use the services of members of the Labor Party to help in its distribution.' It did not discipline Keon and Mullens, reportedly because of Evatt's intervention on their behalf.

Archbishop Mannix denounced the ban in a statement to *News Weekly* of 28 November as a 'hasty and ill-advised act of repression'. He said *News Weekly* was a 'valuable and well-informed organ of opinion' which had rendered notable service in Australian affairs. *The Advocate*, the official organ of the Archdiocese, said, 'Whatver its shortcomings, whatever the personal enmities it may have aroused in the enthusiasm of the moment, *News Weekly* . . . is the most vigorous, well-written and effective anti-Communist paper in Australia.' It said the ban was 'an insult and an outrage to the Catholic community' and that unless the ban was immediately lifted, the Catholic community 'will despair of the ALP and regard its formal rejection of communism as merely a miasma of words.'

News Weekly's own comment on the ban, in a front-page article, was: 'The pattern is crystal clear. The ban on *News Weekly*, the destruction of the ALP groups, appeasement of the Communist Party are the policy of the clique which today controls the Federal Executive.' A more restrained editorial inside said, 'No matter what any political party resolves . . . truth and the Christianising of society remain the constructive ideals of the paper.'

The 'narrow-minded skunk' exchange between Mullens and Pollard, described in the previous chapter, occurred the day after the ban on *News Weekly*, giving a further indication publicly of the tension in the ALP. However, the external signs suggested a greater strife than actually existed. *News Weekly* would have had at most half a dozen supporters in Caucus. Keon and Mullens were the only two Federal members who made spectacular attacks in anything like the *News Weekly* style, on the right of the Party, although Chambers had been summonsed—without further action—before the South Australian Executive for lack of support for the Referendum campaign. The Tasmanian Premier, R. F. Cosgrove, had also been clearly opposed to the 'No' case. A section of branch opinion and a much smaller section of union opinion had supported this attitude and some had refused to work on the booths on polling day. A 'Yarra Vote Yes Committee' had appeared in Keon's electorate of Yarra. All these incidents were to a large extent isolated, and no great or significant ground swell built up in favour of the Bill, as distinct from a lack of enthusiasm for political suicide.

Evatt adopted a 'forgive and forget' attitude towards the right wing, whose backing he had received for re-election as Deputy Leader before

Chifley's death. He transferred his enormous energies and ambition into the famous 'honeymoon' with the right. The wounds of 1950-51 appeared to have healed, but they had flowed into, aggravated—and were aggravated by—the fierce faction fighting of the Federal bodies. Events only three years later were to show that the tensions of this period were fundamental.

Chapter Seven
The Unions, The Movement and the Cain Government

The first majority Labor Government in the history of Victoria came to power in the state election of 9 December 1952. It had a record 37 seats in a Legislative Assembly of 65, after a swing to Labor of 7 per cent. The election came after a split over electoral reform in the previously governing Liberal and Country Party, and after a series of unstable minority governments; it had been the era of 'hole in the corner' government in Victoria, when no party could get a working majority. The election also came towards the end of the economic recession of 1952, the aftermath of a period of violent inflation.

In contrast to the warring inside the Liberal Party between the factions led by T. T. Hollway, the defeated Premier, and L. G. Norman, and a split a few years earlier in the Country Party, Labor in Victoria appeared to be united. Its rank and file membership was large, its organisation good. Relations with the Catholic Church had never been better.

The apparent unity of Labor, however, concealed serious divisions. These were most pronounced in the faction fighting at the Trades Hall and on the Federal Executive, but flowed into the State Parliamentary Party.

There had more often than not been skirmishing between 'in' and 'out' factions in the State Party. As far back as the early 1940's, mistrust had built up between John Cain, the Party Leader since 1937, and his Deputy, Herbert Cremean. The death of Cremean in 1943 at the age of forty-three has been widely held, however, to be one of the great tragedies of Victorian Labor. It is often argued that as Deputy to Cain, even though there were differences, he alone had the strength and stature to hold the factions together.

Cremean's death intensified an already existing clash of personalities between Cain and W. P. Barry, MLA for Carlton, most prominent 'out' and the man who was to lead the break from Cain in 1955. William Peter Barry, born in Melbourne in 1899, was a warm, colourful, ambitious man regarded, with as much affection as criticism, as a 'hard doer'. A former Secretary of the Tobacco Workers' Union, he entered State Parliament in 1932 after a pre-selection contest in which he defeated the Cain-backed candidate, W. Slater, who had been defeated for the country division of Dundas in a previous election. As it happened, Slater subsequently was returned in Dundas through a technicality, but the controversial entry to politics marked Barry as a storm centre.

In Parliament, Barry eventually became something of a favourite of John Wren, who, between the wars, exercised great influence on ALP branches in the northern districts of Melbourne. His partisanship for Barry was at the expense of established Party figures such as Cain, under whom the Party had been edging away from Wren's influence by the late 1930's. Wren had tried to use Cremean, Barry and the more Catholic section of the Party to counter the Cain faction.

Relations with Wren and the Church lay at the back of much of the earlier division in the State Caucus. Through his financial power and discreet gifts and assistance, more often than through outright bribery, Wren was able to play politics inside the ALP, controlling branches and promoting protégés. H. M. Cremean, for example, was a friend and protégé of Wren; but intimate friends accept his assurances that he obtained no personal enrichment from the relationship. Archbishop Mannix, the realist who had in his complex nature a streak of sympathy for the Irish larrikin and wheeler-dealer who had yet not strayed too far from the Church, also enjoyed a long friendship with Wren. In the Victorian ALP of the twenties, thirties and forties, friendship with Wren (and better with the Archbishop as well) was a source of power and influence more than of personal enrichment. This dual patronage went to Cremean rather than Cain, who had been christened but not reared a Catholic. Barry sought the Deputy Leadership when Cremean died, but Cain successfully promoted instead Francis Field, an independent-minded Catholic from the outer suburbs. Under Cain and Field, the Party now moved rapidly away from the influence of the ageing Wren.

Labor came to power at the end of 1945, governing with the support of independents for two years until it was voted out over the Bank Nationalisation issue. Wren's attempts to exert influence over this Government, often on relatively minor issues, and sometimes trying to force trivial concessions for the Church, were a constant divisive issue, even if only at the level of an irritant. The government also had to take the brunt of the post-war surge of communist-led strikes, and the concessions and 'deals' used to settle some of these caused dissatisfaction from the right in Caucus and at the Trades Hall. There were claims that some ministers would not 'stand up' to the communist leaders.

The Government's major issue with Wren was over the control of trotting. Wren had virtually held a personal monopoly over this sport between the wars. Under pressure from other sporting interests, the Cain Government instead placed post-war trotting under a non-profit public instrumentality, the Trotting Control Board.

Wren swore vengeance and it was rumoured that he contributed heavily to the funds of other parties when the Cain Government fell over Bank Nationalisation a year later. There were signs, impossible to be sure about, that he tried to stir up local trouble for Cain and Field, the Deputy Premier who introduced the legislation and lost his seat of Dandenong in 1947, and for Slater, the Attorney-General and Chief Secretary who drew it up.

In the new Parliament, it became clear that not only the more secular trend represented by Cain, but also a new Catholic, right wing force, was rising against Wren.

Its spokesman was the inimitable S. M. Keon, who had become MLA for Richmond in 1945. Barely two years in Parliament and only thirty-one years of age, he stood for the position of Deputy Leader, previously held by the defeated Field, and drew enough votes away from Barry for the Cain candidate, William Galvin, to win.

The following year, on 27 July 1948, Keon 'tipped the can' on Wren in one of the most outspoken speeches in the history of the Parliament. Keon was then engaged in a bitter fight against the Wren-dominated forces in Richmond and Collingwood for both local hegemony and pre-selection for the Federal seat of Yarra. He chose the Race Meetings Bill for his attack. This Bill, introduced by the new Hollway Liberal Government, merged Wren interests in the Williamstown Race Club and the Victorian Trotting and Racing Association.

'It is no secret,' Keon told an aghast Parliament, 'that because the Labor Government took night trotting from Mr John Wren, he set out to destroy that Government and he financed the campaign of the Country Party.'

Mr Hyland (Gippsland South) : 'That is a deliberate lie.'
Mr Dodgshun (Rainbow): 'It is a deliberate lie and it is the type of statement that the Hon. member makes.'
Mr Keon: '. . . I have no intention of being a "stooge" for Mr Wren or any other interest in gambling or otherwise. If my seat in Parliament is to be held at that price I will not pay the price. I have no illusions as to what is likely to take place in relation to my seat in this House in due course. . . .
'The new (racing) club will be as much the creature of John Wren as was the Victorian Trotting and Racing Association. The same methods and the same technique will be used. Those who can be bought will be bought. Those who can be intimidated will be intimidated. Those who have honour and integrity will be won over by donations to some charitable cause. What is badly needed is a Royal Commission to investigate Mr Wren and his ventures.'

A few months later, in November, Keon was suspended from the House after making a Nazi salute to the Speaker during an incident. In his defence Cain said, 'There may be a great deal of objection in this Parliament to the Hon. Member for Richmond; he may have many opponents . . . but he has a great deal of natural ability.'

In fact this statement concealed Cain's growing dislike of Keon. The Leader, then sixty-one, was irritated by the brash newcomer. He had become suspicious of intense young Catholics who seemed to have the run of Raheen, the Archbishop's residence, of The Movement and of the rising trend against his friend and protégé, Kennelly, at the Trades Hall.

These feelings were reinforced when Keon entered Federal politics in 1949 and was succeeded as Member for Richmond by his own friend and protégé, Francis Raymond Scully. While Keon was a sympathiser and

collaborator rather than member of The Movement, Scully was a dedicated member of the inner group of The Movement, an intense, tireless
young man who had come up as secretary of the Industrial Group in the
Australian Railways Union, a job he retained while in Parliament. He
developed as a parliamentarian of outstanding energy and enthusiasm and
of considerable ability, while perhaps lacking Keon's unusual edge of
intelligence. However, his dedication, burning anti-communism and obvious links with both The Movement and the Industrial Group complex
made him the object of some hostility in the Caucus.

During the two and a half years of the McDonald Government, these tensions found new issues around which to grow. An anti-Cain faction
pressed on several occasions for the McDonald Government to be defeated, before the decision to withdraw support was finally made in the
spring of 1952. The manoeuvring to succeed the ageing Cain also intensified in this period, the main contenders being Barry and Galvin. Galvin,
a non-Catholic from Bendigo, had pro-Cain support and tried to attract
more right-wing support by building up a base of fellow country members. Barry, who enjoyed fair relations with Galvin despite the rivalry,
worked for Trades Hall and other right-wing support to bolster his position as potential Leader or Deputy Leader. Yet another divisive issue was
the personality of Kennelly, Labor Leader in the Legislative Council.
Many considered him too close to Cain and this produced tension—which
Kennelly's pre-selection defeat did nothing to minimise.

Victory at the polls at the end of 1952 only aggravated the internal
troubles. While the old Barry faction was declining, the win greatly
increased new right strength in Caucus. Scully's tireless organising
produced a youngish, aggressively Catholic, Movement-influenced faction,
militantly opposed to Cain and the old wheeling-dealing traditions he
stood for. The Protestant or agnostic, moderate faction around Cain reci-
procated the hostility; the feeling that a handful of young Groupers were
leading others on to make life difficult for Cain produced bitter memories
for years to come. Compromises between the factions produced a broadly
accepted Cabinet, about two-thirds pro-Cain and a third 'right wing' and
evenly divided between Catholics and Protestants. Barry became Minister
for Health. The Movement and Industrial Groups were strong enough
to have Scully, at thirty-two unusually young for a minister, included and
he became Honorary Minister, in effect an assistant minister without a
portfolio. The actual intervention with Cain on his behalf was by Lovegrove who reflected the wishes of the Groupers to have one of their
hard-working members in Cabinet. Scully was then also Secretary of the
Young Labor Association and was elected to the Central Executive of the
ALP in 1954.

John Galbally, who became Minister for Electrical Undertakings and
Forests, was a Catholic fairly loyal to Cain. Leslie Coleman, Leader in the
Upper House and Minister for Transport, was one of the few acceptable
to all three groups. Archibald Fraser, a Barry supporter, was Minister for

Labour. Samuel Merrifield, Minister for Works, was the Minister most opposed by the Groupers. He had been named at the Royal Commission of 1949 by the defector, Sharpley, as a Communist Party contact in the State Parliamentary Party. This was news to most of his friends who regarded him as a mild mannered, fairly conventional moderate socialist, but it made some Groupers bitterly opposed to him. Another significant figure in the Cabinet was the Minister for Lands, R. W. Holt, son of a Presbyterian minister and sensitive to organised Catholicism.

The sectarian atmosphere that developed in the first year of the Government became a chronic weakness, leading to mistrust, personal animosity and secret faction meetings. The leaders of the new right faction, Scully and Bert Bailey (who had defeated Kennelly in the 1952 pre-selection ballot and replaced him in the Legislative Council) organised intensely and formed some working arrangements with the Barry faction to build up a recognisable 'right wing' in Caucus. Protestants such as E. Morton, the Chairman of Committees, began tentative counter organisation. Many of the pro-Movement men such as George Fewster (Essendon), George White (Mentone) and Charles Murphy (Hawthorn), a former business manager of *News Weekly*, were not looked on as being particularly controversial; but the build up of sectarian feeling made it harder for men on all sides to avoid entanglement in alliances.

Cain, who was sixty-six years old when he attained office, became worried that a Barry-Scully alliance would seek to replace him, though in this parliament he still had 'the numbers' in Caucus. The ability of The Movement and Groupers to control pre-selections, as shown in the Kennelly affair in Melbourne West, unnerved many members. This was aggravated by the Government's own redistribution which reduced the number of low population country divisions and increased the number of Melbourne seats. The border changes and rearrangement of seats produced by this meant a general instability and rivalry for several new seats.

In the previous Government, Cain had had his brushes with the Trades Hall, anxious to influence the Government. This conflict developed again by 1953 and 1954, at first with the Grouper-dominated Central Executive and later with Stout and the THC.

Lovegrove had enunciated a policy early that he did not want to see the Central Executive become a 'court of appeal from Caucus', ordering the Parliamentary Party to reverse decisions made in Caucus. However, the Caucus 'out' groups had many sympathisers on the Executive and sometimes were able to use it against the Cain faction. Grouper union officials and The Movement also from time to time tried to use the Executive against Cain's faction.

The issues involved were usually secondary enough in themselves, with Executive discussions—often not taken to the point of a vote recorded in the minutes—only part of wider tactics. Grouper union officials pressed the Executive for more favourable workers' compensation legislation, The Movement pressed for land settlement and co-operation. Cain came under a number of such pressures, with the Executive right sometimes caucusing against him. They were pressures with which he was quite able to live, but his friends thought he would have been happier without them. His relations with the Grouper Executive were neither good nor especially bad, but his association with the Kennelly-dominated machine had certainly been far better. His relationship with Lovegrove and McManus, Kennelly's political enemies, was unenthusiastic.

The irony of all this factionalism was that there was little disagreement except of emphasis and timing over specific issues, and practically no broad ideological division. There was no Marxist-influenced left in the Caucus and even potentially divisive issues such as State Aid for independent schools did not seriously arise.

But the internal atmosphere encouraged bitterness and suspicion over trivial issues. The factions organised against each other over an appointment to the Public Library Board. There was even an argument over a gift of firewood to pensioners. Scully was thought by many to be attending too many Communion breakfasts and Church functions. To their colleagues, some Movement men seemed obsessive in their attitude to possibly obscene literature. Groupers were irritated by the lack of interest of many others in the fight in the unions, while to some Cain supporters the Scully group seemed to have an anti-communist obsession and to want the Government to deal unnecessarily harshly with communist-led transport strikes. The Movement's enthusiastic, ideologically based support for a Co-operation Act, increasing the scope for co-operatives in Victoria, surrounded it with a measure of suspicion, although it was based on one introduced in New South Wales in 1923. The measure was in line with traditional ALP policy and eventually proved to work modestly but well in Victoria. Hundreds of small co-operatives were formed under it.

In spite of these background disturbances, the Cain Government's record in the first year was of good administration and a solid legislative program. It introduced the 'two for one' electoral reform, which provided two State seats for every Federal constituency and ended domination of the State by country electorates of relatively small population. The Workers' Compensation Act was liberalised, quarterly adjustments to the basic wage retained in State awards after the Arbitration Court eliminated them in Federal awards, and Long Service Leave was introduced. Reforms to the Shops and Factories Act improved working conditions. The Co-operatives Act opened the way to as many co-operatives as the people would support. The Tattersalls lottery was transferred to Victoria to provide more finance for hospitals. Serving of liquor with meals was allowed until 10 p.m., instead of the previously restrictive 8 p.m. Jurors' fees were increased, and there were reforms in State housing, slum clearance and the provisions governing Wards of State.

The Party was broadly united on almost all of these issues, but one important piece of legislation did cause perfectly genuine division that in the atmosphere of the time was explosive. This was the Land Settlement Bill, 1953, a portmanteau piece of legislation which made a number of— apparently small—changes in the Victorian land laws, to provide for a variety of changes of circumstance. Many had been suggested by the

Crown Law Department. Other changes were necessary in law for soldier settlement because of the rising value of land.

As originally intended and approved by Cabinet, however, the legislation was to provide for two rather more controversial changes which would have been 'sneaked in' in a technical and seemingly non-controversial Bill.

These were to place employees of the Soldier Settlement Commission, which administered soldier settlement in the State, under the Public Service Board; and to provide for Crown land not required for soldier settlement or conventional closer settlement to go to unspecified 'organisations' at the discretion of the Minister for Lands.

The reason for the first of these changes was that many public servants were resentful of higher salaries in the Soldier Settlement Commission, available because of its special conditions. There was a feeling that favourites of the Commission could get these good jobs: and there was also a feeling that it was much easier for Masons than for Catholics to get them. 'Masons versus Catholics' in the battle for promotion in the State Public Service had been an issue—how important is difficult to judge—in the Service for many years. Cabinet agreed to end the controversy, at the request of the Victorian Public Service Association, by placing future appointments to the Commission under the Public Service Board.

The provision to give land not wanted for other settlement to 'organisations' was a stratagem designed to hand over a tract of poor land at Caradale, in the South Gippsland hills, to the National Catholic Rural Movement for a land settlement project. Santamaria had asked Cain for the land earlier in 1953, in a deputation with the Italian Consul and an Italian land settlement expert.

The origins of this particular scheme were, despite the ideology of the NCRM, conventional enough. Italian migrants had been entering Australia in record numbers in the early 1950's. Most were of peasant origin and in the recession of 1952 many were unemployed. Santamaria's standing in the Italian community and the Church, and his enthusiasm for land settlement, led to him attempting to see if migrants could be settled on the land. The situation accorded with his own ideas, though he had come to realise the natural priority that would go to returned servicemen and farmers' sons in any closer settlement scheme on the scale then being considered by Australian governments.

In accordance with wider NCRM policies he approached the Victorian, New South Wales and Queensland governments for grants of land, while European Catholic migration bodies agreed to provide capital and people. The NCRM hoped to attract Italian and Dutch and possibly other nationalities as well, and some Australians. It hoped that if the modest schemes envisaged worked, bigger things would be possible. It was hoped—at least in theory—to have some non-Catholics as well.

The Premier of Queensland, V. C. Gair, refused to grant the land and the Premier of New South Wales, J. J. Cahill, made no decision. Robert Cosgrove in Tasmania and Cain in Victoria both agreed to give otherwise unwanted land to the NCRM.Cosgrove agreed in principle to land in the foothills of the north-west of Tasmania, inland from Burnie; and Cain agreed to the Caradale proposition. He invited Santamaria to discuss it further with R. W. Holt, as Minister for Lands.

Shortly afterwards Santamaria visited Holt in his office, accompanied by Scully at Cain's suggestion. Versions of the interview given later by the parties differ markedly.

Santamaria and Scully have insisted that it was amicable, lasted longer than they expected, and that Holt readily agreed to the scheme. Holt, on the other hand, charged a year later at the height of the split that he had refused to agree and that Santamaria had said he (Holt) 'might not be in the next Parliament'—presumably a reference to his seat of Portland being abolished in the redistribution.

There were misgivings about the proposal in Caucus from members who feared a 'peasant community' and were scandalised by the idea of an unassimilated foreign community. Most, however, agreed that the NCRM should be given a chance to develop the land if nobody else wanted it and there was no cost to the state. The measure passed through Caucus and Cabinet with limited controversy, considering its background and subsequent events. Some believed the scheme too impractical to get off the ground.

Holt introduced the Land Settlement Bill into the Legislative Assembly on 24 November and explained it in his second reading speech on 10 December, a few hours before Parliament was due to rise for the Christmas break. The two controversial sections were completely missing from his speech and the Bill, however. He said it was an uncontroversial measure, and after brief debate it went to the Legislative Council.

The Leader of the Government in the Council, Coleman, and Minister in charge of the Bill, Fraser, noticed then that the two provisions approved by Cabinet were missing. They called a special late night meeting of Cabinet, which agreed to Fraser introducing amendments in the Council to insert the missing sections into the Bill.

This he did, and Holt then brought the amendments before the dying assembly, when it resumed at 3.40 a.m. on 11 December after a two-hour supper break. The debate on the first amendment is hard to follow as members were obviously tired from the succession of late-night sittings and one speaker even confused his bills. However, it lasted nearly an hour, with Opposition members asking for more information and apparently trying to embarrass the Government over its 'ingratitude' to the employees of the Soldier Settlement Commission. Holt spoke only briefly in support and the main defence then fell to Cain.

Eventually the amendment passed on the voices and then, at about 4 a.m., Holt introduced the second amendment, reading it out without any supporting speech.

The Hansard record then goes on:

Mr Bolte (Leader of the Opposition): Surely the Government cannot admit an amendment without an explanation that members have seen now for the first time. This procedure is the culmination of the deplorable tactics that we have witnessed. The submission of the amendment is

typical of what has happened to the Bill since it appeared on the Notice Paper three weeks or a month ago. It remained on the Notice Paper for a fortnight without a second-reading speech being made.
Mr Holt: I cannot go on with this!
Handclapping and 'Hear Hear' on Opposition benches as Mr Holt left the Chamber.[1]
The Speaker (the Hon. P. K. Sutton): Order! We have witnessed a most unseemly uproar.
Mr Bolte: I was saying that for a fortnight the Bill appeared on the Notice Paper. . . .

Holt had torn the amendment up before leaving the Assembly. The episode missed all but the final edition of the *Argus* in the morning press, but was prominently headlined on page one of that afternoon's (Saturday) *Herald* and followed up in the Monday morning papers. Correspondents said it was the first time such an incident had occurred in any Parliament.

An interesting sidelight in the publicity was a strangely vague article in the *Herald* explaining the land settlement scheme. It went into considerable detail, but was entirely in the passive voice and omitted any reference to the NCRM. This was typical of the hushed tones in which Santamaria's activities were described at the time.

The debate on the controversial amendment continued after Holt's walkout until Parliament rose about 9 a.m. Cain took over the amendment and defended it eloquently, though many felt he did not like it. The main attack came from the Country Party, where anti-Catholic feeling was strong among some members. Gradually vague references to 'sectarianism' crept into the debate. For example:

Mr Brose (Rodney): . . . We do not want any persons to be settled on poor land. So I am full of suspicions concerning this measure. I now propose to say something straight out. I feel that sectarianism comes into this measure, and I am sorry to have to say it.
Mr Galvin: There is no greater sectarian bigot than you.
Mr Brose: I read in the newspapers about last Easter of a Conference that was held at Albury by a group of people who put forward a certain policy. It amounts, in effect, to peasantry and poverty. I do not want to see any good people put on the land under a policy of poverty and peasantry. . . . Sectarianism is a horrible thing to get into this House. However, it has come here in recent days in my experience. The former member for Richmond displayed and preached that sort of thing. I do not like it. I know the Government is unhappy because the proposal comes from down the street, from an outside group of people who control the destinies of the great Labour party for which, over the years, I have had a considerable amount of respect. . . . I feel sure that this proposal has been foisted on the Government by a group of people outside who have control of the Labour organisation. I utter my protest. . . .

After leaving the Assembly, Holt returned to his home at Portland for the weekend and on the Monday resigned from Cabinet. 'I found myself out of step with my Cabinet colleagues on what I considered to be a

[1] Some claim that the clapping and 'Hear Hear' calls came also from Soldier Settlement Commission employees in the galleries.

matter of principle. . . . I intend to support the Government,' he said in a brief statement to the press.

His action, and the whole atmosphere surrounding the legislation, had given another twist to the sectarian spiral in Caucus and the election for the Cabinet vacancy created was particularly bitter. With the support of the Scully and Barry groups, Malcolm Gladman (Warrnambool)—Holt's potential rival for the new constituency to be created in the south-west of the state—won the Cabinet vacancy from a field of seven.

Cain wished to let the affair pass over, but a section of the Central Executive sought to discipline Holt. At the meeting on 18 December, Keon moved that business be suspended so the Executive could hear a report from Cain and Fraser on the incident. M. J. Travers seconded the motion, and a heated debate followed in which differences then developing in the Executive could be seen. Lovegrove, Woodhouse, Devlin—interestingly, as one of Santamaria's main supporters on the Executive—Cameron and Cain opposed the motion, while Hoban and Peters supported it. Hoban then moved the adjournment. R. E. Wilson supported him and it was carried by 12 votes to 9.

What made Holt act as he did? He has argued consistently that he simply objected to the notion of 'peasant farming' in communities and to Santamaria's influence and alleged threat to him. Others claim he was more influenced by pressure from officials of the Soldier Settlement Commission. There was also a widespread feeling that, as a practising Presbyterian and son of a minister, he was, perhaps unconsciously, hypersensitive to Catholics. But certainly before this incident Holt was not regarded as being particularly anti-Catholic and there were some strongly Catholic districts in his electorate. He developed a subsequent reputation as being somewhat erratic and highly emotional. Another point is that he was something of a protégé of Kennelly, who had recruited him into the ALP after the war and backed his pre-selection for Portland as a 'horse for the course'. Coleman had also been something of a mentor to him. He had little sympathy from Caucus colleagues over the incident and many were angry with him. They did not place much intrinsic significance on the incident, except in its potential to cause trouble.

In 1954, the sectarian problem continued to plague the Cain Government, while more serious trouble came in challenges from the unions.

The 1953 Conference had adopted a resolution that children attending independent schools be given full rights to use transport available to State school children. The previous provision had been that they could use it if the State school headmaster concerned considered it practicable; interpretation of this had caused sectarian trouble in some country districts.

The sponsor, Reginald Hoban, had the impression at Conference that the Minister for Education, Shepherd, was not enthusiastic about it and on 23 October he moved successfully on the Central Executive, that Cabinet be requested to implement the Conference decision immediately.

This apparently simple proposal provoked a 'State Aid' controversy, one of the traditional troubles of all Australian political parties. The fear of such a controversy had been a reason why Cain, Shepherd and others were unenthusiastic about the measure. In Caucus, the Scully group took it up and Shepherd and Cain got the impression they were being 'hounded' over it. They eventually passed the regulation required, but the affair left a stronger flavour of sectarian bitterness than the more spectacular Holt walk-out.

The left wing of the trade union movement had always been amenable to the idea that the unions should put 'stomach' into nervous politicians on radical social changes and the communists wished to expose the 'capitalist' nature of the Cain administration. These inevitable pressures led into a feud of extraordinary bitterness which had developed between the Trades Hall Council and ALP officers and by the middle of 1954 the Cain Government was facing severe hostility from the Trades Hall.

Most of the ostensible issues over which this bitter spirit arose were genuine. The unions, naturally, wanted to use the Cain Government as an instrument to get better conditions for their members and to uphold the interests of the industrial wing: just as naturally, the pressures from much wider sections of the community on a new, reforming government limited the time it had to consider issues the Trades Hall considered vital; and more importantly, the financial limitations upon it dampened enthusiasm for wage rises.

There was a strong element of malice in the union attitude, inspired by the troubles at the Trades Hall. There also was, and remained, a half-conscious contempt by some industrialists for the necessarily compromising, dealing political wing. In Victoria, this feeling had been encouraged over several generations by the 'pure' Marxism taught to aspiring young unionists at the Victorian Labor College. A contempt for 'compromising with capitalism' was developed early, and while most outgrew the overt stage, this feeling remained as a lingering prejudice. It should be added that there were faults on both sides. The political wing was often less sympathetic than it should have been to the genuine interests of its industrial partners, and among some middle class elements in the ALP a lack of sensitivity to the susceptibilities of the industrialists was marked. The predominantly Catholic nature of the ALP middle class sections only increased feelings of estrangement from the mainly Protestant or secular union men.

The principal issue around which the troubles of 1954 developed was the Arbitration Court's refusal early in the year to increase margins in keeping with basic wage rises. This led to an intensive union campaign for the State Government to pay voluntarily the increased margins sought. To add to the conflagration, part of the then anti-inflation mood of the Arbitration Court was attributed—in an atmosphere of growing hysteria— to the influence on the Court of 'Catholic Action' economic doctrines.

The Australian Workers' Union, which covered many construction workers employed directly and indirectly by the State, sought margin increases for these men, and in protest at what it considered a slow response, on 22 March announced that it had suspended from union membership twenty-four members of the State Parliamentary Party, including two ministers—C. P. Stoneham (Agriculture) and J. Smith (Lands). The District Secretary, H. O. Davis, announced that in future membership would be confined to those engaged in industry under AWU awards. This followed an earlier decision by the AWU not to send delegates to the 1954 ALP Conference. Although a genuine industrial issue was involved it is difficult to believe that two other factors were not involved—the changed attitude of the AWU to the Industrial Groups since the previous year and the longer resentment of Davis against the ALP Executive, since his argument in 1951.

About the same time another, superficially trivial, dispute broke out when the Tramway Employees' Association directed its members not to man 41-seater buses on the Point Ormond-Clifton Hill run unless there was a driver as well as conductor. Coleman, the Minister for Transport, backed the attitude of the Tramways Board that at off-peak times the bus could be worked by a driver alone, who would collect the fares. Despite communist influence in the union, this appeared to be another genuine industrial dispute as the bus crews themselves strongly supported the union attitude at mass meetings. Nevertheless, this curious and debilitating dispute went on for nearly a year until an independent arbitrator agreed to by the parties, Mr G. S. Featonby, ruled on 7 January 1955 in favour of the union attitude.

It was actually an issue rich in background malice. Lovegrove and the Groupers feared the Tramways Union, one of the last under mainly communist control, was the spearhead of a new communist-instigated attempt to 'stand over' the Cain Government, in the spirit of the post-war years. Lovegrove pressed Coleman to stand up to the union leadership, especially its secretary, C. O'Shea, at all costs. His attitude may have been reinforced by memories of O'Shea from his Communist Party days. On the other hand, Stout seized on a sound industrial issue to beat Lovegrove and the ALP. A puritan, Stout also disapproved of Coleman being in a Labor Cabinet because of his profitable hotel interests.

At monthly meetings in mid-July, the month after the State ALP Conference, where a new dispute over Industrial Groups had flared up, the AWU and the Moulders' Union announced within a couple of days of each other that they would disaffiliate from the ALP—the AWU because of the construction margins dispute and both because of the 'activities of the Industrial Groups'. The Moulders' Union decision followed a report to the meeting by delegates to the ALP Conference.

By this time yet another issue had developed between the unions and the State Government. In June, the Industrial Group candidate J. W. Neill had finally succeeded in defeating the communist State Secretary of the Australian Railways Union, J. J. Brown. On leaving office, Brown applied to rejoin the Victorian Railways, where he had been employed prior to becoming secretary of the union in 1943. The State Cabinet, under pressure from the Industrial Groupers, asked the Railways Commissioners not to re-employ him; it was felt that a return to the rank and file would only give Brown a base from which to organise a return to office three years later. The decision angered the Union Movement where majority opinion was that, whatever the inconvenience and personalities involved, it was a vital industrial principle that a man's activities in a union should not prejudice his chance of re-employment in his industry.

At a tense meeting of the Trades Hall Council on 22 July, the ever intensifying discord broke violently into the open, when Stout declared that the Victorian ALP was 'almost in a state of fascism'. Jordan, in a second report, said the attitude of the Government 'bordered on contempt of the union movement'.

Stout said the unions had been seeking appointments for deputations to the Government on margins, compulsory unionism, the re-employment of Brown, appointment of the Tramways Industrial Group Secretary K. Brennan instead of a man chosen by the union itself as employees' representative on the Tramways Board and the one-man bus dispute. He said there were 'fascist tendencies in Victoria'. There were apparently people with sufficient strength and ability to determine whether State ministers should confer with the unions. The THC would have to determine whether it would function purely as an industrial organisation, if the present position continued. Many Labor people were young and inexperienced and would have to 'take a tumble'.

Jordan told the meeting that the THC had been seeking a conference with Cain for six weeks on claims for higher margins for employees in state instrumentalities, but had been unable to obtain an appointment. But a few hours after the THC Executive had convened a special conference of unions on the issue, Cain had notified the THC officials that he would receive a deputation within a few days.

The bitterly anti-Grouper J. P. Brebner, of the Pulp and Paper Mill Employees' Union, said the ALP was being run by a small clique. The unions were loyal to the Labor Party, but they could not continue to be loyal when the clique running it were taking every opportunity to embarrass officials of the THC.

The following Thursday, 29 July, Cain met representatives from twenty-three unions. In his warm, placatory style, he told them the Government would examine the question of increasing margins for Government and semi-Government employees, and would support claims for increased margins before the Arbitration Court later in the year. 'All you have put forward is more than justified,' he said. There may have been misunderstandings in the past, but he welcomed the round-table talk and looked forward to working together for common aims. But he refused to relent on the J. J. Brown affair, and said it was closed.

Stout said a Labor Government had a normal duty to fight for the sort of industrial conditions the unions advocated, even if it lost its place as the Government in doing so. Otherwise it 'would not be worth a bad two bob'. He said the action against Brown had been 'distinctly anti-union'. 'Personally I would not care twopence if he worked on the Siberian Railway for the rest of his life,' Stout said, 'but a basic union principle is involved.'

On the same day, Cain also met a deputation from the ARU, led by Neill, and said he would consider payment of service grants to railway employees.

July was also the month for some key pre-selection contests, for vacated or re-distributed seats for the State elections due at the end of 1955. There were fears in some sections of the Party that The Movement would try to manipulate these to its advantage. The fears proved unfounded.

For the Melbourne North province of the Legislative Council, J. Little, the past-President of the ALP, a Protestant but strong supporter of the Groups and militant anti-communist, won 2,500 votes of 5,000 in a field of nine. He had the indirect backing of The Movement in that Norman Lauritz, who was interested in the seat, did not contest the pre-selection against Little. Little had the support of his union, the Boot Trades, which had many members in the province and could usually control the pre-selection.

In Warrnambool, Gladman defeated Holt for the new, enlarged seat. A Catholic, Gladman had the support of the State Executive not only because of his ideological alignment but because he lived in Warrnambool, the most populous part of the new electorate, and was judged to have a better chance than Holt, a Portland man, of winning it. He had also been a shop steward at Nestles milk plant where there were many union votes.

A Scully associate, Michael Lucy, whose seat of Ivanhoe was to be abolished in the redistribution, won pre-selection for the new seat of Evelyn against P. R. Connell, another Catholic right wing sitting member. The Country Organiser, John Tripovich, won Dandenong, Larry Floyd won Williamstown from a field of eight, Roy Schintler won Footscray and George Poyser, Geelong. None of these four was Catholic, and all stayed with the ALP after the split.

K. Hayes, a son of the Minister for Housing, Tom Hayes, beat pro-Movement activist, Maurie Keady for Coburg by a margin of only seven votes. A prominent right winger, T. V. Hartnedy, won Preston.

The trouble between the political and industrial wings declined temporarily after the meeting with Cain, but the one-man bus dispute dragged on to provide an issue around which the deep-seated animosity could centre. The unions had agreed to accept Coleman, the Minister for Transport, as arbitrator, but rejected his decision that one man could handle the contentious buses. A THC Disputes Committee, in which militant influence was strong, recommended to the full THC that the Victorian Branch of the Labor Party was 'no longer worthy of financial support or association'. This was in September 1954, when the Federal Parliamentary Party in Canberra was bitterly divided and unsettled over Evatt's appearance before the Petrov Royal Commission and subsequent ejection, and when factional rivalry on the Federal Executive was approaching a climax. In the branches, the restraint imposed by two impending Federal elections, in the late autumn of both 1953 and 1954, had been superseded by disillusion and a sharpening of factional and personal rivalry.

The one-man bus issue came before a stormy meeting of the Melbourne Trades Hall Council on 16 September. In a report to Council, Stout said the Disputes Committee had made its decision and unions could now do what they liked with it. The Committee felt it had been sufficiently patient over the past ten months of the dispute, he said. He believed the Committee would have to take industrial action.

Lovegrove was the chief speaker against the decision. The Government, he said was being asked to repudiate its actions before Parliament, and possibly be turned out of office. The union movement had gained more from the present Government than from any other. One element in the dispute aimed to smash the Labor Party and the Government. F. J. Riley, supporting him, said the Disputes Committee's decision was aimed at sabotaging and white-anting the Labor Party.

The Council voted by 95 votes to 54 to support the Disputes Committee recommendation. This was fairly typical of the two-to-one majority Stout and his supporters could now command against the Industrial Group unions and supporters of the ALP Executive. The far left and communists had declined to a small minority, and, on the surface, were not operating as a faction in the Council at all, allowing the Stout-ALP fight to grow without hindrance.

The resolution which the Council adopted, with grave potential for trouble in the ALP, read:

We again affirm our belief that the manning of 41-seat buses by a driver-conductor is against the interests and welfare of the men employed by the Tramways Board and the travelling public.

We regard the actions taken by the Minister for Transport, Cabinet and the Parliamentary Labor Party in upholding the Board, rejecting the opinion of the Trades Hall Council and supporting the use of punitive sections of the Arbitration Act objected to by the ACTU and trade unions as being so subversive of trade union and Labor principles as to warrant condemnation.

Such conduct forces us to express the opinion that the Victorian branch of the Labor Party is no longer worthy of financial support or association.

On this minor issue, the vicious circle of division that had been turning in an ever more intense spiral in Victorian Labor for eight years appeared to have reached a climax. One or two more straws and the camel's back would break.

The land settlement question, which Holt had raised so dramatically in the State Parliament, had for many years been a key part of Santamaria's Distributist ideas. This 'back to the land' notion—sometimes scathingly though inaccurately referred to as the 'peasant on every acre' policy—often impinged on both the political and industrial wings of the Labor Movement in the late 1940's and early 1950's, and is an example of how apparently fringe issues can have a snowballing effect in politics.

It arose out of the Distributist movement of the 1930's and was formalised in the National Catholic Rural Movement, under the National Secretariat of Catholic Action, in 1940. Santamaria was its first secretary and Bishop Henschke, of Wagga Wagga, was its Episcopal Chairman for twenty-five years.

A pamphlet by Santamaria, *The Fight For the Land*, on the objectives of the NCRM was published in 1942. A monthly newspaper, *Rural Life*, began publication in 1940. By the mid-1950's, according to the *Australian Encyclopaedia*, there were 3,714 members, in 200 groups in 20 dioceses. A handbook published as late as 1958, *Fruits of the Vine*, showed that the ideas of the NCRM had changed very little, except in one aspect, since its foundation, though it mellowed considerably during the sixties.

The objectives of the NCRM were to create a climate in favour of agriculture and smaller communities as the way of life most suited to mankind; to encourage a more spiritual approach both to farming and life in general by Catholic farmers; and to encourage better farming practices and a more dignified attitude to rural life among Catholic small farmers.

Many of its non-spiritual ideas were relatively uncontroversial: farmers should spend more money on their houses and less on cars. Cooperatives should be developed so there would be less dependence on other forms of credit. Education in the country should pay more attention to rural needs and interests. Light industry, often run by cooperatives, should be developed to create employment in small towns, thus helping farm families to stay together. There should be more provision for employees in country towns to own small blocks outside the town, where they could live and work part-time.

The idea of 'diversified farming' was preached with zeal, to reduce dependence on one crop, such as wheat.

A much more controversial NCRM idea was 'Independent Farming'—
another way of describing semi-subsistence farming. Farmers should concentrate more, it was argued, on producing their own household needs,
and be less dependent on the vagaries of overseas and domestic markets for
their produce. It was posed as the alternative to 'commercial, exploitative
farming'. Apologists for it argue that it was a meaningful idea in the
1930's, when prices for many products were disastrously low and unemployment trapped men on their farms, while at the same time agriculture
was less mechanised than after the war.

Santamaria wrote in *The Fight For the Land*:

The term 'independent farming' is newly coined, and it is an attempt to
link up the technical policies involved in diversified farming with the
desire for personal independence, which is the objective and indeed the
very 'raison d'etre' of the Catholic attitude to the land. It is neither
Specialised nor Subsistence farming. Its objectives are two-fold:
1 That the farm should primarily be regarded as the granary from which
all the family food is produced. This should be the first objective which
the farm family should set itself so that, whatever the economic vicissitudes
of the outside world, there would always be a living for the family from
the land.
2 To secure the money income which the family will need for education
and the other necessities which cannnot be produced on the farm itself,
the family will diversify the production of the farm as far as possible, so
that there will be money coming in all the time. . . .
Thus there is imported in our attitude to the land that Catholic and
European tradition which has founded a permanent agriculture in the Old
World. On the other hand, by aiming in addition at a regular money income, provision is made to enable the family to better its position economically and to make the land attractive to the children because it promises
tangible economic returns which allow it to compete, even to the superficial eye, with the financial allurements of the city.

Perhaps revealing a fear for the future, Santamaria added later, in explaining why the NCRM should not tackle the problem of rural debt in its
early stages:

This delay is not only one of necessity. In certain respects it is fortunate. The
farmer is proverbially politically minded and there would have been a
real danger, had The Movement allowed the problem of debt to be its first
consideration, that it would have become its only consideration. In other
words, The Movement would have been plunged into the maelstrom of
party politics—a sphere which is completely forbidden to Catholic Action.
The delay enables The Movement to educate its members so that they
keep party politics in perspective. Whatever decisions The Movement
arrives at in matters which concern public authorities will be formulated
not through one or other parties, but for the consideration of all governments and parties, whatever their nature. The role of the Christian within
these parties will be to persuade their particular parties to adopt the
Christian plan.

Apart from the vague references to 'diversified farming', 'independent
farming', 'commercial, exploitative farming' and the like, it is difficult to

pinpoint the agricultural ideas of the NCRM. The language in *Rural Life* and other publications was so ideological and doctrinal that it was virtually a different language from that of the mainstream of agricultural discussion in Australia. The NCRM used economics and preached them with zeal when they suited its ideas; when economics did not suit, they were dismissed with contempt.

Santamaria published his only full-length book, *The Earth Our Mother*, in 1945. It repeated many of the ideas of *The Fight For the Land* and went into more technical detail, but was not a satisfying book. Much of it was devoted to attacking a report of the Rural Reconstruction Committee, which had proposed the 'economic unit' as a farm size in the post-war reconstruction of agriculture. This would have meant elimination of some of the smaller holdings. Santamaria pleaded the case for 'the family farm' as an alternative concept, but he often seemed to be attacking the Commission for its choice of language as much as indicating concrete areas of disagreement. He made vague references to the development of handicrafts as a supplement to 'independent farming' in keeping the smallest holders on the land, but again the ideological rather then technical bent of the argument made it another rather than an alternative case.

NCRM publications were always vague about the size of small farms. Once there was a reference to 'eighty acres' as the ideal and one got the impression that it generally wanted holdings a little smaller than secular authority would have considered a living area. The scale of land settlement it sought was also kept vague. *News Weekly* wanted a policy of 'a million migrants a year' immediately after the war, when Europe had many displaced people. A powerful supporter of this policy was the Managing Director of the *Argus* newspaper, Sir Errol Knox, who entered the Catholic Church shortly afterwards.

Various post-war issues of *Rural Life* called for settling 'possibly millions' of migrants, and 'half a million a year, including migrants'. It talked of opening up great stretches of the North and envisaged a vast, dense agriculture in the valleys of the Murray and Murrumbidgee using the water from the Snowy River diversion scheme. The NCRM wanted hydro-electric power from the Snowy scheme to be used to support small industry and regional centres in these valleys, rather than supplement metropolitan electricity supplies.

The factual situation in which the NCRM was working was that there had been about 250,000 rural holdings in Australia for many years, with new land settlement schemes roughly cancelling out the decline from amalgamation of small holdings. Well over 90 per cent were owner-occupied and 'family farms'. There had been a history almost from the beginning of Australia of severe distress caused to individuals by ill-conceived land settlement schemes, with under-sized holdings the major cause and the unreliability of overseas markets the next most important. This had been as evident as ever in the soldier settlement schemes that followed the First World War, when British migrants as well as Australians, both often with little experience, were settled on farms too small to pay for their development and return a worthwhile living as well. The mainstream of economic opinion in Australia was that post-war development should be geared to fast industrialisation, to reduce national dependence on fluctuations in seasonal conditions and overseas markets and to provide the only practicable base for a greatly increased population.

Yet the NCRM was inclined to regard its opponents as having an anti-Catholic bias, if indeed it noticed them at all.

'In Praise of Peasantry', an editorial in *Rural Life* in April 1952, said:

The fact that Australia does need a vast number of additional primary producers is undeniable. A surprising degree of unity already exists on this particular point. But as soon as a type of small-scale, intensive agriculture is advocated a hornet's nest of opposition is stirred up in some quarters. . . .

What is the basis of this hostility? More often than not it has a subconscious religious motive. . . .

The NCRM's main strength was in rural dioceses such as Wagga Wagga, Ballarat and Armidale, where the bishops were strong supporters. Santamaria built up a strong personal following among provincial bishops, such as Bishop O'Collins of Ballarat and Bishop Doody of Armidale, as well as Bishop Henschke. These were to provide a crucial religious-political base for him after the split in the ALP.

NCRM members were active in the Murray Valley Development League, with headquarters in Albury, and the New England New State Movement, with headquarters in Armidale. Many members had also been active in primary producer organisations and the Country Party and in none of these was there much sign of resentment against them. Others were in The Movement and the ALP; but if Conference agendas are any guide, the NCRM did not exert much influence on rural branches of the ALP. However, *News Weekly* and *Social Survey*, as well as *Time*, were the three main political papers recommended for reading and libraries in *Fruit of the Vine*.

NCRM ideas were based on the Distributist philosophy and came from the usual Chesterton-Belloc and Continental sources. However, certain differences can be distinguished. The NCRM looked, if anywhere, to Central Europe and Western Canada for its model, rather than to the Middle Ages and Southern Europe, as the English Distributists did. Even Protestant Scandinavia was sometimes an inspiration. Much American Populist writing, arising from the rural distress of the 1930's and early 1940's, influenced it. Dutch migrants were emphasised rather than Italians—possibly a sop to the Australian mood of the time. There was an emphasis on modest prosperity, and poverty was emphatically rejected—though at times the NCRM was vague about how poverty might be avoided on small holdings. The ideas showed an eclecticism typical of the Australia of the time—appealing notions from all over the place were pieced together with some reference to Australian conditions, but rarely, one feels, much attempt to think them through in the light of genuine Australian experience.

The practical achievements of the NCRM were two small settlements, in which its ideas were put into practice. Maryknoll, near Tynong in the

Gippsland region of Victoria, was a Catholic community centre of small husbandry and handicrafts. San Isidore, near Wagga, provided small homestead plots in a Catholic setting for people employed full-time in Wagga itself.

Whatever the economic and technical ideas of the NCRM, its main purpose was always spiritual. It claimed that the farm and small community provided the organic community in which the regular practice of religion thrived. *Fruit of the Vine* quoted a survey in the diocese of Port Augusta, South Australia, which showed that only 48 per cent of Catholics in the industrial city of Port Pirie practised their religion, while in the country 80 to 90 per cent and more practised. Surveys from other countries showing a similar two to one ratio of Catholic religious practice between city and country were often quoted by the NCRM. A secondary attraction was the high birth rate in rural areas, which *Rural Life* and the other publications said would help populate Australia.

Santamaria himself stated the policies of the NCRM with his customary lucidity at the annual Conference in April 1951, when it had approached the peak of its power and influence. His address was published in *Rural Life* of May that year. He said in part:

What are the qualities necessary for Movement membership?

They are, first of all, a sense of the apostolate; a willingness, if I may so express it, to take your feet down off the mantelpiece at night and work.

The second, once that has been achieved, is a sense of loyalty and of discipline in carrying out the policies of the Movement. Thirdly, a sense of perseverance against the frustrations which are absolutely inevitable in an organization like this. Lastly—and this has not yet been called for from members of the Rural Movement—but it will be called for, when you really begin to be active and you are subjected to direct attack—a great reservoir of moral courage which will make you stand up when it is much easier to sit down. . . .

Let us deal briefly with the question of why we began. We begun our work about the year 1940—at perhaps the worst time in which we could ever have begun—and we began to drive home one single doctrine, the primacy of the land, and of rural life, and of agriculture in Australia. We said then—and it was our central thesis—that whatever else might be done in this country; whatever else might be left undone; however many great industries might be built up; whatever economic arrangements might be made—that the land had to come first.

We had three vital and fundamental reasons. The first was religious, the second was national, and the third was civic.

The religious reason was this. All the observation and experience, all the reading that one could do, showed that the fervour and the regularity of religious spirit, the fervour and the very life of Catholics depended upon the strength of rural life in this country. I think it is a general rule, to which there are very few exceptions, that whenever your society becomes urbanized and your Catholics become urbanized, it becomes almost physically impossible to keep up the level of Catholic life among them.

That was the first reason why the Rural Movement was begun. It was the vital reason, the fundamental reason; because with rural life there went the strength of religious practice. If you destroyed rural life, no matter how many Churches you built in the cities, you could not keep Christian life going at the proper level.

The second reason was national. Professor Macdonald Holmes proved to us that the birth rate, the very strength, the very numbers of our community depended upon the strength of rural life. We were given time and again the relative birth rates in metropolitan, provincial, and country areas; and it has been proved, not only through Australian experience but through world-wide experience, that any increase in population must come from the rural areas. Therefore if we hope for the survival of this country everything has to be done to build up those areas which have been given us Australians.

The final reason for emphasising this central theme of the primacy of rural life was civic. You find that when Stalin wanted to establish his dictatorship in Russia he seized the political machine first; but he was never safe until the moment when he destroyed—and when I say destroyed I mean killed—11 million peasants, because so long as the peasant system lasted, a system of people attached to their own holdings, his totalitarian regime could not endure.

I don't care whether it is Russia, or Germany, or whether it is Australia, in proportion as you destroy your rural life, in that proportion you destroy your free institutions.

If you have had in Australia totalitarianism in another way, totalitarianism without a shirt, through social services, through the social service state, it is tied up absolutely with the decline of independent proprietorship, particularly on the land.

You cannot ignore these general principles; because in the end, if you ignore them, they will hit home to you in the lives of yourselves and your families in a very brief time.

We were formed to put forward this one central theme of the primacy of agriculture. You will admit, everyone will admit, that if we said just that and did not explain the methods, the policies, we would not have got very far. We did put forward a policy and a programme in 1940.

Very briefly it was this. We stood for more farmers and greater agricultural production; we stood for smaller farms; we stood for diversified agriculture; we stood for co-operatives; we stood for a particular system of rural education.

We were attacked from three centres. We could ignore the people who rather annoyed us at the time with the appellation 'Collins Street farmers', for we soon realized that these people were trying to cover a guilty conscience in themselves.

The second attack came from those practical farmers who said this doctrine of diversification was a lot of nonsense, that if a man was a good wheatgrower, specialization in wheatgrowing was the best business he could undertake.

The third line of attack came from academic circles, which deprecated all this talk of extending agriculture because of the uncertainty of outside markets for Australian agricultural produce.

Now we can see how the wheel has turned full circle. If today we are able to invite to this conference economic experts like Barbara Ward, experts on regional development like Professor Macdonald Holmes, we can do it because we are sure that the economists and the rest will reiterate the same doctrine which we proclaimed in 1940 and 1941.

Now the second question—how far have we come? This can be summed up under three heads:

1 Our doctrine has been established and is today the doctrine of the agricultural experts.

2 We have discovered a technique of action through the work of influencing local public organizations.

3 The government, through its policy of developmental works—the Snowy,

the Clarence, the Burdekin and the rest—has opened up what I may call the flower of the Australian countryside in which new farms and industries will be established and in which our doctrine can actually be made concrete.

I say that our doctrinal postion has been established.

I said at the beginning we stood for more farms and greater agricultural production.

The Second Report of the Rural Reconstruction Commission poured cold water on our ideas because it declared that there were no markets for Australia's agricultural products. Today what do we find?

We find Professor Crawford, prominently associated recently with the Bureau of Agricultural Economics, pointing out that unless Australian agricultural production was increased under the different heads of production by about 40 per cent, by the time that we had a population of 11 million—and we have 8 million today— we would lose any possibility of exports at all.

We find an eminent economist like Colin Clark predicting—as he predicted in 1945—that for the next 20 years at least, and certainly longer, the prices offering for Australian agricultural products will be high and remunerative, and therefore it pays to have greater agricultural production.

The reason why Australia's inflation is so great today is that over the last 20 years there has been a diversion of the labour force from agriculture to industry. If we could divert 100,000 people from industry to agriculture—and they will be diverted—events in the world will be so shaped that they will be diverted—this central problem of inflation in this country could be cured, because you would have your labour force working where the returns are highest. So that if in 1940 we stood for more farms and greater agricultural production, that stand is accepted today by the world's leading economists.

We stood for smaller farms. The Rural Construction Committee was with us on that because it recognized that erosion was practically a function, a result of large-scale farming. Only a few weeks ago the Senior Agronomist in the New South Wales Department of Agriculture pointed out that if we were going to have 20 million people in Australia—and I tell you that 20 million is the very least that we can afford to have—you would have to divide Australia's farms two and three times. He said that it can be done and that agriculture would be improved thereby, so that the large farm has gone out of fashion.

With regard to diversified farming, in very many areas of Australia your own group members themselves, and through their influence on others, have been pushing the idea of diversification with profit, with financial profit to the districts involved. Beyond Australia, the Food and Agricultural Organization, which represents the Departments of Agriculture of every country affiliated with the United Nations, last year declared in favour of diversification by a unanimous vote, and warned countries establishing new agriculture not to depart from diversification if they were not to face ruin.

So you see that all of the things we stood for from a moral and ethical standpoint are today backed by economists and soil scientists. Now that would be a very empty victory if we had not been able to discover how that doctrine could be incarnated in the life of our community.

Strangely enough, we found the answer not within our own organization but by learning the lesson of what was happening in the trade unions. In other words, the unions were the weapon of social change. They could make a revolution. They could also make a Christian social order.

Then we discovered if we applied that analysis to the farming industry, to rural occupations, that it was farmers, rural and regional organizations which stood in exactly the same position to agriculture as trade unions stood to industry; and that the strength of your doctrine was in proportion to the way in which you could influence your own local public organizations with that doctrine.

Your rural organizations, wool and wheat growers' associations, graziers' associations and so on, are not only the defensive organizations of those sectional interests; they are the weapon whereby you can have a Christian or an unchristian social order.

Accordingly, the strength of this Movement was determined not by the number of members, nor by the number of financial members, but by the influence which its trained and apostolic members could have in local and public organizations.

When the Government began work on the great Snowy River scheme, we suddenly realized the significance of what was going to happen to Australia. The Government, as it were, was about to strike a match, and out of the fire a new social order could be built. If we were strong enough it could be a Christian social order based on the small farm, the small industrial unit, the small social unit, the small town.

Western Europe as we well know is strained to near her limits in primary production, and her livestock industries are far too dependent on imported concentrates including feed grains. The United Kingdom is even dependent on the USSR for 800,000 tons of coarse grains.

This brief analysis should serve to indicate that it is quite safe on economic grounds to launch a programme of agricultural development in the year ahead of us.

What more do we need than the opportunity, the obligation, the economic advantages.

This speech came at a time when the NCRM was markedly changing the emphasis of its work away from Independent Farming, which became increasingly more obviously irrelevant, to the affluent agriculture of the 1950's, towards a broader notion of land settlement.

These were the years of the decisive swing in Australia to an industrial economy. Inflation, a serious problem in the late forties, began 'galloping' in the early fifties under the double strain of fast industrialisation and the boom in wool prices caused by the start of the Korean War. Wool prices dropped back to normal in 1951, at a time when industrialisation was causing a record inflow of imports. This produced a balance of payments and inflation crisis. The new Menzies-Fadden Government administered its first dose of deflationary medicine, and caused the first post-war recession, with unemployment rising to 4 per cent for several months in the second half of 1952.

Agricultural production was showing a much slower rate of growth than industry, and in some products it fell. The fear arose that Australia would soon not be producing enough food for its fast-growing population, let alone enough to maintain the exports needed to pay for industrialisation.

The Bureau of Census and Statistics Index of Farm Production, based on an index figure of 100 in 1936-39, fell to 91 in 1946-47, after the great drought of the middle forties, and had risen to 115 by 1949-50. It fell back again to 109 in 1950-51 and 103 in 1951-52. By 1952-53 it soared to a record 123 and after that climbed steadily throughout the decade to reach

149 by 1958-59 and as high as 187 by 1964-65, before drought again produced a decline.

The temporary decline in production in the early 1950's was due partly to a shift away from wheat (which had reached record acreages after the war) and meat, towards wool following the price boom. Declining fertility in some dairying districts, particularly in Northern New South Wales and Queensland, was another reason. Government economic policies favouring industry at the expense of agriculture were probably more important than either.

Declining production more or less coincided with a quite dramatic 'flight from the land'. In July 1939, total males employed in rural industries (excluding unemployed) had numbered 502,000; by the Census of June 1947, the number had fallen to 435,200 in a much bigger population, and the Census of 1954 showed that it had remained at this level until the first half of the 1950's, when a further decline set in—from 435,900 in 1954 to 396,500 at the Census of June 1961. Rural employees as a percentage of total employees declined from 23·8 per cent in 1939 to 17·6 per cent in 1947, 15·3 per cent in 1954 and 12·5 per cent in 1961.

The combination of declining rural population and falling production produced a short-lived campaign for closer settlement. It was argued that industrialisation should be cut back and men and resources, including migrants—many of whom were unemployed in the 1952 recession—transferred to building up agriculture. This would obtain the production needed, and also provide the steady increase in exports so badly needed.

The chief prophet of the closer settlement campaign was the talented, lucid but highly ideological Colin Clark. After the war, Clark had pressed the Queensland Government—he was its economic advisor and Director of Development—to break up the big leasehold estates on the coast, mostly used for extensive cattle raising, in favour of small holdings for more intensive beef production and the cultivation of grains. He told a Royal Commission on pastoral lands in Queensland that Queensland alone could take a quarter of a million new farms in the ten years of the 1950's—almost as many as then existed in the whole of Australia. The Government (under E. J. Hanlon, a Catholic in the Chifley tradition) refused to accept his ideas, however, and a mutual disenchantment led to Clark's resignation from the Government service at the beginning of 1952. Ironically, this came shortly after Hanlon died and Vincent Gair, a right-wing Catholic eventually to become Parliamentary leader of the DLP, became Premier. Though a strong supporter of the Industrial Groups, Gair intended to pitch his Premiership towards industrialising Queensland.

After leaving the Public Service, Clark set up as a consulting economist and contributor to newspapers for about eighteen months, until he accepted an invitation to become Director of the Institute of Agricultural Economics at Oxford and left Australia.

In articles in the Brisbane *Courier-Mail,* Sydney *Daily Mirror,* Melbourne *Herald* and other newspapers, in public lectures and private conversation, Clark expounded the need for more agricultural production, and more land settlement to get it. He also campaigned for a clamp-down on the growth of the cities and the development instead of regional centres of around 100,000 people. He forecast, accurately as it turned out, that there would be an expanding world market for meat and for feed grains. But others of his forecasts were disastrously astray. 'Meat, dairy products, eggs and fruit are the agricultural commodities for which an expanding world market is to be expected,' he wrote in his book *Australian Hopes and Fears*,[1] published as late as 1958. In *The Economics of 1960*,[2] written in 1941-42, he predicted—again quite inaccurately—that the terms of trade would turn violently towards primary products by 1960.

The distinction should be made, however, that Clark, unlike Santamaria and the NCRM, always used economic analysis in his arguments. On economic grounds, he opposed further development of the Queensland sugar industry years ahead of public opinion in the state. Unlike the NCRM, he was opposed to further irrigation—again, years ahead of public opinion.

Industrially at this time, Clark argued strongly in favour of abolition of the quarterly automatic adjustment to the basic wage, on the grounds that it was a principal cause of inflation. He supported wage schemes designed to increase the productivity of the individual worker. On both these questions, he is open to the criticism of over-emphasising the place of individual workers and under-estimating the role of technological development and good management, though productivity later came to have an important place in wage fixing.

Throughout his work, one finds much the same flavour: Colin Clark the visionary, sometimes brilliantly perceptive about the needs of the future, at other times hopelessly wrong and all too often apparently influenced by his ideological, romantic Catholicism. He was to see years ahead of others the possibilities for export from Australia of meat and coarse grains to a world market, rather than the traditional British market. He was equally a prophet ahead of his time in advocating 'decentralisation' in the sense of building up selected regional centres to an economically viable size; more than a decade later it was to become a common notion. But the export market for dairy produce, eggs and fruit was to become steadily tighter throughout the fifties and sixties and the terms of trade were to turn steadily against agriculture. The result was that agriculture in general, and dairying, poultry and fruit in particular, were to become problem industries by the mid-sixties. Land settlement at the expense of industry, on the scale advocated by Clark and, much more exuberantly, by the NCRM, in the early fifties would surely have brought economic disaster to Australia within a decade.

The Santamaria weakness for seeing crises was a recurring theme of *Rural Life* in the early 1950's. 'The coming crisis caused by over-industrialisation', the 'unbalanced economy', 'the disaster of excessive industrialisation', were discussed in almost every issue.

[1] Colin Clark, *Australian Hopes and Fears*, Hollis and Carter, London, p. 264
[2] Colin Clark, *The Economics of 1960*, Macmillan and Co., London, 1942

The editorial in the December-January issue of 1950-51 said in part:

. . . And as for Australia, what does the record show? It shows a nation which faces imminent doom, perhaps the last 10 years of its life before it, too, becomes a geographical expression, and it shows its citizens behaving as Nero did, fiddling while their earthly city burns. . . .

The scandal is that there is no difference in any of these essential things between the Christians, between the Catholics and the pagans. There is no distinctively Catholic approach to any of the problems which, left unsolved, must destroy this nation as a people of Christians and European culture. We are as involved in the worship of Mammon as our most Godless neighbour.

The 1952 Social Justice statement of the bishops was entitled 'Food—or Famine?' and echoed the Clark-Santamaria call for massive land settlement.

The campaign for closer settlement impinged on the ALP both through the conventional pressures of ALP country branches and through The Movement.

At the 1951 Victorian Conference, a long motion originating from the Ararat branch and coming to the Easter Conference from the Country Conference, committed the Party to closer settlement on big estates and Crown land. It was moved by R. G. Hoban, a Kilmore solicitor, member of the Central Executive and a non-Movement Catholic representing not Santamaria and policies of the NCRM but rather conventional rural interests in the ALP. The seconder was C. P. Stoneham, a non-Catholic, subsequently Leader of the Opposition in the State Parliament. Broadly sympathetic amendments were put by H. Hawkins (Moe) and seconded by Gordon Bryant, later a left wing MP, and by J. J. Ryan and A. McLeod. Although The Movement's D. Devlin spoke in favour of the original motion, it was mainly the work of conventional rural interests.

The 1952 Easter Conference agenda, however, carried a number of motions in favour of closer settlement and decentralisation, quite obviously inspired by the Clark-Santamaria campaign and coming as often from Movement-influenced city branches, such as North Richmond, Glenhuntly, Elsternwick and Camberwell, as from the country.

At this stage The Movement 'line' on these subjects had become: there must be a massive campaign of land settlement, of migrants as well as Australians; further siting of industry in the metropolitan areas should be forbidden, on the lines developed by the Uthwatt Royal Commission in Britain; 'non-essential' industry should be curbed in favour of basic industry; and industry should be developed in regional centres rather than in the big cities.

In the event, a relatively innocuous resolution was adopted, with E. W. Peters, seconded by Arthur Calwell, having successfully moved an amendment which deleted a mildly worded section opposing 'unessential industry'.

A further crop of both conventional and Movement-line motions appeared on the agenda for the 1953 Conference, at which The Movement was considerably stronger than in earlier years. But this time the Agenda Committee selected for debate by Conference a motion from the Frankston Branch calling for development of secondary industry in the interests of full employment. It was moved by K. Ewert, who had been elected MP for Flinders at a by-election the previous year, and seconded by G. Sowerbutts. Both could be classed as 'anti-Grouper' in a broad sense. Movement members L. Fitzpatrick (AEU) and J. P. Maynes (Clerks) immediately moved an amendment supporting previous Conference decisions on land settlement and priority in men, materials and capital for 'basic industry', including agriculture. The amendment was carried on the voices and then put, successfully, as the motion.

By 1954, the 'crisis' in primary production had passed and the agenda carried far fewer items on land settlement than in the three previous years. There were no Movement-line motions on the subject from metropolitan branches, though a motion that 'effective measures be taken to prevent the accumulation of land, by limiting future land purchases to persons who do not possess a suitable living area' was moved by W. Findlay, Benalla, a Movement and NCRM man, and supported by Movement interests.

Naturally enough for an Opposition Party seeking to embarrass the Government, the Federal Parliamentary Labor Party adopted, desultorily, the 'food production crisis'. In his 1952 Budget speech on 12 August, Evatt called for the opening up of the land as a matter of urgency. He said much land was not being used as it could be and said there was a 'good possibility' that a large number of New Australians could be absorbed by full realisation of the land. Keon, Bourke and others also called, in their Budget speeches, for land settlement and more agricultural production.

Within a year or two, the 'crisis' had disappeared under the impact of financial policies designed to encourage greater productivity from the land and of technological developments. Agricultural production increased by nearly 50 per cent during the fifties—from a rural work force which steadily declined, despite various land settlement projects of a much more conventional and modest type than urged in the Clark-Santamaria campaign.

The great mistake of this campaign, of course, was its obsession of equating increased production with increased manpower. Increased production came from mechanisation, more and better use of fertiliser, better breeding and cultivation, pesticides, decimation of the rabbit and pasture improvement, not from settling more men on the land. Australia's experience in this was broadly the same as those of other industrialising countries. European countries with a high proportion of rural manpower to production, such as West Germany, suffered economic disability in the 1950's and 1960's through high-cost food production.

One aspect of the campaign that was to have far-reaching repercussions was its influence on the Chief Judge of the Commonwealth Court of Arbitration and Conciliation, Sir Raymond Kelly. A Catholic, Sir Raymond met Santamaria, was interested in Church social principles and philosophy and apparently was influenced by the economic ideas of Colin Clark.

A continuing problem, and source of controversy, in this Court, as the main National wage fixing authority, has been how far it should confine itself to the original purpose of settling industrial disputes, and how far it should develop economic and social policies in the public interest. In practice, since the Second World War, this has meant how far the Court should concern itself with the danger of inflation in wage rises. Broadly, a narrow interpretation of its role as a settler of disputes tends to work in favour of the unions; while the more it concerns itself with inflation, the more employer interests are suited. Employers argue that any but small wage increases will cause inflation, while the unions object to the idea that wages should be controlled to check inflation, while prices, profits and monopoly practices in business are not affected.

It is a dilemma without any easy solution. In practice the Court (later Commission) has tended to swing a little in each direction at various times, with some judges being known for their concern with inflation and others with their relative disregard of it.

Sir Raymond Kelly became Chief Justice during the 1949-50 hearing of the union claim for a £10 basic wage, on the death of Chief Justice Drake-Brockman. He moved from Adelaide to Melbourne. In his judgment of 12 October 1950, he declared himself a strong proponent of the anti-inflation role of the Court.

'The rapid deterioration in the value of money must, perhaps even with some serious sacrifice on the part of all, be arrested,' he said. 'Failure to arrest it will surely endanger this unbalanced economy to the material detriment of our established industries and to the general unhappiness, perhaps the early poverty, of large numbers of our people. I am not prepared to take any risks about this matter. . . . I believe that today its [the Court's] duty is to give a lead to the other instruments of adjustment by taking a firm stand to stabilise, as well as lies in its power, the value of wages; for it is undoubtedly principally owing to the rapidly increasing level of wages, both nominal and real, that costs and prices are now tending to become out of control.'

As preparations for his first major case as Chief Justice, the Standard Hours application of 1952-53, got under way, Sir Raymond sent a circular letter outlining his views to all the employer organisations and unions respondent to the awards concerned. In the case, as it developed during 1952, the employers sought a reduction in the basic wage and increase in standard hours of work on the grounds that these measures would be needed to curb inflation and lift productivity per worker.

Dated 1 February 1952, and covering seven and a half pages of closely typed foolscap, Sir Raymond's letter was one of the strangest documents in the history of the Arbitration jurisdiction. It was a rambling, philosophical letter, alternating between discussion of the issues and speculation on the nature of authority and moral codes.

'We need a far greater proportion of our population than there is at present to be engaged in primary productive pursuits,' he said at one point. 'We need from abroad many more good peasants than good artisans, shop-keepers or train-crews.'

. . . For, with his knowledge of the transitory nature of his life on earth, as well as of the differences of opinion and of action amongst even his good fellow creatures, man naturally seeks a philosophy of existence, of its purpose and of the means of fulfilling that purpose. Lest, however, I digress, let me return to my proposition that happiness can only be found in conforming to a code of right conduct, in other words to a moral code. To the Christian and the deist, the source and nature of such a code proceeds from his belief in a supernatural and eternal Law-giver.

. . . My own humble study has been of my fellow men and women and I confess that such a study can never proceed beyond a beginning. But this I do believe: that I have discovered that contentment and peace and happiness is only to be found in the acceptance of authority.

Sir Raymond suggested that the parties try to agree on a number of points before proceeding to court and went on to make fourteen specific suggestions.

Some of these were:

Can we agree upon some such principle as a reduction by, say, 10 per cent per annum over a period of, say, three years of the incomes of shareholders? (This could, I think be effected by a special taxation, the proceeds of which might be paid into a national resources development trust fund.)

Can we agree upon a reduction by, say, 10 per cent per annum of any adjusted basic wage during a period of, say, three years?

Can we agree that award margins should stand fixed at present rates for a period of, say, three years?

Other suggestions were for a paring of overtime rates, a reduction in the number of public holidays, progressive modification of tariffs on imported consumer goods and 'less reliance upon Governmental aid to secondary industries'.

Sir Raymond said that the national resources trust funds he proposed, to be financed from some of the savings outlined and additional tax derived as a result of any further upward adjustment of the basic wage, should go to assist agriculture. It should be applied to loans or advances for the purchase of land, implements, seed, grain, etc., for new and existing primary producers.

'It is my belief that the substantial adoption of such suggestions will inevitably bring about a reduction of retail price-levels, secure substantially the level of our basic standards of living and secure us against the risks of unemployment,' Sir Raymond concluded.

The reaction of trade unions, including some of the most ideologically militant in the world, to proposals for cuts in wages and conditions, can be imagined. Sir Raymond's attempts to bring the parties together in the spirit of the corporative state were completely unsuccessful and the case went through the usual procedure of drawn-out hearing and judgment. The Court (Sir Raymond and Justices Kirby, Dunphy and Morgan) handed down a collective judgment on 27 October 1953, rejecting the employer application for cuts in the basic wage and increased standard hours of work. It, however, agreed to their application that the quarterly adjustments to the basic wage be suspended.

The Chief Judge's letter, with its unfamiliar language, proposals for wage cuts and apparent pre-judging of the issue had caused wide resentment among union officials, many of whom reacted violently to philosophical Catholicism of this kind. Its contribution to the gathering hysteria about 'Catholic Action' can hardly be under-estimated. Abolition of the quarterly adjustments served to renew this hostility and suspicion. The 1953 judgment went down in trade union lore as one of the most anti-union in the history of the Court, and for many years afterwards the unions claimed that the abolition of regular, automatic adjustments to the wage reduced the share of Gross National Product going to wages throughout the 1950's.

A few months later, in February 1954, the Full Bench infuriated the organised Labor Movement once again, with a judgment 'freezing' margins above the basic wage, on the same grounds of holding back wages to curb inflation.

There was, in fact, considerable sympathy in the community for measures to break the 'wage-price' spiral, but certainly not among the unions, who naturally objected to their members being singled out for sacrifice.

Evatt took up the issue and promised that a Labor Government, if elected in the general elections due in May of that year, would intervene before the Court to have the margins judgment reversed. He had the strong backing of the unions.

Chapter Nine
Fissures in the
Machines, 1953-54

The Melbourne Trades Hall attacks on the Cain Government throughout 1953 and 1954 showed a return to the political-industrial wing troubles that had disfigured the late 1940's. Even ostensible issues are difficult to find; the affairs of the McDonald Government and 3KZ obviously were part of it, but such issues were hardly important in themselves. The feud, rather, seems to have been an extremely deep-seated one, with the trade union movement having a characteristic tendency to split into rival factions and the two centres of trades hall power, the Trades Hall Council and ALP offices, becoming the focal points for them. The clashing personalities of Stout and Lovegrove, and many of those around them, exaggerated the internal divisions.

In this atmosphere, what should have been an unemotional, machinery matter after the election of the Cain Government became instead a blazing controversy.

On 12 December 1952, the Central Executive met to decide a procedure for unions to approach the new Government. Memories were strong of the way communist union leaders—and some non-communists—had tried to exert individual pressure on Cain ministers in the post-war Government, and there was wide agreement in the political wing that there should be some formal machinery for approaches.

Lovegrove, with Reilly seconding, moved that affiliated unions and the Trades Hall Council should approach the State Government through the Central Executive direct and that unaffiliated unions should approach it through the THC first and then the ALP Central Executive. This was carried, but against the opposition of Clarey and Jordan (who wanted it referred to the THC and ACTU for discussion) and Keon.

Predictably, the THC and to a much lesser extent the ACTU, bitterly opposed the procedure; and a series of talks through the summer did not solve the problem.

The 1953 State Conference was held on 29 May, in accordance with a new procedure of holding the Conference on Queen's Birthday weekend instead of at Easter. It was the weekend of the Coronation of Queen Elizabeth II, and eight months before her historic tour of Australia. Despite the optimistic spirit of Britishness then enjoying a short-lived revival in Australia, the Victorian Conference was marked by a spirit of acrimony and bitterness approaching that of 1948.

The Trades Hall Council had sponsored a rival 'ticket' to that of the Executive officers, designed, if elected, to give the industrial wing the balance of power between the Parliamentary and Grouper factions. Tripovich, Kennelly, H. O. Davis of the AWU, L. M. Fennessy of the Clerks' Union, W. Divers of the Municipal Employees, R. Balcombe of the Fuel and Fodder Employees, the former minister J. J. Dedman, and Senator J. Sheehan were among those nominating. All were defeated, with a margin of about 40 votes between the lowest polling of the winners and the highest polling of those not elected to the Executive.

The ticket was largely in the nature of a gesture to assess strength. It was publicised as a protest against the THC having to approach the Government through the Central Executive, with Stout and Jordan stating that they would continue their resumed boycott of the Executive.

The Conference in fact was marked by strengthening power for the Industrial Groups, with large delegations from the newly affiliated Ironworkers' and Clerks' unions appearing for the first time. Under Industrial Group pressure, the Railways, the largest union, had affiliated to the ALP in May, but did not send its twenty-man delegation until the following year. By that time it had passed completely under Grouper control.

The appearance of the Clerks' Union delegation was a fillip for Movement strength at the Conference. About half the Clerks' delegation were in The Movement and J. P. Maynes, one of its leaders, was active in getting round the Agenda Committee obstructions to promote Movement policy on land settlement.

Although the 1953 Conference showed prominent Movement people more active than in previous years, in both 1953 and 1954 Movement people not on the officers' ticket polled poorly.

The 1953 Conference in New South Wales, held a fortnight later, saw the same bitter debates as in Victoria, caused by the presence of a rival group of candidates for the Executive. Memories of the coup of a year earlier, and the depositions and change of power flowing from it, were keen and acrimonious.

With Ferguson gone, the man emerging as new 'leader of the opposition' in Sydney Labor was another pugnacious Scots Australian, Frederick Hugh Campbell, born in Sydney in 1908. Campbell, a gentlemanly man nevertheless given to fiery and vehement political in-fighting, was regarded by his critics, but not his friends, as being disposed to Calvinistic anti-Catholicism. He had come up through the Electrical Trades Union, was active with Jensen and others in the early years of the Industrial Group in the union and had been close to Ferguson. Ernie Wright, the dismissed ALP secretary, was also active in the opposition, as was J. D. Keenahan, a Catholic and Assistant Secretary of the ETU, Robert Erskine of the Textile Workers and Tony Mulvihill, later a Senator, of the ARU, who had been secretary of the Industrial Group at the Eveleigh railway workshops.

The presence of two other figures in the Group was of incalculable importance—James Ormonde and A. G. Platt.

James Patrick Ormonde, born in Scotland in 1905, was a journalist with many contacts in journalism, the Labor Movement and the Church. He had been close to Chifley and Ferguson and was for some years editor of *Standard Weekly*, the New South Wales branch newspaper. Under the Chifley Government, he became Public Relations Officer of the Joint Coal Board. He had become a strong critic of The Movement and the Groups in the early fifties, and seemed to many to have almost an irrational obsession on the issue. He publicly attacked the Groups at an Adult Education Summer School in January 1953, and repeated the attack in the left of centre monthly, *Voice*, the following month. His anti-Group activities had led to him being dropped from the official Executive 'ticket', to make way for men from newly affiliated Group unions.

A. G. 'Barney' Platt, the affable, First World War 'digger' who was State Secretary of the Transport Workers' Union, had been under attack in his union for a decade from a rebel group, the best known and most active member of which was J. T. Kane, the new Assistant Secretary of the ALP. The rebels considered Platt bureaucratic, too friendly with the employers and something of a Tammany Hall character. He considered them power-seeking wreckers. Over the years, the feud became extremely bitter.

John Thomas Kane was born in Lithgow in 1909 and was a miner for several years. Later he became a truck driver and was active in the Lang Labor Party in the 1930's. A friendly, kindly but aggressive and somewhat devious man, he had a talent for organising and a strong instinct for reform. Ironically, as he later became Federal Secretary of the Democratic Labor Party, he was considered by many union leaders in the late 1940's to be on the far left wing and even a 'comm'. It was on these grounds— but the real reason was presumably the internal feud—that Platt excluded him from the foundation Industrial Group in the TWU in 1945. Platt treasured a 'unity ticket' for the TWU, on which Kane's name appeared with those of several communists, but Kane was adamant that it was prepared without his knowledge; he said he had disowned it in a *Sydney Morning Herald* advertisement. (He would have been obliged to do this under ALP rules anyway.)

Kane subsequently grew close to The Movement and in 1952 became Organising Secretary of the ALP and Secretary of the ALP Industrial Groups. Although he became a leader of the Industrial Group faction, he had been looked on with less than disfavour by Ferguson.

The Printing Industry Employees' Union (under moderate left control), the Timber Workers and others joined those committed by their leaders to the front rank of the fight—the Electrical Trades, Textile Workers' and Transport Workers' Unions. The result was nevertheless a win for the big battalions supporting the Grouper Executive. The President, W. Colbourne, was re-elected, defeating Ormonde by 390 votes to 98. The Secretary, C. W. Anderson, defeated H. Jensen, 367-107.

The press described the winning team as the 'AWU-Labor Council' ticket, a good, brief description. The AWU and the newly affiliated Ironworkers now under Industrial Group control, had the two biggest delegations to Conference. Ferguson's old union, the Railways, now had Dr Lloyd Ross, an ex-communist intellectual, as its Secretary, and he supported the Grouper cause despite a long-standing friendship with Ferguson. Ross had been hired as a Special Writer on union and Labor affairs for the Melbourne *Herald* in 1950, after dissolution of the Post-war Reconstruction Department for which he was Public Relations Director. He strongly supported the Industrial Groups in his *Herald* column—to the annoyance of many unionists who considered the paper an 'anti-Labor rag'—and also became friendly with Santamaria. Ross and Laurie Short, the Ironworkers' Secretary, had been added to the 1953 official ticket for the Executive, replacing Ormonde and Mulvihill, who were dropped.

The anti-Executive faction was increasingly adopting the claim that the Executive was dominated by 'right-wing clerical groups' and 'Catholic Action'. This was always a suspect claim, and the addition of the Protestant, militantly anti-communist ex-Marxists, Short and Ross, in place of the anti-Grouper Catholics, Ormonde and Mulvihill, tended to produce much the same broad Grouper faction as in Victoria. But its position was significantly stronger, as it had the full backing of the Trades and Labor Council and was working well with the much more established State Labor Government.

The Deputy Premier, R. J. Heffron, addressed the Conference on the Saturday in the absence of Cahill (who was absent at the Coronation), and announced that the Government would shortly legislate for compulsory unionism. Compulsory unionism had long existed in Queensland, but was opposed by many in and out of the Labor Movement in other states as interference with a basic freedom; 'preference to unionists' was a more widely accepted approach.

The legislation for compulsory unionism, introduced and passed in the spring session of the State Parliament, was to become a source of considerable controversy, and of embarrassment to the Cahill Government. There was a political motive for it. 'Blue collar' employees were already overwhelmingly union members, but membership was low among 'white collar' employees. Some observers estimated that membership of the Clerks' Union in New South Wales would go up seven to eight times if membership was compulsory. It would have immensely strengthened this by now most Grouper- and Movement-dominated of unions, especially in its influence in the ALP. Freed from the need to recruit and hold membership, the union could also afford to be much more ideological in its style. In practice, however, the legislation was never enforced. When the split started a year later, it was soon forgotten.

It was now High Noon for the Industrial Groupers. Their control of the ALP in the two biggest states had been established against powerful opponents. They had strong supporters in Gair and the AWU, together able to dominate Queensland Labor politics, sympathisers in other states and, the seeming ace in the pack, the firm support of Evatt. There were now Labor governments in every state except the gerrymandered South Australia and, in the period after the 1952 recession, every indicator pointed to a Federal Labor Government being elected in 1954.

The remaining nationally powerful opponent of Grouper control, who was able to organise the varying dissident elements, was Kennelly. He had been forced out of the Legislative Council at the end of 1952, only to re-emerge as a Senator. (He was elected in the May 1953 Senate election and officially became a Senator for Victoria on 1 July.) He was thus in an even better position to carry on the feud—and as far as anybody knew, had never renounced his 1952 threats to produce changes in Victoria. He had even linked up with his old Trades Hall Council enemies to run on the anti-Executive ticket at the Victorian Conference.

A tough, if risky, way to end the faction fight and ensure both Grouper control Federally and a reasonably united party would be to drive Kennelly from the Federal Secretaryship. This the Groupers decided to do.

At the meeting of the Victorian Central Executive on 26 June, Lovegrove moved, 'That delegates advise the Federal Executive that the office of Federal Secretary should be vacated.' Keon seconded it and Peters then moved an amendment, 'That the position of Federal Secretary be vacated and not filled by a member of the Federal Parliament.' R. E. Wilson seconded the amendment. Clarey opposed both the motion and the amendment. Meere supported the amendment, Lovegrove accepted it and it was carried.

Keon then moved, with Meere seconding, 'That the collection and dispersal of moneys in the Federal sphere be discussed by Federal Executive.' This also was carried.

The Federal Executive met in Melbourne on 13 July 1953, and the Groupers, or 'right wing', appeared to have the 'numbers'. Lovegrove and J. P. Horan, the new state Vice-President, represented Victoria, and Colbourne and Anderson, New South Wales. E. E. Reece, Federal President and Deputy Premier and Senator G. R. Cole represented Tasmania; J. M. Schmella, the new State Secretary and H. Boland, State Secretary of the AWU, Queensland; H. Webb and C. Gough, Western Australia; and J. P. Toohey and J. F. Walsh, South Australia.

With the support of the AWU and Cole, a convert to Catholicism and intensely anti-communist, the Groupers were able almost to control the vital vote on Kennelly. But to secure adequate support from Western Australia they had to compromise and accept an amendment that, although a Federal Parliamentarian could not be Federal Secretary, the job would not be vacated until the next meeting of the Federal Executive. Once this vote was taken and the 'numbers' were clear, Reece did not contest the Presidency. It went to Lovegrove. Walsh withdrew as Senior Vice-President and the job went to Boland, while Colbourne, the Grouper choice for Secretary, became junior Vice-President of the ALP. The Industrial Group-AWU, pro-Evatt faction now held all the offices except Secretary; and Kennelly was destined to go at the next meeting, due in November. Kennelly, predictably, fought back in the few months remaining to him and the factional bitterness intensified yet again.

It is tempting to discuss this fight in terms of ideology, but the ideology involved was minor; yet it was not simply a crude power struggle.

With Victoria and New South Wales now quite lost to his cause, and Queensland tottering, Kennelly's base lay in the three smaller states. The objective situation of the Labor Movement in these three states was:

South Australia: The dominating figure in South Australian Labor politics, in their relations with other states, was C. R. Cameron, MP for Hindmarsh. Clyde Robert Cameron, born in Adelaide in 1913, had worked in the outback of several states and become an AWU organiser. He was a man of considerable intelligence, but fond of gathering and using power and, in the Caucus, a strong supporter of E. J. Ward and the old left. Although a Parliamentarian, he was still able to dominate the South Australian Branch of the AWU and clashed nationally with Dougherty. The South Australian Branch of the ALP elected its officers and executive by the 'card' system, under which disciplined union delegates could vote in thousands on behalf of all their members. The AWU controlled well over 10 per cent of this vote in the South Australian Branch and, with Cameron's powerful personality exercising influence over other big unions, a small group of men in large unions could control the destinies of the branch. Toohey, then the Secretary, and J. F. Walsh, MHA and former President of the Trades and Labor Council, were lapsed Catholics, but were influenced by Cameron's power, Chifley era ties and by a slightly stronger suspicion of Catholicism in South Australia, which had an unusually high proportion of Methodists and low proportion of Catholics in its population. All these factors made for a predisposition to anti-Grouper feeling, reinforced by the knowledge that Industrial Groups would tend to undo the neatly packaged power system of the state. Cameron and the South Australian officers thus came to enjoy a good working and personal relationship with Kennelly.

Western Australia: There was an incipient, though at this time not very strong, cleavage in Western Australia between the Perth Trades and Labor Council on the one side and the Parliamentarians and AWU on the other. The Secretaryship of the TLC and the ALP was then vested in one man, the authoritarian F. E. Chamberlain. Hs power was reinforced by the large number of small unions which had part-time officials and in practice delegated much of their work—and influence—to Chamberlain.

Tasmania: The intimate politics of Tasmania then mainly concerned personalities; there was little division built into the structure. The Premier, (later Sir Robert) Cosgrove, J. O'Neill, secretary of the Trades Hall, and Senator Cole tended to back the Groupers nationally; while Reece, despite an AWU background, was personally close to Kennelly.

Working on the base of the South Australian branch, Chamberlain and Reece, Kennelly set out to change the 'numbers' for November. He was able to get a tighter rein on Western Australia and Tasmania, and thus delegates changed.

The Executive met in Canberra on 9 November, and on 11 November voted that the July decision that a Member of the Federal Parliament could not be Federal Secretary, was unconstitutional. The 'numbers' were reported to be 7 to 5, though the actual vote—as in July—was on the voices.

The *Age* reported on 12 November:

Senator Kennelly was pointedly asked to withdraw his candidature, because of a statement he was alleged to have made on Monday, that if reinstated he would set out to break Dr Evatt's leadership of the Party.

He refused to stand down and today's decision must be regarded as a personal triumph for him, as every effort was made to swing the vote against him.

An Executive member who voted against him complained angrily after the meeting that Dr Evatt had done too much 'meddling' in the matter.

However, to secure his win, Kennelly had had to compromise again and announced after the vote that he would resign his position after the next general election, due in the late autumn of 1954. The Executive decided that the Federal Conference, due in January 1955, would elect a new Federal Secretary by ballot.

The years of faction fighting and intrigue had, inevitably, aroused deep personal animosities and ugly passions within the Labor parties. The saw that 'all's fair in love and war' applies also to Labor faction fights, and both sides appear to have taken every step to vilify the other in private conversation. A perilous tendency developed for them to forget the original, complex causes of the struggle and to believe the simplified, dramatised versions with which they sought to blacken their opponents.

Thus, to the anti-Groupers the Grouper faction became the tools of clerical reactionaries and bigots, trying to foist a peasant economy if not a corporate state on Australia in the interests of 'Catholic Action'. At best, they were pawns in the hands of an 'outside organisation'. They were also trying to destroy the Chifley tradition, socialist policies and even the British heritage. The anti-Groupers, by contrast, were the Chifley men, the keepers of the traditions and the socialist faith.

To the Groupers, on the other hand, their opponents were vulgar opportunists, anti-intelligence, prepared to wheel and deal with the communists and corrupt influences, yet proclaiming a meaningless socialist rhetoric and outdated ideas like nationalisation of industry at home and isolationism abroad. The Groupers tended to see themselves as more interested in ideas, aware of the danger communism threatened to the independence of the Party and to the Asian-Pacific region, prepared to bring the Party into the second half of the century.

There was something in these mutually hostile images—but not much. Factional division over issues other than industrial groups and the like, involving redistribution of power, was slight at either executive or conference level, nationally or in states. Foreign affairs, though potentially a divisive issue, were usually left to the Parliamentarians and did not much interest the men of the machines. On domestic policy, there were differences in the rhetorical postures, but they did not show up much on specific issues.

Despite the lack of ideological content, the faction fight was nevertheless compelling on bodies as small as Federal and State Executives. To be neutral under the intense pressures building up was not to be trusted and to risk impotence. Movement could only come through factional backing. And in the 1950's, the Federal Executive was becoming a much more powerful organisation than it had been in the previous decade, when strong Labor leaders and the men round them could exercise informal control. Evatt had not been able to get the loyal backing of the old Chifley power structure and was caught in spiralling mistrust in trying to build up his own. The resulting vacuum tended to heighten the importance of the bitterly divided Federal Executive.

The year 1954 thus became one of great danger for Labor. The great hope and expectation was of a victory in the autumn elections. As the Party of Government, the internal tensions would find new outlets. If the election was lost, the resulting disappointment and rancour could fan the grass fires burning merrily throughout the Party into a mighty conflagration.

In the months before the election was lost in May, however, the Industrial Group faction began to develop its own internal cracks. By 1953, the industrial battle against the communists had been substantially won, communist power being replaced by a diverse range of Grouper power. The common industrial purpose had cemented the faction together and as this purpose declined in importance other purposes began to make themselves felt.

The Movement, its industrial role now becoming marginal, showed no signs and indeed appears to have had no intention of disbanding. Santamaria made it clear at the annual convention of The Movement at the beginning of 1954 that he intended to continue to use his and The Movement's influence in the Industrial Group faction to push Movement social and foreign policies. He and his supporters had for some time been using whatever pressure and influence was available to get policies adopted by ALP branches and unions.

Elected union and political office bearers, however, did not see things the same way. The feeling that people were meeting outside secretly and trying to impose the decision reached on a wider body now began to produce something of the same deep antagonism within the Groups that others had felt earlier. Once installed in union offices, Grouper leaders were much less dependent on The Movement and this began to reflect in the priority they gave its views. And there were many Catholics who had supported or joined The Movement in its role as an auxilliary to the Groups, but who had no intention of joining it in a crusade for the implementation of Santamaria's cataclysmic and urgent view of Christian social principles and foreign relations.

In Sydney, this inherent division was strengthened by physical distance from Santamaria, a less emotionally involved Archbishop and the personality of Bishop Lyons. Bishop Lyons, who had a flair for personal trouble, clashed with Dr Ryan and in 1953 replaced Ryan as Movement chaplain with Father Harold Lalor, a Melbourne Jesuit who had been transferred to Sydney. A priest of strong ideological bent, Father Lalor had been a leader of the Institute of Social Order, a Jesuit social studies and training organisation close to The Movement. The Institute of Social Order had its first office in the Catholic Action offices at Curtin House, though it later moved to the aptly named Belloc House in Sackville Street, Kew. Father Lalor was the foundation editor, in 1951, of the Institute's periodical, *Social Survey*, which was virtually a theoretical journal for The Movement. Its first business manager was H. R. Slattery, the Victorian Secretary of The Movement. Father Lalor was also the best known, in both Melbourne and Sydney, of the orators at confidential Church meetings on the melodramatic theme of 'Ten Minutes to Midnight'—the threat from communist Asia.

The dismissal of the personally popular Ryan and his replacement with a man who seemed the very embodiment of Melbourne-based ideology dramatised and intensified the incipient split in The Movement in Sydney, as well as causing much resentment.

In this atmosphere, many men began leaving The Movement in 1953 and 1954, a proportion of them deeply hostile to it. This hostility in reaction was particularly marked in Sydney among some students who had been in The Movement group at Sydney University. Most of them were attracted to the liberal Catholic trend, then just beginning among a few young Catholics in Sydney and Melbourne. They became intense and articulate critics of The Movement.

In Melbourne, some of the defectors from The Movement found understanding friends in the *Catholic Worker* group, who had been drifting away from their *News Weekly* counterparts in lengthening steps ever since 1940. In Sydney, the more vocal dissidents had talks with Ormonde and with the anti-Movement, anti-Grouper front building up around him. The obsessive Ormonde worked frantically at his cause, creating hostility by word of mouth and warning a number of Protestant leaders. Some of the statements by Protestant leaders, warning against 'Catholic Action' in 1953 and 1954, can be traced to Ormonde's zeal.

In 1953, the *Catholic Worker* group finally sent a long letter to the Bishops of Australia complaining about the activities of The Movement in the name of Catholic Action. About the same time the Sydney student group submitted a document of complaints to Cardinal Gilroy.

The main theme of such complaints was that The Movement was trying to impose one view in the name of the Church, that this tended to create a form of moral blackmail where a 'good' Catholic should do as The Movement wanted, and that it was distorting the purpose of Catholic Action. Other complaints referred to specific instances of over-zealous behaviour by Movement people, of 'stacking' meetings, membership of several unions, posing Movement membership as a sacred duty, claiming Infallibility for Encyclicals and the like. Behind much of it lay an instinctive dislike for the ideological fervour and intolerant fanaticism that distinguished at least one strand of Movement membership and support. Many Catholics feared The Movement would damage the Church, by involving it in political controversy and questionable tactics. Others objected to a tendency for it to make strictly political issues into moral questions—more often by implication than by outright statement. *News Weekly* illustrated this tendency in its typically cataclysmic page one article on 2 January 1952: 'Australia Facing a Tough Fight in 1952', the headline read, 'Only a Moral Revival Can Save the Nation. It will be a Testing Year for Labor.' A related article on page two said:

News Weekly believes in an absolute code of morals, which apply to all political parties and all political acts, irrespective of the Party concerned. It regards politicians not as an end, but as a means to an end. When it sees a Party tying itself to a policy which is wrong, whether it relates to Communism, monopoly, the tariff, revaluation, primary production or any of the main heads of legislation, it will point out the error, adopting as its standard always the National rather than the Party interest.

At the beginning of 1954, an episcopal leader emerged for these diverse elements to unite around. James Carroll was born in Sydney in a strongly Labor family. Unlike most clerics, he had grown up surrounded by politics and had many friends at the heart of New South Wales Labor politics; he had an instinct for the complexities, sensibilities and foibles of Labor. A thrusting, genial man, though hardly an intellectual or Church liberal, he became parish priest at Enmore and in February 1954, was consecrated Auxiliary Bishop of Sydney. This was at the height of the internal diocesan crisis over The Movement, with complaints about it growing in Sydney from various quarters. He set out to study The Movement—and became convinced that, in its existing form, it had to go from the Diocese. He became an influential proponent of a growing view that it should be placed under firmer episcopal control and emasculated to an innocuous body for the social training of Catholics.

Father Duffy[1] quotes an anonymous memorandum on The Movement in Sydney, circulated in early 1954, on differences of view between some of the Sydney region officers and the National officers. It said Sydney wanted more stress on individual initiative and greater freedom of action within the region and education and persuasion as the means of cooperation rather than direction from a centralised and unitary body at the top. It said a Federal type of organisation would suit Sydney. The National officers were using Movement power too quickly, gripped as they seemed by a sense of urgency to achieve their objectives.

'They assumed they had the right to give directions to politicians, they had too much contact with certain Cabinet members, which would eventually embarrass the Church; their use of *News Weekly* led to "excessive" and often profitless criticism of Labor politicians, which multiplied enemies unnecessarily,' Duffy paraphrased the memorandum as saying. It said Sydney wanted more cautious use of political power, with the direction of politicians left to the Hierarchy, who alone had the power to do this.[2]

[1] P. J. Duffy, 'Catholic Attitudes to the ALP Dispute'
[2] Archbishop Carroll assured the author in 1970 that there was never any question of either the Hierarchy or Movement directing politicians. He could not remember how or why the reference arose. Some observers believe it may have been a Sydney reaction to the Holt Land Bill affair in Victoria.

Duffy commented: 'It expressed—almost exactly—the known views of a very few influential ecclesiastics and lay figures in Sydney, notably Bishop (now Archbishop) James Carroll'—whose appointment had coincided with the writing of the memorandum.

Duffy said the Sydney region's view was stated officially to the rest of The Movement at a National Executive meeting in July 1954, attended by Santamaria. The meeting had decided unanimously, however, that it would 'never compromise' on the issue of disbandment of the Industrial Groups, then becoming a white-hot issue within the ALP.

The sort of issue suggested by the memorandum had arisen dramatically at the meeting of the Victorian Central Executive of 23 October 1953.

Devlin moved, in the course of a busy night when the Executive was preparing for the forthcoming Federal Executive meeting, the following prepared motion:

In view of the ALP's support for the United Nations, whose Charter dedicates the organisation to insure peace by promoting freedom and respect for human rights, and because the Chinese Communist régime is unable by reason of its Constitution, which describes itself as a dictatorship, to subscribe to the Charter, and because of our concern with the future security of Australia, which must depend to a large extent on the holding of Formosa itself, and the loyalty of 11 millions of Chinese throughout Asia who owe allegiance to the Free Chinese Government in Formosa, should the question of recognition for Red China be discussed at the Federal Executive, we instruct our delegates to oppose recognition and support a proposal consistent with this resolution to deny such recognition under any circumstances at any time.

Keon seconded the motion and a row of important and memorable dimensions started.

The first to oppose the motion was Lovegrove. He had shown annoyance on occasions before when Devlin produced typed motions on ideological questions, thus interrupting carefully prepared programmes for Executive meetings. Lovegrove had also shown increasing divergence from The Movement on questions such as migration and land settlement. A widower for many years, he had recently remarried and with regular home life was living less for politics than he had. He was also strongly opposed to executives making Party policy.

The record shows Brennan supporting the motion, Clarey and F. J. Riley opposing it and Travers supporting it. Horan moved an amendment for deletion of 'under any circumstances at any time', which McManus seconded.

The amendment was lost and the motion carried. The Chairman, Little, then ruled that Devlin's motion was not an agenda item, but for the guidance of delegates if the matter was raised. The record states that Lovegrove—whose fury was well remembered years later—'raised the question of his position in view of his opposition to policy making by Federal Executive'. Some interpreted it as a threat to resign. Little ruled that the matter should be determined by reference to decision of Federal Conference.

About the same time, the New South Wales Central Executive also passed a motion against recognition of Communist China. This caused another memorable row and opened up divisions among the Groupers.

At the subsequent Victorian meeting, on 6 November, an ominous argument developed over attempts to discipline Don McSween, the left wing Secretary of the Clothing Trades Union and *bête noire* of the more intense Groupers, over a public statement he had made attacking the idea of industrial Groups. Lovegrove had tried to smooth this over with a conciliatory report and a statement of explanation from McSween, who had recently been endorsed as ALP candidate for Isaacs. This attracted strong criticism from Keon, Brennan and Travers. The Executive instead, on the motion of Cremean and Meere, voted to call McSween before it to explain his attitude to the Groups.

McSween attended the Executive meeting on 20 November and, after he had made a statement and answered questions, Lovegrove moved that the explanation be accepted. The motion was carried, but against strong opposition from Keon, Riley, Frank Reilly, Brennan, D'Arcy, Meere and Woodhouse.

Then on 18 December the issue of R. W. Holt's walk-out from State Parliament came before the Executive. Keon moved suspension of Standing Orders to hear a report from Cain and Fraser on the incident, with Travers seconding. Lovegrove and Cain opposed it, and a heated debate followed. Eventually, on the motion of Hoban, it was adjourned indefinitely, with a 12-9 vote.

The position was thus developing where the Victorian Executive was fighting on three different fronts—federally against the Kennelly anti-Groupers, against Stout in the Trades Hall, against both in its branches and now was cracking within its own Grouper ranks.

The fight in the Trades Hall was the bitterest and most omnipresent of these, and spiralled. There were angry factional scenes on the Trades Hall Council most Thursday nights, with the once-powerful communists cut back to a rump, and instead Stout taking the fight to the ALP Executive supporters and vice versa.

Stout's obvious allies were on the left—the communists, those entangled with them and the traditional leftists; and his own body of personal support began to merge with them in a new anti-Grouper faction. As the new alignment developed in 1953 and 1954, the bitterness on the Council floor became reminiscent of nearly a decade earlier, with the difference that this time the humiliating Grouper invective was turned on Stout and his allies. It was highlighted towards the end of 1953 over the election of a Melbourne THC delegate to the 1953 ACTU Congress. Stout backed Fennessy, a dissident Clerks' Union organiser, against Little, the Grouper choice. Grouper reaction against Fennessy for accepting Stout's invitation was such that he was 'rolled' from the union's Political Committee and became so unpopular he had to resign his job. He became an ALP MLA in the split.

The idea began to develop incipiently among a few Groupers that Stout, now nearing seventy, might be squeezed out and that this would end their troubles. There was now strong personal feeling between Stout, who was showing no inclination whatever to go, and his assistant, Jordan. Jordan, though hardly in the Lovegrove camp, was not in the Stout camp either. Stout now hated him. Some of the Groupers thought that, with changes in a few unions, they would be in a position to replace Stout with Jordan. Quietly they began probing for weak spots among the Stout supporters, looking for the incompetent, the lazy, the unpopular secretary, preferably with an ambitious frustrated underling. This was all done on an informal basis and did not go very far; the ALP Executive as such had no part, nor did The Movement, though some Movement men took part and there was certainly no objection raised.

Naturally, the Grouper assessment of weak spots did not coincide with the view of the alleged spots themselves; and there seems to have been a tendency for Groupers to regard vocal opponents on the Trades Hall Council floor as suitable for attack.

In fact, few, if any, officials were 'rolled', though some attempts were made. But whispers of the strategy got about and by the end of 1953 fear, hysteria and factional bitterness were reaching new levels. Like most people, union officials were rarely stirred more than by threats to their self-esteem, way of life, and, most of all, their jobs. Fear of a mysterious underground intent to 'roll' men for their jobs was probably the biggest background reason for the emotional campaign against the ALP that developed in 1954. At the same time, the Stout supporters began steps to 'roll' Jordan and replace him with someone closer to the faction.

A somewhat similar situation was developing in Sydney, though not on the same scale. Partly it was the decade-old feud inside the Transport Workers' Union, but the key to the whole split that was to develop was also building up in the Australian Workers' Union.

In November 1953, a number of members of the TWU, including the President and Secretary of the dominant Sydney sub-branch, asked the ALP Executive to re-form the disbanded ALP Industrial Group in the union. The request was granted, against the objections of Anderson and others.

Although this affair related to a years-old union feud, the reactions to it were far-reaching. Kane enlisted the support of The Movement for the fight on the Executive and in the union, on the basis of combating corruption. With the dismissal of the former ALP Secretary, Wright, only a few months before, the apparent cleansing zeal of the Groupers—which was not always accepted by others as without ulterior motives or an element of threat to them—caused widespread hostility in the Sydney Trades Hall. The breach between Kane and Anderson over it was also an indicator of things to come, including the breach in The Movement itself.

This incident followed a contentious election campaign in 1952 and 1953, in which the Assistant New South Wales Secretary, Carling, stood against Platt, unsuccessfully. Carling subsequently complained to the Industrial Commission that the records of five men on Platts' ticket had been tampered with to make them appear eligible for election when they were not. A drawn-out inquiry followed, with Mr Justice de Baun finding it the 'worst case of fraud and forgery in Union affairs in the history of the Industrial Commission', and that there had been 'wholesale systematic forging and faking' of records.

Carling subsequently began further proceedings in the Commonwealth Arbitration Court, seeking an order for Platt to account to the union for secret profits he had made, by having union cars serviced and occasionally sold, at a garage owned by himself and his senior clerk, Miss P. Herbert. The Court found the facts proved, but said there was no evidence of a profit being made.

When under attack later for approving an ALP Industrial Group in a union led by an ALP member, the New South Wales Executive said:

The ALP groups owe much of their success in defeating Communists to their exposure of corruption, ballot-rigging and other forms of dishonesty in Communist-controlled unions. If the Groups stood idly by while similar dishonesty took place in Unions controlled by ALP sponsored candidates, they would betray the trust reposed in the name of the ALP by rank-and-file unionists and would be forever discredited.

The breach with the AWU was of fundamental importance, and decisively swung the balance of power against the Groupers in 1954. As early as the end of 1952, there had been signs of uneasiness between Dougherty and the Groupers and the growing trend culminated in him walking angrily out of the last Executive meeting before the 1954 New South Wales Conference.

The AWU in the mid-fifties suggested a vast mediaeval kingdom, with a haughty, tough, hard-living king presiding over regional barons of like temperament. With many of its members itinerant bush workers and much of it scattered in small parcels, the officials were dominant and felt little rank and file pressure. Other unions often sneered at the AWU as a union 'of officials for officials by officials'. There were shifting patterns of allegiances among the regional officialdom, but all owed fealty to Dougherty; apart from any personal loyalty, he had the power to organise the rest of the union against any recalcitrant baron who was not well entrenched. It was a powerful weapon to hold in a union where rank and file opinion counted for little. Conversely, the very lack of substance in AWU membership, despite its huge numbers, often made its officials abnormally afraid of any counter-organisation against them. The ability to command organisation seemed to count for everything.

This abnormal fear of rival organisation provided much of the background to the AWU's breach with the Groupers and their own web of organisation. However, it was complex and cannot be put down to any one factor. Some of the factors involved were as follows:

1 Dougherty had tried to enter the Sydney City Council as a Labor candidate and there were reports that part of his plan in linking with the Groupers in 1952 was to become Lord Mayor of Sydney. However, in late 1952 the Grouper Executive was instrumental in the legislation which changed the system of election, from a Lord Mayor chosen by the Council to one chosen by the electors, much as a United States President. This was largely a strategy devised to cut across corruption in the City Council. P. D. Hills became Lord Mayor and Dougherty withdrew his nomination for the Council. It is recalled that he was obviously upset.

2 Several incidents seem to have given Dougherty the impression that the Groupers might be up to something in the AWU. In the AWU paper *The Worker* of 23 February 1955, Dougherty claimed that Keon had told an AWU organiser from Sydney, J. S. Bielski, that he should help to 'get rid of Davis and men like him in the AWU'. Keon had invited Bielski to Melbourne to help organise migrants in the ARU Industrial Group campaign. The alleged remark was a reference to H. O. 'Brahma' Davis, the Federal President and Victoria-Riverina Secretary of the Union, a cantankerous official who was then fighting with Stout against the Groupers in Melbourne. Davis claimed later that D'Arcy and Devlin of the Victoria Executive had also tried to organise some kind of group against him, and at one stage he appears to have informally approached the Executive to form an Industrial Group, against left-wing and communist attempts on the union. There is no doubt of bad blood between Davis and the Victorian Grouper faction. At the same time, Kane seems to have muttered the occasional veiled threat against the AWU when Dougherty was being difficult.

Some observers claim there was at one stage some form of organised Grouper activity in the AWU, but there is no evidence of it and it has never been admitted on the Grouper side. The AWU was certainly a rich prize; it had long attracted the attention of the far left and its rulers must have felt uneasy about similar organisation and dedication on their right. The brand of clean, efficient 'new unionism' the Groupers were proclaiming was far from the AWU tradition.

3 An unexpectedly bitter feud over the legal business of the Ironworkers' Union, after Short and the Industrial Group won office. The AWU solicitors, J. J. Carroll and Cecil O'Dea, who were prominent in Sydney Catholic circles, had handled the Ironworkers' Industrial Group business, including the appeals to the Arbitration Court against ballot forging. Most of the fees came from Commonwealth under the Arbitration Act. When Short became Secretary, he gave the business instead to one of his old ex-Trotskyist friends, J. R. McClelland, who had done a Repatriation law course. McClelland—who, oddly, had sat next to Santamaria at school—was then a rising industrial lawyer who was resented by many of the old guard. The extreme bad blood raised by this affair would seem, to the outsider, quite disproportionate, though the Ironworkers compensation business was most lucrative. Dougherty was always close to his lawyers.

This dispute was against a traditional background of tension between the two unions because of competition for members among workers on steel construction jobs. Periods of peace between them had long alternated with rivalry and by 1954 rivalry was returning after initial quiescence by the Grouper leaders.

4 A genuine dislike and mistrust by Dougherty towards the activities of The Movement. Christened a Presbyterian but in practice a man for the good things of life, he had little in common personally with the devout Movement types. He claimed later that he was 'going along' with the Groups to find out what was going on.

5 The traditional dislike between the AWU and the orthodox unions

that dominated the Sydney Trades and Labor Council began to reassert itself, in clashes of personalities.

6 With such big unions as the Ironworkers', Clerks' and Railways now supporting the Grouper Executive and more being won from the communists, the AWU was no longer so critical to the balance of power *in New South Wales*. Dougherty found himself much less dominant on the Executive in 1953-54 than in 1952-53. The passing of control to such people as the intellectual ex-Marxists Ross and Short, the blunt reforming zealot, Kane, and representatives of the anti-AWU unions, such as Kenny and Shortell of the TLC, intensified his feeling of alienation from the ALP 'establishment'.

The Victorian Central Executive of the ALP in 1953 and 1954 was very much a collection of individuals, though several broad tendencies could be distinguished. Three of these would be covered by the broad heading of 'Groupers', while a fourth might be categorised as 'moderates'.

The three types of 'Groupers' would be the Catholics of the Old Right, those of the New Right and Movement and the secular, industrial Groupers. The Old Right Catholics would include the Parliamentarians J. L. Cremean and E. W. Peters; A. M. Fraser, MLC, Mary Barry (wife of W. Barry, MLA, and a woman of notably independent and outspoken mind) and J. Meere. They were mostly born before the turn of the century, had had close associations with the ALP since the First World War and while usually intensely anti-communist and even anti-left, they tended to be pragmatic but very radical on the issues that interested them. They mostly had little to do with The Movement, which mainly worked with younger people, though they were strong supporters of the Industrial Groups. As an example, Mrs Barry, who was for many years Secretary of the Women's Central Organising Committee, led the opposition to National Service at the 1951 Conference, though such military training was Movement policy.

The New Right included The Movement members and individuals such as Keon and T. W. Brennan, a solicitor, former journalist and an MLC after the 1952 State election. The Movement members on the Executive for most years of the first half of the 1950's were McManus and J. J. Roberts (the Treasurer), who in many ways were probably closer to the Old Right; L. F. D'Arcy, a farmer and MLA for Grant; M. J. 'Jock' Travers, a Scot and Vehicle Builders' Union activist from Geelong; Frank Reilly, of the unofficial group in the Amalgamated Engineering Union; and D. Devlin, a railwayman stationed in the Goulburn Valley and later Gippsland. Until Scully joined the Executive in the middle of 1954, Devlin was the only one of these who might be said to regularly reflect the highly ideological approach often associated with The Movement. Keon was always extremely active on the Executive and took the militant right wing approach on most questions, which was usually The Movement approach, though he was not consistent. Brennan, regarded as a rather lovable demi-intellectual figure who would go to almost any trouble for the ALP, was also influential and mostly took the militant right wing approach.

Lovegrove, of course, was the best known and most influential of the secular Groupers. Little, a vigorous and aggressive debater, also became prominent and was President in 1953-54. Woodhouse, of the Amalgamated Society of Carpenters and Joiners, was active on the Executive once his union was established and by 1954 was emerging as an independent, intelligent Industrial Group leader, distinct from both the political wing and The Movement. Fred Riley, Secretary of the Manufacturing Grocers' Union, was a veteran of the Executive, a strong anti-Communist who knew his Marx and had come from the old non-Leninist Marxist Socialist Party. He was an active Melbourne Rationalist, a self-made intellectual and prolific writer on Trade Union affairs. Riley, with a common feeling for the ex-Marxist, had fathered Lovegrove politically in his early years out of the Communist Party. R. E. Wilson, Group-sponsored Federal Secretary of the Vehicle Builders, joined the Executive in 1953. J. P. 'Jack' Horan, Federal Secretary of the Transport Workers' Union, had been close to Stout in the late forties, but went with the ALP Executive in the feud of the fifties and became President of the ALP in 1954.

The 'moderates' were regarded as being led by Cain and Clarey, and would probably include Broadby, L. W. Galvin in the years he was on the Executive, Arthur Kyle of the Storemen and Packers' Union, Roy Cameron of the Miscellaneous Workers, and Senator J. M. Sheehan, a member of the Executive in the earlier part of the 1950's. These people mostly opposed the moves against Kennelly and supported the State Caucus majority on the issues where there was a clash. Cain and Galvin usually confined their Executive activity to questions affecting State Parliament, however. Stout and Jordan, in the years they were on the Executive, were 'moderates' of a different kind, and really a separate classification.

The labels should not be taken too far, however, as the records show little evidence of bloc voting and much evidence of individualism. What was known as a 'general right wing line' could be distinguished, covering the three classifications of Groupers, who often would vote together on things they might not agree with in the hope of getting similar consideration from others later. This explained some of the defeats Cain, and in turn Lovegrove, suffered. Votes that individuals regarded as important were often well canvassed and organised for, and the right sometimes held caucus meetings before important votes.

In New South Wales, the three most important Party officers after 1952 —Colbourne, the President, C. W. Anderson, the Secretary, and Kane, the Assistant Secretary—were all close to The Movement. But all might have been regarded as having their first loyalty to the Groups and ALP and were hardly of ideological bent, though Kane was close to Santamaria about this time.

William Regis Colbourne, born in Sydney in 1898, had become Secretary of the pro-Federal, anti-Lang Labor Party led by Chifley in New South Wales in 1931. He was a casualty of the rapprochement between the warring elements of Labor and in 1940 became Federal Secretary of the Industrial Life Assurance Agents' Union—hardly a satisfying job for a man who had made the early progress in Labor Movement that Colbourne had, and who was a favourite of Chifley. Close to The Movement and Groups in 1952, he became Research Officer of the Ironworkers' Union and then State President of the ALP.

Charles Wilson Anderson, born in Sydney in 1918, showed early promise in the Plumbers' Union and became Assistant Secretary of the ALP in 1949 and Secretary in 1952, when Wright was dismissed. He was a convert to Catholicism, but was regarded as being close to the AWU and even something of a Dougherty protégé, as well as a keen supporter of the Industrial Groups and a discriminating supporter of The Movement.

Vice-Presidents of the New South Wales Branch at this time included James Henry Shortell, who became President in 1954 after Anderson resigned and Colbourne became Secretary, H. J. Blackburn, a Catholic and friend of the Kane family from Lithgow, and F. Bowen of the Furnishing Trades Union. Shortell, born in Liverpool, England, was President of the New South Wales Branch at the height of the split and had been regarded as a major organiser for the Grouper faction nationally. A bluff north of England Protestant, Shortell was secretary of the small Sugar Workers' Union and had come up through the Sydney Trades and Labour Council. The Sugar Workers was something of a 'company union' as it dealt with only one employer, the Colonial Sugar Refining Co Ltd, a fairly paternalistic employer. This meant that its interests were often different from many of the big militant unions.

Apart from the officers, the main Movement group on the New South Wales Executive in the Grouper years included Milton McCarney of the Vehicle Builders' Union and C. J. (Chris) McGrane, of the Postal Workers. A few other industrialists and branch members were in The Movement, making a total of eight or nine out of the 41-man Executive. As many again could be regarded as rather close to The Movement and influenced by its anti-communism and to a minor extent by its social policies. Those who might be regarded as 'moderates', or in a mild way anti-Grouper, probably totalled about 20 to 30 per cent of the Executive, as in Victoria.

The Victorian and New South Wales Executives will be seen, then, to cover the broad spectrum of the Industrial Group faction, from Movement men, who were not unduly prominent and tended towards the less ideological stream of The Movement, through people of in many ways similar views to the more secularly minded Groupers. There were also minority groups of 'moderates' who found they could work with the Groupers. Almost everybody involved had long histories in the Labor Movement and this was as true—despite later assertions to the contrary—of Movement people as of anybody else. The Movement could hardly be said to 'control' either branch—except in malevolent and distorted political propaganda—but it could have been said to have influence.

In Victoria, Santamaria used his weekly lunches at the Latin with Keon,

McManus, Mullens, Scully and the others to exert some influence, but this rarely went beyond what the others agreed with anyway. At times, too, he used Devlin and other Movement members to influence the Executive, but again it was influence of a minor kind.

In New South Wales, Santamaria's influence tended to be more wide reaching, but not so deep. He enjoyed more friendship with non-Catholics such as Short and Ross, and Movement people occupied more high posts. But as has been shown, while they might like him and admire his intelligence, these people were rarely willing to do his bidding unless it suited them or they agreed with the purpose. His own base of dedicated followers was even smaller at significant levels in the Labor Movement in New South Wales than in Victoria. He also, of course, did not have the same invaluable relationship with the Archbishop.

This pattern of his influence was difficult to discern at the time, however. Few outsiders knew who were Movement people and who were not, and tended to assume there were more than there were. And knowledge of who was a member and who was not was not always important, because some members did not seem like the popular conception of 'Catholic Actionists', while some non-members—the classic example is Keon—did.

The Movement's own activities in these years hardly discouraged the groundswell against it. Apart from the higher levels of Santamaria's influence, the innumerable secret church meetings, the widespread reaction against a barely perceived 'party within a party', The Movement did not tread very carefully in smaller things. There are many stories, difficult to pin-point exactly, of Movement people becoming especially ruthlessly aggressive at this time, at the union, branch or personal level. Partly this seems to have come from a heady feeling of power in victory, partly from a struggle to maintain this power and to push The Movement's policies now that its ostensible role in the unions was declining in importance, and partly from the logical extension of its threatened feeling over Asian affairs. In one example, W. M. Bourke, who had become a critic of The Movement, felt it had tried to upset his pre-selection for Fawkner for the 1954 elections. There might be the feeling that a Movement man's ties would lead to him getting preference in his union, or that another was using Movement contacts to further his local political career.

The reaction amongst some Protestants, Masons, liberal Catholics and moderates began to intensify, occasionally reaching the level of embryo organisation. When Evatt attacked The Movement in October 1954 there were few who did not have some idea, however vague or distorted, of what he meant.

While communism had declined in the unions by this time, objectively, some form of defence by the ALP was still needed. There were still a few bastions of communist power and the occasional union—the Watersiders' in Victoria, for example—had fallen back under communist control.

More importantly, it was becoming apparent that the quiet of the communists, who had all but ceased to operate as the core of an industrial faction, was strategic. Several articles in the Party's theoretical journal the

Communist Review, in 1952, 1953 and 1954, indicated a return to greater emphasis on the united front strategy and 'isolating the right wing'. The most important of these was by the General Secretary, L. L. Sharkey, in the issue of August 1952. Here Sharkey laid down suggestions for showing up the 'capitalist nature' of the ALP and discrediting it with the workers if it won office in 1954. The communists, as the vanguard of the proletariat, would then try to isolate the 'right wing'—including Evatt and most Parliamentarians—and build up a left wing. Fear of how the communists would use union strength against a Labor Government was always an important consideration with the Industrial Groupers.

The New South Wales and Victorian ALP conferences of June 1954, were held in a critical atmosphere, for Labor had lost the 1954 election and the factionalism was still intensifying. The Party was still without a credible Federal Secretary.

A week before the New South Wales Conference was due, *Century*, the Lang organ which had once supported the Groups, appeared with a splenetic attack on them. Though outside the ALP, Lang at seventy-eight was still an influence, if a secondary one, to reckon with in New South Wales Labor. He still—unsuccessfully—sought re-admittance to the ALP. Several left-wingers had lately, according to popular rumour, been gathering influence in the *Century* circle. *Century* accused the Groups of principles 'completely repugnant to the basic principles of Australian trade unionism' and of planning to introduce into Australia 'the Mussolini pattern of the corporate state'.

On the Tuesday before the New South Wales Conference, the Transport Workers' Union announced that it would disaffiliate from the ALP, until it received an assurance that the Party would not be used against ALP men in the unions.

The Conference itself was stormy and Dougherty, C. T. Oliver, the State Secretary of the AWU, and three other members of the Executive did not re-nominate for the Executive elections. 'I must have forgotten,' Dougherty told the press. J. Williams, of the Builders' Laborers' Federation, who was close to Dougherty, was also believed to have joined the Dougherty boycott. Two others, J. Allport (Timber Workers) and G. Neilly, the Group-backed secretary of the powerful Miners' Federation, withdrew on the grounds that they did not have enough time for the Executive meetings.

The opposition, now with Dougherty virtually among their numbers, attacked the Groupers over the Transport Workers' affair and Campbell said he had documents that proved Kane had stood for office on the same union ticket as a communist. He also said he had documents showing that Kane had told the Transport Workers he had 'unlimited money and thousands of workers' to remove Platt from the union.

In Victoria, there was an early clash on the Friday night, 11 June, when Frank Crean, an MP who had economics qualifications, attacked Evatt's promise in the election to abolish the means test. He had asked for the

Conference to be closed to the press during this attack, but McManus opposed the suggestion. Lovegrove rose to defend Evatt's policy, which, he said, would have been carried out had Labor been returned to power.

Evatt received rousing cheers from the Grouper-dominated Conference when he addressed it on the Sunday afternoon in one of his rare appearances since the election defeat. He would never tolerate the communists using Eureka—it was the centenary year of the Eureka Stockade—for their own ends, Evatt told the cheering Groupers.

But shortly afterwards, there was pandemonium when Kennelly rose and attacked the means test promise. Labor would be 'haunted for years' by the promise, he said. He defended Crean and added, 'I have no objection to abolishing the means test if you can prove to me how it can be done without taxing or risking inflation.'

'Utter treachery!' cried E. W. Peters, MP, an interjector.

'The sooner we get back to the position of years gone by when we were not labelled "comms." if we had different views to anybody else, the better for the Party,' Kennelly said amid continual interjection. 'The Party is not as united today as it was in past years. Unless we can get to a basis for tolerance that gives the right to at least take a point of view, we'll find a great body of people will continue to wonder where this Party is going to finish up,' he said. 'Please let us get a bit of tolerance into it.'

'Drivel!' 'Go home!' were the interjections recorded by the press.

'I agree that there are differences of opinion, but there are no disagreements that cannot be dissipated over a glass of beer,' Lovegrove said.

The next day, 14 June, saw the debate on the report of the Industrial Groups Committee. Again there was violent dissension, despite an overwhelming vote of confidence in the Groups.

Kennelly, to more loud and indignant interjections, said the Industrial Groups were being used by an 'outside influence' in an attempt to dictate the Party's policy. They had gone far beyond the purpose of fighting communists in the unions. There was uproar when Kennelly said the outside influence using the Groups was also active in pre-selection ballots.

To end the debate, McManus rose heatedly: 'I might expect communists to get down into the gutter but I don't expect leading members of the Labor Party to get down there with them.' The Groups had not been successful when Kennelly had a chance of using them, he said.

It was with this background that the Federal Executive met in Canberra a month later. The difference was that here Kennelly, after compromises, had 'the numbers'. The joker in his pack was the defection from the Grouper cause of the AWU, as well as success in getting the right delegates —Reece and Gil Duthie, MPs—from Tasmania and Chamberlain and H. Webb (in the absence of Beazley on a Moral Rearmament tour abroad) from Western Australia.

Kennelly had promised to stand down as Federal Secretary. Quite apart from 'the numbers' on the Executive, there had been a considerable body of opinion in the Federal Parliamentary Party Caucus against a Caucus member also being Federal Secretary. It was felt that this position would give him too many advantages over fellow Parliamentarians in dispersing campaign money at election time and in elections for Cabinet.

Colbourne had been the 'Grouper pea' for the job for more than a year. Evatt had originally wanted McManus or Lovegrove, but Colbourne wanted the job and there was a feeling that he deserved it after the difficulties he struck when the Chifley-Lang troubles ended in 1939. But Colbourne was quite unacceptable to the Kennelly faction.

Kennelly's choice for Secretary became Jack Schmella, the Queensland Secretary since 1952. John Mathew Schmella was born at Charters Towers in 1909. He was in turn a teacher, journalist, bush worker and trainee metallurgist in North Queensland and became an Industrial Officer there for the AWU and a protegé of the old AWU leader, Clarrie Fallon. The Northern Branch of the AWU, under the secretaryship of Edgar Williams, had indifferent relations at that time with the great Southern Districts branch of Queensland, where R. J. J. Bukowski, virtually the number two man in the AWU, was secretary—and boss. Nevertheless, AWU influence got Schmella, who was literate and educated by AWU standards, the job of State ALP secretary in Brisbane. Partly, the motive was to get him out of the AWU. A capable man, Schmella was nevertheless a famous hard drinker and had in him something of both the folksiness of a North Queensland politician and the *angst* of a driven man never fully at home in the society he mixed in with superficial gaiety. He enjoyed a rollicking friendship with the Deputy Prime Minister, Arthur (later Sir Arthur) Fadden. He was a Catholic, ambivalent towards his religion.

Schmella wanted the job of Federal Secretary, he was getting on well with Kennelly and Dougherty's change of direction finalised the eligibility. On 14 July, the Federal Executive chose him, by eight votes to four, ahead of Colbourne as its acting Secretary. With the 'numbers' up, Reece then returned to the National Presidency without a fight, replacing Lovegrove. Chamberlain became Senior Vice-President—in line to succeed Reece the following year—and Toohey withdrew to give the Junior Vice-Presidency to Colbourne as a 'consolation prize'.

The appointment as Federal Secretary was to be confirmed at the Federal Conference due in January—and therein lay more trouble. Federal conferences of six delegates from each of the six states were notoriously more difficult to predict and manipulate than the twelve-man Executive. Any reasonable count of the likely 'numbers' in January would have shown them almost evenly balanced, with one or two changes or defections either way likely to be decisive. The organising, manipulating and plotting between the factions still had a while to run. And both were intent on victory.

Evatt, unsuccessful six weeks earlier in his bid to be Prime Minister of Australia, was now in a parlous position. His backing of the Groupers, in an attempt to achieve a solid base of support in the machine, had ended only with men in control who were seemingly determined to drive him from the leadership, and more bitterly hostile to him than ever.

As a first instalment the Executive, recalling the means test affair, passed the following resolution:

It be a recommendation to Federal Conference that prior to all future Federal elections the Federal Executive assume its required responsibilities and set out, after consultation with the Leader and his deputies, the policy that Labor will submit to the people of Australia.

And that very week, Evatt was taking his first steps into the disastrous trap of intervention before the Petrov Royal Commission on Espionage.

Chapter Ten
Petrov and After:
The 1954 Election

Evatt's leadership set the Federal Parliamentary Labor Party on a more markedly 'right wing' course than for some years, after defeat of the referendum on the Communist Party Dissolution Bill. This was partly a result of his alliance with the Groupers against Kennelly in the party machine, partly a strategy to improve internal harmony in Caucus and partly a strategy to hold 'swinging' votes from the 1952 recession until the half-Senate election of 1953 and the 1954 General Election.

The Menzies Government's first exercise in internal money management to control the inflation of the Korean War period and a balance of payments crisis had caused the brief recession of 1952, when unemployment reached 4 per cent during the winter. The result was a swing to Labor, with a win in a by-election for the outer Melbourne division of Flinders, followed by election of the Cain Government in December. If Labor could maintain this momentum, it would win control of the Senate in 1953 and of the House of Representatives the following year. Such an outcome would make Evatt Prime Minister of Australia.

A stronger, more secure Leader than Evatt, or one who had more time, might have tried to give a firm leadership from the centre, dramatising around his personality the policies with which there was general agreement and encouraging rational discussion of others. But Evatt, unsure of touch and pressed for time, tended more to the tactic critics often called 'playing the ends against the middle'. He tried to cultivate all sides, playing them off against each other and only aggravating the tendency to mistrust him. He had bad relations of mutual distrust with his Deputy, Calwell. His conduct would reach the extent of taking members aside and asking them what others thought of his leadership. It was a general erraticism of conduct in small things—for another example, not answering letters—and lack of confidence in his tactical ability rather than ideology that caused rumblings against his leadership between 1951 and 1954.

Publicly, Evatt's policies turned to the right after the referendum on the Communist Party Dissolution Bill. He became anti-Chinese and in favour of land settlement. In April 1952, he praised the anti-communist record of the Victorian Branch in his address to the Easter Conference. About the same time he helped in getting the Federal Executive ban on *News Weekly* lifted. In May 1952, Evatt led Calwell, Keon and others in a strongly worded attack on the Government and the liberally-inclined

Immigration Minister, Harold Holt, for allowing five Australians headed by Evatt's old protégé, John Burton, to visit a peace meeting in Peking during the Korean War. The rumpus raised by the Opposition and right wing Liberals together was sufficient for the Government to reverse its position and refuse passports to a larger group who wished to attend a full-scale peace conference, for which the earlier meeting had prepared.

Unfortunately for Labor, by the time Menzies called the Senate election in May 1953, the recession had lifted. Evatt campaigned, with a vigor that surprised the commentators, on unemployment, inflation, lagging social services and the like. Menzies emphasised the need for stability in Government if the rising prosperity was to be maintained. Evatt called for a 'watchdog' Senate, Menzies for a stable, pro-Government one.

The election, on 9 May, resulted in a slight swing to Labor which, nevertheless, was not as great as the state and by-election results of the previous year had suggested. Labor was losing momentum. It had twenty-nine seats to the Government's thirty-one in the new Senate, a reduction of two in the Government's majority compared with 1951-53. The critical State had been Queensland, where the Country Party vote was high and Labor's share of the vote only 44·7 per cent. In New South Wales Labor had won 52·7 per cent of the vote, in Victoria 51 per cent, South Australia 52.8 per cent, Western Australia 49.1 per cent and Tasmania (where there had been a third party) 45·9 per cent. In the Melbourne *Sun* of 12 May, the Canberra correspondent, Frank Chamberlain, wrote of Evatt's 'rising popularity'. The country had become politically almost perfectly balanced.

Apart from ephemeral issues like the peace conference passports and the political rights of Australians such as the left-wing war correspondent, Wilfred Burchett, the ideological issues dividing Labor had not pressed heavily in 1952 or early 1953. But shortly after the Senate election the Korean War ended and the issue of recognition of Communist China and a 'settlement' in East Asia arose once again.

A violent ideological debate broke out around rather than in the ALP. A new left developing around Burton and a lobby of academics supporting a conciliatory attitude towards China was pressing vigorously for recognition, admittance to the United Nations, a generous settlement of oustanding territorial issues and no military cordons. The Catholic right, especially *News Weekly*, was vehement in its opposition to such a course. Probably majority opinion in Caucus would have favoured the conciliatory approach. Only the widespread apathy to and ignorance of international affairs kept the temperature comfortable inside the Party.

Evatt probably supported the conciliatory approach and recognition personally; but his public stance was to keep quiet about it at least until the elections, due in less than a year, or else make vague anti-recognition noises.

Henry S. Albinski in his book *Australian Policies and Attitudes Towards China,*[1] relates that on one occasion Evatt was confiding to a small

---

[1] H. S. Albinski, *Australian Policies and Attitudes Towards China*, Princeton University Press, 1965, p. 117

circle of friends in Perth that of course Australia's China policy needed a realistic overhaul. 'There would need to be recognition, a vote for Peking in the UN, etc. Then a stranger approached the group. Discovering that the newcomer was a newsman, Evatt reversed gears and began to preach against the very proposition he had just laid down.' Evatt had been in London for the Coronation in the winter and when he returned the extra-parliamentary debate was well under way.

Albinski also claims that Evatt prevaricated heavily, much more so than Chifley, on China recognition in 1949-50 for similar internal and external political reasons.[2]

As described above, the far right and Movement got anti-recognition votes through the New South Wales and Victorian executives in the spring, while Keon took the initiative in Parliament. On 24 September, he broke Labor's China ice publicly with a strong anti-recognition speech.

'The Government is now obviously engaged in trying to soften Australian opinion to accept the fact that sooner or later the Goverment will sucumb to pressure from other quarters and, in return for a promise that they will be good boys in the future, provide for the recognition of the Peking Red Government,' he said. The Government would succumb to 'the world-wide campaign through the multifarious avenues by which the Communist Party infiltrates public opinion'. It would also succumb to pressure put upon Menzies in London to follow Britain in recognition. This would be the 'worst thing possible' for the Australian people. If it recognised Peking, the Government could not also continue to support what would become a 'small group of disgruntled exiles' on Formosa.

'If Formosa falls to the communists,' he said in a clear presentation of the Catholic right viewpoint, 'the whole Pacific defence line, from Japan to Korea and down to the Philippines will go. That defence line, which is manned mainly by the United States, will be compelled to fall back thousands of miles across the Pacific.' Recognition would be an insult to every member of the United States Congress, which had voted unanimously against it. Australia would be placed in a precarious position if its friendship with America was broken. Finally, Keon mentioned the effect on the morale and views of the twenty million overseas Chinese in South East Asia, should the organisational and propaganda facilities offered by Nationalist embassies disappear.

A few days earlier, on 15 September, another right winger, Kim Beazley, had said in a much milder speech that America's China policy was more realistic than Britain's. About the same time, Keon and Beazley appeared on public platforms at non-Labor gatherings to protest against Australian recognition. Beazley was an Anglican, whose anti-communism came from intellectual conviction, an educated interest in Asian affairs and recent embracing of Moral Rearmament.

Keon and Beazley remained lone parliamentary voices for Labor on China, while Evatt's strategy was to keep this perilous issue out of sight.

[2] op. cit., pp. 25-70

Fortunately for him, the Government had its own problems of international pressures and a vociferous right wing and was happy to join him.

The China issue having been kept under control during the spring, Evatt entered post-holiday 1954 energetic and confident about the elections due in May. Throughout the late summer and autumn, he was rarely absent from the newspaper columns and radio news, as he issued statement after statement attacking the Government—on margins for skill, wheat marketing, failure to take initiatives to control the hydrogen bomb and the like.

This preliminary campaigning showed great energy and drive, but in restrospect comes over as displaying little skill or imagination. Too often Evatt's statements got him into public wrangles with ministers, who were better informed. He ignored issues like socialisation, nationalisation and Government intervention in industry, among the rocks on which the Chifley Government had foundered. But inevitably, with Calwell, Pollard and Ward appearing in print as his lieutenants, Labor must have seemed to the public little different from the Government rejected five years earlier. There was little to give the Party what would be known in the more conceptual 1960's as a 'new image'.

Evatt followed up his public campaigning with three private conversations with Santamaria in the autumn of 1954. As only the two of them were involved, Santamaria was the only living witness to the nature of these talks when this work was being written. Nevertheless, the general outline is widely accepted. Dalziel tells in his *Evatt The Enigma*[3] how Albert Grundeman, a member of Evatt's secretariat, used to say that he accompanied Evatt to a private meeting with Santamaria.

Evatt himself said, in a press statement replying to Santamaria two years later, on 25 April 1956: '. . . I entirely reject Mr Santamaria's claim that I was inconsistent in attacking him in October 1954. It is true that I was acquainted with him six months earlier. I had not the slightest idea that he was head of the secret "Movement" aiming at control of the Labor Party from without. . . .' He also admitted the conversations in considerable detail in his statement to the Federal Executive inquiry into the Victorian Branch later in 1954 (see Part 2, Chapter 13).

Santamaria's version of the incident accords with the impressions of others who heard about it later, and who could be expected to be reasonably critical in their approach to vital statements by Santamaria.

Santamaria told the author that Evatt had asked Keon for an introduction, or for his (Santamaria's) phone number several times, and that he first met Evatt—briefly—at a reception for visiting Church dignitaries, Cardinals Agaginian and Gracias, after the Eucharistic Congress of April 1953.

In February 1954, Evatt invited Santamaria to his (Evatt's) suite in the Hotel Windsor, in Melbourne, and after consultation with Archbishop Mannix, Santamaria accepted. Evatt was flattering and expansive, talking about what he would do when he was Prime Minister. Evatt's attitude was: 'I think we'll be the Government. I want to tell you my ideas.' He

[3] Alan Dalziel, *Evatt The Enigma*, Lansdowne Press, Melbourne, 1967, p. 142

said he favoured compulsory unionism, migration and government aid to church schools. He mentioned a grant of £2 million for land settlement. He spoke highly of Keon's ability and said he would back him for a seat in Cabinet. Evatt also said he thought it very important to get rid of Kennelly as General Secretary, and to replace him with someone 'reliable' from Victoria like McManus or Lovegrove, rather than Colbourne or Anderson from New South Wales.

In a second private discussion in April, this time at new Movement offices being prepared in Gertrude Street, Fitzroy, Evatt talked to Santamaria about foreign policy, and agreed with him about almost everything.[4] Santamaria says Evatt appeared to over-estimate his (Santamaria's) ability to deliver Catholic votes, and that the obviousness of the manoeuvre deepened the mistrust he already felt for Evatt. However, an independent source told the author that Evatt's tactic seemed to have succeeded with the Archbishop, who had also been visited by Evatt from time to time. The Archbishop was in a very pro-Evatt mood before the election, delighted most of all by the possibilities of State Aid. Evatt appears to have privately promised Mannix almost unlimited amounts.

While Evatt's approaches to one section of the Catholic right may have been successful, he was falling out with an independent-minded colleague who represented another strand of it.

In a Melbourne 'Labor Hour' broadcast on 14 March, W. M. Bourke, the MP for Fawkner, said certain people were trying to trap Evatt into including abolition of the means test for pensions in his policy speech for the elections. Such a promise, to win a few votes in short-term political expediency, would be at a terrible cost, he said. Complete abolition of the test was a fantastic, impossible and undesirable proposal. It would wreck Australia's social security structure. A worthwhile increase in pension rates was long overdue, but complete abolition would cost £100 million a year. Bourke said the Commonwealth could not stand 'new and fancy' benefits unless the people were prepared to pay for them with higher taxes. Abolition would be undesirable from a social viewpoint and impracticable from a financial angle. It would almost completely destroy the country's financial capacity to provide worthwhile pensions to the needy and dependent pensioners.

The same afternoon, Evatt was with Menzies at the opening of the new St Edmund's Christian Brothers High School in Canberra, and both took advantage of the opportunity to praise church schools.

Evatt's effort to avoid the divisive communist issue before the election was not to be successful. In the last hours of the session, on 13 April, as Parliament was preparing to rise for the elections, Menzies announced the defection of Vladimir Mikhailovich Petrov, Third Secretary and Consul in

---

[4] Santamaria gives a similar, shorter version of the interviews in his essay, 'The Movement 1941-60, An Outline', first published in *Catholics and the Free Society* (Cheshire, Melbourne, 1961), while Evatt was still alive.

the Soviet Embassy in Canberra since 1951. 'It is my unpleasant duty to convey to the House some information which I this morning laid before the Cabinet for the first time,' the Prime Minister said. He said Petrov had voluntarily left his diplomatic employment and made to the Australian Government, through the Australian Security Intelligence Organisation, a request for political asylum.

Evatt had left Canberra for Sydney by plane late that afternoon to be guest of honour at the annual reunion of the Old Fortians, the ex-students' organisation of Fort Street High School, his old school. Calwell, Evatt's deputy, was not told of the announcement until shortly before Menzies made it. Evatt was bitterly angry at not being told in advance of this information, which could conceivably affect the election result.

He flew back to Canberra next morning and in the course of a statement to the House said: 'I had a very important engagement in Sydney, but I did not leave Canberra till 5 o'clock in the afternoon, and I would have cancelled the engagement had I had any inkling that such an announcement was to be made. I heard of the statement just before 9 o'clock [Menzies started speaking about 8 p.m.] and I made a statement to the press which was unanimously endorsed this morning at a meeting of the Parliamentary Labor Party.'

This statement was:

The Federal Parliamentary Labor Party will support the fullest inquiry into all the circumstances connected with the statement made by Mr Menzies tonight and the matters contained in, or relevant to, the statement. If any person in Australia has been guilty of espionage or seditious activities a Labor Government will see that he is prosecuted according to law. That has not only been our established policy, but we have acted in strict accordance with it. In short, we shall see to it that no guilty person escapes, that no innocent person is condemned and that the whole matter is dealt with free from all questions of party politics and on the basis of the established principles of British justice.

By this, Labor supported—it could hardly at that time do otherwise—the Royal Commission Menzies had announced to inquire, without delay, into 'what are already beginning to emerge as the outlines of systematic espionage and at least attempted subversion'. Petrov had also been the MVD secret police representative in Australia and had been part of the faction of Lavrenti Beria, the Soviet police chief executed soon after Stalin's death a year before. Petrov brought with him a pile of papers and documents allegedly relating to Soviet espionage in Australia and the formation of a spy ring. Menzies announced—after the election—that Petrov had been paid £5000 to help him establish in Australia.

The same day as Evatt's statement in the House, 14 April, Menzies brought down a short bill to provide for the appointment of Royal Commissioners for the inquiry. 'This kind of thing,' Menzies told the House, 'indeed presents embarrassments to a Government in this sense, that happening as it does through circumstances beyond our control—because it happened when the man concerned had finished his term of duty with the

Soviet Embassy and had left—not long before a general election, some people might be disposed to think it has some electoral significance. I want to tell the House that I should have been very happy if this matter had not arisen in this way for two or three months, and, so far from feeling that it involves any party considerations, I want to make it abundantly clear that it concerns something far superior to party.'

Days of excitement, edged in some anti-communist quarters with hysteria, followed. There were many conflicting rumours about who was involved in the alleged spy ring and police rescued a distraught Mrs Petrov from the hands of Russian couriers at Darwin Airport, while she was being flown back to Moscow, apparently against her will.

News Weekly of 21 April trumpeted in its main headline, 'Lid Blows off the Red Spy Ring'. It forecast mass exposure of communists in the universities, Department of External Affairs and the like. Elsewhere there was speculation that Petrov may have been the 'White Rabbit' Menzies would pull out of the hat for the election—as forecast some weeks earlier by the *Sydney Morning Herald* correspondent.

Menzies eventually arranged for Mr Justice (later Sir William) Owen, of the New South Wales Supreme Court, Mr Justice (later Sir George) Ligertwood, of South Australia, and Mr Justice Roslyn Philp, from Queensland, to be the commissioners.

Although Menzies denied that he had any prior knowledge of Petrov's defection, later evidence showed that the security service, which was under his personal control, had been aware of the impending defection for some time. Menzies avoided any mention of the affair during the election campaign, but it could hardly have other than helped him. For one reason alone, headlines on the Petrov affair and the melodramatic rescue of Petrov's wife from Soviet couriers at Darwin Airport, effectively blotted out public political debate for the next month, virtually until the start of the campaign. And of course the melodrama of the whole affair in this early stage, with the repeated references to Soviet espionage in Australia, must have engendered a degree of patriotic conservatism in the community, though one remembers a good deal of scepticism as well.

The Royal Commission held its first hearing on 17 May, only twelve days before the election, in the Albert Hall, Canberra. It was a preliminary hearing to prepare for the main sessions. 'The note struck was just the right one to give the impression that a great spy drama was about to unfold,' wrote Dalziel, Evatt's biographer.

Communism from another Continent also threw a shadow over the election campaign, though it was one both sides, as with Petrov, largely ignored on the hustings. In Indo-China, in the region that was to become North Vietnam, the French and loyalist troops throughout the early months of 1954 had been in imminent danger of defeat from the communist-dominated Viet Minh nationalist forces. By May, collapse seemed certain. The United States, Australian and British Governments—not to mention *News Weekly*—believed that decisive support, in arms and back-up facilities, was going to Ho Chi Minh's Viet Minh from an expansive Communist China. The powers convened at Geneva on 26 April to discuss the possibility of a settlement in Indo-China, while in the background there was much inspired speculation about American, British and Australian armed intervention. *News Weekly* was strongly pro-intervention and highly critical of British 'appeasement', claiming Britain had no vital interests to protect in the area. Majority opinion in the Parliamentary Labor Party and the unions would probably have been as strongly opposed to intervention. On 28 April, Menzies said defensively that a report that Australia would follow American policy on Indo-China was 'completely untrue'.

Menzies opened the election campaign on 5 May in the Canterbury Memorial Hall in Melbourne. He mentioned neither Petrov nor Ho Chi Minh, but concentrated on the stability and prosperity his Government had brought the country. He sought a mandate to continue. However, the *Age* next morning said Menzies 'looked momentarily uneasy' when Fadden, the Deputy Prime Minister, asked if the Government should not continue 'in the light of the Espionage Royal Commission and the events that brought it about'.

Menzies said the people could not put his government out without 'putting an Evatt Government in'. He promised tax cuts in the 1954-55 budget and a series of minor reforms, including raising the maximum permissable income for receipt of an age pension from £2 to £3.10 a week, and the property limit from £1,250 to £1,750. He said the social service bill had increased from £75 million in 1949 to £153 million.

Next day at Hamilton, Victoria, Fadden, a lovable personality known off stage as 'Artie' but a crude political fighter, was much blunter about the implications of the Petrov affair.

Only the present Government, he said, could be trusted to carry out with the rigour of the law the findings of the Royal Commission. 'Could you trust the destiny of Australia in the hands of Dr Evatt, pledged to carry out a policy on all fours with the communistic manifesto, whose objectives are to socialise the means of production, distribution and exchange?' he asked. 'Can you afford to make Dr Evatt the nation's trustee after his association with communists and communism over the years? Communism interferes with the social and Christian life of Australia.'

Bourke's foreboding that Evatt would promise to abolish the means test proved well placed, when Evatt opened the Labor campaign at the Rivoli Hall, Hurstville, Sydney, on 7 May.

The aspirant Prime Minister promised to abolish the means test within the life of the ensuing parliament, to repeal immediately the property disqualification for pension entitlement, and to raise pensions by 10 shillings a week to £4. He also told the cheering audience of about 3,000 that he would immediately, as a step to complete abolition, increase the income limit from £2 to £6 a week and increase child endowment and maternity allowances.

Evatt spent comparatively little of his time on the details of his pension proposals, devoting most of his speech to detailed proposals for more abundant and cheaper housing finance. Labor would arrange with the Commonwealth Bank to advance funds to co-operative housing societies, with advances up to 95 per cent of the total cost contemplated. Other promises included even lower interest on War Service home loans, intervention before the wage tribunals, abolition of sales tax on furniture and a farm support scheme on American lines.

Evatt was vague about how he proposed to finance the programme, or what it would cost. His only specific proposal here was to end the practice, adopted during the inflation and recession of 1950-53, of using tax funds to pay for capital works. Labor would charge the cost of capital works to the loan account, where it properly belonged, he said, relieving the annual budget of a charge far exceeding £100 million a year.

Next day, in speeches at Bundaberg and Rockhampton in Queensland, Menzies denounced Evatt's promises as a 'jumble of nonsense', which to implement would cost £357,800,000 in a single year. This compared, he said, with total receipts from income tax in Australia of £350 to £400 million a year. Income tax would have to be doubled. 'I don't know,' said Menzies, 'the state of mind of a grown man who can put such drivel before the people. Financially speaking, it is criminal. Dr Evatt's ambition to become Prime Minister is so great that he made it clear last night he would rather become Prime Minister of a bankrupt country than Leader of the Opposition in a solvent and prosperous one.'

'A series of insults,' said Evatt in reply. 'He [Menzies] does not try to analyse my policy. He says it is disgraceful. Just imagine Mr Menzies saying that. He used the word "puerile", but he does not use facts to support himself.'

And so—as the fort of Dien Bien Phu was falling to the Viet Minh in Indo-China—the undignified war of words went on throughout the campaign, which Menzies managed to make turn exclusively on the practicability of Evatt's promises.

'Dr Evatt is as innocent of financial knowledge as a frog is of feathers,' said Menzies, returning to the attack; while Fadden called Labor's proposals a 'Wizard of Oz policy', a 'crackpot, jackpot financial revolution' and a 'bottomless and ever-expanding dilly bag'.

On 10 May Evatt's nemesis, Bourke, said in an election speech at Prahran Town Hall that the means test could be lifted now, but would have to be reimposed as a basis for future pension increases. 'I am not happy about everybody getting pensions, irrespective of their incomes,' he said. 'We'll have to take another look at that.' What was most urgent was to abolish the property section of the means test, which penalised thrift. 'In my view, we'll have to have another look at the speed with which the income section of the means test is taken out.'

Bourke was called immediately before the Executive Officers of the Victorian ALP and warned, while Menzies then quoted him from time to time. Evatt asked that no other action be taken against Bourke.

The same night Fadden had made what was billed as his policy speech, but devoted it almost entirely to a stinging, witty attack on Evatt and his proposals. According to the *Age*, Evatt's voice was 'trembling with anger' when he replied in a ten-minute National broadcast the next evening:

These are the people who dare to criticise me, the smearers, the slanderers. . . . I speak with indignation because these people are only the agents of powerful forces in this country, the shipping combines, the great monopolies from whom they receive their party funds, and whose will they carry into effect . . . behind Fadden is Mr Menzies. He does not do anything himself. He smears through his agents, the Faddens, Wentworths and Harrisons . . . I am leader of the Labor Party and I want a new deal for our people. They have no answer and therefore they try to smear me. . . . Sir Arthur Fadden does not even write his speeches. He cannot write them.

Foreign affairs came briefly, if with little dignity, into the campaign on 9 May when Calwell warned that a Chinese Communist Embassy might be built in Canberra if the Menzies Government was returned to power. Menzies was only waiting, he said, until the fighting in Indo-China and elsewhere died down before he recognised Communist China. 'He promised to do this after talks with Sir Winston Churchill [then British Prime Minister] at the Imperial Conference in London early last year,' said the ALP's super-nationalist. At Richmond, Keon said the Liberal Government would be in trouble if a 'nest of traitors' was found in External Affairs, a reference to the Minister for External Affairs, R. G. (later Lord) Casey having said in 1952 that there had been such a 'nest' in the Department.

Menzies' strategy throughout the campaign was to challenge Evatt to state the cost of his promises, and not at any stage did Evatt attempt to do so, or to explain further how he would implement them. Instead, towards the end of the campaign he promised to implement the proposals from 1 July instead of from the Budget, due early in August.

The truth about Evatt's promises seems to be that there was no real enthusiasm for them in the Party and that Evatt simply had convinced himself they would be 'a winner'; he had no idea how much they would cost or where his government would get the money from.

He either did not foresee Menzies' skilfully worded charges of financial irresponsibility, or decided that the promises were good enough to risk the cry, which Labor had risked often enough before, of 'where's the money coming from?' His only reply to Menzies was 'smear!', to up the ante, and to accuse Menzies and Fadden of financial irresponsibility themselves. This he said, consisted of using taxes to fill out the money needed for capital works and usually raised from loans, and also of 'talking about inflation' when the Government had increased the average weekly note issue from £220 million on taking office in 1949 to £340 million in March 1954. Both practices were part of the perfectly respectable techniques of Keynesian economic management which had been developed in the Treasury in and since Chifley's day.

Could Evatt have financed his promises? In retrospect, the irresponsibility of his promises is staggering. The Financial Editor of the *Sydney Morning Herald* estimated in an article in that paper on 13 May that a 'truly minimal' estimate of the cost of implementing Evatt's promises would be £200 million a year, with abolition of the means test and the 10 shilling rise in pensions together costing £126 million. He estimated that, given a recovery in the loan market and certain financial changes, Evatt might have been able to implement the promise to abolish the means test and to introduce initial depreciation allowances; but he would not have been able to implement the other promises without distorting the economy, and any implementation would have to be spread over three years.

Three days before the election, Calwell issued a press statement also giving the estimate of £200 million as the cost of Labor's promises, and provided a breakdown of 'Labor's Estimates' compared to the 'Menzies Story'. Calwell said 'Labor's policy' of charging capital works to the loan fund would enable most of this to be found. Menzies retorted on 27 May, 'Dr Evatt has never had to handle the financial affairs of a pie stall.'

Even if part, or all, of Evatt's promises had been capable of implementation without creating severe inflation, the result would have been to restrict Government spending in any field other than pensions, and to make rises in pensions more difficult to finance, and therefore less likely to be made. Spending on education, foreign aid, national development or defence, all of which in the subsequent years were to place genuine and heavy demands on public funds, would have been much harder to provide for. The beneficiaries of Evatt's policy, on the other hand, would have been the financially better-off aged. Summing up the election on 13 June, the Melbourne *Herald*'s political correspondent, E. H. Cox, wrote, 'Labor fought the election on the most right-wing policy for decades.'

There was violent disagreement about Evatt's character, even among those who knew him. Nevertheless, there were several observable traits in his complex nature in this part of 1954, indeed as throughout his leadership of the ALP. Although a man of great intellectual attainments, he seemed to lack feeling for social and economic issues and, one suspects, plain common sense. His talents were very much for the law, for history, for knowledge of literature, at all of which he was outstanding in his generation in Australia. The phenomenon of the intellectually gifted but mercurial and egocentric man who lacks insight into the results of his action is common enough in politics.

Evatt's own writing, particularly *Australian Labor Leader*, his biography of W. A. Holman,[5] shows an acute awareness—and implied condemnation—of the empty rhetoric and opportunism of politics in Australia prior to the rise of the Labor Party. His own formative years in the ALP were in the cynical period after the First World War, when something of the same spirit began to affect the ALP. One of the many tragedies of Evatt's career was that, in political practice, he would not be able to lift the Party above the depths in Australian politics of which he must have been intellectually aware. It is also possible that the decline in his faculties, which became much more noticeable after the election, was already having its effect.

[5] op. cit.

In the event, Labor narrowly lost the election. Labor won six seats and lost two, for a net gain of four. In the new House, the Liberal and Country Party coalition would have 64 seats, against 68 previously, and Labor 57, against 53. However, Labor won 50·03 per cent of the votes, against 47·07 per cent for the coalition parties—a vote of nearly 200,000 more for Labor than for the Government. It compared with 47·63 per cent for Labor and 50·34 per cent for the Government in 1951. Labor's share of the vote in the various states in 1954 was: New South Wales, 52·31 per cent; Victoria, 50·29; Queensland, 42·46; South Australia, 55·13; Western Australia, 47·51; Tasmania, 49·61. These figures showed a slight turn from Labor in New South Wales and Victoria and towards Labor in the smaller states, compared with the Senate election a year earlier. Then the Labor proportion of the vote had been: New South Wales, 52·74; Victoria, 50·92; Queensland, 44·72; South Australia, 52·76; Western Australia, 49·08; Tasmania, 45·91.[6]

The state of the new House of Representatives would be:

	1954-57 Parliament			1951-54 Parliament		
	Liberal	Country Party	Labor	Liberal	Country Party	Labor
New South Wales	15	7	25	16	7	24
Victoria	15	3	15	14	3	16
Queensland	8	5	5	9	5	4
South Australia	4	–	6	5	–	5
Western Australia	2	2	4	3	2	3
Tasmania	3	–	2	4	–	1

Labor had lost two seats in Victoria, Flinders (won in a by-election during the recession of 1952) and Wannon in the far south-west of the State. It won St George and Lawson in New South Wales, Griffith in Queensland, Sturt in South Australia, Swan in Western Australia and Bass in Tasmania.

On 30 May, Evatt issued an embittered press statement:

The Government did not win the election fairly. . . . Throughout the campaign it resorted to the smear and hysteria technique adapted from the police states of Germany and Russia. In spite of that, Labor outnumbered Government votes by more than 250,000. Yet Labor did not win the election. This was because shifts of population and other factors had completely distorted the distribution of seats and denied democratic rights to the people. Under these conditions, the will of the minority could easily prevail over the will of a large majority. Nevertheless, it is still by no means certain that the Menzies-Fadden coalition will secure a chance majority in the House of Representatives. But if it does, it will be a minority government. Even if the Government does survive for a while, the returns show that a clear majority of Australians have deliberately censured its record of broken promises and have given a popular verdict in favour of Labor's positive programme.

[6] Slight distortions are caused by the failure of Labor to contest some seats in New South Wales and of the Liberals in South Australia, and of the appearance of splinter groups in the 1953 election, mainly in Tasmania.

The imbalance between voting strength and seats in the House of Representatives was caused mainly by more people voting Labor in the middle-class and rural districts that return non-Labor MPs than voting Liberal in Labor's industrial strongholds. The distribution of seats which provided this result in 1954 had been made under the Chifley Government, in which Evatt was then Deputy Prime Minister. The first redistribution under Menzies was made later in 1954. The resulting small changes in the distribution of seats would hardly have worked in favour of Labor, since it eliminated mainly inner city seats.

In 1954, however, an additional factor aggravated the imbalance. There were no contests in about half a dozen 'blue ribbon' Liberal or Country Party seats, mainly in New South Wales, thus taking probably 150,000 or so Government voters out of the election. Nor were there contests in some 'safe' Labor seats in South Australia. The new government would have been a 'minority' one by a lower margin, had these voted. In general, the result showed the country still to be in a state of fine political balance, as in 1953. Differences of a few hundred votes in a dozen key electorates decided the future government. Labor's decisive failings were in Queensland, where it failed to recapture the vote that had gone from Labor to defeat the Chifley Government in 1949, and in Victoria.

In Victoria Labor lost Flinders, normally a safe anti-Labor seat on the southern environs of Melbourne running into the Mornington Peninsula. It had gone to Labor in a by-election in 1952. Labor also failed to win Corio, covering Geelong, where there was rapid industrial expansion, an influx of migrants and where the sitting Liberal, H. L. Opperman, the former world cycling champion, had worked hard at developing a personal following. The other seats Labor had to win to improve its showing in Victoria and become the Government had been outer metropolitan ones such as Latrobe and Deakin, and changing inner city ones such as Isaacs, running south from St Kilda. Although Evatt spoke in such marginal seats during the campaign, Labor made no substantial headway in them. A common characteristic of most of these seats was that they contained the seeds of the emerging Australia—the new outer suburbs, the districts of flats, the migrant centres. The lesson must have been that Labor was not making the headway it needed in new segments of the community.

The Gallup Polls taken at this time reinforce the impression that the community was in a fine state of balance politically, but that Labor was not making or holding the advances it required to break through the post-1949 electoral mould. The Gallup Poll estimated the Labor vote at 51 per cent in December 1953, 52 per cent in February 1954, 52 per cent in March (from a poll taken at the height of the Royal visit), 50 per cent at the beginning of May, after the Petrov defection, and 51 per cent on 27 May, two days before the poll.

Alternatively, a poll taken by the less experienced Market Research Consultants of Australia Pty Ltd, as a National Forum Poll, published by the *Argus* on 28 May, the eve of the election, showed Labor winning 11 to 16 seats, on a vote of 51·1 per cent.

The implication of these figures is that neither the Petrov defection nor Evatt's promises greatly affected the outcome of the vote, which most commentators and the pollsters had for months expected to be determined by close contests in a few evenly balanced divisions. But, as the outcome was to be determined by such a narrow margin, factors which could influence it even a little had unusual importance. In this sense, Petrov might have influenced the result, as the balance of favourable and unfavourable reaction to Evatt's promises—and personality—may have.

After his petulant attack on the Government's return, little was heard of Evatt until August. Except for essential appearances, such as at the Queen's Birthday weekend Labor conferences in June, and an early brush with the Petrov Inquiry in mid-July, he was as absent from the headlines as he had been present in the two months before.

On 14 June he received what the Melbourne *Sun* called a 'tumultuous welcome' from 450 people, 400 of them delegates, at the right-dominated Victorian Conference in the Melbourne Trades Hall Council chamber. The *Sun* said Evatt was 'visibly moved'.

'I do not feel we have anything to apologise for, to extenuate or to explain,' he told the Conference. Alluding to the split then developing between the Trades Hall Council and the Cain Government, Evatt said it was absurd to say the political and industrial wings of Labor were separate; 'they started together and they go forward together'.

Evatt returned to his public silence after the Conference, until 16 July, the date of his first clash with the Petrov Commission. A further three weeks of silence ensued, until the new Caucus met on 3 August. But already the divisions in the Sydney and Melbourne Trades Halls and with the Parliamentary Party were becoming a regular part of the news. With the meeting of the new Federal Caucus, Labor was to enter three terrible years, when is was to provide weekly, if not daily, sensations, and when men were to become parodies of themselves.

Chapter Eleven
Petrov and After: Evatt Before the Inquiry

Evatt's appearance before the Petrov Espionage Royal Commission was to be one of the last straws that finally broke Labor unity. On 13 July 1954, Fergan O'Sullivan, a former *Sydney Morning Herald* reporter who had been appointed Evatt's Press Secretary in April 1953, was called before the Commission. He had resigned from Evatt's staff a few days before, after having informed Evatt about the allegations against him. In the box, O'Sullivan admitted that he was the author of 'Document H', an exhibit before the Commission. It was a typed document giving personal, often unflattering, details about a large number of journalists in the Federal Parliamentary Press Gallery. O'Sullivan said he had written it in 1951, when he was twenty-three, at the request of the Tass representative in Canberra. He said he thought it would help Tass to get more Russian news into the Australian press, thus helping international relations. O'Sullivan denied that he had ever been a member or supporter of the Communist Party.

Two days later a new document, 'J', was being discussed at the inquiry. This was a thirty-seven page article, in three parts, said to describe Japanese and American penetration of Australia and aspects of local politics. Counsel assisting the Commission, W. J. V. Windeyer, QC (later Sir Victor), had described it earlier as a 'farrago of facts, falsity and filth'.

In the last hour of the hearing on 15 July, Mr Justice Owen told O'Sullivan, still in the witness box, that some of the information in Document J was alleged to have come from O'Sullivan and others of Evatt's staff. 'It is very disturbing that the writer claims to have got information from the secretariat of a man who holds a very high position in public life,' the judge said. Earlier, in response to another question from the judge, O'Sullivan had named the other three members of Evatt's secretariat— W. I. Byrne, his Canberra private secretary, Alan Dalziel, his personal private secretary living in Sydney, and Albert Grundeman, the assistant private secretary.

Next day Evatt sent a strongly worded telegram to the Commission, challenging Owen's propriety in mentioning his staff without, as had been agreed, their being notified beforehand that their names would be mentioned. 'The first that Albert Grundeman and I knew of Owen's comments was when we heard our names blaring forth in a radio newscast as if we were deep in a great espionage plot,' Dalziel wrote.[1]

Evatt's telegram, addressed to the secretary of the Royal Commission, K. Herde, read:

I request that you draw the attention of members of the Royal Commission to the following communication:

Yesterday the Chairman of the Commission was reported as stating that the document known as Document 'J' quoted as sources for various matters, some of which were very confidential, three members of my secretariat.

As a result of this statement I have made enquiries of all members of my present staff. Each one of them has unequivocally denied having given at any time any such confidential information to the alleged author of Document 'J' or to any person. I therefore feel it is my bounden duty to protest at once at the making of defamatory and injurious imputations reflecting upon members of my staff. These statements have been given the widest circulation by press and radio. Moreover the imputations appear to have been made without any evidentiary support and upon the assumption that events and sources said to be contained in Document 'J' are truly and accurately stated by the author thereof. The course taken in naming persons by obvious reference to a small group is quite opposed to the basic procedures of justice which were outlined at certain stages of the Commission. No notice having been given, injury to individuals is immediate and may be irreparable.

I therefore request that a copy of this communication be embodied in the proceedings of the Commission.

According to Dalziel,[2] Evatt decided that weekend to appear before the Commission as counsel for his staff, but despite vague rumours, nothing of this decision was known when Caucus met in Canberra on 3 August to elect office bearers—including the Leader—for the new Parliament.

Evatt's opponents at this stage appeared to be his traditional ones on the left led by E. J. Ward, the Kennelly group in the ALP machine and, perhaps, his ambitious deputy, Calwell. Press commentators said the Ward group would like to get rid of Evatt, but not for six months or so. There was a common feeling in Caucus that—as the slogan became soon afterwards—'Evatt must go', but that he should be eased out gently and with dignity over a period, not defeated by a Caucus vote immediately. Hardly anybody expected a challenge in the first Caucus meeting. There was surprise, and not a little anger, when a challenger appeared at the last minute in Thomas Patrick Burke, the member for Perth.

Burke, born at Moora, Western Australia, in 1910, entered the Parliament in 1943. It will be remembered that for some years he was something of a favourite of Chifley, but that Chifley broke with him after Burke's part in securing the reversal on the Communist Party Dissolution Bill. A friendly, energetic man and trained accountant, Burke was active in securing right-wing votes for Evatt in the Deputy Leadership contest against Ward in 1951. Though the right felt Evatt was a little naive about

[1] Alan Dalziel, *Evatt The Enigma*, p. 92
[2] ibid. p. 93

the extreme left, particularly in the way the left-wing 'old boy network' got to work in the Department of External Affairs in the late 1940's, they thought a man of his stature was worth the gamble as leader—it then seemed likely that Chifley would go in a year or two—and certainly preferable to Ward.

Under Evatt, Burke was elected to the Caucus Executive and became spokesman on finance. It was principally because he held this role and had not been consulted about the promise to abolish the means test, that Burke decided to oppose Evatt for the leadership. He decided to stand, while flying to Canberra from Perth, mainly as a protest because nobody else would. It was a quixotic gesture, unorganised and by a comparative young-ster who was mistrusted by many of the older members of Caucus both for his rapid rise in the Party and for helping humiliate Chifley over the anti-Communist Bill.

Evatt won the ensuing ballot by 64 votes to Burke's 20. Calwell was returned unopposed as Deputy Leader. Then the Ward group won a sur-prise success in getting a tied vote, 43-all, for its candidate, Senator Wil-liam Ashley from New South Wales, against the sitting Senate Leader, Nicholas McKenna. McKenna got back by 46 votes to 41 (with one infor-mal) in the second ballot. It was a surprising victory for the Ward group, however, who now began organising hard for their own 'ticket'.

The left candidate, Dan Curtin, scored 35 votes against 53 for Frederick Daly for Party Whip. Sydney O'Flaherty scored 41 votes against John Armstrong, 47, for Deputy Leader of the Senate. J. O. Critchley was un-opposed as Senate Whip and T. Sheehan as Party Secretary. Several can-didates backed by Ward then won places on the Caucus Executive, and in a minor sensation the Ward-backed Senator Dorothy Tangney, from Perth, beat Burke for his place on the Executive.

Next day the *Age* reported the 3 August balloting as 'a great reversal for Evatt', and many members said it was 'the writing on the wall' Ashley's near-victory 'is held as another victory for the growing anti-Evatt group in the Party'. The correspondent said many members had entered the Party room refusing to believe rumours that Burke would stand. An at-tempt had been made to dissuade Burke, but it was believed the Victorian vote had figured largely in the twenty for Burke. Evatt's election promises had been criticised by many and there was no doubt that resentment at them influenced the vote. 'Many said Victoria and Queensland will never vote Labor back into power with Evatt,' he wrote.

Most newspapers considered the twenty votes for Burke—nearly a quar-ter of Caucus—to be unmistakably high, considering his lack of organisa-tion, relatively junior standing and his unpopularity with some over the events of 1950 and 1951.

Indeed, the implications for the future of Evatt's leadership were im-mense. Burke's relative success meant that Evatt had lost the confidence of much of the right, and it was freely reported that the Ward group wanted to replace him in six months or so. At the same time, the Kennelly-AWU axis now dominating the Federal Executive opposed him. Except for a few personal supporters, Evatt now had no base in the party.

Apart from the resentment at his election promises, the isolation in which Evatt found himself was partly the result of his own failure to build a strong centre in the party. The movement to the left was partly a reaction against the dominance of the right before the election. The lack of social meaning in Evatt's promises, and indeed the lack of convincing leadership on social questions during his leadership, helped attract support for the belief that 'Labor must turn to the left and become more radical.'

The trouble with this theory, which was to become increasingly popular over the next few years, was that the left had little to offer. In Caucus, as represented by men like Edward John Ward, the left was rhetorical and obscurantist, with its roots in the myths of the Australian workers and small farmers of the twenties and thirties. Ward, born in Sydney in 1899, represented something of the Australian larrikin tradition in politics. An ex-boxer and footballer, he was in perfect physical condition even in late middle age. He habitually wore light suits and 'loud' ties that harmonised with his cheeky, larrikin face rather than the tousle of white hair above it. He not only refused to wear dinner suits, but even to mix socially with conservatives. 'The only good Nat. [from the Nationalists, as the conserva-tives were known in the 1920's] is a dead one,' he would often say. He was a relentless asker of embarrassing questions in Parliament, a producer of juicy scandals in the Wednesday night debates on the adjournment. But for all his energy and skill in Party in-fighting, he had few ideas, limited understanding of the post-war world and seemed unable to break from his pre-war style.

Outside Parliament, intellectuals like Dr John Burton were trying to de-velop new forms for the left, combining both the rhetorical tradition for which Ward and J. T. Lang stood and the various Marxist and 'pink' strands which were little represented in Parliament. Burton's book, *The Alternative*,[3] published in the middle of 1954, was a milestone. It heralded the shift of emphasis in left-wing thinking away from aggressive nationali-sation of industry towards a rather anti-Western posture in foreign affairs. The book was ostensibly an argument that communist expansion in Asia was not necessarily 'aggression', as the Liberals and Labor right claimed, but the result of social circumstances. The 'alternative' of the title was pro-vision of massive and forced aid through the United Nations, rather than military containment. But the 116 pages of the argument were coloured by acceptance of many Marxist views about the 'imperialist' motives of the West in Asia, hostility to existing Asian societies and an assumption of mass support for communism. One might summarise its underlying feeling as incipient neutralism.

Interestingly, the book contained one of the frankest—and most doc-trinaire—attacks so far published on 'Catholic Action'.

Economic and financial interests are concerned more in influencing elec-tions than in pre-selection of candidates to represent the Liberal Party, for any pre-selected candidate of that Party will pursue their interests. The Roman Catholic Church has a different problem in relation to the Labor

[3] John Burton, *The Alternative*, Morgan's Publications, Sydney, 1954

Party for it opposes that Party's objectives, even though its members dominate the Party. It is strongly organised to influence, not only elections, but
the pre-selection of Labor Party candidates, the election of party executives, and even the election of trade union officials. In this way it can
ensure that pre-selected candidates will not pursue socialist and other
policies contrary to its interests. At the headquarters of Catholic Action,
which is the organisation established for this purpose, there is the most
elaborate card index system. . . .[4]

But at this stage the left was mainly concerned with emotional anti-
capitalism, a protest against 'the system' and its beneficiaries. Its feeling
about international affairs, in as far as it cared, was instinctive isolationism.
What could be a better immediate object of attack, with renewed zeal, than
the Petrov Commission, with its connotations of righteous patriotism and
action by the security service? And what, in the longer run, than the anti-
communist right within the Party?

While a highly ideological view of the world dominated all these stirrings on the left, there and to some extent in the centre, there was a groping towards a distinctive Australian approach to relations with Asia,
beyond simple isolationism and the '1942 complex'. There was a recognition that land wars in Asia, mixed up with revolutionary feelings, could
prove complex, bloody and dirty. There seemed to be no recognition of this
among the conservative parties or on the Labor right.

Compared with the increasingly cohesive left, the centre was more
numerous but it had little sense of direction and no organisation. Many of
the moderate centre held muted, less ideological and extreme versions of
the ideas of right or left. There were skillful manipulators of the political
machinery like Kennelly and Calwell, who had few ideas, and Fabian intellectuals whose ideas were often irrelevant. Chifley ministers dominated,
and often showed a disinclination to understand the post-Chifley world.
Much of the life of the centre was sapped by a debilitating woolly
idealism, or by an excessive interest in internal politicking. There was a
tendency, especially by natural supporters of the centre outside Parliament,
to be dominated by consideration of non-issues, such as that it was a choice
of 'Rome versus Moscow' or 'conservatives versus radicals' in the Labor
Movement, 'London versus Washington' and 'nationalism and socialism
versus imperialism' in Asia.

In 1951 the monthly magazine *Voice* was founded and it became something of a forum for the centre. But *Voice* itself, though a fair pioneering
effort, reflected some of the faults of the centre and it alone could hardly
restore the life that was needed. From another direction, the *Catholic
Worker*, reflecting the left-liberal tendency in the Church, contributed to
the restoration of the centre, but its efforts were still weakened by a fuzzy
background of Distributism.[5] Between 1951 and 1954, Evatt, whose
natural place was in the centre, showed little, if any, understanding of
its weakness and its need to understand the modern industrial state and the

[4] ibid. p. 103
[5] See also Alan Davies and Geoffrey Serle, *Policies for Progress*, Cheshire, Melbourne, 1954, a Fabian Society publication

post-colonial world. It is surprising, in retrospect, how little the Australian Labor Party in these years seemed to comprehend—or like—the developing Australian industrial society, and consequently how little it was able to identify the real problems and propose solutions. It snatched eagerly at minor recessions and marginal interference with civil liberties, but said hardly a consistent word about education, town and regional planning, capital for national development, defence spending, tariffs, foreign aid, the decline of the public sector. On such questions, its attitude was rarely other than being 'agin the Government'.

The Caucus meeting at which Burke opposed Evatt for the leadership was the first of a series, lasting with few breaks until the end of the parliamentary year, when Caucus was perpetually 'on the boil'. Few members of the Caucus were ever to forget those months.

At the next Caucus meeting, on 11 August, the Party had to decide its attitude to a Government Bill strengthening the powers of the Espionage Commission. Among other things, the Bill, in Section 24, provided that a person should not bring the Commission, or a member of the Commission, into disrepute.

The Caucus Executive recommended that Section 24 be opposed. Executive members strongly attacked the Bill at the general Caucus meeting, but Mullens complained that members had not seen the Bill. He said they had not had a chance to examine it properly. The meeting was adjourned until the dinner break, and in the meantime members discovered that the section closely followed the terms of Section 111 of the Conciliation and Arbitration Act of 1947, passed when Evatt was Attorney-General. Its objective had been to protect the Arbitration Court against the violent attacks communists were then making on it.

The Executive held a special meeting at 6.30 p.m. and recommended to the full Caucus meeting half and hour later that opposition to the section be withdrawn. Mullens told the meeting he had had 'an intuition' that morning and events justified it. But Ward then moved that the Executive recommendation be disregarded, claiming that Labor should not perpetuate a mistake it had made in 1947. Senator J. P. Toohey (South Australia) and E. G. Whitlam supported Ward, while Leslie Haylen, E. J. Harrison and A. D. Fraser attacked him.

The result was a huge vote against Ward—so great that no count was taken—and commentators interpreted this as a personal rebuff to Ward for the intolerant methods he was using to win influence in Cabinet, as much as a vote on the issue. Then Haylen, who had a longstanding dislike of Ward, told Ward to 'stop beating his chest as if he was running the Party'. Ward retaliated by hitting at Haylen—a much smaller man than himself—and Haylen hit back.

Next day the Royal Commission on Espionage Bill came up for debate in the House. Tense, bitter exchanges occurred throughout the debate, with the Speaker refusing to allow Evatt to comment on events before the Commission. Then the Liberal extreme anti-communist, W. C. Wentworth, accused Evatt of pro-communist bias. Ward, following, called Wentworth Parliament's 'chief entertainer and clown' and Pollard interjected, 'The dirty mongrel'.

Following the Speaker's refusal to allow him to speak on the Commission itself, Evatt issued a Press statement outside the House saying that the £5000 payment to the Petrovs, which Menzies had revealed in his speech on the Bill the previous day, was one of the keys to the Petrov matter. The picture Menzies had painted in April, Evatt said, was one of a man seeking individual freedom in a democratic state.

The sinister facts were that the man received £5000 for the sale of certain documents which the Government bought to unduly and improperly influence the people of Australia at the general elections, and that the people of Australia were kept in ignorance of the 'deal' until after the elections. . . . I believe that when the tangled skein of the matter is finally unveiled, the Petrov-Menzies letters case will rank in Australian history as an equivalent to the notorious Zinovieff letter, which was used to defeat a Labor Government in the British election of 1924, or the burning of the Reichstag, which ushered in the Hitler régime in 1933.

On the adjournment of the House that evening, Menzies read out Evatt's statement and scathingly attacked it point by point. It was, he said, 'so hysterical as to indicate a grave state of panic'. It contained 'a farrago of ideas, mostly following the communist line'.

Menzies said any security service had to pay its agents and added:

I would like to say this. The name of Petrov became known to me for the first time on the Sunday night, April 10, or the Saturday night, one or the other, when the head of the security service came to see me with the first two or three literally translated documents Petrov handed over. By April 13, after consulting with Cabinet, I announced the position in the House. On the following day we had established a Royal Commission. Therefore the whole idea of some cunningly concealed plan falls to the ground. If this was an election stunt, then I must say that I performed it very badly. If this was an election stunt, then I must say that it was a remarkable thing for the Leader of the Government to say to every Government candidate that there is to be no reference to the Petrov incident.

I learned about the £5000 payment for the first time on Sunday, May 9, during the course of the election campaign. It is now said that I should have said something about the £5000 but that I should not have said anything about O'Sullivan. . . . So the right honourable gentleman, having enjoyed all the advantages of my silence during the election campaign, is now hysterically complaining that I did not produce the one thing which he may have been able to use and twist on the public platform. . . .

Evatt's reply, in which he said Fadden and others mentioned the Petrov affair in 'nearly every electorate', was equally vitriolic. It seemed that the long-standing and well-known personal detestation between the two Party leaders had spilled more strongly then ever before into public debate.

The correspondent of the *Sydney Morning Herald* wrote on 17 August:

He [Evatt] acted with the desperation of a cornered man when he accused the Government of having bought the Petrov documents for political purposes . . . Mr Menzies, being personally involved in Dr Evatt's charge, had justification for making a bitter reply. But the reaction of other Government members was one of the most merciless spectacles the House of Representatives has ever presented. Government back-benchers, in one chorus, hounded Dr Evatt with derisive laughter, like a bullfight crowd at the death scene.

He also added that the situation was no more creditable to many of Evatt's supporters, who had been 'sniping' at him, though they had been too busy manoeuvring for their own position to attack him at the proper time—the first meeting of Caucus after the election. The correspondent said Evatt and Calwell had 'dropped all pretence of harmony', and Calwell appeared to be dissociating himself from Evatt 'probably as a preliminary step to a bid for power if Dr Evatt's position should come unstuck.'

Parliament rose next day, with Labor members deeply concerned not only over the lack of perspective in Evatt's attack on the Petrov affair, but over persistent rumours that he would appear before the Royal Commission in person. 'Senior party members, when they heard rumours that Dr Evatt might appear before the Petrov Commission, said that if he did he would lose the leadership within 48 hours,' the *Age* reported on 16 August.

The same day Evatt indeed did appear before the Commission, as counsel for Dalziel and Grundeman. It was a heated first day, in which Evatt dominated the proceedings. He claimed that the pattern of proceedings had been used to embarrass him, in that he was not informed of the imputations to be made against his staff. He also brushed several times with the commissioners, on various matters.

The following day Evatt indicated that a strong part of his case would be that Document J was not written, as counsel assisting the Commission claimed, solely by the Sydney communist journalist, Rupert Lockwood. Over the subsequent days, Evatt probed away at Document J and climaxed his argument on 1 September. He then claimed the document was a forgery and that inclusion of the names of two members of his staff was 'the basest conspiracy in political history'. He said Petrov was the centre of the main conspiracy. Mrs Petrov was some party to it, though she may not have supported it all through. Evatt said Fergan O'Sullivan, his former press secretary, had been forced to take some part in the fabrication of it because the Russians had been able to put pressure on him after he supplied Document H (about the Canberra press gallery) to them. He said the Deputy Director of Operations for the Australian Security Service, G. R. Richards, was 'not in the Petrov's main conspiracy, but had been negligent in not having tested the authenticity of Document J.'

Senior Counsel assisting the Commission, W. J. V. Windeyer, QC, replied that Evatt had tried to 'redeem the vagueness and irrationality of his allegations by his vehemence in making them. No-one who had read the whole of Document J would suggest, unless some sense of persecution warped his mind, that it was brought into existence solely to make it appear that two of Dr Evatt's secretaries gave information to the Russians.'

Mr J. A. Meagher, a solicitor appearing for O'Sullivan, said the whole of the evidence put before the Commission supported O'Sullivan's denials that he had anything at all to do with Document J. He said O'Sullivan was now without the means to pay for legal representation, and would be kept interminably at the Commission while Evatt's allegations were investigated.

The communist barrister E. F. Hill, appearing for Lockwood, said Lockwood also had been the victim of a 'foul conspiracy' and that Richards of the security service, at least, was concerned.

The Commissioners would not allow Evatt to see the whole of Document J, which they were treating as a confidential document, but did allow him to see the last three pages, which had the references to his staff. His basis for this claim was, first, that the literary style of 'J' was inferior to other examples of Lockwood's work, and second, that notes in the margin of the pages he inspected were not Lockwood's handwriting. Inspector J. Rogers, the New South Wales police expert on handwriting, gave evidence that in his opinion the handwriting was that of Lockwood. Evatt then applied for permission for an independent handwriting expert, Dr Monticone, to give evidence, but after several hesitations, the Commission refused the application on 3 September. 'The question of handwriting seems to us to be assuming an importance which it does not warrant, and further evidence of that description will unduly prolong our inquiry,' the Commissioners said. In a written opinion offered the Commission, Monticone later said he believed the handwriting was not that of Lockwood.

That weekend, a new sensation developed when Evatt issued a press statement attacking the treatment of Madame Rosemarie Ollier, until a few days previously Second Secretary of the French Embassy in Canberra. On 3 September, the Secretary of the Royal Commission, Mr K. Herde, told the press—verbally, in a guarded house at Rose Bay—that Madame Ollier had been arrested and would be tried in France for an alleged breach of security. Mr Herde said Petrov had said Madame Ollier had given him secret information about loading of arms in Australia and New Zealand aboard the *Radnor* for French forces in the Indo-China war. On 19 May her Ambassador, M. Louis Roche, had ordered her to leave Australia, and she was taken aboard the French liner *Tahitien* to the French Colony of New Caledonia. The Royal Commission subsequently took evidence about her at a secret session in Melbourne on 19 July, and on 22 August she was informed of the charges against her.

Madame Ollier was originally charged with treason, but the charge was eventually reduced to one of 'indiscretion'. About eighteen months after the start of the affair she was exonerated even of this. Quite apart from doubts raised in evidence about Petrov's version of the events, the *Radnor* incident itself was trivial, as the equipment involved was obsolete, the agreement to provide the equipment was public knowledge, and a couple of months after the alleged passing of information the passage of the arms was mentioned in the press.

Evatt's statement said Madame Ollier had been defamed as a spy 'apparently on the say-so of two paid informers' and that she was probably completely innocent of any wrong-doing.

Evatt's statement said of Madame Ollier: 'Today she will find herself defamed through the world as a spy, apparently on the say-so of two paid informers who, on their own admissions, have been treacherous to both Russia and Australia. Surely this is worse than McCarthyism.'

Next day, the Ambassador replied—in a statement again featured prominently in the press—that the French Government had made its own independent investigation before arresting Madame Ollier. Evatt sent a cable to the French Premier, M. Pierre Mendes-France, appealing directly to the French Government to intervene and investigate the Petrovs' charges.

This exchange appeared in the morning newspapers of 7 September and a few hours later the Commissioners withdrew Evatt's leave to appear. Referring to the Ollier exchange, the Commissioners said there was too much conflict between Evatt's roles as politician and advocate. Three-quarters of an hour of legal argument followed, Evatt arguing almost frantically to be allowed to stay, and after a two-hour adjournment the Commissioners announced their decision.

In a statement to reporters otuside the Court, Evatt said in part:

I feel that being outside of the Commission, I am free and under a duty to say this:
During a period in the Commission, I, with my juniors and Mr Barkell, instructing solicitor, have carried the case to this extent—that when the evidence is studied by the Parliament and people of Australia, they will have an opportunity of being convinced that many of the documents in the case have been fabricated and that my clients, Albert Grundeman and Alan Dalziel, are not only completely innocent, but that they have had their names dragged into a concocted document for the purpose of injuring the Federal Labor Movement and the Leader of the Federal Opposition.

A few hours later Evatt flew back to Canberra and resumed his place in the House of Representatives after an absence of three weeks.

The Commission eventually reported that Document J was authentic, and that Lockwood was, despite his denials, the author. After Evatt's departure there was never again any suggestion of fabricated documents.

What stands out about the Petrov affair in retrospect is not so much a sinister quality as sheer triviality. For months after Evatt's departure the Commission went on hearing evidence about document after document in the series known as the 'Moscow letters'. Again and again, incidents which on the surface appeared to have some element of espionage turned out to be inconsequential. Typical was the case of a Russian-born manufacturer who, a letter from Canberra to Moscow said, had offered to sell to Russia a design for ball-bearings suitable for aircraft. In evidence, he said he had offered the design to the Russians only after Australian, British and American officials had rejected them.

The reference to Dalziel in Document J quoted him as telling somebody that a visiting American professor of Russian Affairs had told him that there was a strong pro-Russian influence in Australian universities. Grundeman and O'Sullivan were named as giving Lockwood some piece of information about ALP funds in an hotel bar conversation in Canberra. All three denied the incidents, and the Commissioners absolved them of any part.

In their report, the Commissioners suggested impropriety only concerning minor leakages of information from the Department of External Affairs in the late 1940's—when Evatt was Minister. They pointed out that, other than the Official Secrets Act covering public servants, the law did not cover disclosures of non-military information to another country in peacetime. Since Petrov's position did not cover military information, no leakages of military secrets were ever suggested.

The overwhelming impression one gets from the evidence is that the succession of Russian non-military secret police representatives in Canberra after the war habitually 'padded' their reports to Moscow to give the impression that they were working harder than they were. People who they met socially or professionally, often of left-wing sympathies, were described in an effort to get as many names of 'sympathisers' as possible back to Moscow. Much of the information collected was the ordinary intelligence collected by any embassy, but often with a garnishing of the conspiratorial crudity the Russians used in these matters. The main exception was attempts by the Petrovs to get Madame Ollier to give information about the French cypher system. The author's impression from the records is that she was a sociable widow, friendly with the Petrovs, but often pestered by them, and gave them a harmless titbit eventually as a gesture of friendship.

Should Menzies have appointed the Royal Commission? Ideally, no, since there was an element of smear and embarrassment and an innuendo of disloyalty for the people mentioned in the various documents and called before the Commission. But politically it was easier to appoint a Royal Commission than allow a secret investigation by the Security Service, because of the penchant of all Oppositions for seeking as many Royal Commissions as possible. It is difficult to imagine Labor not calling for a Royal Commission, had Menzies decided against one, and even more difficult to imagine an Evatt or Calwell, with as good an opportunity to embarrass Menzies, not using it fully.

Ideally, Evatt's strategy should have been to laugh at the whole affair and try to reduce its importance, rather than exaggerate it. Quite possibly, as he claimed, he was motivated by a desire to use his talents to defend his staff. Certainly, there was much in his career to suggest both a courageous defender of liberty and reputation, and even more the old professional who could not bear to be away from the action in the courts for too long. Yet he also, objectively, had important personal interests in appearing. One was to shift as much blame as possible for Labor's defeat onto the Petrov affair, since an alternative explanation must have been his leadership. The other was to increase his attractiveness to Ward and the left, who now had increased influence in Caucus and an obsessive hatred of the whole Petrov affair. Generally, it would create an issue around which support for Evatt's continuing leadership could be built.

In Evatt's absence, the Parliamentary Party was little quieter. Most reports at the time, and recollections since, suggest there was little support for his going before the Commission, without serious reference to his colleagues. This was not only because of the political embarrassment to Labor, but because Evatt was needed in Parliament to give the lead in important debates on foreign policy and the Budget. A further point was that conventional lawyers regarded a barrister appearing as counsel in a case in which he was personally interested as undesirable.

On 25 August—the day Calwell had to lead the Budget debate in Evatt's absence—Caucus voted overwhelmingly to refer back to the Caucus Executive a recommendation to grant Evatt leave from his parliamentary duties while he was appearing before the Commission. This meant that the recommendation had been rejected, though not directly. It was a critical censure of the Leader.

Even more seriously, a subject which had long been taboo started to be openly discussed by members of the Caucus. For some time there had been private reservations about Evatt's sanity. Now it was freely discussed, and some members sought the opinions of psychiatrist friends, without coming to any conclusion.

The Caucus meeting of 8 September, the day after Evatt was barred from the Commission, was unprecedentedly tense. Early in the meeting Evatt opened the subject by reporting to Caucus on his actions. He spoke, emotionally and with an unsuspected talent for showmanship, for seventy-five minutes, claiming it was the greatest case he had ever been engaged in. He said it gave him supreme confidence and joy of heart that he had gone into the Commission. The Zinovieff letter was trifling compared with the Moscow letters. Mrs Petrov had probably learned the art of forgery at an MVD school. Ominously, he waved a copy of *News Weekly*, saying it had hinted at the Petrov defection in January 1953. This proved that the knowledge was common in some circles that Petrov sought asylum.

To the anger of some members, Evatt spoke until after 1 p.m., the time at which Caucus meetings had under the rules to adjourn. When he finished speaking Ward tried to move a vote of confidence in him. Members began clamouring for the right to speak on it. Evatt strode quickly from the party room, thus ending the meeting, while the hubbub continued. Shouting down protestors, Ward said it was now or never for the Party to declare its confidence in the Leader. Albert Thompson, an ageing Salvation Army officer from South Australia, shouted that he had the right to speak, and Keon supported him, saying the matter demanded full and immediate discussion. At least a dozen others were shouting their insistence on the right to speak, when Ward angrily charged Thompson with being a party to the 'Premiers' Plan' of the depression, under which wages were cut. 'You ought not to be in the Labor Party,' Ward said. The two then moved together in a scuffle, with other members pulling them apart.

Next day Evatt called a Press Conference in his office and charged that the press reports of the Caucus meeting were not correct. 'I denounce the people who gave it to the press as deliberate falsifiers of what happened at the party meeting.' The *Sydney Morning Herald* said Evatt 'appeared to be excited' and said he 'did not blame the press.'[6]

A similar report of the Caucus incident had been carried by most news-papers. The practice of 'leaking' information from the supposedly secret Caucus meetings to the press was as old as the ALP and all other Australian parties. Both sides would agree that it would be plain incompetent report-ing for a journalist to accept a biased version of such a meeting, without full checking.

Evatt followed with another, extremely long statement on 10 September calling for the Petrov Commission to be reconstituted. He said the new Commission should have five, instead of three members. It should have the power to review the activities and decisions of the present Royal Commis-sion, which had 'departed at times from the safeguards of established judicial procedure'. The Commission had 'assumed such dimensions and importance' that this was necessary in the public interest.

The turmoil in Caucus during September reflected not only the immediate, distressing enough, issues of the Petrov affair and Evatt's behaviour, but more deep-seated differences as well. The changes in the machine and de-velopment of the Kennelly-AWU axis had radically altered the power posi-tion in the Party as a whole, while hysteria about The Movement was getting out of hand. The whole situation—machine, Movement, Petrov and Evatt—had led to a round of faction fighting extending to the local branches of the party, now the discipline of impending elections had passed. Differences over foreign affairs increasingly began to reflect the wider differences.

The first full-length foreign affairs debate since the Korean War had been held in the first half of August, with the House debating statements by Menzies and Casey on the Indo-China settlement. Most of the speeches were unexceptional enough, though both sides were prone to generalities about 'communist aggression' and the assumption that in some unexplained way Australia was threatened by 'aggression' resembling that of the Second World War. This was particularly true of Menzies' statement on 5 August; but Casey showed a much better grasp of the complexity of Asian politics.

Calwell said Labor had been seeking a security pact resembling NATO since the end of the Second World War, while Ward showed an under-standing many would not have suspected in the stirrer from East Sydney. He attacked the Vietnamese Emperor, Bao Dai, who had stayed in France during the recent war, and also Chiang Kai Shek. He showed little enthu-siasm for a South-East Asian pact that included Britain, France and America but few Asian nations, and called for a more independent Australian foreign policy. These ideas were to become commonplace a decade and a half later, but had little support in the Parliament of 1954.

---

[6] The accounts given of Caucus meetings at this time are based on a comprehensive selection of material from the press, checked against the recollections of several who were present.

Then, on 11 August, in an astonishing, penetrating speech, Keon virtually called for a 'preventative war' on China. Blaming the influence of communist and fellow traveller propaganda, Keon said Australians often seemed to approach international affairs with a guilty conscience. He went on:

We need have no guilty conscience when we ask the Asian people to stand with us in the defence of freedom. Some people believe that our efforts should be confined to helping Asian people to raise their standard of living rather than asking them to join us in military organisations. We all hope to help them raise their standard of living, but this is not a world of our choice . . . let us tackle our task with a clear conscience, uninhibited by the fellow travelling, screaming press and communist propaganda, with which we are deluged from all parts of the globe.

'If there is ever another generation of free, white Australians—a possibility which I beg leave to doubt—they will live to revile the governments that participated in the Geneva surrender,' Keon continued. He attacked many of the fashionable, conciliatory arguments of the left and said we must realise Britain would withdraw more and more to Europe and the Mediterranean. If action similar to that taken in Greece (a Western intervention) had been taken in Indo-China, the country might have been 'held'. 'We talk about organising defence pacts and so on,' he said, 'but any weapon is only as strong as the person whose finger is on the trigger.'

Mr Pollard: Why don't you join the Foreign Legion and go yourself.
Mr Keon: I suggest that the Hon. member for Lalor should do so.

Keon said those who placed much confidence in a SEATO organisation were merely deluding themselves. The 'suicidal policy of containment simply means waiting while we are picked off bit by bit.'

'The sooner we begin to look for allies among the countries of Asia and have started in a policy of liberation, the sooner shall we enable the free world to begin to take heart and believe in its ultimate survival,' he said.

Next day Pollard devoted his speech to traditional anti-colonialist rhetoric and Gough Whitlam, in a notably intelligent speech, analysed the nature of guerilla movements in Asia, called for recognition of China and warned that SEATO might not be a success unless it included more Asian nations.

In general, the speeches from both sides of the House had been uninspiring and ill-informed, but among the best-informed and most interested Labor members sharp differences were now evident.

T. W. Andrews spoke on 17 August, and said a line should be drawn in Asia, inside which communism should be contained. While this speech was less extreme than that of Keon, the members who lunched regularly with Santamaria at the Latin in Melbourne showed a fear of communism and its apparent southward spread quite different in order to that of other interested Labor members, and for that matter all but the extreme right in the Government parties.

These differences were dramatised in the middle of September, when the British Labour Leader, Clement Attlee, arrived in Australia after a visit to Communist China. The visit, in conciliatory form, to China and suggestions that Formosa should be 'neutralised' had roused some criticism of the British Labour Party and there was some suspicion that Attlee was seeking to placate the growing Bevanite left tendency in his Party.

The Australian Labor Party officially welcomed the proposed visit, but shortly after Attlee's departure from Britain, Keon had attacked what he called a 'mission of shame', on the Labor Hour broadcast in Melbourne. Then on 24 August in the Budget debate, Mullens made a witty, allegorical speech about a Greek figure named Attleus who, fortified by red wine, could not hear the cries of the tortured and decided things were not too bad after all.

When Attlee arrived, Mullens boycotted the parliamentary luncheon for him on 9 September, after a public statement protesting at the 'junketing with the red leaders'. It had been reported earlier that Keon also would boycott the luncheon, but he went, claiming that a frank statement to British leaders of Australia's perils in the Pacific was long overdue.

In the event, the tolerance and modesty of Attlee's style made a deep impression on members of the Parliament, and when he moved on to Melbourne Lovegrove made a point of issuing a statement of welcome on behalf of the Victorian branch of the ALP. However, a rumour went round that Attlee, hurt by the Keon and Mullens episodes, told Evatt he believed Catholic influence in the ALP was too great.

Evatt had still not finished with the Petrov Inquiry. The Caucus meeting on 15 September—just after Attlee's departure—decided to ban leakages to the Press and members claimed this decision had brought the Party closer together than for some time. Evatt addressed the meeting and did not mention the Petrov affair. Then, quite unexpectedly, he flew off to Sydney and next day his junior, Gregory Sullivan, applied to the Commission for Evatt to be readmitted as counsel. After legal debate and an adjournment of twelve minutes, the judges said nothing had occurred to change their opinion that Evatt as a political leader could not take the impersonal attitude they demanded from a barrister.

Evatt's decision to seek leave to reappear created a furore in the party in Canberra, which was not helped by its ignominious rejection.

'He had played on every man's natural loyalty to avoid discussion of what had taken place in the last few weeks,' the *Age* correspondent wrote on 16 September. 'Almost every man present was ready to accept this for the sake of immediate peace. Later in the day they had been played for sucker by their leader and tempers are running high . . . matters must come to a head when the Party meets again next week.' Three days earlier, the same correspondent had written that Calwell, after his performance in Evatt's absence, 'is now openly accepted by most of the Party as its potential leader'.

In a disorganised way, matters indeed came to a head at the following Wednesday's Caucus meeting, on 22 September.

Evatt introduced the subject of his appearance and said he was making a stand on principle. He believed Labor principles were being upheld by his actions. Suddenly the normally mild-mannered W. M. Bourke once again returned to the attack against his Leader. Standing only a few feet away from Evatt, Bourke said he was taking a stand on the principle that it was unprecedented and wrong for the Leader to appear as counsel before the Espionage Royal Commission. Evatt was the Communist Party's greatest asset. In effect, he had been senior counsel for Rupert Lockwood and the Communist Party, doing the work of the communists and rallying them throughout the country. 'Your attacks on the Commission judges are the most unworthy thing I have heard from a High Court judge,' he said. 'If any conspiracy exists, you are the leading conspirator.'

As tension built up, Pollard said, 'There are some here not fit to lick the Doctor's boots.' He said Bourke had been disloyal to the Party during the election campaign and helped the return of the Liberals by attacking Evatt's means test promises. He was the best friend the Liberals had. Labor members appeared to be forgetting the traditions on which the Labor Movement was built, traditions of justice and of defending a man, no matter what his political beliefs, until he was proved guilty. 'If Dr Evatt walked across the Sea of Galilee, a number of you would say the communists were holding him up,' he shouted.

Attacks on Bourke followed from Gil Duthie from Tasmania, Bill Edmonds, a former AWU organiser from North Queensland and Senator Ashley, Ward's associate.

The debate swung back to the right, with Ted Peters moving that: 'The Leader should not apply to appear as counsel, nor make any public statements on its operations or constitution without the consent of the Parliamentary Labor Party, expressed by Caucus.'

'I plead with you, Ted, to withdraw the motion, or else it can be termed a censure on me,' Evatt said. Evatt said his part in the Commission had finished with Document J, and he would not be appearing before it again. Peters then withdrew the motion, at Calwell's additional request.

There was almost continual uproar, with Tom Burke trying to say amid jeers that Evatt had none of the qualities of leadership and was no good to the Party.

There were shouts that some members ought to be in the Liberal Party, and Evatt charged amid surging uproar that he had heard rumours of a plot to replace him and the aspirant was Calwell. He asked what Calwell had to say.

Calwell said there were a number of factions operating in Caucus. He urged members to do their best to destroy these factions so the Party could be welded together again into a powerful and cohesive force.

Evatt closed discussion on the motion at 1 p.m., after a torrid hour-and-three-quarters, with protests from members who claimed they wanted to speak and that the debate should be adjourned.

The consensus of next day's press was that, despite the tension of the meeting, the question of Evatt's appearance before the Commission was now closed, and with it the threat of an immediate challenge to his leadership.

This was not quite right because Mullens attempted again to raise the issue the following Wednesday, but Evatt refused to allow discussion of the subject. 'What has happened to the champion of civil liberties?' Mullens asked sourly. Evatt replied that those who wanted to talk about the Petrov Commission only wanted to disrupt the Labor Party.

Parliament adjourned for a week's break the following day. Although Evatt's position now seemed secured for the present, in the longer-term he was plainly finished. Except for a few personal supporters, like Haylen, he had no base of support left in the Party. It would be difficult for him to go to the country in 1957 without repeating his promise to abolish the means test, but even more difficult for him not to do so. The trouble with the Royal Commission must continue, for there would be interim and final reports and debates on it in the Parliament; the probability was that these would further discredit Evatt. In the machine, he was losing the support of the right, while the Federal Executive had drawn closer to the Kennelly-Calwell-AWU axis; his enemies would be able to use the machine against him at will.

There had been suggestions after the election that Evatt would withdraw from politics and that some international job would be found for him. None eventuated, but Calwell's supporters once again began to look for a means of dignified exit.

Evatt was thus at the mercy of his enemies, if his career was not to end in ignominy. It had been one of the most spectacular careers in Australian history. The brilliant storekeeper's son from Maitland had hardly known a setback in the sixty years of his life, until the elections four months earlier. Now the setbacks were piling up, despite his stubborn fighting. Even his best friends were concerned at his mental health; a common explanation was that his nerve had cracked under the strain of office and defeat. The great career was disintegrating. Only the courage of the man, the determination and ingenuity, remained.

Part
Two

Once a learned Doctor sat down in Canberra,
He was the Leader of the ALP.
And he sang as he watched and waited till election day,
Labor Must have Solidarity.

Santamaria, Santamaria, Keon and Mullens are faithful to me
And he sang as he watched and waited till election day,
Labor Must have Solidarity.

Down came Petrov, and Menzies was in power again,
The Doctor cried, 'It's a Conspiracy!'
And he wrote out a statement, saying most emphatically,
Labor Must have Solidarity.

Santamaria, Santamaria, Keon and Mullens are getting at me
And he wrote out a statement, saying most emphatically,
Labor Must have Solidarity.

Up came Chamberlain, mounted on Executive,
Down came the Groupers, one, two, three!
Oh, where's that jolly Santa you've got in your Movement,
Labor Must have Solidarity.

Santamaria, Santamaria, Keon and Mullens and Bourke make three
Oh, where's that jolly Santa you've got in your Movement,
Labor Must have Solidarity.

Up jumped the Doctor and sprang across the stormy sea,
Bound for Hobart and unity,
And he sighed as he sang in that very nearly empty hall,
Labor has lost Solidarity.

Santamaria, Santamaria, Keon and Mullens are all up a tree,
And he sighed as he sang in that very nearly empty hall,
Labor has lost Solidarity.

Now Keon and Mullens and Bourke are back in Canberra,
In the Anti-Communist ALP,
And they hide behind the skirts of their Leader, Mr. Joshua,
Singing Labor Must have Solidarity.

Santamaria, Santamaria, Keon and Mullens and Bourke make three
And they hide behind the skirts of their Leader, Mr. Joshua,
Keon and Mullens with Liberals agree.

Chapter Twelve
'Once a Learned Doctor . . .'

During his Petrov troubles, in Court and in Caucus, Evatt had come under intensive lobbying by Ormonde and the anti-Movement front in Sydney. Ormonde was a frequent visitor to the Court while Evatt was appearing in Sydney. The anti-Groupers sensed a possible new ally and Ormonde was able to provide a boost of tremendous importance for his case with a verbatim copy of a speech 'The Movement of Ideas in Australia', made by Santamaria at the annual Movement convention at Albury at the beginning of 1954.

In this typically Santamaria speech Santamaria analysed with brilliant ideological clarity the situation that was developing as the anti-communist battle in the unions neared its end. He said the battle in the unions had had absolute priority, and the next task was to beat, in ideological argument, those inclined to a 'soft', anti-American attitude on foreign policy and reduced defence spending. Santamaria made frequent use of the words 'we' and 'us' and the speech had the clearest possible implication that he expected Movement members to influence the ALP on these questions. It could have been construed as hinting that Santamaria wanted the Movement to 'take over' the ALP, but only by assiduous 'reading between the lines'—a practice that was prevalent on this question at the time, however, and was to become more so.

In one resounding political gaffe, Santamaria referred to the foreign policy softliners using what he called the 'Chifley legend' to reinforce their viewpoint. 'People might not follow Dr Evatt or Mr Calwell, but the Chifley legend is held to be strong enough to make orthodox any policy that they put forward and to condemn any policy that we put forward,' Santamaria said. He said Movement members should work to destroy the 'Chifley legend' and replace it with the pro-American 'Curtin legend'. Within a few months, Santamaria was to be dubbed throughout the country as the man who had not only tried to subvert the Labor Party, but perhaps worse crime, the 'Chifley legend' as well.

About the time Ormonde was starting to lobby Evatt in Sydney with this speech, Broadby had visited Canberra in the course of a routine visit at Budget time, and had spoken privately to several members about 'getting rid of one intolerance only to replace it with another'—a remark he often used at this time. Partly it was inspired by the Attlee visit incidents, which deeply upset many orthodox Labor men.

With this and the attacks on Evatt in Caucus, tension had reached an unprecedented pitch, and the name of Santamaria was being whispered around with both frequency and fear.

On 28 September the Sydney *Sun* published an article by its well informed, though at times melodramatic, Canberra correspondent Alan Reid, which mentioned Santamaria's name in association with the Industrial Groups for the first time in any newspaper. Reid wrote:

In the tense melodrama of politics there are mysterious figures who stand virtually unnoticed in the wings, invisible to all but a few of the audience, as they cue, Svengali-like, among the actors out on the stage. Such a figure appears to be Bartholomew Augustine Michael Santamaria, of politics but not in them, a man dedicated to an unrelenting crusade against communism, reputed by his enemies (who include some powerful men) to exercise a major influence on the course of Australian politics, yet out of the public eye and seemingly a casual by-stander. When his name is mentioned, as it is frequently, by politicians, it is usually in a guarded whisper behind a hand muffling the mouth, for they appear to fear speaking aloud of him, just as medieval men feared to speak aloud of bogies. . . .

Although about this time Evatt appears to have spoken to some senior newspaper executives in Sydney about The Movement, and the need to expose it, Reid's article was essentially good journalism. The 'Santamaria story' was interesting and waiting to be written; the remarkable thing is not that it was written as soon as it was but as late. In the spring of 1954, however, it was a significant contribution to the build-up of hysteria and one whose impact on political opinion did not go unnoticed by the embattled Evatt. It also resulted in Reid arranging to interview Santamaria in Melbourne for an article for *People* magazine, published by the owners of the *Sun*. However there were rumours about this time that Evatt was about to attack the Groupers or The Movement.

Next day in Caucus, Mullens attempted to renew the attack on Evatt over the Petrov appearance and the anti-Santamaria climate was a soothing balm to Evatt's ravaged ears.

The coming weekend was Labor Day weekend in Sydney. Evatt used the opportunity of his address to the Labor Day dinner on the Saturday 2 October, to call for loyalty and justice—an obvious, if indirect, attack on his Caucus critics.

The principle of common justice had become a crucial question in Australia, Evatt told the crowd assembled in the Sydney Trades Hall. 'Things we accepted in previous years may have to be fought for over and over again,' he said. 'Even more important than economic justice is the ordinary notion of justice in the community between man and man. One hundred years ago we fought for it [it was the year of the centenary of the Eureka Stockade] and do not let anyone take away from us the achievements of Eureka. If we give up the search for truth and justice, this community is not worth living in. I hope that in this country there will never be any interference with the fundamental principle of trial by jury.'

Evatt told the audience not to believe everything they read in the news-papers about meetings of the Labor Caucus. 'Two Caucus meetings are held every Wednesday,' he said. 'One is at Canberra, over which I preside, and the other is the one you read about in the Press. Sometimes, I regret to say, they correspond very closely, in which case you can draw your own inferences.'

'We must insist on active and regular loyalty in the Labor Party,' he concluded to the cheering crowd of diners.

Politically lonely and near defeat, Evatt appears to have been heartened by the warm response of many union leaders to this speech, both formally after delivery and in informal talks later. Dougherty, controlling the big-gest single union in the ALP, gave warm praise. Enthusiastic support for Evatt's viewpoint was also coming from other major unions, such as the Electrical Trades and the Transport Workers'.

Next day Evatt had a further talk with the ubiquitous Ormonde and was reassured that a section of Catholic opinion was strongly opposed to The Movement.

In the next two days Evatt drafted a momentous Press statement at his Mosman home. In close confidence, Ormonde, Haylen, Reid and Dalziel, all of whom had had journalistic backgrounds, and others were asked to comment. They assisted him with some passages and suggested changes, but the basic text and tone remained Evatt's.

He brought the final draft to town with him in the afternoon of Tues-day, 5 October. He took it first to a small party to mark the anniversary of Morgan's Bookshop in Castlereagh Street, whose proprietor, A. E. Shep-pard, was John Burton's father in law. He showed it to the surprised, but not displeased, crowd there and then went to his office in the Common-wealth Parliament offices in the Commonwealth Bank building, around the corner in Martin Place. Shortly after 4 p.m. Dalziel, his eyes alight with excitement, visited the Press room a few doors from Evatt's office and told the reporters there that a very important statement would be coming shortly.

The statement was reported in the late radio bulletins, and was the main page one item in almost every newspaper in Australia next day. 'New Evatt Sensation', the Melbourne *Argus* headline said, in a not untypical reaction. In the Sydney *Sun* Reid called it Evatt's 'hydrogen bomb'. It was to unleash such passion and force that the Labor Party would be hope-lessly rent within months.

The text of Evatt's statement was:

The strong and determined desire of the overwhelming majority of trade-union officials and membership for solidarity within the movement has been given eloquent expression at the Labor Day celebrations in New South Wales.

But the matter is of such Australia-wide importance to the Labor Move-ment that I have come to the conclusion that I must say more about the present position, especially so far as the Commonwealth Parliament is concerned.

At the recent Federal elections on May 29 we put forward a policy of development and we polled a majority of the people in Australia. We made gains in every State except Victoria.

All this was achieved by the self-sacrifice of tens of thousands of voluntary workers for Labor.

It was achieved, too, despite the thinly-veiled use against Labor of the opening speech before the Petrov Commission—the statement of which seemed to be distant many poles apart from the truth of the matter so far as it has been more recently revealed by the sworn evidence of many witnesses.

But in the election, one factor told heavily against us—the attitude of a small minority group of members, located particularly in the State of Victoria, which has, since 1949, become increasingly disloyal to the Labor Movement and the Labor leadership.

Adopting methods which strikingly resemble both Communist and Fascist infiltration of larger groups, some of these groups have created an almost intolerable situation—calculated to deflect the Labor Movement from the pursuit of established Labor objectives and ideals.

Whenever it suits their real aims, one or more of them never hesitate to attack or subvert Labor policy or Labor leadership.

A striking example of this at the elections was the attack upon Labor's proposal to abolish the means test. That proposal had been approved, not only by myself but by the authorized representatives of the Federal Executive, the ACTU, the AWU and the leaders of the Parliamentary Labor Party in both Houses.

In spite of that, there were further attacks on the agreed policy. These attacks were eagerly seized on by anti-Labor parties, as though by a preconceived plan, and advertised from one end of the country to the other.

Since the elections, nothing has been done officially to deal with those responsible for the disloyal and subversive actions to which I refer.

In addition, it is my clear belief that in crucial constituencies members of the same small group, whether members of the Federal Parliamentary Labor Party, or not, deliberately attempted to undermine a number of Labor's selected and endorsed candidates, with the inevitable and intended result of assisting the Menzies Government.[1]

Similar attempts at subversion have recently been taking place in the Federal Parliamentary Labor Party. In that Party the group concerned is small, almost minute, in numbers. But repeated attempts have been made to make use of minor and unimportant incidents in the Caucus.

For instance, it was falsely reported to the Press that three members, having nothing to do with the group, were resorting to fisticuffs.

Incidents were deliberately created and then followed by an almost instantaneous relay of distorted and sometimes invented accounts to a naturally receptive anti-Labor Press.

It seems certain that the activities of this small group are largely directed from outside the Labor Movement. The Melbourne *News Weekly* appears to act as their organ. A serious position exists.

---

[1] This was probably a reference to some extreme right-wingers refusing to work in the campaigns of Donald McSween in Isaacs, Geoffrey Sowerbutts in Higinbotham and J. J. Dedman in Corio. They claimed McSween and Sowerbutts were too close to the extreme left. Although some Movement people did not like Dedman, the trouble in Corio was minor and local. Corio and Isaacs were seats where Labor conceivably could have won, but Higinbotham was just short of being 'blue ribbon' Liberal. Upset by the campaign of some Groupers against McSween, Mrs Mary Barry led a team of her own to help him, on the grounds of solidarity behind endorsed candidates.

Since the referendum of 1951 Labor leadership has become very patient with some of these outbursts, solely in the interests of solidarity. But our patience is abused and our tolerance is interpreted as a sign of weakness.

The Labor Party cannot yield to the dictates of any minority which functions in a way contrary to the overwhelming majority of the rank and file of the Labor Movement.

The procedures adopted cannot be accidental. They are deliberately planned. They are causing a rising tide of disgust and anger throughout Labor's supporters.

I cannot overlook the fact that in somewhat analagous circumstances Mr Chifley was subject to sniping and snide attacks which helped to undermine his health and strength.

The feeling of the rank and file of Labor throughout Australia is strong and determined. Thousands of messages have come to me from Labor leagues and trade unions.

They are almost all to the effect that this planned and somewhat desperate attempt to disrupt and injure Labor leadership is really intended to assist the Menzies Government, especially in its attempt to initiate in Australia some of the un-British and un-Australian methods of the totalitarian police state.

Having in view the absolute necessity for real, and not sham, solidarity and unity within the movement, I am bringing this matter before the next meeting of the Federal Executive, with a view to appropriate action being taken by the Federal Labor Conference in January.

Ninety-five per cent of the rank and file of the Parliamentary Labor Party are absolutely loyal to the movement. There is not the slightest reason why their efforts should be undermined by a tiny minority.[2]

Why did Evatt do it? It is not possible now to accept what was accepted by many by the time the dust began to settle three years later—that Evatt was being an honest man of principle, courageously gambling his career and reputation on a bid to check a trend that would turn the ALP into a near-Liberal, if not fascist, Catholic Centre Party. Granted that the activities of The Movement were a cause of concern, the attempt to check it should not have been made in the panic-stricken, unscrupulous and highly public manner Evatt chose.

The statement says almost nothing; it relied for effect on copious use of innuendo. The suggestions are that Keon, Mullens and Bourke, whom Evatt subsequently named, were directed by Santamaria to subvert the leadership of himself and his predecessor. Yet this does not withstand any examination.

Bourke was well known as a bitter opponent of The Movement, and had become much more vehement since its attempt on his pre-selection. Ironically, much of his anger with Evatt at this time was a result of his discovery that Evatt had been talking with Santamaria. The suggestion that the means test proposal in Evatt's policy speech was in accord with Labor Movement policy was not true; abolition of the means test in the broad sense was, but the main disagreement in 1954 was over Evatt's proposals for the timing and conditions of abolition. Evatt's timetable and conditions appear to have been purely his own idea and not made in consultation

[2] Text from Alan Dalziel, *Evatt The Enigma*.

with any of his colleagues. Certainly, several people who should have been informed emphatically told the author they knew nothing of the proposals beforehand.

It is difficult to discover what Keon's crimes were supposed to have been. Although on the anti-Evatt side in the Petrov debates, he was not especially active in them. His foreign policy speech in August and his radio attack on Attlee may have been controversial incidents, and the August speech brought him fulsome praise in *News Weekly*,[3] but neither was against Labor policy. The only serious points that could be made against him were the boycotting of Evatt's referendum meeting in Melbourne in 1951 and the attack on Chifley in Parliament in 1950. These incidents were then years old and in the meantime Evatt had not only been friendly with Keon but had promised to back him for Cabinet.

Mullens' misdemeanours boil down to the referendum and Attlee boycotts and an attempt to reopen the Petrov wounds in Caucus—again, incidents which, though perhaps unattractive like some of his anti-communist oratory, were hardly breaches of discipline.

It could hardly be alleged against these three alone that they irresponsibly 'leaked' to the press to subvert Evatt's leadership. 'Leaking' from Caucus was extremely widespread at that time, as at any time of Party crisis, and all sides were involved. The atmosphere was indeed so electric that it could hardly not have been noticed in the intimate atmosphere of Parliament House. Evatt himself rarely scrupled to use the press, both openly and confidentially, for furthering internal Party causes. And, at any rate, the press reports were substantially accurate, though some may have been incorrect in detail or incomplete, as must happen with information gleaned informally from a private meeting. The 'fisticuffs' incidents certainly occurred, though—as most papers reported—it was a pushing scuffle rather than a fight. 'Leaking' certainly did not stop with the departure from Caucus of Keon, Mullens and Bourke. The fact is that it is such a powerful weapon in a faction fight that no side can afford not to use it.

The author's impression, gained from many interviews and some minor personal recollection of the time, is that Evatt was at that time extremely disturbed. Always an unusually suspicious man with indifferent judgment in long-term political strategy, the less attractive side of his nature became exaggerated under extreme pressure. Although he could be genuinely idealistic to the point of naivety, under pressure he tended to adopt in a clumsy way the cheap demagoguery and bullying that were among the less attractive features of his political apprenticeship in the dark Sydney ages that followed the First World War .

The desire to become Prime Minister in 1954 had become an obsession with him, and with little regard for long-term consequences he adopted dishonest tactics to gain his objective. He had rarely known a setback until his narrow defeat at the 29 May election. The defeat seemed to warp his judgement utterly.

There is no doubt that Evatt believed with a passionate and obsessive

---

[3] Interestingly, it called him Stanley, not Standish Michael Keon.

sincerity in his Petrov appearance and arguments, yet it is difficult to think that he was not also trying to create a scape-goat for his failure in the election. Petrov *did* defect and Evatt's staff *were* named in the documents. The incidents with which his staff were connected were trivial, but so were most of the other incidents investigated by the Royal Commission.

Evatt's continued reverses while he was in a state of shock heightened his natural tendency to believe that there were conspiracies against him and made him receptive to any talk of new conspiracies that would help explain his troubles. This became a desperate need by the end of September. The elements for a 'Catholic plot' could conceivably have been real enough to a man in this condition. Evatt's chief rival for the leadership, Calwell, was a Catholic, as was the persecuting Kennelly, Tom Burke, who opposed him, Peters, Calwell's friend and active in the Petrov attacks, and Keon, Mullens and Bourke. The excitable attitude of *News Weekly* towards the Petrov affair, the circumstantial evidence for links with Security, well supported by rumour, the incidents in Isaacs and Corio, the attentions of Ormonde and Dougherty and a distaste for Evatt by the New South Wales machine were all other elements pointing in this direction.

It is also reasonable, though distasteful, to suspect that Evatt may have been suffering from a deeper paranoia, perhaps aggravated by his recent experiences. His behaviour was most erratic for some years, and became worse after he left Parliament in 1960. His frantic energy and the extraordinary cunning and insight of his propaganda in the years 1954-56 are also consistent with deepening instability. But he did not give the impression of unbalance to the men he was cultivating and using to promote the split; rather, with his patronage, tireless prodding and occasional flattery, he seemed able to inspire them. Cunning concealment of the condition for much of the time would also be consistent with paranoid behaviour. The judgment of mental illness is one men seem more likely to make of Evatt in retrospect than in the desperate heat of the mid-fifties, but never with any certainty.

The statement of 5 October seems to be mainly a rehash of much of the gossip of the Sydney anti-Movement front, moulded to Evatt's purposes of the moment and his Caucus troubles, without any attempt to check its accuracy. The references to unity, loyalty to the leader, the press, vigilance against fascism and subversion of Party principle are the standard, largely meaningless stuff of propagandist appeals to the Labor rank and file. Such propaganda was commonly used after 1954. In fact, a reasonable hypothesis about the years since the War might be that Labor men in trouble tended to go for the pseudo-principled ground of the obscurantist left, whereas they had once gone to the respectable right. A Labor leader with memories of the copious use of the word 'rat' between 1916 and 1939 could hardly be expected to take the rightward course.

Sensing the atmosphere of the spring of 1954, Evatt may even have had no other motive than to jump over onto the winning side, for a change, and identify himself with it. It is difficult to believe he could have foreseen and wanted the devastation that occurred. Some have the impression that he seemed to falter as the strength of the gathering storm became apparent. But once having acted, he was stuck with the situation. He had to fight it through and win if he was not to leave politics utterly discredited. His old zest seemed to return for a while, and for two years he fought the split through with amazing energy, persistence, cunning and not a little courage.

In Melbourne and Sydney, the headlines of the morning press of 6 October landed like a bomb on the Trades Halls, bitterly divided into warring camps. The effect of Evatt's statement was to act as a catalyst in bringing the various streams of discord together in one mighty, snowballing avalance of emotion, self-interest and hysteria that was to feed on its own internal conflicts for three years.

In Melbourne, there was nervous, excited activity for much of the day as politicians, big and small, visited or telephoned the ALP office, while the Executive Officers, with many willing assistants, drafted a press statement.

The rival faction, however, was just as active. Conversations in the passages and on the telephone soon started bringing the pro-Stout men together in small but growing groups. The left-wingers Don McSween, from the Clothing Trades Union, Albert McNolty, from the Sheet Metal Workers' Union and J. P. (Bob) Brebner, from the Pulp and Paper Mill Employees', were active early. Their most notable moderate colleague was W. J. (Bill) Divers from the Municipal Employees' Union. 'Brahma' Davis of the AWU was also active. Divers telephoned the Federal Secretary of his union, Terrence Winter, in Sydney and Winter's office in the basement of the Trades Hall became the nerve centre for the anti-Executive campaign. Contact was quickly established with like-minded unions interstate and with friendly Parliamentarians. Organisation to recruit support for some kind of, at first vaguely conceived, campaign against the 'establishment' of the Victorian ALP began.

In Sydney, Dougherty, Platt and the ETU became the base for a similar attack on the New South Wales 'groupers'.

A Press statement from the Victorian ALP office went out that afternoon in Lovegrove's name:

Dr Evatt's newspaper attack on the Victorian Labor Party displays an intemperance and disregard for fact which is particularly regrettable because of the Party's traditional custom of confining inner Party criticism to properly constituted meetings of the Party. The attack appears to be motivated by Dr Evatt's difficulties before the Royal Commission on Espionage. Victorian Labor considers that it should not be made the victim of a diversionary tactic designed to provide scapegoats for a situation for which the Party is not responsible, and indeed, in connection with which the Party was not in any way consulted.

Lovegrove's statement said the attack had made some public reply essential, and attention was therefore drawn to the following facts:

1. Months before the Petrov disclosure, a Federal Labor Parliamentarian from another State made certain allegations concerning Evatt's staff, and

these allegations were known to members of the Federal Labor Caucus and Dr Evatt.

2. Following the Petrov disclosures, the Federal Parliamentary Labor Party supported the appointment of the Royal Commission on Espionage and has not since sought any alteration of the Commission.

3. The Labor Party, through its properly constituted Executives, has made no allegation of a conspiracy against the Labor Party.

4. Following the last election, the Campaign was discussed by the Victorian Annual Conference in June, which Dr Evatt attended, by the Federal Executive in July, which Dr Evatt attended, and by the Federal Parliamentary Labor Caucus. The charge of deliberately attempting to undermine a number of selected and endorsed Labor candidates was not made by Dr Evatt on these occasions, nor was advantage taken of the ample provisions made in the rules for the hearing of charges of disloyal and unworthy conduct which may be made by any member of the Party against any other member.

5. The Victorian Labor Party believes that evidence before the Royal Commission on Espionage has disclosed a conspiracy against Australia, and that persons who entered this conspiracy should be exposed and dealt with according to the law.

6. The Victorian Labor Party further believes that persons so exposed should be dealt with irrespective of whether they have any connection with any Party or Parliamentary Leader.

7. Members of the Parliamentary Labor Party have complete freedom of discussion in Caucus without direction by the Victorian Central Executive.

8. The Federal Executive of the Party has declared its opposititon to members of the Party attacking other members in the Press.

9. It is hoped that Dr Evatt will refrain from further Press statements and express his views in conformity with the constitutional opportunities afforded him by the Labor Party.

The same day, in Sydney, Short issued a statement saying Evatt was a 'millstone round the neck of the Labor Party', and it would never win with him as Leader. Short said he had once praised Evatt, but had not 'since his inglorious entry into the Petrov Royal Commission'. His statement followed telephone conversations with Santamaria and others.

Any hope of the Victorians that a sharp reply to Evatt would encourage an end to press statements was not fulfilled, because they proliferated in the next few days, almost like wheat pouring into a silo. Evatt continued to issue regular, very long press statements. One might guess that between 1954 and 1956, Evatt issued more words in press statements—simple written 'hand outs' to the press, as distinct from speeches at functions—than all other Labor leaders before him combined.

Evatt's very long retaliatory statement on 7 October said both Lovegrove and Short were ex-communists and some of the language employed indicated Communist jargon. He said a straightforward public discussion was infinitely better than discussion in Caucus, from which 'informers— whether paid or not is immaterial'—gave distorted accounts to the press, with subversive intent. Neither Short nor Lovegrove could speak for the rank and file of the Labor Movement, from which in the last few weeks he had received literally thousands of supporting messages, Evatt said. 'It is plain that Mr Lovegrove and Mr Short were compelled to speak by a political group which is outside the Labor Movement,' he said. 'It is highly significant that in each case the central feature of their criticism of myself, and their implied praise of the Prime Minster, Mr Menzies, relates to the Petrov Commission. . . .'

Other statements at this time came from the AWU leaders Dougherty and Davis, supporting Evatt (Dougherty also attacked Bourke); from various Victorian Labor MPs saying they did not believe the statements referred to themselves; from Protestant leaders attacking—in the 'Moscow versus Rome choice' tradition—'the political wing of Catholic Action'; from Catholic leaders denying that any such 'wing' or organisation of Catholic Action existed; and from Anderson, the New South Wales ALP secretary, saying Short would have to go before the State Executive.

By Friday, it was the turn of the State Executives. The Victorian Central Executive adopted a resolution endorsing, and accepting responsibility for, Lovegrove's statement. The resolution said Evatt's attack was on the Victorian branch, and was unworthy of a Federal Leader of the ALP. Evatt, in reply, said the Victorian resolution was 'against all conceptions of a just decision' and that it had come to its decision without any examination of the matters he had raised. 'Who would expect otherwise from the Santamaria-Keon-McManus group, to which justice and fair play seem to be alien principles,' Evatt said, naming people for the first time. 'Labor supporters in Victoria know that *News Weekly*, the press organ of this inner group, was formally declared to be an anti-Labor organ by the supreme governing body of the movement for its persistent attacks on Labor leadership. . . .'

Evatt said Lovegrove's statement was endorsed, but Lovegrove was 'little more than the reluctant spokesman of a controlling group which is disruptionist of Labor's Federal Policy and assists anti-Labor by condoning disruption'.

In Sydney, the New South Wales Executive, which felt itself to be less under attack, took what the *Sydney Morning Herald* called a 'rail sitting' attitude, and deplored public attacks by Party members upon each other. It did not take the predicted action against Short.

While the controversies seethed in the Press, organisation among what became known as the 'rebel' anti-Executive unions proceeded rapidly in both Melbourne and Sydney.

An original group of six Victorian unions had elected Divers as their spokesman soon after Evatt's statement and on 11 October he announced a conference of affiliated unions for the following afternoon, 12 October. Unions which had recently disaffiliated were also invited.

Secretaries of twenty-five unions attended the meeting, or indicated their support, and with fevered unanimity decided to urge the Federal Executive of the ALP to 'immediately review the position in this State in accordance with Rule 9 (K) of the Federal Constitution'.

This rule, under which the Victorian Executive was to be dissolved within a few weeks, stated:

9 (K) In the case of any State Executive, State Branch or section of the ALP acting or having acted in a manner deemed by the Federal Executive to be contrary to the Federal Constitution, Platform and Policy of the Party as interpreted by the Federal Executive, the Federal Executive may overrule such State Executive, State Branch or Section and/or may declare that same no longer exists, and shall set up in place thereof organisation competent to carry out the Federal Constitution, Platform and Policy of the Australian Labor Party.

Such decisions shall be subject to appeal to Federal Conference, but pending the hearing of such appeal the decision of the Federal Executive shall operate. In the event of the Federal Executive taking any action under the last preceding paragraph hereof, the Federal Executive shall be the body to approve of any selection which otherwise would have been made by the body affected by the Federal Executive decision.

The decision to call the Federal Executive into Melbourne subsequently was endorsed by meetings of the committees of management of many, though not all, of the unions represented, and Divers sent it to Schmella with a letter dated 21 October.

The 'rebel' unions varied in number at various times during the crisis, but the biggest number involved at any one time was twenty-seven. They were sometimes known as the 'twenty-seven unions', or the 'pro-Evatt unions'. Some were communist-influenced, but their base lay in pro-Stout union officials who felt themselves and even their jobs to be under attack from the Groupers in the Trades Hall faction fight. This was not true of all of them, however. Some weak officials seem to have felt they could not afford to be unaligned in the fight that was brewing; that if they were, one side or other would try to undermine them. A form of anti-Catholicism, the tendency to be unquestioning about allegations against The Movement and to associate it with aspects of Catholicism they disliked, was a common motive. Others, as members of the Masonic Lodge, were involved in some degree in the Catholics versus Masons antagonism. Divers himself was a prominent Freemason. Most felt the bitterness of the 'outs' and their passion was aroused by the sudden vulnerability of the 'ins'.

Most probably genuinely believed, in the hysterical atmosphere of the day, that The Movement was a threat to the good order of the Labor movement in Australia. But what should not be supposed is that they had a burning concern for the welfare of the political wing, the Australian Labor Party. Most of the union officials involved in the appeal to the Federal Executive had shown over the years little constructive interest in the affairs of the Party and had not bothered to make their views felt very vocally in the past. Very many were men who had little interest in affairs outside their own union and the walls of the Trades Hall.

This was not true of their leaders, however. Divers had sought preselections for Parliament on two occasions, against Mullens in Gellibrand and Randles in Brunswick West and eventually he became MLA for Footscray. His interest appears to have lapsed for a few years prior to 1954, however. He was close to Stout in the early 1950's, and there was organised—though informal and not very effective—pro-Grouper activity against him in his union. McSween, always a left-wing leader at Conference, had often sought Parliamentary office and had stood for Isaacs in 1954. Bob Brebner was a colourful, pugnacious individualist who usually voted with the left both in the ALP and Trades Hall Council and frequently—partly a function of his personality—clashed bitterly with the Groupers. Davis, a rather cantankerous personality, had supported the Groups until 1951 and fought with them subsequently.

Brebner became Secretary and Divers President of the 'pro-Evatt' unions, which avoided forming other than the losest organisation.

The main unions supporting the 'pro-Evatt' faction were: Plasterers', Amalgamated Engineering, Municipal Employees', Tramways, Teletechnicians', Brick Tile and Pottery, Textile, Australian Workers', Liquor Trades, Boilermakers', Fire Brigade, Bricklayers', Meat Workers', Miscellaneous Workers', Vehicle Builders', Tanners and Leatherdressers', Plumbers and Gasfitters', Sheet Metal, Fuel and Fodder Trades, Clothing Trades, Locomotive Enginemen's, Cigar Manufacturers', Timber Workers', Waterside Workers'.

Divers' complaint to Schmella was accompanied by a twelve-point case against the Victorian branch of the ALP and a ten-point case against the Industrial Groups, together covering ten pages of foolscap. Both give the impression of hasty preparation, based on little actual information and not much careful thought. They were accompanied by summaries, which read:

Against the Victorian branch of the ALP:
1 The Victorian Executive considers the 'minority' group attacked by Dr Evatt to be synonymous with itself.
2 The Central Executive attack on Dr Evatt protected Liberal Party.
3 Much Party fighting strength has been diverted from Parliamentary elections to trade union elections.
4 No action has been taken against Santamaria's influence in Party affairs.
5 Failure to act against 'unofficial' groups in affiliated unions.
6 Party monies have been (illegally?) diverted to assist groups.
7 Victorian Trade Union Movement has declared Victorian ALP 'no longer worthy of support'.
8 Union principles have been flouted.
9 Opinions of membership ignored when Victorian Executive tried to gain a 'yes' decision by Party re 1951 Referendum.
10 Weak Referendum campaign.
11 Loyal branches were penalised: disloyal ones allowed to go 'scot free'.
12 Failure to take action against unfair use of local papers.[4]
Against the Industrial Groups:
1 They lose votes for the ALP.[5]
2 They infringe democratic principles. ('Less than one unionist in 20 is an ALP member . . . this 5 per cent of membership shall control the destinies of the other 95 per cent.')
3 Their rules are totalitarian.
4 They rob union members of the right to control their own officials.
5 Non-unionists help to control ALP Groups and unions.

[4] The detailed case said that Keon and Bourke had used local papers against other Labor Party members. This was presumably a reference to Bourke's means test statement to a paper in his electorate and Keon's influence in the *Richmond News*.
[5] The full case said union faction fights biased some unionists against the ALP.

6 Outsider Santamaria admits 'united front' in Group activities.
7 Groups not open to *all* ALP unionists.
8 Central Executive can determine who has right to vote for it. (By influence in the Groups organisationally.)
9 Groupers have supported anti-Labor *News Weekly*.
10 Gains relatively small—Destruction of ALP unity and strength great.

In Sydney, a group of twenty-four 'pro-Evatt' unions emerged more slowly, allowing the spotlight to fall on the more vulnerable Victorian ALP. Its complexion was much the same as the Victorian group, though its base lay in the old anti-Executive committee headed by Ormonde, Dougherty, Campbell, Platt and the others. The New South Wales unions adopted a more formal organisation, and were known at various times as the 'Steering Committee' and the 'Organising and Convening Committee'. Dougherty usually appeared in the press as their spokesman—and a very florid spokesman he was. The New South Wales unions became more active after the dismissal of the Victorian Executive on 3 December.

The campaign against the New South Wales Executive began in earnest in the issue of the AWU paper *Australian Worker* of 1 December; one not untypical paragraph of the main article alleged 'Domination by anti-Labor opportunists, spawned in the gutter by the Ku Klux Klan Movement, and incapable of rising above their own unsavoury environment.' Dougherty was subsequently summonsed before the Executive over this article.

The Committee eventually lodged complaints against the New South Wales Executive to the Federal Executive. At the height of the controversy, the chairman of the Organising and Convening Committee was R. Erskine, of the Textile Workers' Union, and J. Williams, of the Builders' Laborers' Federation, who was close to Dougherty, was Secretary. A circular letter against the Executive, sent out to secretaries of affiliated unions and branches in January 1955, was also signed, as 'members', by Dougherty, Ormonde, Platt, Campbell, C. Oliver (New South Wales Secretary of the AWU) and I. Wyner, a former Trotskyist associate of Short at Balmain.

The name of Santamaria crept slowly into general press usage in the fortnight following Evatt's statement. Press reports, too often reflecting the mystification of many leaders of both churches and the Labor Movement, indicated a considerable confusion as to what Santamaria and The Movement were all about, and about their relationship to both Catholic Action and the Industrial Groups. The Movement itself adopted a 'low posture' public strategy at this time, partly because of the division in Sydney and partly because it did not wish to provide scraps of information upon which its critics could seize. Its statements were cautious and not very informative. Considering the use in fact made of anything said, this was hardly surprising, but it did tend to convey an impression of lack of candour, which did not win much positive sympathy or help abate the inflammation of feeling. In general, anti-Movement propaganda, spearheaded by Evatt,

Dougherty and the pro-Stout unions in Melbourne, emphasised the secretive aspect of Movement activities, simplified its attempts at influence to attempts at 'control' and represented its views on policy as attempted subversion of all Labor held dear.

Innuendo built up a public 'image' of Santamaria associated with all that Anglo-Saxondom instinctively disliked about Southern Europe. Santamaria had often mentioned that the Lipari Islands, where his parents came from, had had a considerable influx of Spanish blood at one time, and this enabled not only the build-up of a 'stiletto' legend, but coupled with his name an inference of association with the Spanish ultra-clerical tradition stretching from the Inquisition to Franco. The *Australian Worker*, often referred to 'Santa-stiletto' or 'cloak and stiletto', usually associated with the attack on the 'Chifley legend'.

The public quiet of Santamaria and The Movement, however, covered intensive private activity. Santamaria's view of Australia's position in Asia and the threat to his own personal power were cause enough for him to fight back; but the crude, hurtful attacks on his name and ancestry reinforced his determination to use all his influence against the Evatt-Dougherty-Stout alliance.

The Sydney *Sun* and Melbourne *Argus* were among the first newspapers to feature profile articles on Santamaria. Alan Reid of the *Sun* was much the best-informed reporter on The Movement. By a stroke of journalistic fortune, the *Sydney Morning Herald* was able to publish a well-informed and notably balanced series on The Movement within two days of Evatt's attack. They were by its editor, John Pringle, who had been, by coincidence, investigating The Movement for some time and interviewed Santamaria about the time of Evatt's attack.

On 20 October Dougherty published most of 'The Movement of Ideas', suitably embellished with melodramatic comments, in *The Worker*, and substantial extracts were reprinted in the general press. This produced a fairly detailed statement from Santamaria, in his capacity of Secretary of the Rural Movement. It was the first public statement by Santamaria on The Movement. He said:

The picture Mr Dougherty has presented of the activities of my friends and myself is totally untrue. Since there may be some who may wonder as to the facts, let me recite them and make the issues clear. As long ago as 1943, I was fully engaged upon the work of the Catholic Rural Movement, endeavouring to create a public conscience favourable to agriculture and the rural way of life. I was approached by a number of trade unionists, including responsible officials, many not of my own persuasion, with what they held out to be an urgent crisis. They said the trade union movement was already largely in the hands of communists and that if this process was not checked, it would fall completely.

They said they were endeavouring to energise their own sections of the people. Could I do the same where Catholics were concerned? Unwillingly —for my existing work was far more congenial and I doubted my own capacities—I said I would try. From this approach, there was built up over the years a united front of Australian trade unionists to fight the communists in the unions. No one was asked his religion. Love of country, opposition to communism, and readiness to work were all that was required.

The results are well known. Many trade unions, till then securely in the hands of communists, were won back. My own personal part in all of this was minor. Nothing which I did compared with the efforts of thousands of rank and file unionists of all religious persuasions—and of none. Nor was I attacked, victimised, expelled from my union and driven from my job as so many of them were. To say that in this great crusade I was 'the master-mind', as Mr Dougherty does, is to import the atmosphere of the 2d. novelette into a life and death controversy.

It is a very different picture today. Many trade unions, particularly on the waterfront, have remained in the hands of the communists. Use of the sectarian weapons has all but destroyed the unity of the opponents of communism. In those circumstances, those unions would not be regained. In months to come, other trade unions which were brought back will fall to communism again. The sectarian poison will continue to work. Let us be under no illusions as to who first used this ignoble weapon. There is nothing in what has been said by the Leader of the Opposition and his supporters in recent days about my friends and myself which has not been said in the communist press for months past. If all Australians were united, our backs would still be to the wall.

Santamaria's statement notwithstanding, the *Worker* article was shortly afterwards distributed as a pamphlet by the Victorian pro-Evatt unions, under the authorisation of F. Carey, Secretary of the Victorian Branch of the Australian Federated Union of Locomotive Enginemen, one of the more active of the union 'rebels'. It carried on the front page the *Worker*'s flamboyant headlining:

SANTAMARIA UNMASKED! Master-Mind Behind Industrial Groups CLOAK AND STILETTO METHODS EXPOSED.

The Federal Caucus erupted into what had become its usual ugly turmoil when Parliament resumed on 12 October, after a week's break. There were urgent and hurried meetings on the Tuesday, many following on earlier telephone calls, and again before Caucus met on the Wednesday morning, 13 October.

One of the results of these was that Senator G. R. Cole, from Tasmania, moved at the meeting the traditional 'spill' motion, that all positions be declared vacant—the most effective way to challenge Evatt's leadership. Cole moved this in the knowledge that, following representations from himself, Keon and others, Calwell was prepared to stand for the leadership and Alan Fraser, of New South Wales, for deputy.

Evatt had the tactical advantage of being chairman, and ruled amid loud protests that Caucus meet at 9 a.m. the following Wednesday to deal with Cole's motion. Evatt said notice was required so that members could nominate for any position, if the motion were carried.

The meeting saw more angry, embittered attacks on Evatt. The veteran Western Australian, Victor Johnson, said Evatt had been the greatest failure as a leader that any section of the Party had ever chosen. Evatt,

Johnson said, had neither the technique nor the capacity to handle and consolidate a team. Peters accused Evatt of 'running to the newspapers' and challenged him to state any charges. Tom Burke said Evatt was 'weak and he was vicious, he was mean and contemptible'.

Ironically, but politically logically, Evatt's strongest defender was Ward, Calwell's incipient opponent for the Leadership in the seemingly likely event of the discredited Evatt being deposed. Calwell, who followed a policy of neutrality at this stage, did not speak in the debate, and nor did Fraser.

Many members contend that, on the division of opinion that day, Caucus would have gladly deposed Evatt by a considerable majority—a contention that, of course, cannot be proved. But in the next week the 'pro-Evatt' unions and anti-Grouper State Executives intensively organised to pressure MPs into voting against the spill, as Evatt was too powerful an ally to their own factional cause. A faction backing Ward for leader against Calwell also clearly emerged and, needing time, drained support away from the spill.

When the numbers went up at the next, again tense and embittered, Caucus meeting on 20 October, the spill motion was thoroughly defeated, by 52 votes to 28.

These twenty-eight, many of whom came to be treated with disdain as 'Groupers' in the years that followed, were:
New South Wales: Fraser, W. P. O'Connor, D. Minogue, G. Anderson, A. S. Luchetti, F. Daly, F. Stewart, Senator J. I. Armstrong.
Victoria: Calwell, Keon, Andrews, Bourke, R. Joshua, Peters, Cremean, Mullens, Senators C. Sandford, A. Hendrickson and J. M. Sheehan.
Queensland: J. Riordan, Senator C. Byrne.
South Australia: P. Galvin.
Western Australia: Burke, Johnson, Senators D. R. Willesee, J. M. Fraser and J. Cooke.
Tasmania: Senator Cole.

Clarey and Beazley were among key parliamentarians absent from Canberra at the time .

In the fierce debate which preceded the vote, Evatt spoke for twenty minutes, with most of the speech again given over to the Petrov appearance. 'I cannot understand how any person can say I should not appear for my staff, who are completely innocent,' he said. He said *News Weekly* had consistently campaigned against Labor and eulogised Keon.[6]

Keon: 'The *Tribune* eulogised you.'

Perhaps the most violent attack on Evatt came from Mullens who, amid persistent, loud and often violent interjections, called him a 'smear merchant', a 'phoney' and a 'colossal ego'.

The Sydney *Daily Mirror* (which often had good sources in the right wing) said in its report:

---

[6] There were also times when *News Weekly* eulogised Evatt. Over the years, he was in both its good and bad books at various times, but from that day on he was always in its bad books.

There were shouts of protest and some derision, but although an organised attempt was made to 'down him', Mr Mullens declared dramatically: 'If you want Dr Evatt, then you are gluttons for punishment.'

Mr Mullens said that Dr Evatt posed as a crusader for justice and civil liberties and added laughing, 'This champion of human rights—the smear merchant', as he pointed to Evatt.

There was uproar when he referred to the 'noisy lamentations of this man in accordance with the well-established theory that the bigger the lie, the bigger the news'.

Rejecting pleas from some members to discontinue his line of speech, Mr Mullens said: 'This man is jittery. He is obviously moving for a Moscow trial.'

Another particularly tense moment in the meeting came as members were taking their places on both sides of the Caucus room for the division on Cole's motion. Several members hesitated in the middle of the room, and Evatt jumped angrily on to the Chairman's table to watch them closely. Ward, amid shouted protests, began taking names and several papers next day reported that a number of hesitant New South Wales members who, in fact, had considered voting against the spill, supported it in protest against Ward's action.

In the meantime, the trunk telephone lines had been busy with the preliminary organising for a Federal Executive meeting.

A significant feature of much of Evatt and the pro-Stout group's recent propaganda had been to represent Lovegrove as a reluctant prisoner of The Movement, and Evatt had worked tirelessly in telephone calls to Melbourne to talk his Grouper protégé into a conciliatory approach. He appealed to Lovegrove's instinct for secular radicalism, to his difficulties with the more extreme rightist faction in Melbourne and to his sheer self-interest in being on reasonable terms with what must inevitably be a winning line-up.

The *Argus* was thus able to report, somewhat incredibly, by 23 October: 'Last minute support for the pro-Evatt forces is expected from one Victorian Federal Executive delegate, if the Executive moves to expel the Victorian branch.'

And on the previous day, the same paper had reported that Kennelly had left Canberra on 21 October and was 'believed to be on a mission to ensure favourable voting for Evatt at the Federal Executive meeting'.

Chapter Thirteen
The Federal Executive
Moves In

On 18 October—three days before the vote on Cole's 'spill' motion in Caucus—Schmella dispatched telegrams from Townsville to members of the Federal Executive calling them in his own name and that of Reece to a special meeting of the Executive, in Canberra from 26 October. The next ordinary meeting had been fixed for 15 November, but a majority of members agreed to go to Canberra for the special meeting 'to deal with urgent matters affecting the Party welfare'.

The Executive assembled at the Hotel Kingston at 3 p.m. on 27 October. Lovegrove and the new State President, Jack Horan, Federal Secretary of the Transport Workers' Union, represented Victoria and Colbourne and Anderson New South Wales—the only two (it seemed) reliably 'pro-Grouper' state branches. E. J. Walsh, an old friend of Kennelly and respected State Minister, came with Schmella from Queensland. Senator J. P. Toohey and J. F. Walsh represented South Australia, while Chamberlain and a surprise choice of the State Executive, Harry Webb, MHR, represented Western Australia; Tom Burke would have been the expected choice, in the absence of Beazley on an MRA trip abroad. Reece and Duthie represented Tasmania.

The official record says: 'The purpose of the meeting was to consider correspondence and statements made by Dr Evatt, Messrs Mullens, MHR, Keon, MHR, Bourke, MHR, R. Holt, MLA, W. Divers, secretary, Municipal Employees' Union, Victoria, and the New South Wales Executive.'

Briefly, the specific issues put before the Executive were:
1 A lengthy 'submission' by Evatt, which followed closely the pattern of his press statement earlier in the month, but elaborated on 'disloyalty' and 'deliberate acts of sabotage' alleged against Keon, Mullens and Bourke, who were now officially named for the first time. Evatt said Keon and Mullens had been guilty of 'gross disloyalty' in refusing to support his case in the anti-communist referendum in 1951, and that Bourke had been guilty of disloyalty with his publicly expressed doubts on the promise to abolish the means test.

Repeating the 5 October allegation about Victorians 'never hesitating to subvert or attack Labor policy or leadership when it suited their real aims', Evatt said Bourke's attack on the means test proposals was a striking example of this. The Victorian group, he alleged, had attempted deliberately to undermine a number of Labor's selected and endorsed candidates. He also quoted their attacks in Caucus on his leadership at various times.

2 Counter-charges by Keon, Mullens and Bourke. The main point of the charges of all three was that Evatt used press and radio rather than conventional Party channels, to attack Caucus colleagues, by inference which soon became direct, the three of them. Keon, in his letter to the President and Secretary of the Party, said Evatt had offered no evidence in support of his charges and had not taken up a challenge to specify them in writing. 'If the charges have not been made in the correct form, in view of the widespread damage done to my personal and political reputation, I desire to ask that an immediate public statement to this effect be issued,' Keon wrote. He also said Evatt had disregarded Caucus over the Petrov appearance.

In addition to these points, Bourke said Caucus had approved setting up of the Petrov Commission, which Evatt subsequently attacked. He also went in detail, as the major part of his letter to Schmella, into his case against Evatt over the means test.

He said Evatt had promised not to raise taxation, although the year before Menzies had reduced company tax to seven shillings in the pound, which was appreciably lower than the UK and US rates. 'Not satisfied with this unwarranted concession to big business interests', Evatt had also promised to consider an industry depreciation allowance. Bourke then outlined his means test arguments, and said Evatt had not submitted any of the proposals to Caucus prior to the election, because he had been criticised in Caucus for putting forward similar proposals in the Budget debate of 1953 and he knew that a majority in Caucus was against him on these points.

3 A submission through Divers by the twenty-two Victorian unions, claiming that genuine Labor forces could only be re-united by disciplining the Victorian Executive, which had recently attacked Evatt. The submission expressed concern at the disaffiliations from the ALP which had occurred in Victoria and said more were contemplated, all the result of influence exercised on industrial and political matters by an outside-dominated pressure group. The twenty-two unions said 'genuine Labor forces' could only be re-united if the industrial groups were dealt with.

4 A letter from Holt, who had resigned as Minister for Lands in Victoria in 1953, stating that: 'My charge is that the Victorian Branch is controlled and directed through Mr B. Santamaria.'

Holt's letter was 'leaked' and published widely in the press the following weekend, giving a fresh boost to the hysteria generated by Evatt's statement and the accompanying pandemonium.

The letter read:

Dear Mr Schmella: If the Federal Labor Party executive should during its forthcoming deliberations (to examine Dr Evatt's charges about an 'outside influence') have reason to discuss the position of the Victorian Labor Party executive, I feel that the factors affecting my decision last December to resign from the Victorian Cabinet, irrespective of the merits of such decision, have a direct bearing upon the extent to which sectional control has become paramount in the Victorian branch.

My charge is that the Victorian branch is controlled and directed through Mr B. Santamaria.

I make this statement without prejudice and without any personal animus whatsoever. My criticism is not personal. It is levelled against those ideas which are contrary to what I believe Labor policy to be.

Moreover, I have been requested by numerous and trusted friends who happen to be Catholics, to fight against the influence of Mr Santamaria and those he represents, when he seeks to implement his ideas through an abuse of a political movement, designed to serve a truly political purpose.

This statement is based on my own evidence, of my own knowledge, and without recourse to hearsay.

First, I listened to a speech by Mr Santamaria delivered to the National Catholic Rural Movement Convention, at Albury, in the early part of last year. There he stated, among other things, that Industrial Groups were charged with the carrying out of *our* aims and ideals.

Secondly, in August of the same year, 1953, I, as Minister for Lands, was approached by Messrs Santamaria and the Honourable F. R. Scully, MLA, and asked if I would amend the Land Bill to enable land to be made available to the National Catholic Rural Movement, to enable the settlement of Italians with foreign capital on our Crown lands in Victoria.

When I refused to make the necessary amendment, Mr Santamaria stated that I might not be in the next Parliament. His remark was endorsed by the Honourable F. R. Scully, who accompanied him to the Lands Department on this particular occasion.

This I regarded as a direct threat. My convictions were confirmed when Mr Gladman, MLA, later approached me and stated that he was having pressure from 'certain quarters' put upon him to oppose me for selection which he did not think he could resist.

Subsequent events which happened during the selection ballot all combined to make the obvious conclusion that the Victorian branch is not free to implement Labor policy and connives with these methods.

I have no ulterior motive or political aspiration for the future, but I do feel that our task is to make the Labor Party fit to govern by a re-assertion of the positive ideal of service. This can only be done through a party machine, which permits the true expression of opinion of its members, regardless of who or what they may be. The only requirement is loyalty to Labor ideals and principles. This is not possible in the present circumstances in the Victorian branch.

5 A resolution from the New South Wales branch, requesting the Federal Executive to direct members to use the constitutional channels of the Party to settle their differences, and requesting a Special Federal Conference if unity could not be restored by a meeting of the Federal Executive.

This last was the only document that could have been in the Secretary's office before he called the special meeting of the Federal Executive. The Divers document was dated 21 October, that of Holt, 25 October, and that of Keon, Mullens and Bourke, 27 October.

Although there had been speculation about a 'pro-Evatt' majority on the Executive, Evatt's treatment hardly warranted this tag. He arrived at the Kingston on the afternoon of sitting, only to be told that his request to attend and present a document was refused, until the document—summarised above—had been obtained and read by members of the Executive. After members read it, the Executive unanimously resolved, on the motion of Senator Toohey and Mr Chamberlain:

That Dr Evatt be sent a copy of the specific charges that had been made against him by Messrs J. Mullens, S. Keon and Wm. Bourke, MSHR, and that he be informed that the general submissions he had placed before the Executive are not regarded as specific charges and, consequently, if he desires to proceed with any charges against individual members, the Executive requests that he do so in specific terms.

Next morning the Executive received a letter from Evatt, in which he declined to lay specific charges against individuals. For the next five hours the Executive heard the 'submissions'—Reece refused to describe any of the allegations made as 'charges'—of Keon and Mullens against Evatt, but Bourke asked for hearing of his charges to be deferred until Evatt made more explicit the charges against Bourke.

With the Executive having made little progress on the charges either by or against Evatt, the allegations by Holt and Divers became central to its task. Lovegrove and Horan, claiming there was little to fear from a full and impartial investigation, voted in favour of a motion, adopted unanimously, that the Federal Executive investigate the allegations against the Victorian Executive.

Since the first exchange of attacks between Victoria and Evatt after the 5 October statement, Evatt and his supporters had made a point of 'working' on Lovegrove and also Anderson, the New South Wales secretary. They were told of documentary evidence of Santamaria's intention to take over the ALP, and of the complaints against The Movement in Sydney that had led to the breach with the Cardinal. The strength of the AWU determination was made clear. The 'numbers' were there, it was claimed, and there was no chance of winning. But if there was a quiet surrender to the anti-Grouper faction, nobody would be seriously hurt. No jobs would be upset, though there would have to be a reshuffle on the Victorian and New South Wales Executives and of delegates to the Federal bodies, to end the faction fighting.

Horan, in a pamphlet, 'The Broadcast that was Banned', issued in March 1955, said:

There had been persistent rumours and press allegations that even at that early stage, the line-up on the Federal Executive was seven to five against the Victorian Executive, and that it was intended to bring down a decision adverse to the Victorian Executive, whether or not there was just cause for making that decision. Because of that, the Victorian delegates (Messrs Lovegrove and Horan) requested and received assurances from every other delegate that any decision made by the Fedral Excutive would be made after proper charges had been laid and substantiated by proper evidence. Knowing that the Victorian Executive had nothing to fear from a full and impartial investigation, and believing that unity could be achieved by that means, they accepted the assurances given by their fellow delegates, and therefore voted in favour of a motion that the Federal Executive investigate the allegations against the Victorian Executive.

The Federal Executive adopted unanimously two decisions:

That this Executive is of the opinion that the references to the Central Executive of the Victorian Branch of the Party as contained in the written submissions of Dr Evatt, W. T. Divers, and R. W. Holt constitute grave charges against that body which affect the well-being of the Labor Movement; as a consequence of this opinion we agree that the fullest investigation of the Victorian Branch be undertaken by this Executive sitting in Melbourne on a date to be fixed when the aforementioned persons and any other or others agreed upon by this Executive shall be called before it.

That the Federal Executive of the Australian Labor Party views with concern the general lack of discipline which is having an adverse affect on the Labor Movement generally throughout Australia. We therefore call upon the Federal Parliamentary Labor Party, the State Branches, affiliated bodies, and all members to refrain from any public comment or action related to the present dispute.

The investigation was fixed for 9 November, and it eventually started on 10 November 1954, in the ACTU board room, opposite the Melbourne Trades Hall. It dragged on for one hundred tangled hours, and eventually split the Party.

The precise hopes and fears of those guiding the majority on the Executive will probably never be known. It is unlikely that they were ever committed to paper, and memories of ideas conceived in passionate political intrigue are never reliable. From mid-October, Kennelly was pulling many of the strings and master-minding much of the strategy, with Dougherty and Evatt also prominent. Schmella was a comparative novice as Federal Secretary and Reece, a rather gentle man, was a busy State Minister in Tasmania. The next few weeks were to be Kennelly's last, and some might say finest, hours as a machine politician, however, because already a new figure was rising to influence and within a few months was to have superseded the old master in backroom power.

Francis Edward Chamberlain, known best as 'Joe', was born in London in 1900 and emigrated to Western Australia with his family after the First World War. He became active in the ALP in the 1920's but, apart from unsuccessful attempts to enter Parliament, did not become prominent until the war years, when he was State Secretary of the Tramways Employees' Association. In those years he was regarded as extreme left-wing and pro-communist. In 1949, he was elected Secretary of the Perth Trades and Labour Council and Western Australian branch of the ALP, a combined office. He had become, in the meantime, strongly anti-communist, despite occasional apparently Marxist influence in his ideas. Although he was to become a superb committee politician, it took him some years to acquire a 'feel' for national backroom politics—years he spent quietly improving his style and position. But he had an authoritarian cast of personality and was obviously keen to exercise his talents to their full on the wider, national scene. He had acquired a contempt, perhaps inspired by his own failure to win a seat, for parliamentarians, and this strongly coloured his views. By the mid-fifties he was ready to become a national figure, and for two years the erstwhile militant anti-communist had been indicating in private conversation his view that 'we have to get the Groups before they get us'.

All these men were well aware that the Federal Conference was due in Hobart in January 1955—three months away. It would see the permanent appointment of a new Federal Secretary and yet another round of the power struggle between the old Kennelly wing and the Grouper wing. The danger of communist penetration of the unions was much reduced through the work of the Industrial Groups, and a decision in 1955 to restrict or abolish them would destroy the *raison d'être* and sense of purpose of the Industrial Group faction, without much danger of a communist revival. But the Groupers had been working hard, and Evatt's attack had put issues in a starker shape than they might otherwise have had. Men such as Burke and Beazley from Western Australia, and Cole from Tasmania, would be much more involved than they might have been. In short, there were real prospects of a pro-Grouper victory. This gave the anti-Groupers a vital interest in securing a change in the Victorian delegation—which otherwise would have voted solidly against Kennelly—before the Hobart Conference.

No doubt many, if not all, believed an investigation into Victoria would unearth enough to sack the Executive; certainly they must all have hoped it would. A grand strategy was evolved—change the Victorian delegation to Hobart, confirm Schmella as Federal Secretary, end the factionalism with a decisive defeat for the Groupers at Hobart. Then, most felt, Evatt would have to go. He would be replaced by Calwell, a Catholic, and something approaching the unity of the golden age would be achieved long before the Federal election due in 1957, and even before the Victorian State election due towards the end of 1955. Far from being 'pro-Evatt' in any sense other than as a temporary tactical alignment, most of these men regarded him, as a Leader, as a good fighter for civil liberties.

The Federal Executive met in Melbourne from 10 November to 12 November, when it adjourned until 29 November. It met again on that date and continued meeting until 1 a.m. on 4 December, in sessions lasting from the morning until well into the night.

There were two significant changes in its membership since the Canberra meeting. From New South Wales, Kane replaced Anderson, who suddenly resigned as Secretary. Gair, also a much more reliable pro-Grouper, had replaced Walsh from Queensland.

The inquiry heard evidence from twenty-four witnesses, all members of the Victorian Branch of the ALP. The evidence can be conveniently broken into several distinct sections:

1 Keon, Mullens and Bourke pressed their charges against Evatt and defended themselves against his earlier allegations.

2 Evatt did not go on with his allegations against the three Victorians, but confined himself to the Victorian Executive, charging that it was unduly influenced by an 'outside organisation' and *News Weekly*. In his evidence on 29 and 30 November Evatt made a long statement attacking The Movement, claiming that it did not stop at communists but also harrassed left wingers. He said it had infiltrated the Victorian branch, and that the Labor movement could not survive if there was a party within a party. His statement, conveniently leaked to the press, made few precise allegations, however, and offered no evidence of Movement influence over the Victorian Branch.

A second part of Evatt's evidence was Santamaria's 'Movement of Ideas in Australia' speech, which Evatt claimed was proof of The Movement's intention to take over the ALP and subvert its policy. This speech with its attack on the 'Chifley legend', was widely used at this time to whip up feeling against The Movement. Whether, for all the clarity of its analysis, it could be construed as a blue-print for conquest or merely as over-enthusiastic, inept politicking is a matter for debate. But it certainly did not provide any specific evidence of Movement control of or influence over the Victorian Branch.

Evatt said statements made by Keon, Mullens and Bourke would have been impossible had there been any proper administration in Victoria and control over them. These statements included the Keon and Mullens statements on Attlee and Bourke's on the Means Test.

The official Victorian Executive summary of the inquiry, circulated to all members of the Executive, describes the questioning of Evatt:

In reply to questions, Dr Evatt said that he had made his statement to the press on October 5th, instead of to the Federal Executive through constitutional party channels because of the attacks which had been made upon him inside the Federal Caucus and published in the press. A Federal Caucus Executive story re SEATO was also given to the press. Dr Evatt defended his appearances before the Petrov Commission and said he adhered to everything he had said in various press statements. Some of these were not included in his statement to the Federal Executive.

Asked what other evidence he had, Dr Evatt said the composition of the Victorian Central Executive showed that Mr Santamaria's representatives were increasing. Handed a list of members of the Victorian Central Executive and asked, 'Who are they?', Dr Evatt said he could not answer the question because Mr Santamaria's organisation was a secret society. Asked, 'Can you indicate them?', Dr Evatt said, 'I believe Messrs Devlin, McManus, Keon, Scully and Horan are in the organisation.' Mr Horan, who was present as a Victorian delegate to the Federal Executive, then denied Dr Evatt's statement and Dr Evatt immediately accepted his denial. Regarding the other people named, he had no evidence.

Dr Evatt was then asked, 'Did he think Mr Santamaria was a fit and proper person to have any contact with the Labor Party?' He replied, 'I have met him once or twice.'

Dr Evatt denied he had asked Mr Santamaria for support prior to the elections, but admitted meeting Mr Santamaria twice and, asked what he had discussed with Mr Santamaria, said he had discussed the Colombo Plan, Land Settlement and *News Weekly*. He had spoken to Mr Santamaria about an article in *News Weekly*.

Concerning the statement made by Mr Bourke, MHR, re the Means Test, Dr Evatt was asked, 'Did you not request that nothing be done about Mr Bourke after the elections?' and he replied there was an element of truth.

3 Holt, Scully and Gladman gave evidence on the Land Act affair, Holt repeating his claim of Santamaria's threat to his pre-selection and Scully repeating the gist of earlier press statements by himself and Santamaria, emphatically denying it. Holt and Scully were called before the Executive singly, and together, in a quite searching examination.

The Victorian Executive summary of Holt's evidence says in part:

During Mr Holt's selection ballot, sectarianism was used against him. In reply to questions, Mr Holt said that Mr Santamaria had too much influence in the Victorian Branch ALP. Asked what evidence he had that Mr Santamaria controlled the CE, Mr Holt said only Lovegrove's statement that it was no use bringing the matter to the CE and that he was informed that when Cabinet was formed there would be no trouble if Mr Scully was included in the Cabinet because the CE wanted him there. Mr Holt said Mr Scully was close to Mr Santamaria, that the Land Settlement Bill was evidence of the control exercised by Mr Santamaria over the Victorian Branch ALP and the carriage of Catholic school children on buses was also evidence of this control. . . .

Mr Holt said he regarded the Land Settlement Bill as opposed to the Platform and policy of the Labor Party and that the whole Party including the Parliamentary Labor Party is controlled and directed by Santamaria. This was his belief and he had no evidence except hearsay evidence, which he did not wish to submit.[1]

4 Stout addressed the Executive on relations between the unions and the ALP. The Victorian summary states:

Mr Stout addressed the Executive and referred to the tram dispute, the report adopted by the THC thereon, Mr Galvin's failure to co-operate with the THC re the Workers' Compensation Act, the Government's selection of an employees' representative on the Tramways Board, the ALP Conference decision re a representative on the Harbor Trust Commission, the Government's circularisation of members of the AWU, Mr Stout's ticket in the THC ballot against Mr Little when President of the ALP, the Victorian Central Executive's procedure (afterwards withdrawn) for Union approaches to the Government, Mr McManus and the Radio Session, Mr Sowerbutts, *News Weekly*, the dispute between the ASC & J and the communist-controlled BWIU, blamed the Victorian Central Executive for not directing the Parliamentary Labor Party from carrying out the wishes of the THC,

[1] There is an obvious bias in the tone of the Victorian Executive summary, but as an official report of the hearings it would presumably be correct in facts. There appears to be no other documented detail of the evidence to the inquiry. However, the evidence of Holt, Cain and Galvin impressed some interstate delegates as making a strong case against the Victorian Executive.

objected to the Victorian Labor Party's support of the McDonald Government, objected to the Labor Party radio session at 6.55 p.m., stating the majority of unions object to ALP Industrial Groups and said he had no confidence in the Victorian Central Executive to carry out ALP platform and principles.

5 Divers, McNolty, McSween and Parry put the case for the anti-Executive unions, amplifying and being questioned upon their earlier written complaints.

6 Coleman stated the Government position on the one-man bus affair.

7 Davis repeated the allegation that Keon had suggested Bielski form a Group in the AWU. He said Devlin and D'Arcy had also tried to set up a Group.

8 Cain and Galvin gave evidence of relations between the Government and Executive. Cain said the Executive had successfully opposed the Government on some questions, but that relations between the Parliamentary Party and the Victorian Branch were 'reasonably good'. He said there must always be some differences between two such bodies.

9 Kennelly and Broadby gave general evidence on the character of the Victorian Branch. Broadby criticised its record on the recent industrial questions.

10 R. J. Corcoran, Secretary of the Dandenong Branch of the Party, submitted a sworn declaration from his wife, saying she had attended a meeting of The Movement which McManus had attended. A second declaration submitted by Corcoran was from a person who did not wish to give his name because his financial and working circumstances laid him open to suffering. This person was invited to join a secret organisation in the Labor Party, irrespective of whether he believed in Labor principles or not.

Corcoran said he had submitted a number of questions about a secret Catholic organisation to the Central Executive in 1951, after the anti-communist Bill referendum. He said no satisfactory reply had been received. The President of the Dandenong Branch had told him he (the President) had spoken to a member of the Central Executive. The President stated that if Corcoran again raised the question of the secret organisation, the Dandenong Branch would be disbanded by Central Executive.

11 J. F. Cairns, later MP for Yarra, but then a lecturer in Economic History at the University of Melbourne, gave evidence of the closing of the Toorak Branch in 1952. This incident arose out of the Communist Party Dissolution Bill troubles, and is described in Chapter 6, above.

In a letter of complaint to Schmella, Cairns said the position of the Toorak Branch had been before the Disputes Committee for about two years, and this was not satisfactory. He had been in England at the time of the suspension. As a result of the unsatisfactory position of the Toorak Branch, he had had to join the Brighton Branch, when he moved to Brighton at the end of 1953, as a new member. This was by the decision of the Brighton Branch Secretary, Mr Dunn, and the result was that Cairns had no continuity of membership.

I have the impression that somewhere in the ALP machinery there are people who were concerned to destroy the Toorak branch because of embarrassment its members might have caused, Cairns wrote. This impression I have known to be shared by others. It is undesirable that a situation giving rise to impressions of this nature should be allowed to continue for over three years without determination.

In addition to these letters, there were also letters from branch members complaining about suspension of the Mount Dandenong Branch in 1950, a row with Lovegrove over membership tickets in the Healesville Branch and dismissal by the Executive, without precise reasons, of a complaint alleging abuses in the July 1954 pre-selection ballot for the Southern Legislative Council Province. The other two complaints also had their background in factional competition in pre-selection and imputed a bias by the Central Executive towards pro-Executive candidates.

12 Devlin and D'Arcy answered questions on Davis's allegations of interference in the AWU, substantially denying his charges.

13 McManus answered questions about the Victorian Branch, and denied allegations of Movement control or influence.

14 Little gave evidence about the dispute in the Mount Dandenong Branch controversies.

Finally, Lovegrove and Horan presented a case in defence of the Victorian branch, stressing its successful record in both general and trade union elections and the industrial legislation the Cain Government had introduced during two years of office.

The evidence was entirely lacking in any proof, as distinct from assertions, of control or substantial influence in the branch by The Movement. In any strict sense, the allegation simply was not true, though The Movement was a powerful influence moulding the overall character of the branch.

The Victorian Executive of that year contained six members of The Movement—McManus, Roberts, Scully, Frank Reilly, Travers and Devlin. A careful study of the records over several years indicated that these, and other Movement men such as D'Arcy, did not act at all as a team. On the rare issues where a Movement 'line' might have been expected, such as the disciplining of Holt and McSween, they were to be found on different sides. Travers, for instance, supported a conciliatory approach to McSween's statement on Industrial Groups, while Devlin opposed Keon's motion for the Holt affair to come before the Executive. Roberts, Reilly and D'Arcy had been rather quiet members of the Executive, while Scully had been a member only since June, when his union, the ARU, attended Conference for the first time since the war. On the Executive, McManus usually adopted a conciliatory attitude, being adept at the modifying amendment or the gentler rephrasing to take the edge off controversy.

The 'militants' of the Executive, as far as they could be singled out in a fairly homogeneous body, were Keon, Peters, Little, Devlin and Travers. Only the last two were in The Movement.

With no evidence of Movement control, the task of the Federal Executive became mainly political rather than judicial. Obviously there was a *prima facie* case of grave dissension in the Victorian Branch. The evidence given before the inquiry, however, could amount to no more than this. A proper sifting of all the available evidence would have taken an inquiry on the scale of the Petrov Commission, with the same length of sitting, legal representation and background research.

Already, Reece had had to return to Tasmania for a period for a personal bereavement and a just inquiry would have been quite beyond the resources in money and in time of the members of the Executive, few of whom could spare more than a few days away from their home cities.

The slightness of the evidence against the Victorian Branch had caused considerable hesitation about the future course during the hearing, and there were several reports in the press from usually well-informed journalists that the charges would collapse. However, in the overall political situation a number of other factors commanded attention:

1 The compelling attractions of Kennelly's grand strategy for unifying the Party, with a defeat for the Groupers at Hobart.

2 The Sydney and Melbourne groups of 'rebel' unions and the AWU nationally had informally threatened to disaffiliate from the Party, unless the Victorian Executive was dismissed. The Victorian unions had even threatened to set up a rival Industrial Labor Party. Whichever course the Executive took, it would be risking a split, but the threat from the left may have seemed greater than that from the right.

The Sydney 'rebel' unions sent Dougherty, Platt and Campbell to Melbourne early in the inquiry. They set up headquarters at the Melbourne Trades Hall and lobbied intensively for several days.

The threat of the AWU to disaffiliate could not be taken other than extremely seriously in Queensland, South Australia and Western Australia, where it provided a major part of the financial and organisational backing of the Party. The AWU had already disaffiliated in Tasmania, in a dispute with the State Government. As a former organiser for the union, Reece had excellent prospects of bringing it back into the Party there when, as seemed soon likely, he succeeded to the Premiership.

3 A new Executive in Victoria could include Calwell and Kennelly, increasing their strength Federally and placing Calwell in a good position for the Leadership.

4 Broadby had indicated dissatisfaction by the ACTU with conditions in Victoria.

5 The atmosphere of mounting suspicion and hysteria about The Movement, particularly that generated by free distribution of 'The Movement of Ideas' speech, had produced a situation where some kind of action was needed. A back-down would have gravely weakened the anti-Grouper faction's position. Under pressure, Group supporters were admitting very little about The Movement. The seeming lack of candour created the suspicion that the truth was not being told. In particular, the Groupers dismissed the 'Movement of Ideas' as having been 'circulated by the Communists on the Yarra Bank 18 months ago'.

6 Men from the smaller states were genuinely shocked by the rancour, discord and high-handedness they found in Melbourne. It contrasted sharply with the more gentle and intimate climate of their own Labor politics.

7 Chamberlain, not by nature a compromising man nor one to care greatly about the fate of politicians, had begun to emerge in Melbourne as a commanding figure on the Federal Executive.

8 Skilful press leaks had created a public opinion for action. There was just enough publicity to keep the pot of sectarian suspicion simmering, and to let Catholics know its power, without it being heated sufficiently to boil over.

9 The whole situation was affected by lack of a strong fight by the Victorian Executive. Lovegrove, believing he knew the rules of the game and subject to intense lobbying by Evatt, had advised against any organised opposition. He believed the temperature should be kept down, the coup accepted and that the crisis would work itself out within a few months.

It is not possible to more than guess at which of these factors carried the greater weight. Nor is it possible to know what transpired at the secret meetings, informal conversations and on the innumerable long-distance and intra-city telephone calls.

The culmination of the hundred-hour investigation is described by Horan in his pamphlet 'The Broadcast That Was Banned':

Mr Chamberlain was absent from the Federal Executive meeting during most of the time that Messrs Lovegrove and Horan were replying to the submissions made against the Victorian Executive and at the conclusion of the session at 10.35 that evening, announced that he had prepared a document which he would present to the Executive for discussion the next morning. That document was discussed and amended in some respects. The contentious portions were carried by seven votes to five.

Mr Chamberlain and Senator Toohey both said that no evidence which could be taken into account by any judicial body was presented against the Victorian Executive, but a 'frame of mind' which was adverse to the Victorian Executive had been created.

Briefly, the Federal Executive's decision was to hold a Special Conference of the Victorian Branch on 26 and 27 February to elect a new State Executive. The Federal Executive was to supervise the Conference and the rules were to be amended for the Conference to allow as delegates people without the usual Victorian qualification of two years continuous membership of the Party; in effect, delegates would be eligible if they joined the ALP on the day of the Conference. Affiliated unions were directed to hold new elections of Conference delegates.

Evatt's allegations against Keon, Mullens and Bourke, which had started the whole crisis, were virtually dismissed, on the grounds that Evatt had made no specific charge. (See Appendix for text of the finding.)

The suspension of the two-year membership rule was devised by Chamberlain, in association with various Victorians, as a means of obtaining the 'numbers' at the Special Conference to elect a broader Executive and an at least partly anti-Grouper delegation for Hobart. It would enable the secretaries of several key unions, which previously had been politically apathetic, to ensure a reliably anti-Grouper vote from their delegations at Conference by a more careful selection of delegates.

The Executive set the date for the Federal Conference at 14 March 1955, although it had been originally intended for the middle of January. It gave no reason for the postponement—but the obvious one was that the Federal Conference should be after the Victorian Special Conference, so a predominantly anti-Grouper delegation would come from Victoria. Another decision was that unions which had disaffiliated in the preceding twelve months would be invited to attend the Special Conference—in effect an invitation to the AWU to come back.

The jobs of the three paid members of the Executive, Lovegrove, McManus and the Women's Organiser, Mrs Barry, were to be preserved, but all other positions on the Executive would be declared vacant at 9 a.m. on the morning of the Special Conference. All present members of the Executive, however, would be eligible for re-election.

In a final decision, the Executive ordered that the provision in the Victorian Constitution governing Industrial Groups be deemed to be non-existent after 31 December 1954. The effect of this would be to withdraw ALP official backing for the Groups and leave them as mere bodies of individuals. The Executive said it would submit a recommendation to the Federal Conference on the overall question of Industrial Groups.

Chapter Fourteen
The Long,
Hot Summer

Hardly had the ten interstate members of the Federal Executive packed their bags and left Melbourne on the morning of Saturday, 4 December, when the shape of the great split that was to take place became clearer. Already that weekend, events began to polarise around the two figures of Evatt and Archbishop Mannix.

Although the Federal Executive had repeated its ban against party members making public statements, Evatt issued a statement saying that the organised groups and individuals who were exercising influence on the ALP from outside in many cases had objectives foreign to Labor and, operating secretly, had the effect of a fifth column operating within the Labor movement. Evatt said he had received thousands of letters from Labor branches and unions and from men and women who constituted the heart of Labor. These, he said, convinced him that Labor people were overwhelmingly in favour of revitalising the Labor party on the basis of the principles and platform embodied in the party's constitution for the benefit of the Australian people. The Federal Executive had set the democratic machinery in motion to give the rank and file of unionists and genuine Labor people an opportunity again to control the Labor movement. He added: 'Labor is opposed to all forms of totalitarianism, communism, fascism or McCarthyism.'

Archbishop Mannix, in an address, said the anti-communist industrial groups had the backing of every Catholic bishop in Australia. He said that whether the bishops did or did not get the commendation of political parties or industrial authorities made no difference. If the groups had not been organised to do in the unions against communists what communists had been doing against them and the community, Australia would have fallen under the domination of atheistic communists directed by Soviet Russia. The ninety-year-old archbishop said the groups might be hampered, but the fight against communists would go on.

On 9 December the seven functioning ALP Industrial Groups in Victoria met at the Trades Hall and adopted a resolution condemning the Federal Executive order as unconstitutional. The resolution said in part:

Through our own bitter experience gained in this struggle over a period of years we have become firmly convinced that communism in the trade unions can be matched and defeated only by a strongly organised fighting body.

The proposed withdrawal of Labor's forces from the unions is tantamount to an expression of apathy towards the outcome of this struggle.

The seven groups operating at that time in Victoria were in the Australian Railways Union, the Federated Clerks' Union, Federated Ironworkers' Association, Amalgamated Society of Carpenters and Joiners, Electrical Trades Union, Tramways Employees' Association and the Waterside Workers' Federation. There were about 350 members in the seven groups.

Next night a deputation from the Groups waited on the Central Executive, with a protest against the Federal Executive order dissolving them. The members of this delegation were: V. Crosbie (ETU), R. Saker (Clerks), J. Neill (ARU), P. Gleeson (WWF) and J. McDonald (Tramways), with Neill and Saker the spokesmen.

The Executive then adopted a resolution—introduced by Peters and shaped through amendments with the assistance of Little, Keon, Brennan, Devlin and Lovegrove—condemning the Federal Executive action, claiming the Groups were the only effective reply to organised communist activity in the unions and expressing gratitude to Group members for their work. The resolution said the disappearance of the Groups must inevitably lead to a great expansion of communist influence in the unions. Ominously, Cain and Cameron spoke against it.

On the motion of Woodhouse, the Executive then decided to call a meeting of affiliated branches and unions on Sunday, 19 December, to hear a report from the Executive and discuss further action.

In the meantime Keon, in defiance of the Federal Executive ban on public statements, had issued a press statement on 7 December saying, in part:

Not one tittle of evidence was produced to substantiate the fantastic charges made by Dr Evatt of conspiracy and disloyalty against him.

In my own case, despite headlines throughout Australia naming me as one of the accused, the only charges with which I was confronted were allegations that three years ago in Sydney I asked a New Australian organiser of the Australian Workers' Union to come to Victoria for a few weeks to help the Railways Union's Industrial Group candidates in the election campaign; and that I criticised to this organiser the Victorian secretary of the AWU, Mr H. O. Davis.

In the face of nonsense such as this, the Federal Executive has torn up the rules of the Australian Labor Party in Victoria.

In Sydney, on 14 December, the New South Wales 'rebel' unions held a meeting at which Dougherty issued a list of seventeen members of the New South Wales Central Executive who, he claimed, were in The Movement. A third of these turned out to be Protestants, some members of the Masonic Lodge. About the same time, Short said in Sydney that the Victorian branch of the Ironworkers' Union was prepared to pay the cost of any legal challenge to holding of the Victorian Special Conference.

The meeting of Victorian branches and unions—each of which was invited to send two delegates—took place at the Trades Hall on 19 December, with a large crowd but both factions claiming different results. Executive and Industrial Group supporters claimed fifty of the seventy-five affiliated unions were represented, but Brebner claimed only twenty-five were present, meaning success for a boycott organised by the 'rebel' group.

Lovegrove, Horan and Cain reported to the meeting, with Lovegrove's rhetoric at its most savage against the opponents of the Groups and Executive.

The meeting adopted a resolution agreeing that a Special Conference of the Victorian Branch was needed, but condemning in detail the Federal Executive proposal that non-members of the ALP and members without two years standing could attend as delegates. The resolution claimed this provision would open the way to communists and liberals attending and passing judgment on ALP men. 'This meeting therefore is of the opinion that the Victorian Central Executive should request the Federal Executive to reconsider its decision not later than 31 January 1955, and failing action by the Federal Executive, Federal Conference should convene to determine the matter prior to the Victorian Special Conference,' the resolution concluded.

This resolution indicated the two main lines of Victorian strategy that were emerging: to have the new membership provision for the Special Conference dropped; and to try to circumvent the Federal Executive by going to the Federal Conference, where Group supporters would quite possibly have 'the numbers'.

Peters and Lovegrove reported to the Victorian Central Executive meeting on 22 December, and on the motion of Woodhouse the resolution of the 19 December meeting was endorsed. Clarey opposed the motion, a further indication of the split developing.

The Christmas and New Year holidays then intervened, and the troubles of the ALP went beneath the surface for three weeks, only to re-emerge more intensely in the second week of the disastrous year of 1955.

When the holiday season started, the expectation on all sides was that the factions would attend the Special Conference and seek to win. The Groupers seemed fairly certain they would win at least a majority of places on the Executive and in the delegations for the Federal Conference and Executive. The size of their majorities in previous years suggested this result, even with the AWU back and tightening of opposition union delegations through the relaxed membership conditions.

During the holidays, however, word got around that the anti-Grouper forces proposed to credential non-members of the ALP as delegates to the Conference, as an extra measure to secure the most reliable possible delegations from the unions now in the process of re-electing or re-appointing their teams. This appears to have been confirmed in unofficial discussions. It alarmed and infuriated many Groupers, who expected to find communists attending as delegates and possibly defeating them. A close study of the wording of the Federal Executive decision suspending the two-year membership rule showed this was permissible, if not expected.

The fear also began to grow among the Groupers that if they allowed non-members to attend as delegates their opponents would stop at nothing to win, with the Federal Executive simply making and interpreting the rules to suit itself. The idea began to evolve that the Conference should be boycotted, to avoid giving it 'respectability'. Those supporting the boycott idea felt several other moves could be taken, in preference to attending the Conference. For instance, the Executive and delegates elected by the regular June Conference of the Victorian Branch could attend the March Federal Conference in Hobart. As Federal Conference was the supreme body of the Party, they could ask it to choose between the two Victorian teams that would be present in Hobart. There was a 1927 precedent for allowing the other five state teams to judge on a disputing state—in that year, New South Wales.

The threat alone of such a course would give valuable bargaining heft in the weeks before the Special Conference and might induce the anti-Groupers to back down.

It was also suggested that there could be a legal challenge to the powers of the Federal Executive to hold the Special Conference, on the grounds of the superior powers of the older, stronger Victorian Branch. And, if a split did develop, the Victorian political wing could be expected to remain solid and team up with New South Wales and sufficiently sympathetic elements elsewhere to provide a more electorally appealing Party than the Evatt-Stout-Chamberlain-Kennelly forces. The threat of this should be sufficient to deter Cain and other Federal and State parliamentarians from conniving in a split in an attempt to get the upper hand. Another suggestion was that if there was any pre-emptive action against pro-Grouper State parliamentarians, the Governor could be asked to withdraw Cain's mandate to govern, as he would have lost his majority. If this happened before Hobart, it would tend to force the Federal Conference into a compromise.

These apparent options all proved illusory, but they had seemed a convincing argument for a boycott in the summer of 1954-55. The strategy evolved in unrecorded private conversations and small meetings, hot with emotion and uncertainty. Keon, Santamaria, Horan, McManus and Scully were among those who pressed for it, mainly in the expectation that it was the course most likely to bring victory. By steadily widening the circle of those supporting the move, and using all the pressures available to them, they were able to be fairly sure of having 'the numbers' for the Executive to support a boycott.

The chief opponent of the boycott move in their own ranks was Lovegrove, who claimed it would amount to surrendering or cause a split. He claimed the Groupers could win and persisted in the belief that at any rate they should lie low until the storm passed. Though at times he showed fury against the Kennelly-Stout forces, he had been adamant for weeks about the conciliatory course and this led to a breakdown in the Grouper majority's trust for him. He became the negotiator between the two sides in January and February, but both appeared not to fully trust him and this seems to have been a factor in the continuing failure of negotiations in those weeks.

The pro-boycott forces chose T. W. Brennan, a relatively uncontroversial figure, to move for the boycott at the first Executive meeting after the Christmas-New Year break.

When the Executive met on 14 January, A. T. Brodney, the senior partner in Maurice Blackburn and Company, the ALP solicitors, addressed members on legal implications of the crisis. Then, immediately, Brennan produced and moved the following typewritten motion, to the surprise and anger of those who were expected not to agree:

That in view of the resolution of this Victorian Central Executive of 22 December 1954, and having regard to the demands of the Victorian, New South Wales and Queensland branches for an earlier meeting of the Federal Conference to resolve the crisis in the Party, and pending clarification of the legal difficulties in which the Victorian branch is involved as a result of the Federal Executive decisions, branches and affiliated unions be instructed to defer until further notice any arrangements now being made for the selection of delegates.

Frank Reilly seconded the motion, but in the long debate that followed only Woodhouse, Keon and McManus supported it. Lovegrove, Peters, Fred Riley, Kyle, Cain and Clarey all opposed it, but the 'numbers' were there and it was adopted by 14 votes to 7. This was the critical vote which was to lead directly to the ensuing split and formation of the Democratic Labor Party.

At this time, two broad attitudes had developed within the Victorian Executive, and were widely reflected throughout the Labor Party. The first was that of The Movement, Keon, McManus, the Scully and Barry factions in State Caucus, and Industrial Group leaders such as Woodhouse and Neill. This view was that Chamberlain and Stout could not be trusted to run a fair Conference; that opponents of the Groups would 'stack' union delegations with left-wingers; and that attendance at the Special Conference would give it respectability, and the chances for fighting on with legal challenges or a breakaway party would be eliminated. It was felt that public opinion would support the more anti-communist party if it ever came to an election.

There was a strong feeling that the Industrial Groups would have to be protected and preserved to complete the job of eliminating Communist influence in Australian unions, and to fend off the planned campaign of the Communist Party to win back its lost power. With some, though by no means all, of these people, the fear of Asian communism propagated by The Movement was a strong consideration; they felt that remaining communist influence in the electricity generating plants, the metal trades and on the wharves would weaken Australian defence preparedness. The attitude of Kennelly, Evatt and the others to foreign policy was thoroughly mistrusted. Essentially the support for a boycott came from those under attack and threatened with loss of influence: The Movement, rightists such as Keon, and Industrial Group leaders who would be deprived of their special role and backing. The Catholic instinct, as a minority group in the community, to show a united front in troubles was an immediate factor.

The main proponents of the other viewpoint were Lovegrove, Cain, Clarey and Broadby. They believed, in various ways, that the ALP had got out of balance during the Industrial Group era. Cain bitterly mistrusted Keon, Scully and Santamaria and all they stood for. Broadby and Clarey, expressing the view of the ACTU and much of the traditional industrial right, were concerned about the influence of The Movement in the Groups, about the climate of intolerance surrounding the Groups and their effect on trade union power lines. Kennelly and Evatt had 'worked' on them thoroughly. Lovegrove was concerned with his lack of control of the Victorian Executive and the zeal of men such as Devlin, and was committed to the idea that the troubles should not be inflated by a fight that could not be won.

These men believed that the old system was finished, and that they should work for a compromise Executive in which four to five of the extreme right wing and Movement men would be dropped and replaced by representatives of the left, the AWU and the Trades Hall Council. No doubt it occurred to these men in the middle that such an arrangement would give them the balance of power.

Lovegrove at that time argued that, on a realistic assessment of how union delegations would be re-shaped for the Special Conference, the old Industrial Group faction would have a majority of at least fifteen, but that the compromise solution he favoured would find a big majority. Other assessments of the likely 'numbers' even suggested that the Industrial Group faction, which had controlled the 1954 regular Conference by nearly four votes to one, would have retained comfortable control of the Special Conference. Part of this argument is that while pro-Stout unions would be able to handpick 'reliables' for their delegations, there would have been considerable room for the Groupers also to tighten their delegations. Certainly, some Grouper assessments were at the extreme pessimistic end of the spectrum.

Representation at ALP Conferences was in direct proportion to union membership, giving control to the big unions such as the Railways, Clerks', Ironworkers' and Amalgamated Engineering Union, which the Groupers controlled or influenced. Trades Hall Council representation, however, limited unions to a maximum of four delegates. This gave greater power to the small unions, explaining the differences in relative strength on the two Trades Hall bodies.

The two broad views about the Special Conference, already well formed, hardened into rigid, mutually mistrusting factions after 14 January. With the lack of trust, communication between them broke down and personal animosities intensified. Even the friendship and good working relationship of Lovegrove and McManus, which had endured since 1950, broke down in deep mistrust.

The sectarian shape that the dispute was inevitably taking, further hardened the factions. The 'compromise' group was mainly non-Catholic, though Peters and Hoban were regarded as possible supporters. The boycott group was overwhelmingly Catholic, though Little and Fred Riley were supporters. The different religious-cultural backgrounds of the two groups not only deepened the mistrust, but led to genuinely different interpretations of the likely outcome. Because most Catholics mixed with Catholics much more than a non-Catholic would, they tended to think of public opinion in Catholic terms, with anti-Communism a major issue. Non-Catholics, however, were more spurred by the typical Protestant mistrust of Catholics in politics, which at the beginning of 1955 was beginning to acquire an hysterical edge.

The undercurrent of disquiet about The Movement and Santamaria among the non-Catholic public and not a few Catholics received an impetus in late January and early February when there were long and colourful attacks on Santamaria and The Movement at AWU meetings. These sensational 'disclosures', although not taken very seriously by those closely involved, received columns of publicity in the press throughout Australia and had an important effect in stirring up and dividing public opinion.

These attacks contained little more than the dropping of a few names, some inaccurately, a few vague and unsubstantiated allegations and copious quoting from the 'Movement of Ideas' speech. In the atmosphere of the time, nevertheless, their effect was electric.

At the Queensland delegate conference of the AWU on 17 January, Bukowski, until then thought of as a Group supporter, strongly attacked the 'outside organisation'. Duly reported in the press, he received a telegram of congratulations next day from a majority of unions affiliated to the Brisbane Trades Hall.

The annual convention of the AWU started in Sydney on 26 January, and saw day after day of 'exposés' from Dougherty, Davis (who was then Federal President), Bukowski and the New South Wales Secretary, C. Oliver.

The following, from Dougherty's speech, was typical:

In the Labor Party and the Trades Unions, the Movement's instructions are carried out by 'cells' of the Movement known as the Industrial Groups.

The Movement also has members who are politicians in the Federal and State Labor Parliaments, and they are required to carry out instructions given them by Santamaria, directed through his trusted associates in the Eastern States.

These members of the 'cell' of the Movement now in control of the New South Wales branch of the ALP, are making strenuous efforts to gain control of the ALP throughout the Commonwealth, and have branded the real Labor people, who are fighting them and endeavouring to restore the traditions of the real Labor Party, as Sectarianists.

I want to say this: That the Movement obviously cannot be a Sectarian Movement. Have a look at the conglomeration of misfits, go-getters and ambitious men, some of whom were communists not so long ago, fellow-travellers and Liberals who should be in the Liberal Party, and general nonentities that comprise this secret organisation known as 'THE MOVEMENT' (*Worker*'s capitals).

Take the New South Wales State ALP Executive. To my definite knowledge, there are two men on that Executive who, though not members of
the cell, are attached to the cell and only through that cell they know they
can continue their progress in life, and achieve their ambitions by this
association. They were leading Communists in New South Wales for many
years.

I refer to Dr Lloyd Ross, who was some years ago secretary of the ARU,
and is going to be elected or appointed to that position again by the
Group—if it is the last thing they do, and I hope it is the last thing
they do.

And little Laurie Short, who was a Stalin Communist and then a
revolutionary of the Trotsky camp. . . .

And Davis:

Now that deals with those two Sectarian cranks [McManus and Keon].
You have heard about the activities of the 'Movement' in New South
Wales and Queensland, and despite what you have heard, I would suggest
that the Movement is only beginning to operate in those two states. They
have operated in Victoria for many years. They have a complete tie-up and
complete control. They have 'The Movement' controlling the Labor Party
in Victoria. There is not the slightest doubt about that. . . .

'The Movement' in Victoria is controlled by Messrs McManus, Scully,
Keon and Mullens. These are the four leading lights as far as the Labor
Party in Victoria is concerned. They have been 'stooging' to my knowledge
as far back as 1947, and possibly before that. . . .

. . . I suggest that Bourke's outburst was designed to sabotage Labor's
chance of winning the Federal elections.

What did the Victorian ALP Executive do? Did they expel Bourke
from the Victorian Labor Party? No, they didn't even bring him before
the Executive because he was 'one of their mob'. . . .

By the end of January, the division and mistrust on the Victorian Central
Executive had hardened and believable communication between the two
camps became difficult. Threats and insults increasingly became the style of
discussion. Each side tended to argue in terms of what the other had to
lose, should it come to a split.

Lovegrove opened the main debate at the meeting of 28 January by
reading a letter from Schmella on the Federal Conference. Woodhouse
with Riley seconding, moved that any request from Schmella or any other
Federal officer for facilities for holding the Special Conference be re
ferred at once to a special meeting of the Central Executive. This was carried
thirteen votes to nine, with the debate breaking along the predictable lines—
Clarey was first to oppose it, with Peters, Cain, Lovegrove, Kyle, Broadby
and Cameron following. Support came from Riley, Travers, Little, Keon
and Meere.

Lovegrove then gave notice of his intention to move at the next Central
Executive—'That the resolution of the Central Executive on 14/1/55
deciding that no Special Conference be held, be rescinded.'

Mrs Barry then moved (the AWU tirades had just started)—'That in
view of the untrue and malicious attacks made on the Assistant Secretary

of the ALP, Mr McManus, this Executive records its complete and utter
confidence in his integrity and devotion to the cause of Labor, both industrially and politically, a devotion which is evidenced by his active participation within the Labor Movement for more than twenty years.' This was
seconded by Hoban, but Clarey opposed it. Riley and Little, and then
Lovegrove and Broadby, supported it and it was carried on the voices.

Hoban gave notice of a more conciliatory motion on the forthcoming
conference—'That the previous decision of the executive against holding a
Special Conference on February 26 and 27 be rescinded and in lieu
thereof this Executive convene a Special Conference on the same dates,
constituted according to the existing rules of the Victorian Branch.'

He further moved—'That the Executive Officers prepare a full factual
statement defending the actions of the Executive on this dispute and a
refutation of the misrepresentation being circulated against it, and this statement be presented at a meeting of the Executive on Friday next.' It was
carried, without a vote, Meere seconding, Travers in support and Lovegrove and Galvin opposing.

Instead of the normal fortnightly meeting, the Executive now went over
to weekly meetings.

On 4 February Lovegrove sought permission to withdraw his notice of
motion, and instead to present a similar motion—to rescind the resolution
boycotting the Special Conference—a week later. On the motion of Hoban,
with Little seconding, permission was refused and Lovegrove instructed to
move his motion, as set out in the notice.

Cremean then moved an amendment—'That the previous decision of
the Executive against holding a Special Conference on February 26 and 27
be rescinded, and in lieu thereof this Executive convene the 1955 Annual
Conference on April 8, 9, 10 and 11, Easter, according to the existing
rules of the Victorian Branch.'

Scully seconded the amendment, and embittered debate began. Clarey
and Cameron opposed both the motion and the amendment, Keon supported the amendment and Peters opposed the motion. Kyle unsuccessfully
moved adjournment to the next meeting of the Central Executive. The
amendment was carried twelve to eleven to become the motion, which was
carried.

On 10 February Lovegrove again opened the debate by reading a letter
from Schmella and reporting on interviews with Schmella and Chamberlain. These reflected intense negotiation, and a slightly more conciliatory
mood, in recent days. The 'boycott' faction had now modified their stand,
and were prepared to drop the boycott in exchange for withdrawal of the
Federal Executive rule allowing irregular delegates. Both factions by now
regarded this rule, and the latitude it would allow in hastily making up
union delegations to the Conference, as crucial to their chances of winning.
In addition, the Cain-Lovegrove faction were demanding that Devlin,
Travers, and others they regarded as 'extreme right wing' be dropped, in
favour of representation for the AWU, Trades Hall Council and the left on
a 'compromise' Executive backed by both sides. In normal circumstances,
this would possibly have had the support of McManus, Woodhouse,

Hoban and probably at least half of the pro-boycott faction; but what appeared to many as a 'sell out' of men intensely loyal to the faction would have been almost impossible to organise in the atmosphere of the time.

Roberts opened the 10 February debate with the following motion:

That the only obstacle to restoring the unity of the Labor Movement is the determination of the Federal Executive to summon a Victorian Conference in defiance of the rules of the Victorian Branch, including in other infringements a provision that unqualified persons should come as members of the Party Conference. The Victorian Central Executive has indicated its anxiety to restore unity by advancing the date of the Annual Conference of the Branch by two months, to Easter 1955, and by holding Conference of the Branch in accordance with the Constitution and rules of the Branch, to enable the entire Labor Movement to discuss and determine all issues. The Central Executive, as the guardian of the rules for members of the branch, must maintain this position. It determines that this resolution be forwarded immediately to each individual Federal Conference delegate, with a request that each of them inform the Victorian office immediately of his attitude to the Victorian Executive's proposition.

Brennan seconded this motion and it was supported by Woodhouse, McManus and Devlin. Opposition came from Lovegrove and Peters.

Scully then moved, 'That this Executive formally appeal to the Federal Conference against all decisions of the Federal Executive.' It was seconded by Little, and carried.

Lovegrove, as instructed earlier, then moved the motion of which he had given notice, and which was to formalise the split: 'That the resolution of the Central Executive on 14/1/55 deciding that no Special Conference be held, be rescinded.' Cameron seconded and the long, climactic debate began.

It was now late in the evening, however. Only Riley and Keon spoke—both strongly and predictably in opposition—before the debate was postponed to the next evening, 11 February, when the Executive determined that it should continue until concluded.

Keon resumed the debate, and informed the Executive that he had sought legal opinion and intended to take legal action to have the Special Conference stopped. Recourse to the law now became the first strategy of the boycotters, as hope for a compromise solution receded.

The official record of the long, often violent debate that ensued reads: 'Clarey supported, Travers opposed, Kyle supported, Woodhouse opposed, Broadby supported, Scully opposed, Peters commented, Hoban opposed, Meere opposed, Cain supported, Cremean opposed, Brennan opposed, Lovegrove replied. Lost fifteen to nine.'

Resignations from the Central Executive were then handed in by Lovegrove, Clarey, Cain, Galvin, Cameron, Wilson, Broadby and Kyle.

The Victorian Branch of the ALP had split—as it happened, perhaps irretrievably—on predominantly sectarian lines. Six of the eight who resigned were of Protestant background. Only Little and Riley were non-Catholics among those who remained.

Peters, a Catholic, resigned shortly afterwards and was the only practising Catholic on the Executive to stay with the ALP. Hoban was the only
Catholic among those who stayed about whose attitude there might have
been doubt. But there could be no doubt about the deeply and funda-
mentally sectarian nature of the catastrophe that now loomed. The split
was not about religion, and even among the Catholics on the Executive, let
alone the Protestants, there were many who were scarcely religious or
devout men. But religion came to oppress and permeate the climate in
which the split ran its course.

The reduced Executive met again on 18 February. On the motion of
Horan and Scully, McManus was appointed Acting Secretary at the Secretary's salary. Scully, with Devlin seconding, moved successfully that the
officers be directed to secure the property, including records. Stout had
given notice that the 3KZ broadcasts were terminated. The Executive decided to insert an advertisement in the press on which State Electoral Councils had notified it they would not be sending delegates to the Special
Conference.

At the meeting on 25 February, Keon raised the question of Peters'
attitude. Peters stated that he would not resign from the Executive but
would be attending the Special Conference. The break was now complete.

The law case came before Mr Justice Martin in the Supreme Court on
21 February. Woodhouse, as the senior Industrial Group union secretary
on the Central Executive, took the action, with Gregory Gowans, QC,
instructed by the Richmond solicitors, L'Estrange and Kennedy, appearing
for him.

The action was taken following opinions—obtained by the Federated
Ironworkers' Association of Australia and its Victorian branch secretary,
R. Lundberg, in December and January—from the Sydney barristers J.
Kerr, QC, and H. Wootten. There was also a second opinion from Sir
Garfield Barwick, QC. The general trend of these opinions was to throw
doubt, because of the traditional strength and earlier origins of the state
components of the Federal Party, on the power of the Federal Executive to
dismiss the Victorian Executive.

Woodhouse took the action against Schmella, Lovegrove and Horan, as
members of the Federal Executive then in Victoria, asking the Court for
an injunction to stop the Conference and prevent him being deposed from
the Executive.

Woodhouse issued a writ seeking, among other things, a declaration by
the Court that the Federal Executive had no power to declare vacant the
office of the Victorian Executive or to hold a Special Conference to elect a
new Executive or to spend the Federal Executive funds on holding such a
conference; and an injunction restraining the Federal Executive from proceeding with the Special Conference, and interfering with the position of
Woodhouse, as a member of the Victorian Executive.

Because of the imminence of the Special Conference, Woodhouse asked the Court, instead of waiting for trial in due course, to make an interlocutory order to stop the Conference, and maintain the status quo until the hearing.

Gowans told the Court the Federal Executive had acted in an arbitrary and unjust way, exceeding its powers and contrary to the rules, in calling a Special Victorian Conference. He said Woodhouse had not been given a full and fair opportunity to be heard at the Federal Executive inquiry, and so was denied natural justice.

Of the three defendants, only Schmella and Lovegrove defended the action, their counsel being R. M. Eggleston, QC, instructed by Maurice Blackburn and Company, who were solicitors to the ACTU, the THC and the ALP.

Eggleston said Woodhouse had failed to make out any legal claim for an injunction. Any injunction granted against Schmella and Lovegrove would be futile, as it could not restrain other persons not before the Court. He said the real purpose of the case was to litigate the internal affairs of the ALP, but the former Victorian Premier, E. J. Hogan, had failed years ago in a similar action. Binding law was that courts, which might interfere in the affairs of other bodies for some or other reason, could not take the same liberty with organisations which had as their main objective the laying down and implementing of political policies. Woodhouse was seeking the Court's help to work the machinery of a political party. That was not something for a court to come into.

The judge refused the injunction on 25 February. He said he was not deciding the complete action, but only the application of Woodhouse for an injunction to stop the Conference. He said the facts put before the Court seemed to show that the Federal Executive had overridden the Victorian ALP rules in a drastic manner, and had usurped many of the functions which State rules gave to the State Executive. 'I feel great injustice has been done to Woodhouse by the Federal Executive resolutions calling the Special Conference before a right of appeal is practicable,' His Honour said. 'Had all twelve members of the Federal Executive been before the Court, I would have considered allowing an injunction unless they agreed to withdraw the resolutions and allow an appeal to Federal Conference before the Special Victorian Conference.'

Dealing with the inquiry, the judge said: 'Except for hearing what Dr Evatt had to say, they [the members of the Central Executive] were given no notice of the allegations made against the Central Executive and were not permitted to question him or to make any statement whilst he was present at all.' On Woodhouse's admitted failure to ask the Federal Executive to be allowed to make a statement, the Judge said: 'His neglect to do so was partly due to his belief that no such application would be acceded to and partly because Lovegrove told him—"Kennelly's boys have the numbers and the whole thing is cut and dried".'

Meanwhile, the previous day Woodhouse had applied to Mr Justice Lowe for leave to serve notice of intention that he would apply for an injunction against three more members of the Federal Executive, Reece,

Chamberlain and Colbourne, who had now arrived in Victoria. This was a tactical move and would only have applied had the first writ been granted.

The court moves were among the last hopes of the right, but they antagonised some of the party, instinctively defensive about washing the considerable dirty linen of the ALP in public. At the Special Conference, Chamberlain described the court actions as 'the most shocking thing to happen in the Labor Party for years'.

Away from the Executive and the Courts, February was a torrid month in other sections of the Labor movement. On 3 February the Melbourne Trades Hall Council had called on Victorian unions to support the Federal Executive stand. The Industrial Group faction, headed by Woodhouse and Neill, walked out of the chamber.

There were embittered union meetings, as the decision was taken whether or not to attend the Conference, and on the composition of delegations. Among non-Group unions, the Shop Assistants', Hospital Employees' and Motor Transport unions joined the boycott, while the Electrical Trades Union, in which a strong Industrial Group existed, decided to attend. Meetings at least as impassioned took place in the branches and State Electoral Councils on the same question, inflaming feelings that had developed with extraordinary rancour in the past six or nine months.

On 13 February Evatt's Canberra-based private secretary, W. I. Byrne, a Catholic, resigned and on 14 February Tripovich resigned as Country Organiser of the Victorian Branch. Leo Fennessy, the Clerks' Union organiser backed by Stout for THC representative at the ACTU Congress, resigned from his job at the same time.

Issuing his first statement as Acting Secretary of the split Executive, McManus said that in America Evatt's actions would be called McCarthyism—a charge that was to be freely swapped in the years to come. Most people would feel there was something repellant, McManus said, in the rejoicings of one who had styled himself Australia's most eminent defender of human rights over the results of the Federal Executive decision.

In late February, Archbishop Mannix declared a special week of prayer because of the communist threat to Australia. The possibility of a communist invasion of Australia was real, he said.

New South Wales was not far behind Victoria in the intensity of its Labor turmoil at this time, but in Tasmania—soon to become a scene of greater battle—the Cosgrove Government was returned on 19 February with an improved proportion of the vote.

Had there been time for a calmer appraisal after the court moves failed, it is possible that the right may have dropped its boycott. This had remained a possibility until the morning of the Conference, and enthusiasm for the boycott seems to have declined among the more moderate right wingers as the size of the impending schism became apparent. Membership qualifications of delegates remained the key issue. A strong belief in the electoral appeal of ALP Industrial Groups—that those supporting the Groups would win at the polls—and the fervent organising in the background of Santamaria, with the support of the Archbishop, were factors maintaining the boycott. Equally, Cain, Lovegrove and their supporters still believed the 'balanced' Executive they would be able to control was in their grasp; they did not believe that the right wingers would sacrifice their futures—as it seemed to non-Catholics they must—rather than see their present power reduced. Cain, who believed his ministers would not resign used to say, 'It'll all be over in a few months.'

Chapter Fifteen
Two Conferences

After the sustained tension of the preceding weeks, the Special Victorian Conference, held at the Melbourne Trades Hall Council Chamber on the weekend of 26 and 27 February, was quiet and uneventful. Some of the most damaging floods in Australian history, in the Hunter Valley and Northern New South Wales, pushed it out of national attention. Yet the change it initiated in the Australian Labor Party was of almost incalculable importance.

Some fifty-three unions out of a total of seventy-six eligible sent 215 delegates. Thirty-one State Electoral Councils, out of sixty-six eligible, sent thirty-four delegates. Of the total 249 delegates, 149 had attended the 1954 Conference and therefore had more than two years continuous membership of the ALP. Many other delegates had more than two years membership, but had not attended the 1954 Conference. Only fifteen members of union delegations were non-members of the ALP, though many others had only joined in recent weeks. The credentials committee checking admissions comprised Chamberlain, Schmella and Lovegrove, with Tripovich co-opted. Chamberlain, as Federal Vice-President, was chairman in the absence of Reece, and impressed delegates by his smooth and firm handling of Conference.

Gone, however, were the big delegations from Industrial Group unions, the eighty or so Movement members who had attended every Conference in recent years and other supporters of the outgoing Executive. Unions such as the Amalgamated Engineering Union, with one of the biggest delegations to Conference and for many years the scene of a left-right battle for power, had swung unchecked to the left.

The Conference resulted in a decisive win for the twenty-seven 'pro-Evatt' (though in reality pro-Stout) unions, who had built up their internal cohesion in the five months since October and carried the Trades Hall Council division directly into the ALP, with predictable results. A suddenly reviving left wing had joined with the THC 'establishment' to forge a powerful new force. They issued their own pre-selected 'ticket', which easily won all positions opened to election.

Stout was elected President unopposed. The voting for vice-presidents was: R. Cameron 214, A. McNolty 204, R. J. Eddy (Furnishing Trades Society) 42. For Treasurer, D. R. McSween defeated N. Gordon.

The new team of six for the Federal Conference was: W. T. Divers 226, H. O. Davis 225, D. Lovegrove 224, J. V. Stout 222, P. J. Kennelly 219,

J. P. Brebner 184. The seventh and unsuccessful candidate, E. W. Peters, for so many years a power in the Party, received only 80 votes. Stout and Lovegrove were elected unopposed as delegates to Federal Executive.

The eighteen positions on the body of the Central Executive went to: J. Cain, R. R. Broadby, P. J. Clarey, L. Galvin, H. O. Davis, P. J. Kennelly, A. E. Monk, V. Delmenico (Castlemaine Trades and Labor Council), W. Divers, R. Balcombe (Fuel and Fodder Workers' Union), J. Petrie (Storemen and Packers'), R. W. Holt MLA, F. Carey (Federated Union of Locomotive Enginemen), L. Higgins (Vehicle Builders' Employees' Federation), J. P. Brebner, F. Courtnay (Plumbers' Union), W. Butler (AEU) and T. Coe (Textile Workers' Union).

Eleven more—mainly on a rival ticket organised by Jordan and others who were aghast at Stout's new-found friendship for the left and hoped to get more moderate and conciliatory voices elected—were unsuccessful, by margins of two and three to one. These were: Peters, Lovegrove, Jordan, Tripovich, E. Moreton MLA, A. Lind MLA, G. M. Bryant (a school teacher and later MP for Wills), C. Connell (Fibrous Plasterers' Union), R. J. Eddy (Furnishing Trades) and W. Hughes.

The unsuccessful ticket represented, in fact, a badly organised attempt to modify the power of the new force, and was in part inspired by people resentful that they were not included on the winning ticket. The rivalry and bitterness between men like Kennelly, Stout, Lovegrove and Jordan had prevented any organised attempt, on a basis likely to win, against the power of the twenty-seven unions. A proposal considered for some time previously, for a conciliatory ticket headed by Clarey as candidate for president, did not come to fruition and in the event Stout was unopposed. Clarey and other moderates appear to have been complacent until too late in the belief that they could control the Conference.

Stout, at 69 years increasingly autocratic and vindictive, against the Parliamentary Party as well as the Grouper forces, set much of the tone of the new Executive. Alongside him, in the key positions as Executive Officers, were the detested and incompatible Lovegrove, Cameron, a man of little fight, and the extreme left wingers McNolty and McSween. Albert McNolty, born in Melbourne in 1892, was an old-fashioned socialist in the 1917 tradition, who despised Parliamentary Labor and the notion of 'working with capitalism'. Donald Raffey McSween was a former Sydney journalist who had been dismissed from the *Labor Daily* there in 1935 for criticising Lang's failure to nationalise big business. Later he became an organiser for the Clerks' Union when it was under left wing control. Though he sought election to Parliament on several occasions, the Groupers regarded him as a principal 'fellow traveller' of the Communist Party at the Trades Hall.

On the body of the Executive, only two or three could be described as left-wingers in this sense, but a frequent characteristic of the new men on the Executive was that they lacked political experience, and sometimes interest. They tended to be men dominated by the internal issues of the Trades Hall and the Trades Union Movement at the local level. Their inclination was to follow Stout rather than Cain or Kennelly.

Predominantly they were men who had been 'outs' while the Industrial Groupers were 'ins'. Often they had clashed with the Group supporters on the floor of the Trades Hall Council and perhaps at ALP Conferences, and had felt themselves to be insulted in the process. Only a few were Catholics and several were members of the Masonic Lodge at the Trades Hall. In background, they were often aggressively working class. Many had felt instinctive distaste for the devout, middle class or socially mobile Catholics who had dominated the Victorian ALP until then. It was a feeling these last shared with equal enthusiasm—in reverse.

Delegates remember some of the more militant anti-Groupers 'drooling with hatred' in their attacks on the former ALP rulers on this otherwise quiet weekend, while many of the more moderate section appeared anxious to placate them.

Broadby, one of the most respected men in the Labor Movement, must have echoed the feelings of many when he said that though he had played some part in the formation of the Industrial Groups in Victoria, with the progress of time he had found people connected with the Groups were merely using them for putting forward their religious objections to communism. For the last few years his association with the Victorian Central Executive had been most unpleasant. Labor had now reached a stage where it could say it had overturned an intolerance. 'Labor has now to make sure not to create another intolerance,' Broadby pointedly concluded.

However, in his presidential address, Stout indicated a very different line, and appeared to have a different set of enemies in mind. He said the Victorian Branch of the ALP was so rotten he thought he would never again be actively associated with it. He hoped now he had again been elected President, he could assist the branch to regain the position it had lost.

'Some of the most disgraceful things in the history of the Trade Union Movement have been done in the past few years,' he said. 'There is no doubt that somebody or something in the Victorian Central Executive has told the State Government what to do and the Government has done it. We reached the stage when the State Government did something on the one-man bus dispute which would not have been done by the most conservative government in the past century. . . . We are not going to permit a form of fascism to develop in the Trade Union Movement.'

While the Conference went on in the hall upstairs, a round-the-clock vigil in the ALP office downstairs continued.

Preparations for the Federal Conference in Hobart now became the preoccupation of both sides. The press began to describe them respectively as the 'old' and the 'new' Executives. In the mutually hostile statements now flowing from both sides, the newly elected Executive described its predecessor as the 'Santamaria-McManus-Keon Executive', or similar variants, while in retaliation the old Executive described its successor as the 'Evatt-Stout-Kennelly bogus Executive'.

The old Executive met on 4 March and received letters from Clarey, Lovegrove and Peters withdrawing as its delegates to Hobart, in answer to letters sent to them. Following its strategy of identification with the Industrial Groups, it selected Neill, R. Saker of the Clerks' Union and Woodhouse to replace them. Cremean was appointed to take charge of the office while McManus was in Hobart.

Meanwhile, the Stout-controlled THC Executive ordered the old Executive out of the offices in the Trades Hall. The Industrial Printing and Publicity Co had, earlier, banned all ALP broadcasting from station 3KZ.

In accordance with the Court judgment and as part of a broader strategy, the old Executive determined on an appeal to the Federal Conference and on 9 March McManus submitted a letter and a detailed statement of case to Reece, as Federal President.

That weekend, two sets of Victorian delegates travelled to Hobart.

On the eve of the Conference, 13 March, the Federal Executive met as was customary to arrange the agenda, authorise credentials of delegates and make other preparatory arrangements for the meeting of the Party's supreme body. When the question of admitting the six newly-elected Victorian delegates came up, the Executive decided by nine votes to three to admit them to Conference, the objectors being the New South Wales delegates Colbourne and H. J. Blackburn, and Gair of Queensland.

The six 'old Executive' delegates, Horan, McManus, Riley, Woodhouse, Neill and Saker, nevertheless arrived at the Conference chamber at the Hobart Trades Hall next morning and demanded admittance. Their tactic now was to try to force a situation where the delegates from the five other states would decide which Victorian delegation to accept. The chances of the six 'old' delegates winning such a vote were excellent. For this reason, Reece, Chamberlain, Kennelly, Evatt and the others were determined at all cost to prevent such a vote.

Amid angry scenes, with Short and other New South Wales delegates loudly calling for admittance of the 'old' Victorians, the doorkeeper, W. Ramsay, Tasmanian Secretary of the AWU and a hugely built former organiser from the North Queensland branch of the union, barred the door against them. He said he would admit only the thirty-six men on the list of credentialled delegates supplied to him by Reece. As tempers grew more uncontrolled and press cameras clicked, the 'old' Victorians formed a tight group around the entrance, effectively blocking it to other delegates who wished to enter. Reece then joined Ramsay at the door and said that only the six Victorians credentialled by the Federal Executive would be permitted to enter the hall. He then called the police to the Trades Hall.

The Secretary of the Hobart Trades Hall, J. O'Neill, now joined the dispute and told the police when they arrived that he would not allow police action against persons in the passages of the Hall, of which he was custodian.

Next Reece and Chamberlain made a personal approach to Horan and McManus, asking them to induce their colleagues to withdraw. Chamberlain reiterated that Federal Executive, not Federal Conference, had the right to determine credentials. The 'old' Victorians insisted that Federal

Conferences were masters of their own destiny. They claimed there was a precedent for decision by the other states on contested claims, from when two New South Wales delegations arrived at the 1927 Conference in Canberra.

Chamberlain next offered to admit the six 'old' delegates when their appeal was before Conference, but he insisted that the six 'new' delegates must be admitted as delegates. The 'old' delegates claimed, then, that this would mean their own prosecutors would also be their judges.

After a period of arguing in the corridors and round the entrance, Reece announced that he would adjourn the Conference until 10 a.m. next day, 15 March, and in the meantime recall Federal Executive to consider the position.

At the Federal Executive meeting, the New South Wales delegates moved that the Victorian issues be resolved by leaving a decision to delegates to Conference from the other five states. This was defeated and instead, after hearing legal advice, the majority voted to proceed with the Conference at a private hall, where police could be used against trespassers. It was left to the Executive officers to engage a hall, the location of which would be revealed to delegates at 10 a.m.

Holy Trinity Hall, North Hobart, was engaged. By an ironic twist of circumstances, this was near 'Katie' Holt's Ingemar Hotel, where Lloyd Ross and Keon, who was not a delegate but was one of several MPs in Hobart at the time, were staying. Ross saw the hall being prepared, while on a pre-breakfast walk.

After the break-up on the Monday, anti-Evatt delegates began counting their numbers and organising a bloc reprisal against the Federal Executive. A total of seventeen non-Victorian delegates—only one short of a majority of the whole Conference, even with the 'new' Victorians present— decided to boycott the Conference unless it agreed to let the five other states decide the Victorian question. On these numbers, the 'old' Victorians would have been admitted in preference to the 'new' by a majority of seventeen to thirteen. The ALP Industrial Groups would have been saved and the Evatt-Kennelly forces decisively routed. Only ruthless use of the Federal Executive and the six 'new' Victorians at Conference would prevent this outcome.

After many meetings, and protracted discussions of alternatives, the new boycott was announced shortly after 1 a.m. on 15 March. The whole New South Wales delegation, two Tasmanians and four Western Australians, signed one letter announcing this to Reece and a second, with somewhat different wording, was signed by five of the six Queenslanders.

The letter signed by the group led by New South Wales read:

We the undersigned, properly credentialled delegates to the Federal Conference, 1955, desire to inform you that we have given careful consideration to the events leading up to this conference, and in order that all disputes regarding the credentials of Victorian delegates can be solved in accordance with the traditional Labor procedure and practice, believe that neither delegation from Victoria should be admitted until conference has decided the appeal of the Victorian ALP Executive regarding the representation of Victoria at this conference.

In view of this, we desire to inform you that we shall not participate in the conference unless we receive an assurance that the traditional Labor practice be followed by excluding both sets of disputed delegates until the remainder of the conference has decided the issue.

This letter was signed by W. R. Colbourne, H. J. Blackburn, J. T. Kane, Lloyd Ross, L. A. North and L. Short, of New South Wales; V. D. Morgan and Senator G. R. Cole, of Tasmania; and T. P. Burke, MHR, D. J. James, Senator Joseph Cook and Kim Beazley, MHR, of Western Australia. The Queensland letter was signed by V. C. Gair, E. G. Walsh, T. Bolger, A. Cole and C. Bushell.

The New South Wales delegates were all members of pro-Group State Executive, while Morgan was active in the Clerks' Union in Tasmania. James was a railway clerk from Collie, Walsh was Deputy Premier of Queensland, Bolger Secretary of the Queensland State Service Union, Cole a member of the ARU Industrial Group and Bushell Queensland Secretary of the Bricklayers' Society. Cole, Burke, Cook and Beazley were Federal parliamentarians on the right of the Party.

A Federal Executive press statement issued about the same time said the six 'old' Victorians had no claim to attend Federal Conference and their effort to do so was a repudiation of the authority of the Federal Executive to control the affairs of the Party between biennial conferences.

'We want to make it perfectly clear that the Federal Executive acted properly in making the arrangements for the special Victorian conference so that it could resolve the difficulties the Federal Executive considered were apparent in that State,' the Executive statement went on. Because of certain technicalities, arrangements were being made for an alternative meeting place where the conference could be conducted without a repetition of the 'unsavoury incident' of the opening day. The statement said the six 'old' Victorians had lost any right to representation for the following reasons: They were members of a body that organised in complete defiance of Federal authority; they refused to attend the Special Victorian Conference; and they failed to submit their names at the Special Conference for nomination to any position.

A third press statement for the day came from Horan, on behalf of the 'old' Victorians. He said the strong stand taken by these delegates resulted from an inflexible determination to fight every inch of the way against moves by a section of the Labor Party to arrange a non-aggression pact with the Communist Party. The delegates he represented knew they could present an unanswerable case to Federal Conference against recent attacks on Victorian Labor. The six delegates of the opposing Victorian group were to be admitted to the conference to act as judges in their own case, contrary to all traditional Labor principles and practices. All the 'old' executive sought was justice and fair play, in accordance with the constitution of the Labor Party. Irrespective of the consequences, Horan said, the Victorian delegates would fight the plan of corrupt and communist influence, in alliance with the move-in on the Victorian ALP.

All forty-two delegates other than Chamberlain were waiting at the Trades Hall at 10 a.m. on the Tuesday and although everybody seemed to know that the conference would be at Trinity Hall, nobody seemed to have been officially informed. Many, ironically, got their information from Keon, who was constantly in the company of the six 'old' Victorians, and often acted as their spokesman. About 10.30 a.m., Reece and Chamberlain drove up and seemed surprised that there had been doubt about the site.

Finally, in the late morning, the conference of nineteen delegates assembled behind barred doors, again with Ramsay as doorkeeper. These delegates were the six 'new' Victorians, Kennelly, Stout, Divers, Brebner, Davis and Lovegrove; the unbroken South Australian delegation, Senators P. J. Toohey and S. W. O'Flaherty, J. Sexton (later MP for Adelaide), C. Cameron, MHR, M. R. O'Halloran (Leader of the State Opposition) and A. J. Shard; Chamberlain and Mrs R. Hutchinson, MLC, of Western Australia; H. Boland, State Secretary of the AWU, of Queensland; and G. Duthie, R. H. Lacey (McKenna's Secretary and later a Senator himself), R. J. Murray and F. Taylor, of the Engine Drivers and Firemen's Union, from Tasmania.

Since religion was playing an important part in the whole crisis, the point can be made that of the forty-two claiming to be delegates, those who attended the eventual conference were non-Catholic by a majority of about two to one, while the boycotters and 'old' Victorian team were Catholic by about the same majority.

While the 'church hall' conference was meeting, the remaining twenty-three met again at the Trades Hall and after considerable debate, the more cautious section led by E. J. Walsh, of Queensland, prevailed and it was decided not to hold a rival conference. This view was that the strong action had not succeeded, and that to proceed to a rival conference would only provoke even greater bitterness and a split of unprecedented magnitude, which on the known position in state branches must be won by the pro-Evatt side.

There was also a feeling, though one more likely to be heard in retrospect than in the heat of that week, that the boycott was unwise. On this argument, it would have taken the switch of one vote to deadlock the conference, and two to produce an anti-Evatt, pro-Group victory, even against the six 'new' Victorians as delegates. Murray of Tasmania in particular was considered quite likely to have switched in a different atmosphere.

The Western Australian, Tasmanian and South Australian delegates had all been 'tied' by their State Executives to support the Federal Executive decisions. The six Western Australian and Tasmanian boycotters risked suspension, which they in fact incurred, by joining the boycott. There was some confusion on actual events and verbal undertakings, however, which allowed argument that they were not breaking the letter of their State Branch instructions, whatever the effect on the spirit.

The final point might be made that the anti-Evatt delegates could all claim that the rule of the supremacy of Federal Conference overrode all other considerations. On such fine points of interpretation in Labor and most other politics, however, the only rule had always been—and remained—the 'numbers'. Those with majorities in the right places could always win, whatever the points of written rules that could be made against them.

Evatt had been visiting the Hobart Art Gallery with his wife on the afternoon of the opening, but by Wednesday 16 March he was very much present.

In his speech as Leader to the conference that day, Evatt said the tactics used to prevent the opening of the conference were scandalous and resembled those of Mussolini's Blackshirts, and that the conference had shown steadfastness and courage in the face of open physical force and attempted political blackmail. Dealing with the boycott, Evatt said there had been flagrant and open defiance of specific instructions to support the Federal authority of the Party. No self-respecting conference could yield to such intolerable blackmail. But for the combination of certain delegates to defy instructions from their own states, the Federal Conference would have shown an overwhelming majority favouring the authority of the Federal Executive. The purpose of the combined manoeuvre was to snatch a false and fictitious majority by delegates defying their instructions.

Evatt said it showed the whole thing was part of an overall plan to dominate the internal government of the Party by secret organisation. Disruptionists from within the Party or outside it were getting support from the recognised enemies of Labor. A notorious anti-Labor organisation called the People's Union, Non-Party, was merely a front for big business interests and it had recently circularised them asking for £25,000 to support forces working against Federal Labor.[1] Dr Evatt said the real object of the present infiltration into the Labor Party was to turn the Party from one pledged to democratic socialism into a right wing conservative party.

Investigations by the Federal Executive into the Victorian branch of the party had shown that the Santamaria Movement and non-members of the Labor Party had combined over a period of years to gain control of Labor, both politically and industrially, and to force anti-Labor policies on the party, Evatt said.

Apart from Evatt's speech, the conference on the Wednesday was mainly taken up with reports from the Federal Executive for the two years between the conferences of 1953 and 1955. The first part, dealing with the period until July 1954, was submitted by Kennelly, and the second part, covering the Victorian Special Conference, by Schmella.

The adoption of Schmella's routine, deadpan report on the Special Conference gave the authority of the supreme organ of the Party to the Federal Executive actions. The 'new' Victorian Executive was now the official one, as far as Federal Conference was concerned, and in a press statement that evening, Reece warned that members of the 'bogus' body who persisted would be expelled from the Party.

[1] The People's Union was an extreme right wing organisation of minor importance.

A deputation of three from the 'old' Victorian delegation had, that day, been invited by Schmella to address the conference, but on their behalf, McManus rejected the invitation. 'This Victorian delegation accepted the view expressed by the seventeen credentialled delegates to the Federal Conference that neither of the opposing Victorian delegations should be admitted until Conference has decided the appeal of the Victorian ALP Executive regarding representation of Victoria at the Conference,' Schmella reported. Once again, Conference refused to accept the 'old' Victorians on this basis.

The growing power of the left did not prevent Conference from passing a motion condemning 'so-called Peace Conventions organised openly or covertly by the Communist Party'. It endorsed a report from the Federal Executive, proscribing a 'peace Conference of Asian and Pacific Regions' the previous year and written in language that showed the Grouper hegemony of the time. 'The Executive now declares that it is communist strategy to use these (Peace) conventions to represent the West as aggressive and the exclusive centre of danger to World Peace,' it said . . . 'it is a characteristic of the Peace Convention propaganda to use legitimate national aspirations for independence to conceal the Communist use of these national aspirations. . . .' Kennelly moved the adoption of this clause of the Executive report at Hobart and Lovegrove seconded. Brebner, a representative of the new Victorians, opposed it.

Despite approval of this relic of the Groupers, next day's session brought drastic moves against the pro-Group faction, when a motion by Chamberlain, successfully amended by Sexton and seconded by Cameron, directed State branches to withdraw official recognition of the Industrial Groups.

This historic resolution read:

Conference endorses the decision of the Federal Executive in removing political recognition of Industrial Groups in Victoria in the belief that such recognition has materially assisted in group organisation entering fields other than those intended by their founders. It is emphasised that this decision of the Executive does not disband Industrial Groups. No authority is possessed by the Executive to so disband.

In respect to the question of Group organisation generally, official ALP recognition shall be withdrawn by all State branches. State branches shall be requested to conduct an educational campaign to expose the international communist conspiracy against democratic trade unionism and democratic forms of government.

We are of the opinion that any form of industrial organisation designed to combat communist activity in the unions should be a matter for the sole determination of the members of the union concerned.

Conference reaffirms its complete opposition to communism and all forms of totalitarianism and emphasises that only a strong united Labor Movement can prevent the growth of these evils.

As an effective force the Industrial Groups, discredited and disowned, were now finished. It was now the turn of their last remaining strong supporter, the New South Wales Executive.

On this and other questions that followed, Kennelly, the architect of the Victorian coup, now found himself in a minority, the victim of his own revolution. Chamberlain, in ambitious late middle age suddenly a National figure in almost daily conference with the alternative Prime Minister, became a more dominating figure of the Conference.

Press reports at the time said that the anti-Groupers had not at first intended moving against New South Wales, and only decided to do so in retaliation for the boycott two days before—an impression widely held. Also, though there is nothing on the record and the secrets have been carried to the grave, the interest of Evatt, Stout, the AWU and others in crushing Kennelly as a force in the ALP is obvious. He and Stout had been bitter enemies in Melbourne, while the real threat to Evatt still came from the Kennelly-Calwell axis.

On this decision to take the split beyond Victoria, the official report of the Conference shows clearly a rising aggressiveness by the left, though some more extreme amendments did not succeed. Conference merely instructed the Federal Executive to 'sift carefully' the allegations of the New South Wales unions, and if necessary to call a Special Federal Conference to deal with its report.

Conference then moved to silence its critics inside the Party, with a resolution allowing 'enunciation' of its own decisions, but not revoking the previous ban on public discussion of the ALP crisis. The effect of this was to allow Party members to state publicly only one side of the argument. This would include both the existing New South Wales Executive and the 'old' Victorians, should they decide to stay inside the ALP and fight. The resolution stated:

That policy having now been determined, which has the complete support of Federal Executive decisions, the Conference now draws attention to the fact that recognised authorities in each state and members who may wish to support and enunciate Federal decisions and policy, are permitted to make public statements directed towards establishing clearly in the public mind the policy of the Labor Movement in respect of the matters in dispute.

The *Age* of Friday 18 March quoted unnamed members of the 'new' Victorian executive as interpreting this as a formula for expulsions from the Party, particularly of Keon, Mullens and Bourke.

The day this report was written, 17 March, had seen an unprecedently unseemly exchange of insults between Mullens and Evatt, with Mullens now the third Parliamentarian, after Bourke and Keon, to attack the Leader in public. In a statement to the press in Melbourne, he said:

The cloak-and-dagger procedure and Moscow technique shown at Hobart demonstrated all too clearly that neither the constitution nor the rules of our Party matter to the pro-Evatt minority junta, and that they stick at nothing in the way of undemocratic gerrymandering and illegality.

The whole of my political life has been devoted to the fight against communism and I do not intend to sit idly by and see Labor become a communist subsidiary.

The bogus Victorian executive, headed by Stout and Kennelly, is honeycombed with Communists and fellow-travellers. I am not prepared to deliver our children's destiny over to them.

(Mullens' statement was headed: 'Evatt a Millstone: Would Be a National Disaster as PM.')

Santamaria also issued a press statement, commenting on Evatt's references to a 'Santamaria Movement'. Santamaria said the reference was 'a figment of a disordered mind, as was his now famed story of the origin of Document J.

'Whenever Hitler wished to distract the attention of the vile forces he led from his own political predicaments,' Santamaria went on, 'he did not scruple to turn the fires of racial hatred and religious bigotry upon the helpless Jewish minority. In the same predicament, Dr Evatt uses the same weapons of racial bitterness and religious sectarianism.'

In the sort of reply that was now typical, Evatt retorted:

Before his entry into the Federal Parliament, Mr Mullens denounced Mr Chifley. He said he was going into Parliament so as to give Mr Chifley 'more guts' to fight communism. Those like myself, knowing Mr Chifley, rightly inferred from this that Mr Mullens was a person of fascist tendency. This conclusion has been completely justified by the treacherous record of Mullens since he became a member of the Federal Parliament.

He did not have the courage to oppose openly the Menzies communist referendum, but he secretly worked in favour of Menzies. He has been a disloyal man from the beginning to the now-approaching end of his political career. He is a prominent member of the Santamaria Movement and is included in the cell or team which has been out to subvert the Federal Labor Party by secret methods. The praise from Mr Mullens is praise indeed to a Labor leader who is carrying on in the Chifley tradition. Mr Mullens is only masquerading as a Labor member of Parliament. Certain defeat awaits such a man at the hands of Labor supporters in the Labor stronghold which he misrepresents in the Federal Parliament.

Next day, the fourth and final snub came for the Groupers from the 'church hall' conference, this time on foreign affairs. A comprehensive motion adopted on foreign affairs took a 'left' line on the two burning issues of the day, recognition of Communist China and sending of Australian troops to Malaya.

These questions came before the last hour or so of the conference in the form of a seventeen-point recommendation contained in the report of the Foreign Policy, Defence and Immigration, Rural and General Committee of the conference. This Committee comprised Senators S. W. O'Flaherty, Toohey and Kennelly and Messrs Lovegrove, M. R. O'Halloran, R. J. Murray, G. W. Duthie and J. C. Sexton.

The resolution on foreign policy reiterated support for the British Commonwealth and United Nations and said co-operation with the United States in the Pacific was 'of crucial importance'. It then said the United Nations should have intervened to stop the fighting in Indo-China, which was typical of many cases of 'inexcusable delay' in recognising a genuine Nationalist, anti-colonialist movement. As a result, the Communists captured it.

The resolution said Labor policy was to oppose the use of armed forces in Malaya. Action towards agreement or amnesty there should begin immediately. The resolution also called for admittance of 'China' to the United Nations as part of a wider appeal for universal membership.

In brief, the seventeen-point resolution was a fairly typical statement of current 'left liberal' views on Asian affairs—stressing the need for material assistance, cultural exchange and vigorous use of the United Nations, while at the same time opposing the use of military force against almost any activity other than outright, conventional military aggression. It ignored the question of indirect aggression or suspect aggression through guerilla warfare—a difficult subject even less faced up to in public discussion in Australia then than a decade later.

While the decisions taken were in keeping with both Labor tradition and the main lines of debate in the Australian community, they were against the main stream of Industrial Group thinking, such as it was, on foreign affairs, and certainly directly opposed to The Movement views. Evatt, who had been assisted by Burton and Dalziel, had taken an important part in shaping them, though he was not officially a member of the Committee. They may have come close to representing his own thinking, yet there was an element of political strategy in the decisions, in using them to isolate and alienate the more outspoken Groupers and The Movement, to force them into the position of appearing 'right wing'. As the Party was not in government and was divided on these issues, there was no need to press them to a Federal Conference decision. It would have been a perfectly legitimate tactic, and one possibly more in keeping with Labor tradition, to have adopted more generalised attitudes and left the details and specific points to the Federal Parliamentary Labor Party.

The Hobart Conference ended not with a whimper, but with a bang when Calwell rose to give the concluding address on 18 March. In a speech which was widely reported in the press though the conference was closed, Calwell said Labor could never win with Evatt as Leader.[2]

Calwell flew from Melbourne that day to speak, and flew back immediately. His speech was largely a conventional call for tolerance, unity and adherence to the Labor platform. However, he spoke in some detail about Evatt's appearance before the Petrov Commission, saying Evatt need not and should not have gone before it. He said the Party's troubles had arisen from this, and from Evatt's failure to take the Caucus into his confidence. But Calwell also attacked breakaway movements and made it clear he intended to remain a member of the ALP.

That evening, Gair returned to Brisbane and publicly attacked Evatt in a statement to the press. He said there was a feeling that many of the Party's troubles would disappear if Evatt was no longer leader. In Melbourne, a crowd—many rounded up by The Movement—including the State ministers Barry and Scully, was waiting at the airport to hear reports from the returning 'old' delegation.

On the Sunday evening, 20 March, Evatt issued two more long press statements on the conference. In one, he announced that Labor would

---

[2] Evatt subsequently denied that Calwell ever made this attack.

launch a nation-wide campaign in support of the new foreign affairs policy. 'Labor has called the bluff of the small subversive clique within its ranks whose ideas on foreign policy are not only inimical to Australia's chance of peaceful and independent survival in the Pacific, but are also alien to the great traditional Anglo-Saxon capacity to bring enlightened and persistent thought to the most complex of world problems,' he said. He emphasised the points in the policy dealing with recognition of Communist China and her admittance to the United Nations, and the opposition to sending of troops to Malaya.

Evatt described the reports of Calwell's attack on his leadership as 'concoction and fabrication'. 'I am satisfied that the purpose of the concoction was to assist the cause of the Santamaria Movement,' he said. He had unequivocal assurances from delegates that the 'we cannot win with Evatt' statement was never made. He also attacked reports in Sunday newspapers saying he had said he would give Calwell a 'hiding' if the report was true. Even if the 'hiding' report were true, he said, it was unethical and monstrous to publish it.

In Melbourne, Calwell refused to confirm or deny the reports. 'I am not saying any more about anything,' Calwell told the press. 'Labor Party differences are for decision in the party council and not for debate in the public forum.' However, one Sunday paper had quoted him as saying—an unmistakable Calwellian quote—'Dr Evatt couldn't flatten an egg with a shovel', when the 'hiding' report was referred to him.

Chapter Sixteen
The Parliamentary
Parties Split

Immediately the two rival Victorian delegations returned from Hobart, the 'new' and 'old' Central Executives set out to 'line up' as much of the body of the Party as possible behind them. The first and most important bodies they had to win over were the State and Federal parliamentary parties.

As early as 21 March, McManus sent out the following circular to Parliamentarians and other endorsed candidates, with supporting telegrams.

Dear Comrade: You are advised that this Executive at its meeting of 20th March, 1955, convened a meeting of Federal Parliamentarians, State Parliamentarians and other endorsed Parliamentary candidates to be held at Victoria Hall Meeting Room, corner Victoria and Russell Streets, on Friday next, at 8 p.m.

A report will be made by the President, Mr J. P. Horan, on the recent event at Hobart, also on other aspects of the present crisis in the Party. Members of the Central Executive will also attend.

You are requested to regard this matter as most urgent, and to ensure your attendance to assist the Executive in its efforts to bring Unity to the Party.

Yours fraternally,
F. P. McManus
Acting State Secretary

On 23 March, a four-page circular went out under Stout's signature to 'all members of the Australian Labor Party, State of Victoria per secretaries of affiliated unions, ALP Branches, State Electoral Councils, State and Federal Parliamentarians, other endorsed Parliamentary Candidates and Labor Municipal Councillors'. This went into extensive detail on the decisions of the Hobart Conference and emphasised in capital letters the following decision:

Conference resolves that complete recognition shall be given by all sections of the Labor Movement to the Central Executive as elected by the Special Conference of the Victorian Branch of the ALP held on 26th and 27th February, 1955, and subject to determination by succeeding State Conferences as convened by the Central Executive so recognised, and that any other body in Victoria claiming such recognition is, and shall be declared, a bogus body.

After calling on branch secretaries to return lists of members and other material to him not later than 12 April, Stout then went on:

Non-Recognition of Bogus Body: In view of the continuation of a body composed of certain members of the Central Executive of the ALP Victoria which existed prior to February 26th, 1955, and issue by that body of unauthorised directions, you are advised in accordance with Federal Conference decision . . . that that body is a bogus body.

No member of the ALP and no ALP Organisation or Affiliated Union can recognise that body or its decisions and retain membership of, or affiliation with, the ALP.

Bogus Conference: The Conference convened by that body in April 1955 is a bogus Conference and cannot be attended by members of or affiliates to the ALP in Victoria.

Bogus Meeting of Candidates: The meeting of Labor Parliamentarians and endorsed Labor candidates convened by that body on March 25th is a bogus meeting and cannot be attended by members of the ALP.

Meetings Convened by Bogus Body: Members of the ALP shall not participate in the organisation or conduct of any meetings convened by or on behalf of any bogus body.

They shall not take the platform at such meetings, and shall not address them.

This decision applies to any meeting convened by any bogus body.

Stout followed this circular with several warnings through the press that parliamentarians and candidates who attended the Victoria Hall meeting called for 25 March would be suspended. But in the meantime the old Executive, helped by the extensive organisation of The Movement in the branches, worked intensively to win over as many parliamentarians as it could. It had a weapon in the potential power of its supporters in future pre-selections. This 'message' was usually conveyed at the local level, through appeals to loyalty to old friends and supporters, and perhaps loyalty to the Church. A further consideration no parliamentarian could ignore at that time was the near certainty, following the Hobart decision to intervene, of a split at least as big as that looming in Victoria in New South Wales as well.

Similar individual pressure and organisation also came, of course, from the other side. But, while ruthless, it lacked the same organisation, belief in its cause—many were hardly enthusiastic about some of the personalities on the new Executive—and feeling of religious solidarity. To those in touch with broad public opinion and political reality, however, the new Executive, supported by the political leaders and most affiliated unions, must have seemed the body more likely to win in the end. Once again, many Catholics appear to have been swayed in their judgments of the likely outcome by a tendency to assume that Catholic public opinion on communism was the same as general public opinion—a tendency that must have been reinforced by the pressures placed on them in March 1955.

No doubt most acted in the end in the way they felt to be honest and right, but assessments of the likely political outcome necessarily had to be considered in assessing what was right. There was nothing to be gained, even in that intensely emotional atmosphere, from being a martyr for martyrdom's sake.

The prior commitment of many parliamentarians to supporting the old Executive was obvious. Among Federal Parliamentarians, Keon, Mullens and Bourke had been too centrally placed in the dispute not to attend the 25 March meeting, and in addition had been privately warned by the pro-Evatt supporters that they would be expelled whatever they did. In addition Keon and Cremean were members of the old Executive. Scully, Brennan and Little, among the State Parliamentarians, were also members of the old Executive, as was Barry's wife. Coleman had been the minister directly under attack from Stout and the unions in the one-man bus and J. J. Brown disputes. Lucy, Corrigan, Bailey, Fewster, Sheehy, White and D'Arcy had been with the Scully faction in the State Caucus. The old Executive and its supporters were a vital part of Barry's base in the developing contest to succeed Cain, now nearly seventy years of age.

All these formed the core of the twenty-five parliamentarians who attended the old Executive meeting on 25 March.

The full list was:

State Ministers: Coleman, Barry, Scully (Assistant Minister) and T. Hayes (Housing).

State MLAs: S. Corrigan (Port Melbourne), L. D'Arcy (Grant), G. Fewster (Essendon), M. Lucy (Ivanhoe), L. Morrissey (Mernda), J. P. O'Carroll (Clifton Hill), P. J. Randles (Brunswick) and G. White (Mentone).

State MLCs: A. J. Bailey (Melbourne West), T. Brennan (Monash), Paul Jones (Doutta Galla), J. Little (Melbourne North) and M. Sheehy (Melbourne).

Federal MPs: W. M. Bourke (Fawkner), T. W. Andrews (Darebin), J. L. Cremean (Hoddle), W. Bryson (Wills), S. M. Keon (Yarra), J. M. Mullens (Gellibrand), R. Joshua (Ballarat) and Senator J. J. Devlin.

Of these, the biggest surprises were Hayes, Bryson and Joshua. Thomas Hayes had been regarded as unaligned and rather close to Cain, and indeed some of the organisers of the breakaway had been surprised at getting any ministers other than Scully at all. Joshua, a practising Anglican though married to a Catholic, was an unobtrusive former bank clerk who had won the seat of Ballarat at the 1951 election. Only he and Little were not Catholics. In Canberra, Bryson had been regarded as close to Ward.

The support of unelected candidates was much greater, and a total of thirty-eight out of the seventy candidates endorsed by the ALP for the 1955 State election attended the meeting.

On the following Sunday, 27 March, an overflow crowd of more than 3,000 attended an old Executive rally at the Richmond Town Hall, notable for its angry, embittered tone and strong attacks on Evatt. 'The greatest misfortune of this Party today,' McManus told the applauding crowd, 'is that it is not being led by a man like Curtin, Chifley or Scullin but by a humbug.' The meeting passed a resolution calling for a 'unity' Conference to heal the split.

Cain spoke the same afternoon on the first 'Labor Hour' radio session on 3KZ since the split. 'I refuse to be associated with those who will not accept Party discipline,' the Premier said. Whatever happened, he said, the Federal Executive would control the destinies of the Labor Movement for the next two years, until the next Federal Conference. Every Labor member must accept discipline. He must not run away and form a party of his own any time a decision did not suit him. The nine members of the old Victorian Central Executive who favoured participation in the Special Conference had been actuated solely by the aim of recognition of the statutory authority of the Federal Executive.

Now Cain had made his position clear, a clash in the State Parliamentary Party room seemed imminent. Caucus met in an atmosphere of crisis on the morning of 29 March. The feeling was that one side or the other might take the initiative to gain a tactical advantage.

As soon as preliminaries were over, V. J. Doube (Oakleigh) moved a motion of confidence in the new Executive and was seconded by R. J. Gray (Box Hill). Little then moved an amendment, with D'Arcy seconding, that Cain should be instructed to seek a conference between the two contending Executives, with the whole Party to abide by the decision reached.

The bitter, emotional debate lasted, with a break for lunch, until far into the afternoon, with Barry and Coleman leading the support for the amendment. For much of the debate, the amendment gained tentative support from a wider group than those who had attended the old Executive meeting. Many members wanted Caucus to refrain from intervening in the dispute at all, but Doube and his supporters argued that Cain must be supported. Equally, others were adamant that Cain must fight to restore the unity of the Party on an acceptable basis. When the acrimonious debate at last ended, Caucus voted by thirty-two to seventeen to support the new Executive. The same seventeen as had attended the old Executive meeting voted against confidence in the new one.

That night, the new Executive met and suspended from membership of the ALP twenty-four parliamentarians who had attended the 25 March meeting. They were given until 7 April, the date of the next Executive meeting, to declare their loyalty to the new Executive.

Mullens was expelled outright, for having sent the following telegram to the new Executive: 'My position is clear. Publicly stated cannot recognise Evatt or bogus Executive and shall continue.'

Cain, apparently strangely optimistic still, the same night forecast an early end to the dispute, to the satisfaction of all concerned. Addressing a campaign meeting for a by-election for the Monash Province of the Legislative Council, he said every Party had its troubles, but they all came to an end satisfactorily. 'There is nothing better than making friends again,' he said. 'Democracy cannot be a Sunday School on the one hand, or a dictatorship on the other.'

Next day, however, the crisis in his Caucus deepened. Cain asked the four suspended ministers, Barry, Coleman, Hayes and Scully, to resign from Cabinet. When they refused, he hastily visited the Governor, Sir

Dallas Brooks, handed in his Commission to form a Government, and obtained a new one. With this new Commission, he excluded the four from Cabinet.

Cain argued that by doing this he was simply following the Caucus decision to accept the new Executive and the authority of the Federal Executive, but the dismissed ministers were incensed at what seemed to them a precipitate action. After some hours of angered organisation, they assembled twelve supporters and formed a breakaway 'rebel' Party, with Coleman elected Leader and Barry Leader in the Legislative Assembly.

After prolonged balloting for positions, a new Ministry was sworn in next day, with Doube, Gray, J. J. Sheehan (Ballarat) and J. Tilley, MLC, the new ministers. Cain gave Sheehan the Housing portfolio, Doube, Health, Tilley, Mines and Forests and Gray became Minister Without Portfolio. D. P. J. Ferguson replaced Coleman in Transport. Holt, the earliest rebel, was not successful in winning election to Cabinet. Ironically, Sheehan and Ferguson, who got the two most senior portfolios, had been regarded previously as inclined towards the right. A more pronounced right winger, Gladman, who had won election to Cabinet with Barry-Scully support after Holt's resignation, also remained with Cain. Catholics of various degrees of attachment still, in fact, formed close to one-third of the Cain Party.

On 31 March the breakaways wrote to Cain, challenging him to call an early election. This challenge seems to have been partly a strategic bluff, with the objective of forcing Cain to fight for a compromise solution in order to save his Government. It was made in a spirit of extreme anger. However, the breakaway group reasoned, should the bluff not succeed an election would enable the 'old' Labor Party to establish the solid base from which it could seek unity again. They thought it was preferable to have an election as soon as possible, as most branches seemed to be supporting the old Executive, which also had control of the ALP office—two claims not only to legitimacy, but to superior organisation in an election. Delay in forcing an election, it was felt, would give the new Executive time to build up its own organisation.

'It is felt that the people of Victoria, and particularly rank and file members of the Labor Party, should be given the opportunity to decide who shall control in the future the political destinies of the State,' the breakaways wrote to Cain. '. . . In view of the urgent need for political stability, it is our wish that the matter should be resolved by an appeal to the people at the earliest possible moment. . . .'

The following Sunday evening, the Labor Caucus in the Melbourne City Council, of which Barry was Leader, voted ten to one to support the old Executive. The lone Cain supporter was Councillor Kevin Holland, a Catholic, later MLA for Flemington. Coleman and Hayes were also members of the Council Caucus. 'The City Council is free from communism,' Barry told the press later. He said the decision would not be conveyed to Stout, as the Caucus did not recognise his authority.

On the 'Labor Hour' of that afternoon, however, Divers—introducing a talk from Schmella—said the 'Santamaria group' must be eradicated from the Labor Party. He said Labor parliamentarians had been endorsed on the understanding that they would accept decision by Party Executives. Some, unfortunately, had forgotten that pledge. The breakaway group could no longer be trusted by the electors and must be replaced by Labor Party members.

Calwell was emerging at that stage as a conciliator. In a statement to the press, he said Labor's forces must sooner or later be reunited and it was most desirable that unity be restored now. 'The necessity for unity in Labor's ranks overrides all other considerations, even the injustices, real or imagined, about which members of the old Executive and their supporters may feel strongly,' he said. He said his own decision to recognise the new Executive was based on the interests of the ALP.

7 April became the 'night of the knife', wielded in the ACTU Boardroom—the old Executive held the official ALP rooms—with ruthless and bitter dexterity.

The minutes of the meeting read:

Acting secretary Lovegrove reported names of members of the ALP to whom letters of suspension had been forwarded, also members to whom requests had been made to affirm their loyalty to the ALP. Report received on the motion of Messrs Butler and Davis. *Carried*

Ex-Central Executive Members: Moved Messrs Brebner and Carey—'That Mrs W. P. Barry, Messrs D. F. Woodhouse, D. A. Devlin, J. F. Meere, J. J. Roberts, R. G. Hoban, J. P. Horan, F. Reilly, F. J. Riley, M. J. Travers, and F. P. McManus be expelled from membership of the ALP.' *Carried*

Melbourne City Councillors: Moved Messrs Carey and Brebner—'That Crs F. G. J. Hardy, H. Lee, J. B. Naughton, W. R. Hunt, J. C. Madden, F. P. Williams and A. G. Cantwell be expelled from membership of the ALP.'

Candidates: Moved Messrs Brebner and Carey—'That the following candidates that have failed to affirm their loyalty to the ALP, viz [a list of eleven MLAs and twelve non-member candidates] in the House of Assembly [sic] and Messrs P. L. Coleman, MLC [and seven other candidates] from the Legislative Council.'

Federal Members: [the names and designations of Andrews, Bourke, Cremean, Bryson, Keon and Joshua followed] 'be expelled from membership of the ALP.' *Carried*

Non-Retiring Members: Moved Messrs Petrie and Higgins—'That Messrs (Sheehan, Bailey, Paul Jones, Little and Brennan) be expelled from membership of the ALP.' *Carried*

Retiring Member: Moved Messrs Carey and Brebner—'That L. Morrissey, MLA, be expelled from membership of the ALP.'

Appeal: Senator J. J. Devlin: Moved Messrs Cain and Holt—'That suspension from membership of the ALP of Senator J. J. Devlin be lifted, following his pledge of loyalty to the ALP.'

F. Carey opposed. A. McNolty opposed. R. Balcombe supported. *Carried*

Messrs Neil and Saker: Moved Messrs Carey and Delmenico—'That Messrs J. Neil and R. Saker be expelled from membership of the ALP for disloyal and unworthy conduct.'

P. J. Kennelly opposed. J. P. Brebner supported. D. Lovegrove opposed. D. R. McSween supported. P. J. Clarey opposed. *Carried*

In addition, on motions moved or seconded by Carey, Petrie, Davis, Brebner, Butler and Coe, thirty-nine members of suburban councils and one from Wonthaggi were expelled, including eleven—the core of the Keon anti-Wren machine—from Richmond, nine from Collingwood and eight from Fitzroy.

Altogether, 104 members were expelled from the ALP. The division indicated by the minutes over the expulsions of Senator Devlin, Neill and Saker were part of a deeper division of approach. The Executive was already divided between the militants of the industrial wing rampant (backed by Stout and out for blood, vengeance and power) and the more moderate members, predominantly from the political wing, who even now wished to minimise the split into which the Party was hurtling. These included Cain, Kennelly, Lovegrove, Clarey, Holt, and R. Balcombe of the Fuel and Fodder Workers' Union, who later became Assistant Secretary. Monk and Broadby, who were absent, would probably have supported their position. They were all but powerless, however, against the collective strength of the new force at the Trades Hall forged from the alliance between Stout and the far left.

The moderates had wished, the previous week, to confine suspensions to those who had made public statements on their attitudes, and postpone action against those who had attended the 25 March meeting but had not otherwise offended.

After the expulsions, Cain reported on the situation in the Parliamentary Party and said he intended to keep his promise to call Parliament together on 19 April.

McSween then moved successfully, with Brebner seconding:

That this Executive commends the Premier on his decision to boldly accept the challenge of the Santa Maria [sic]-Barry Group by not deferring the date of reassembling the State Parliament.

We draw attention of the Labor supporters in Victoria to the fact that the onus is now placed on the breakaway group of dismissing the Labor Government from office.

This Party will not compromise on its principles and we confidently look to the Labor voters of Victoria to appreciate the fact, and also to relegate to political oblivion the traitorous forces which are seeking to destroy the Victorian Labor Government.

Next came a resolution, on the motion of Kennelly and Clarey, declaring bogus those branches which had supported the old executive.

Brebner and Divers then moved: 'That any person holding membership who, since March 27, 1955, has failed to give complete recognition to the Victorian Central Executive of the ALP, as directed by the Federal Conference, and who, since March 27, 1955, has acted in opposition to the authority of the Federal Conference, the Federal Executive or the Victorian Central Executive decisions, is ineligible to remain a member of the ALP and automatically forfeits membership, under Rule 85 (j).' This was carried, with only Clarey opposing.

It was then the turn of the Young Labor Association. Brebner and Coe moved: 'That the YLA of which Mr Clyde Holding is Acting Secretary be recognised by this Central Executive, and that the organisation of which F. R. Scully is Secretary, be declared as a bogus organisation.'

Divers and Butler next moved: 'That the Women's Organising Committee reconstituted by Mesdames Rodan and Hart be recognised by this Executive, and that any other organisation purporting to be the Women's Organising Committee of the ALP be declared a bogus body.' Both motions were carried without opposition.

In the meantime, the old Executive had met on 1 April, after the suspensions, and passed resolutions expelling fifty-three members of the Labor Party, including twenty-one members of the new Executive, thirty-two State Parliamentarians and Kennelly and Clarey among Federal Parliamentarians.

While the Labor Party was closest to the brink of a great schism in Victoria, it was also approaching the brink in New South Wales, where internal feeling was almost as tense, and in other states as well.

In Perth on 29 March the Western Australian ALP Executive suspended for three years the Federal Conference credentials of the four delegates who had boycotted the Hobart Conference, Burke, Beazley, James and Senator Cooke. This was, in effect, a compromise penalty decided on after a prolonged debate, with a militant section of the Executive seeking to expel them. The Executive decided on the voices to give full support to the Federal Executive and Federal Conference decisions.

The Tasmanian Conference was held the week after the Hobart Federal Conference, and resulted in something like a drawn game after intensive organisation. Reece was re-elected unopposed as President and also as one of the two delegates to Federal Executive; but J. O'Neill, the anti-Evatt Secretary of the Hobart Trades Hall Council, beat Duthie for the second position by one vote. Cole topped the poll for the body of the Executive, but 'pro-Evatt' supporters gained seven out of the eleven positions on the body of the Executive. This gave them the strength, which they used, at the next meeting, to suspend Cole and Morgan, the two boycotting delegates to the Federal Conference, for going against instructions.

At the post-Hobart Queensland Central Executive meeting on 22 March, Bukowski demanded that the five boycotting delegates return their fares and expenses. He was unsuccessful in getting disciplinary action against them and in the heated debate he was threatened several times with punching.

The immediate danger of a disastrous split, however, was in New South Wales, where The Movement and Groups had attracted deep-seated hostility of a kind that did not exist in the smaller states. In late March, anti-Groupers organised a well-attended series of regional meetings in support of the Evatt cause, in defiance of Central Executive orders to desist.

Evatt also addressed a series of public meetings in New South Wales country districts, where he took every opportunity for the most violent and melodramatic attacks on the 'Santamaria Movement', apparently caring nothing for accuracy. At a crowded meeting in Wollongong on 24 March, with several Parliamentarians on the platform, he referred to a 'Menzies-Fadden-Santamaria fascist cell', which was trying to force the Labor Party even further to the right than the Liberal Party. 'We know from recent statements at the AWU Convention that the leaders of this outside group are people who worked day and night to defeat the Chifley Government in 1949,' he said. '. . . Unity, yes, we are all for it, but how can you have it if you have people within the Party secretly controlled by others who don't believe in the Labor policy or platform?' At other country meetings, Evatt alleged that the 'Santamaria Movement' had infiltrated the universities and the press, as well as unions and ALP branches.

On 1 April, the New South Wales Central Executive broke precedent by ruling that Evatt was no longer a member of the ALP, following the discovery in Canberra that he had not taken out his 1955 membership ticket in the branch by the appropriate date, 31 March. Had this stratagem succeeded, it would have meant Evatt automatically forfeiting the Leadership and being succeeded by Calwell. However, he claimed that he had taken out a ticket with the Barton Federal Electoral Council, his own constituency, on 18 January and he was also offered membership of the Mosman Branch, his home district in Sydney. He appealed to the Federal Executive, which was to meet in Melbourne in the coming week.

At this time, some hurried behind-the-scenes diplomacy was taking place in an effort to head off the threatening split in New South Wales. Kennelly, still able to influence a section of the Federal Executive, negotiated with R. R. Downing, Attorney-General in the Cahill State Government, an agreement under which both sides would make concessions.

New South Wales was to call off its 'unity conference' set down for 23 April—which had been designed to forestall intervention—broaden its executive, accept the Hobart decisions and dismiss Kane, the *bête noire* of the 'pro-Evatt' unions.

The reasonable harmony that existed between the Executive, the State Government and the Sydney Trades and Labor Council, plus the effect of distance and division in The Movement, were the factors enabling a slowing of the schismatic pace in New South Wales. The right was more broadly based than in Victoria, but the Government must almost certainly fall and there would be chaotic disunity in the industrial wing if the issue was forced. But the resulting anti-Evatt party would inevitably be far stronger than its Victorian counterpart. It was hardly a risk the Federal Executive could take.

The New South Wales Executive split into militants led by Kane, who believed in fighting the Federal Executive without compromise, and moderates led by Colbourne, who promulgated the doctrine of 'stay in and fight'. Colbourne's vivid memories of the splits in New South Wales from 1927 to 1939 had an incalculable effect on his judgment and that of many others in New South Wales. The bitterness and damage of a Party split seemed much more real in their imaginations than that of their Victorian counterparts.

The Federal Executive met in Melbourne on 5 April and accepted Evatt's credentials as a member of the ALP.

That evening the New South Wales Executive met and, with the Colbourne moderates controlling by seventeen votes to fifteen, decided to abandon the 'unity conference' and accept the Hobart decisions to 'bring unity in the Party'. The Executive decided that the State Conference would be held at the normal time of June or July. But it also appealed to the Federal Executive to restrain Evatt from his 'crazy crusading tours' in New South Wales, as his statements were damaging attempts to achieve unity.

This was the beginning of a series of events, lasting eighteen months, through which the split was confined to minor proportions in New South Wales.

The Victorian Parliament was to meet on 19 April, in keeping with a promise extracted from Cain at the end of the 1954 session by the Liberal Leader, H. E. Bolte. Bolte had expected an autumn of trouble in the Government Party and did not want the Government to avoid Parliament.

Barry, Coleman, Cain and others took part in some intensive private negotiations, including sounding out opinion at the Trades Hall, in the search for a compromise.

The breakaway group's proposal was that at some time in the next three to six months a unity conference should be called under the Victorian rules, including the two-year membership qualification for Conference delegates. The Central Executive would be enlarged from twenty-five to thirty-one, with greater representation for the industrial wing and some of the right wing militants excluded. The no-confidence motion in the Government planned for 19 April would be adjourned, and in the meantime Cain must not introduce any legislation which could give him an advantage in any election held if the compromise broke down.

On 13 April the Caucus of the 'Coleman-Barry Labor Party', as the Press was now calling the breakaways, formalised this proposal—for which increasingly little hope was held—with the following resolution:

This Parliamentary Labor Party Caucus compliments the Party executive on its attitude in the face of minority attacks.

We reaffirm our determination to uphold the rules and platform of the Labor Party, emphasise that unity is essential and again invite the Evatt-Stout faction to attend a unity conference.

This and other proposals for a unity conference did not come before the new Executive, but they were emphatically rejected informally. The almost certain result of the rejections was that the Cain Government would fall on 19 April.

Why were they rejected? One important reason is the attitude of Stout, who was in a mood for revenge and who had little sympathy with the ideal of Labor Governments. He despised most politicians—including Cain and Coleman—and believed that a tight, well led industrial wing could extract more gains for union members from a Liberal Government, with proper bargaining, than from a Labor one. A Parliamentary Party firmly under industrial wing discipline, but in opposition, was part of the strategy he conceived. At the same time, Stout was dependent on the left wing in the unions for his new base of support. The left, even when not influenced by communists, shared his contempt for 'reformist' Labor governments and was attracted by the notion of a hard-line Parliamentary Party which would come to office in a crisis and implement sweeping nationalisation of industry.

Barry, who had a union background and claimed better relations with Stout than most, told the author that in the last days of the Cain Government Stout appeared to be relenting, for fear of the damage a split could cause inside the industrial wing. However, the impression of most other observers is that Stout had no compunction whatever in seeing the split proceed.

Among other reasons for the compromise proposals being rejected was the vested interest of members of the new Executive, many of whom would lose their newly gained—and until recently undreamed of—power with such a development. The ideological attitudes of the left reinforced this feeling.

The hysterical atmosphere of the time must also be considered. Many genuinely believed—and the belief was not wholly unfounded, if wildly exaggerated—that the Party was the victim of an unwholesome, zealous outside organisation which was out to destroy all in its path. And on both sides, there were militants who believed the other side was practising blackmail, and who were demanding that bluffs be called.

On 15 April, the old Executive decided to go to the brink. Barry reported to the Executive meeting on the state political situation. McManus, with Meere seconding, then moved as follows:

This Central Executive of Victorian Labor endorses this week's offer of co-operation in a unity conference with the breakaway Evatt-Stout-Cain group. The Executive declares that the Evatt-Stout-Cain group must accept responsibility for events in the forthcoming State Session, caused by its repeated rejection of unity proposals. This rejection is undoubtedly due to pro-communist influences, which are inexorably determined to smash the unity of the Party. In view of the Evatt-Stout-Cain group's actions over recent months to prevent settlement of the Victorian crisis by appeal to a properly constituted State Conference or properly constituted Federal Conference, the Central Executive authorises action by the State Parliamentary Party to appeal to the only tribunal now available—the people.

In another room at the Trades Hall that night, the rival Executive was already preparing for an election. Kennelly was authorised to secure assistance interstate, including from Labor parliamentarians. Arrangements were made for re-forming branches to replace those that had defected, for obtaining finance from supporting unions and the public and for preliminary election organisation. Arrangements even had to be made to purchase material for the office being set up in the basement of the Trades Hall.

.   .   .

Cain went before the Victorian Parliament as Premier for the last time in the late afternoon of 19 April. The galleries of the green Legislative Assembly chamber were packed and the members were tense. Many members of the Upper House—which was not in session—crowded into the galleries nearest the members' seats.

Cain opened proceedings by presenting a message from the Lieutenant-Governor recommending that an appropriation be made for a Bill to amend the Superannuation Acts, and moving that the message be considered by a Committee of the whole House. A division was called for, and the breakaways crossed the floor to vote against it with the Liberal and Country Party opposition, the Country Party and the splinter Victorian Liberal Party led by T. T. Hollway.

The Leader of the Opposition, H. E. Bolte, then rose and moved: 'That as the Government accepts direction from sources which in the opinion of this House endanger the security of the country and the welfare of the State, it does not possess the confidence of the House.'

This motion, and the debating line to be followed, had been worked out at two meetings in the preceding weeks between Bolte and representatives of the old Executive and Coleman-Barry Caucus. For Bolte, then a forty-seven-year-old farmer from Meredith in Western Victoria, it was an astonishing political reversal. He had become Leader of the Opposition in 1953, when the then Opposition Leader, T. G. Oldham, was killed in an air crash. He had assessed then, as leader of a decimated party of eleven, that he would not become Premier until 1961. Instead, he was to become Premier in six weeks and to establish a record for the longest Premiership in the history of Victoria. Bolte made the following statement:

It may seem strange that a motion based on security should be introduced into a State Parliament, but Victoria has been singled out as the State for the first test of strength between the forces to which I shall refer; in my opinion they aim at overthrowing constitutional government in this Commonwealth. A few minutes ago the Premier read to the House a list of new ministers. In my view that is sufficient proof that he was directed to 'sack' certain ministers and that he was further directed to appoint others in their stead.

Mr Pettiona: 'Utter rubbish!'

Mr Bolte: '. . . I claim that the Premier praised the previous Government; yet by direction, he dismissed some ministers and replaced them with others.'

Mr Bourke: 'Where is your proof?'

Going on, Bolte read extracts from the *Communist Review* of September 1952, signed by L. Aarons, Secretary of the New South Wales State branch, on the tactics of the 'united front', the building up of a left wing inside the ALP led by communists and exclusion from the ALP of the right wing. He portrayed Evatt as having had consistent links with communists, from the Council of Civil Liberties before the war through to the recent events at the Petrov Commission. He hinted that the current events in the ALP were the start of the destruction of the right wing, as outlined by the *Communist Review*.

Bolte concluded, 'The Government accepts advice and directions from outside sources.'

Mr Bourke: 'Furnish some proof of that.'

Proof is easily obtainable. On the question of foreign policy, both Russia and Red China announced that no troops should be sent to Malaya, and within a few days the Federal Labor Party announced its policy of no troops for Malaya. In that instance the direction was given by an outside source and accepted by the Labor Party. The *Tribune*, the communist paper, applauded the action. There is no need for the Communist Party to be represented in Parliament when other members are prepared to work for it. This Government has no right to occupy the Treasury Bench; it should resign immediately so as to give the people an opportunity of deciding this issue.

The Country Party Leader, J. G. B. McDonald (later Sir John) seconded the motion, with copious references to Labor's new foreign affairs programme, and to alleged communist influence in the ALP. 'If the citizens of this country are to be expendable, I do not wish to be dealt with traitorously and treacherously by people who would sell me to somebody else in order to assist those who are Godless,' he said.

Cain then rose to defend his Government:

Not one member of the Opposition or the Opposition corner party believes one word of what has been said about myself and my colleagues. . . . My former Labor friends in the corner have run away from traditional principles that have been developed by the Labor party during the past forty years. . . . My former colleagues were reared on the principles espoused by the party to which they previously belonged and which was responsible for their election to this Parliament. However, they have now 'ratted' on that party and have joined forces with their life-long enemies in this country—the members of the Liberal party. They have aligned themselves with members of that party for the purpose of trying to preserve a little group in this State, which is outside the Labor movement. . . .

Everybody knows that the group of members led by the Hon. member for Carlton is the only section in Australia which has not accepted the decision of the Federal Conference of the Australian Labor Party. Some delegates from Queensland, South Australia [sic] and Western Australia boycotted the Federal Conference, but on return to their respective states they accepted the decisions of that Conference, both in Parliament and at meetings of the State Executive of the Labor Party. Those decisions now form part of the policy of the Australian Labor movement. . . .

After tackling some of the arguments of Bolte and McDonald, Cain then quoted from the January issue of the Victorian Central Executive paper *Labor*, in which McManus drew attention in his 'Room 2' column to requirements for the Special Conference. Then he produced nomination forms for the Conference, dated 14 January, signed by Barry, his wife and M. J. O'Reilly, a member of the Carlton-Fitzroy Central Branch of the ALP.

'Although these three people nominated for the Special Conference, they decided, after the Federal Executive decision, not to attend,' Cain said. 'That decision was made because of outside pressure from Keon and others.

They did not want to go because they thought they might lose their seats, and power was their most important consideration. . . .'

Later, Cain said it was true that 'matters were discussed' before the four ministers left Cabinet. 'The Hon. member for Carlton did not mention in his letter that the former Minister of Transport [Coleman] and myself had discussed this matter with a number of individuals from both sides,' he said. 'I had already informed him that there were great difficulties and a conflict of views. As everyone knows, it is not possible for two parliamentary parties to adopt a peaceful attitude without consulting their Executives.'

Mr Barry: 'My people were ready to talk; yours were not.'
Mr Cain: 'The group has never disclosed that willingness to the new Executive. . . . At no time have I had my objection to talking to anybody, but, as the Hon. member for Carlton knows, I cannot talk for two groups of people who will not speak to each other. Whatever eventuates, I have never had any desire to fall out with my erstwhile colleagues. . . .'

Barry began by praising the rank and file workers of the ALP. 'But in saying that, I except the new president of the Australian Labor Party, Vic Stout, and his colleagues,' he said. '. . . From time to time the Labor Party have supported various governments. . . . However, the trouble with Victor Stout is that we are not still sitting behind the Hollway Government.'

Accusing Stout of a war of revenge, Barry said:

On the one hand, he contended that we should have been supporting the Hollway Government, and, on the other, he said that all our factory legislation was presented without consulting him. There can be no criticism of the legislation that was passed dealing with long service leave and workers' compensation. The fact is that we are in this difficulty because we supported the Country Party. Mr Stout, by carrying on a war of revenge, has played the part of destroyer of Governments and the Labor movement. This has been done to satisfy a number of communists, who have a block vote of forty-four on the Trades Hall Council. They have taken complete control and are supporting Mr Stout against those who previously gave him all the assistance he required to control the industrial movement of this community. As a result, the comms. have pushed little Victor along and have swallowed the party which today claims to be the Government of this State. . . .

Barry next went through the relations of Stout and Broadby with Santamaria, defending the Industrial Groups and passing on to attack Evatt and to claim that the 'trial' of the old Central Executive was a travesty.

Barry spoke for nearly one-and-a-half hours. Galvin followed, personal rivalry showing through when he said Barry's remarks were 'typically Carltonian; they were addressed to the House with much noise and little logic'.

There were constant interjections throughout the night, and at one stage the Speaker, P. K. Sutton, had to call for an end to noise in the public gallery.

Hollway, the breakaway Liberal, appeared almost to defend the Cain Government, and there were constant interjections from Doube and others when Scully spoke, devoting much of his speech to the danger of communism.

Mr Scully: 'The Hon. member for Oakleigh moved the resolution which split the Victorian Parliamentary Labor Party.'
Mr Doube: 'I got rid of you.'

The sitting was suspended at a minute past midnight, until 12.50. When it resumed, Sheehan condemned the 'amazing change' in three weeks from those who had been seeking unity with the new Executive and were now accusing it of being tainted by communism.

Doube said the Barry group had 'chosen to follow the dangerous, tortuous and shameful road that was taken by Hughes, by Holman, by Lyons, by Hogan, by Lang and by other Labor traitors. . . .'

White, interjecting in several speeches, kept referring to the communist *Guardian,* and at another stage Sutton, the Speaker, called on members to stop bandying the name 'Santamaria' around.

Holt said the breakaways could 'accept no other name but the Santamaria Party'. He quoted various works of Denys Jackson, a prolific, erudite, right wing Catholic journalist and claimed that Jackson had been a supporter of Hitler in the 1930's.

Pettiona, the last speaker, rose about 3.30 a.m. He said one or possibly two people were responsible for the attitude of the Barry group. 'I refer to Stanley [sic] Michael Keon, a man . . . the Liberal Party have planted in the Labor Party. . . .' He said Keon and possibly Scully would have been the only ones to go off the Executive, if they had not boycotted the Conference.

The Cain Government fell at 4.20 a.m. With Barry in the lead, the breakaway group crossed the chamber in a division and the Assembly carried the vote of no confidence by 34 votes to 23. Barry, D'Arcy, Fewster, Hayes, Lucy, Morrissey, O'Carroll, Randles, Scully and White voted with the non-Labor parties to produce the majority of eleven for the motion.

The fall of the Cain Government, which had lasted two years and four months, cemented both sides of the schism. Except possibly for 'scab', 'rat' was the strongest word in the Labor man's dictionary of abuse, reserved for parliamentarians who crossed the floor to vote out hard-won Labor governments. There was hardly a member or supporter of the ALP who had not been reared on stories of 'Lyons the rat' of the 1930's and 'Hughes the rat' or 'Holman the rat' of the First World War period. Even among those opposed to Evatt and the activities of the Federal Executive—and this might be said even of Cain—bitterness against the Barry group flowed over, all too often to be reinforced by deep-seated religious prejudices, which came to the surface under pressure.

And, on the very day the 'eleven guilty men' crossed the floor of the Victorian Legislative Assembly, the seven expelled from the Federal Parliamentary Labor Party had gone to the cross-benches of the House of Representatives in Canberra and commenced bitter attacks on their former Party.

Cain handed in his commission immediately, and called elections for the Assembly on 28 May.

The emotions of the Trades Hall and Parliament House had been echoed in district branches and State and Federal electoral councils of the ALP all over Victoria throughout late March and early April, as decisions were taken for one or the other Executives. The old Executive estimated that 80 per cent of branches voted to go with it, and its opponents did not put the proportion much lower, though they claimed superior stacking of meetings by old Executive supporters. However, a lower proportion of total membership—probably around 60 per cent—actually went into physical support of the old Executive, as most branches split into two sections— unhappily, one usually predominantly Catholic and the other predominantly Protestant. One of the great fears of Labor men for years had eventuated: the Party had split down the middle on sectarian lines.

On Sunday 29 April the thirty-three Roman Catholic bishops of Australia, in the last controversial political statement they were to make in unity for many years, issued a Pastoral Letter politely but emphatically defending industrial groups in unions. 'It is most deplorable that the only effective way yet found of defeating communism in industrial life has been destroyed for the moment by political intrigue,' the bishops said. The letter, issued after a meeting of the bishops, closely followed arguments familiar to readers of *News Weekly*, including the reference from the *Communist Review* to communists wishing to foster a left wing in the ALP. It caused strong resentment among many Catholics, as well as non-Catholics, who considered it a blatant intrusion into a purely political question, however wise or unwise the views in themselves. Many also thought the letter was rather patently timed for the Victorian election. This Pastoral was to be an important incident in completing the breach between the sees of Sydney and Melbourne on relations with The Movement.

Evatt issued a statement immediately, saying the bishops had no right to interfere in the internal organisation of the ALP. He said they had a right to criticise on matters of national concern, such as the policies of the ALP, but not on organisation. Evatt made several references to the 'Santamaria faction'.

By early May, both Executives had started endorsing candidates for the Victorian election—a precedent that introduced the controversial practice of Executive pre-selections into the Victorian ALP. The new Executive chose Lovegrove to contest Carlton against Barry—reputedly because Stout believed Lovegrove would be ignominiously defeated, though others more friendly claimed he would be the best candidate. Woodhouse was selected from a field of three to contest Northcote against Cain.

The breakaways had originally chosen the name 'Victorian Labor Party', but the Speaker of the Assembly had ruled this out. Their Conference on the weekend of 28-29 April adopted the title 'Australian Labor Party (Anti-Communist)', but in the press and even among themselves the name 'Coleman-Barry Labor' became accepted. The new Executive supporters won by popular usage the title 'Cain Labor'.

Bolte opened the electoral campaign in Victoria in Ararat Town Hall on 5 May before a crowd of about 150, with promises for increased housing finance, penal reform, stricter treatment for car thieves and an overhaul of state transport.

Next evening Barry opened in Fitzroy Town Hall, in one of the rowdiest election meetings for many years. He drew deafening applause from the crowd of 1,000 with remarks like, 'We will oppose communism, Evattism and capitalism', but there was also a barrage of interjections throughout his speech. There were many private arguments in the hall, with individuals and groups shouting at each other. The press reported that at least two fights broke out, both quickly stopped by other members of the crowd.

Barry promised long-term housing loans at two per cent through the State Savings Bank, an increase in the Government guarantee to co-operative societies from £48 million to £60 million, abolition of the Camp Pell emergency housing centre and more urgent slum reclamation. Pensioners would be given free transport at off-peak periods and concession fare at other times. Superannuation for retired state public servants would be increased.

These conventional enough policy points drew little attention, however, except perhaps for criticism that the two per cent housing loan would prove economically impracticable. Rather, the inevitable interest in the election lay in how Barry, Coleman and their supporters would present their case for having the election at all. Much of the style was by now only too predictable, as the following examples of press reports of Barry's speech indicate:

There was both applause and shouts of derision when Barry attacked Lovegrove as a former communist who 'ratted on the communists, ratted on the Labor Party and ratted on his mates'.

Dr Evatt was 'the most dangerous man to the Labor Party in Australia today'.

He had never accused Cain of being a pawn of communists or his colleagues of being communists, 'but I do accuse them of weakness and lack of courage in the face of the communists and something which is just as bad—Evattism. . . . They are lying down to the Reds and the Doctor.'

As the crowd were leaving the hall at the end of the meeting, Cremean, who had been elected President of the new Party at the 29 April Conference and was chairman of the meeting, appeared on the platform. He said there were 'jackals distributing filthy communist literature outside the hall', and added, 'You know what to do'. A shouting, gesticulating crowd then gathered round two young men near the door distributing leaflets from the left-wing Plumbers' Union, but no actual violence developed.

Cain's opening meeting at Northcote Town Hall on 9 May illustrated the huge strategic advantage he had. He opened as the Premier of Victoria asking for a fresh mandate, with his opponent, Woodhouse, relatively unknown to the public. On the platform with him were Evatt, Calwell, Cahill, J. E. Duggan (Deputy Premier of Queensland) and R. J. Heffron, Cahill's Deputy. Most of the former State Ministers were there, and the organs of the Trade Union Movement as well as most unions were backing Cain.

Throughout the campaign, Cain avoided controversy and much mention of the breakaways and kept to election issues of the more mundane type. In his opening speech, before an overwhelmingly loyal crowd of 2,000, he promised immediate reductions in rail fares and freights, roofing of the Jolimont railway yards and immediate establishment of an Institute of Technology; he also said the Government hoped to be able to make an early start on the Melbourne Underground Railway.

Cain said, 'The attempt to link the Labor Party with communism is fraudulent and those responsible for such statements know they are false'; but this was one of his few references to the Coleman-Barry Party. At times there were shouts of 'You sold the Labor Party out' from the hall, and at one stage three police carried a still-struggling interjector from the hall when a fight looked like developing.

Calwell, increasingly firmly committed to the Party he had stayed with, brought applause when he said, 'Nothing can excuse, explain or extenuate the action of those who voted to destroy [the Cain Government].'

A much wilder rival meeting was being held in Richmond Town Hall that night, in support of Scully. Police escorted six men from the crowd of 500 at Richmond Town Hall, and two men started fighting in front of the platform.

These meetings prepared the way for probably the wildest and most embittered meeting of the campaign, when Lovegrove opened his campaign against Barry at Fitzroy. Police broke up several scuffles, while constant cries of 'Dinny the rat', 'You're an ex-comm., Lovegrove' came from the crowd of 1,200. Lovegrove, in turn, said the Anti-Communist Labor Party were 'not Christians, but a lot of bigots'. 'Their philosophy is not Christianity or democracy,' he said. 'What is their philosophy?'—and before he finished the crowd roared 'Fascism'.

And—'There are some people around here who call Mr Barry the "Minister for Power Without Glory", others call him "The Minister for Debney's Paddock".'

An interjector: 'That's a dirty one, Lovegrove.'

The fight in Carlton became the bitterest and most violent of the campaign, with mutual recriminations and smears flying between Lovegrove and Barry, an upsurge of sectarian anti-Catholic feeling against Barry supported by frequent portrayal of him as a 'rat'—a word that appeared scrawled on many of his posters.

Well publicised, this had the effect of making Lovegrove rather than Cain appear to be Barry's opponent. Cain fought a fairly dignified campaign as Premier, leaving the smearing—of which there was much on both sides—to others.

On one side, the word 'Santamaria' was bandied freely about with the innuendo, if not outright accusation, of clerical fascism and a deeply sinister Southern European Catholic Plot. On 12 May, for instance, Gladman said at Warrnambool in his opening campaign with Cain on the platform, 'The Santamaria group would make Hitler's Blackshirts and Mussolini's Fascists pale into insignificance.'

From the other side, there were continual accusations of 'lying down to the communists', 'the pro-communist Evatt foreign policy', 'communist domination at the Trades Hall', etc.

While the two rival Labor groups tore away at each other, the Liberals, who had their own minority problem with the small Hollway group still surviving, campaigned fairly quietly. Menzies spoke before 1,500 in the Melbourne Town Hall on 20 May, with a quiet appeal to the electorate to 'throw out all splinter groups'.

Archbishop Mannix intervened on 20 May, stating that the issue of the election was communism. 'Loss of the Groups and their fight will ultimately mean the end of the Church in Australia,' he said. 'There are two Labor policies, that of Dr Evatt, who hastens to defend communists at home and abroad, and advocates recognition of Red China, and that of those who fight communism wherever possible as the enemy of God, Christianity and freedom.' A correspondent of the *Sydney Morning Herald* covering the campaign said the Archbishop—whose attitude was echoed by the Victorian provincial bishops and the Church press—had 'gone as close to saying "Vote Coleman-Barry" as it is possible, without actually saying so'.

A few days later another twist to the sectarian spiral came when Lovegrove dramatically released a letter from The Movement chaplain, Father Eric D'Arcy, calling 'carefully chosen Catholics in business and professional spheres' to a secret meeting where the 'person best qualified to explain the present crisis' would be heard. 'The next few weeks will see either a great victory or a great defeat for the men working so stoutly to defend the Church in Australia,' the letter said, and ended with the warning that there would be 'strictly no admittance without this letter'. The letter had fallen into anti-Movement hands and been 'leaked' to Lovegrove.

Any faint hope that the destruction being wrought by the campaign might be mitigated went in the last week, when both sides decided the order of their preferences. Under preferential voting, an exchange of second preferences would have allowed a much higher number of border-line candidates of either Labor Party to be returned than if they gave their preferences to the Liberals. But this was a fight to the death, and the more enemy personnel destroyed, the greater the chance of ultimate victory, however pyrrhic.

The Stout-Cain Executive decided its preferences on 23 May giving them to the LCP or Country Party in nineteen out of the thirty-two seats, to the Coleman-Barry Party in eleven; the preferences behind Cain and Lovegrove were left open, without a recommendation from the Party 'ticket'. The Coleman-Barry Executive met on 26 May and gave their preferences against the Cain Party in most seats, including against Cain and Lovegrove. On both sides, there were strong elements of personal vindictiveness in the decisions, though sheer personalities—including anger against those considered 'comm. types', renegade Catholic rightists, Protestant sectarians, or culpable in the development of the split—seemed to play more part in the Coleman-Barry decisions.

These decisions were symptomatic of a far deeper bitterness. Those who took part in the campaign were never likely to forget it. Everybody has his story of being insulted and even spat upon, of doors shut in the face, of scuffles, whispering campaigns and defacement or destruction of rival campaign literature. Barry and some other breakaways received dead rats in the mail. Many on both sides received angry or threatening telephone calls. Men who had been close friends since childhood stopped speaking to each other. Catholics supporting the Cain party were snubbed at church and their children often made miserable at Church schools. Political sermons thundered out from many pulpits, both Catholic and Protestant, and there were some singularly confused and hysterical articles in religious newspapers of all parts of the Christian spectrum. The feeling engendered was so intense that it took many years to die away.

It was clear by the last hour or two of 28 May that the Coleman-Barry Party had been annihilated—and that Henry Bolte would be the new Premier of Victoria. It was the first Victorian election under the 'two for one' redistribution of seats, which had transferred much power from the rural to the city vote, and also increased the size of the Legislative Assembly by one.

The comparative strengths of the parties in the retiring Assembly of sixty-five seats and the post-election one of sixty-six were:

	Old Assembly	*New Assembly*
Liberal and Country	11	33
Victorian Liberal (Hollway)	4	–
Country	12	11
Cain Labor	25	20
Coleman-Barry Labor	12	1
Progressive Labor	1	1

Percentages of the vote were as follows:

	per cent		*per cent*
Liberal and Country Party	37·78	Cain Labor	32·57
Victorian Liberal Party	3·46	Coleman-Barry Labor	12·61
Independent Liberal	0·35	Progressive Labor and Independent Labor	1·45
Total Liberal	41·69		
Country Party	9·53	Total Labor	46·63

Scully, who defeated P. V. O'Connell by a narrow margin in Richmond, was the only member of the Coleman-Barry Party to keep his seat. Randles was defeated by C. Turnbull in Brunswick West and Hayes by A. Clarey in Melbourne, both by narrow margins. Otherwise the defeat of the Barry group was complete. Barry lost his seat to Lovegrove, whom his Party reviled as a traitor. Cain was back as Leader of the Parliamentary Labor Party, with the loss of only five supporters. At the same time, Hollway and his group had been driven from politics. Ironically, Hollway's seat in the last parliament, Glen Iris, had been eliminated in the redistribution, on which Hollway had staked his political life, and he had had to contest a seat where he was unknown.

For Bolte, the election was an easy triumph. With his following in the Assembly tripled and his own splinter Party defeated, he was able to govern without Country Party support. He received his commission as Premier of Victoria on 2 June. Labor's brief triumph, its strongest position in the history of the unstable Victorian Parliament, forged from the wounds of a shattered Liberal Party in 1952, had been destroyed in less than three years by a split that was about—in tangible state political issues —nothing. Stable government had come to Victoria, not out of the ruins of the Liberal Party, but out of the ruins of Labor.

Some of the Coleman-Barry faction had expected a substantial victory, others were not so sure. But hardly anybody had forecast the devastation that occurred; it was supposed that at least a sizeable nucleus of sitting members would be returned. Yet in retrospect it is possible to see that what occurred was the inevitable result of the decision to boycott the Special Conference, taken five and a half months earlier by angry, hurt and worried men.

The inevitable result of the boycott was to give the decisive power in the Victorian ALP to the new Stout-left coalition, whose intransigent mood might have been obvious in a cooler analysis, as must that of the Federal Executive in Hobart. The boycott could only have succeeded if it had been followed by a better showing at the polls than that of the 'machine' backed Labor group, or if the Victorian Executive had remained united and re- tained the support of the Parliamentary Party. The second of these possibi- lities was ruled out largely by the position of Cain, whose cautious belief in working strictly within the rules of the ALP and whose resentment at frequent overruling by the Central Executive, and the general opposition to him of the right, inevitably inclined him against the boycott.

The difficulties of achieving electoral success were monumental, and it is difficult in retrospect to explain the gamble taken by experienced parlia- mentarians except by the fevered mood of the time.

The Coleman-Barry faction went to the State without a leader or an issue and with the certainty of being typed as a 'Church Party'—and a sinisterly dominated one at that. The risk in any splinter party is that it will become over-emotional, obsessed with personalities and internal issues and appear to the neutral observer as sour and fanatical. This is exactly the fate that befell the Anti-Communist Labor Party.

Immediately they broke away, the Barry group had faced impossible dif- ficulties in selecting a leader. The Movement wanted Scully, but Barry was obviously the senior parliamentarian. Barry, however, was simply not a credible alternative Premier. Though a genial, kindly man of little malice, he was inclined to bluster and to adopt an old-fashioned 'boots and all' style of politicking. His speech had a rough, uneducated edge and there was the indelible Wren taint. These failings led the breakaways to make the cooler, more presentable Coleman their Leader, though he was a Mem- ber of the Legislative Council while the election would be for Barry's Lower House.

The onus was on Barry to explain his own position, but instead he was trapped by the dynamics of politics into a slanging match with Lovegrove, while Cain was able to appear as the dignified Premier. The breakaways had no answer to Cain Labor's advertising slogan—alongside a picture of the grandfatherly, pipe-smoking Premier—'Solid, sensible citizens know they can trust John Cain'.

The only issue the breakaways could use was that of communism. Used against a Party led by Cain and a little-known Executive presided over by the, until recently, bitterly anti-communist Stout, it sounded like crude smearing, lending weight to the innuendo of clerical fascism. The argument about the Industrial Groups was impossibly intricate to present in an election, while that on foreign policy had only the barest relevance.

These arguments were not without weight, though, in the longer term. The effect of the disowning of the Groups and their association with both a splinter party and a discredited Movement was to remove the effective barrier to communist penetration of the Trade Union Movement—a penetration to which the most influential group on the new Victorian Central Executive had little objection. Already in April, the Commonwealth Council of the Amalgamated Engineering Union had gone back under communist control. By June, ALP left wingers were running with communists on 'unity tickets'—teams recommended by 'how to vote' cards—for elections to the Australian Railways Union and Waterside Workers' Federation in Victoria. Both were under complete communist and left wing control by 1956. The ARU and AEU had the two biggest delegations at Victorian ALP Conferences, and were able to exercise great influence. The new Executive appeared to welcome them as additional anti-Grouper strength and for many years 'looked the other way' at the breach of ALP rules by those who appeared running for union office on the same platform as members of a rival party. At the same time, the emergent left, working closely with the communists, was able to control many weaker union leaders, who no longer could afford to play the Groups and the left off against each other.

The left showed a keen interest in foreign policy and, with the strongly pro-Western view now discredited, had no trouble in reinvigorating isolationist, mildly anti-Western sympathies in the ALP. Certainly for anybody who shared the Santamaria deep concern at communist pressure in South East Asia, this was an alarming trend.

For technical reasons, the Legislative Council election was not held until 18 June. After the rancour of May, it was a quiet election, fought mainly on the radio and in the press. Coleman, opening the campaign in a radio address on 6 June, went for a 'soft sell'. 'The lesson of the Legislative Assembly election was that Labor cannot have electoral success until it faces the people united,' he said. It could not govern unless the unions were in 'sound and sensible Labor hands'.

All eleven Coleman-Barry candidates, including Coleman himself (the only sitting member) were defeated. Coleman, in Melbourne West, received only about 40 per cent of the vote of the Cain Labor candidate, Machin. In a Council of six-year terms, with half the membership retiring each three years, the other sitting Coleman-Barry members, Little, Brennan, Paul Jones, Sheehy and Bailey, were safe until 1958.

The Council election, however, saw a substantial rise in the combined Labor vote and at the close of Sunday counting the *Age* put the Coleman-Barry share of the vote at 16·53 per cent and that of Cain Labor at 39·42 per cent, compared with a total of only 35·44 per cent for all the Liberal groups and 5·98 per cent for the Country Party.

Chapter Seventeen
'The Seven'

By a coincidence, the Federal Parliament had been set to re-convene for the autumn session on 20 April—only a few hours after the Coleman-Barry group crossed the floor in Melbourne. With seven Victorian members of the Federal Parliamentary Labor Party expelled only thirteeen days before, an electric atmosphere in Parliament was unavoidable.

The expelled seven had met at the Trades Hall in Melbourne on the weekend of 16-17 April, adopting the same name as the State breakaways, 'Australian Labor Party (Anti-Communist)'. To the surprise of many, they elected the unknown Joshua, from Ballarat, as their Leader and Keon as Deputy. Robert Joshua, born in 1909, had been a bank clerk and rose to the rank of Lieutenant-Colonel during the War. He was attracted to the ALP by its promise of ameliorating the social conditions of the 1930's and, rather surprisingly for a private bank employee in the late 1940's, joined because he favoured nationalisation of the banks. Within two years, in 1951, he was MP for the 'swinging' Division of Ballarat, which had gone to the Liberals in 1949 and came back to Labor with a good campaign and a well chosen, highly respectable 'horse for the course' in 1951. A practising Anglican layman, but with a Catholic wife and children, Joshua was a decent, well-meaning man of dignified military bearing, but little schooled in the labyrinthine ways of National and Labor politics.

Joshua had been nominated for Leader by Mullens, on the perhaps naive principle that the choice of a non-Catholic to lead an otherwise Catholic group would be a politically valuable gesture to the non-Catholic majority in the community. National feeling in the climate of 1955, encouraged wherever possible by the ALP, was much more that Joshua was a 'stooge' for The Movement. In the nine torrid months in which he was an active Party Leader, he experienced continual sneers against the authenticity of his leadership.

Arriving in Canberra on 19 April, the 'sad seven', 'soured seven' and 'sacred seven' as they variously became known, were allotted Calwell's Deputy Leader suite in Parliament House as a Party room. This was much to the annoyance of Calwell, who protested at being moved to a less convenient part of the House, where he could less easily maintain the contact he required as Deputy with the Leader of the Government, Sir Eric Harrison. A further irony was that the rooms were only a couple of doors down the passage from Evatt's suite.

The presence of the 'seven' in the corridors was little more than a pin-prick for the troubled Labor Caucus of that week, however. New South Wales was only in less turmoil than Victoria, and there was unprecedented tension in most of the other states. Splits as great as that in Victoria were possible, and the outcome of Federal Executive moves in Sydney and the election in Victoria were anxiously awaited.

Forces in politics are often bigger than the men involved, and one seeming fact of life in mid-April of 1955 was that Evatt was finished. Few thought his Leadership would last more than a few months and even fewer that he could now go before the nation again as an alternative Prime Minister. The inevitable outcome of this was ruthless manoeuvring for the succession. Calwell was the favourite of most Catholics and the right, Ward of the left and the anti-Grouper front in New South Wales. Clarey, whose name was often paired with that of Pollard, as Deputy, was suggested as a compromise. The Kennelly group in the Federal 'machine' leant towards Calwell or Clarey, while the militant, 'pro-Evatt', faction was being cultivated by Ward.

Calwell's difficult strategy had to be to remain unchallenged as Deputy, avoiding antagonising Kennelly, the remaining Grouper faction or the new force in Victoria, which controlled his pre-selection. The Ward strategy had to be early destruction of Calwell's legitimacy of succession, and forcing him towards the right. Clarey had to remain uncontroversial and be ready to step forward if either of the others became too identified with an extreme to be acceptable. The idea of a 'left wing party', which seems to have originated from admiration for the Bevanite tendency in the British Labour Party, had been a subject of speculative discussion for some time, and now began to crystallise around the possibility of Ward's leadership. In as far as it had any aim other than power, it was dedicated to 'socialism' —a concept rarely explained, though the implication of whole-scale nationalisation was there and the suggestion was often made that the Party might have to spend ten to fifteen years out of office before it could educate the Australian public to accept such a platform.

Caucus met on 18 April in full knowledge of the forces rending it. Early, Clarey moved a vote of 'complete confidence' in Evatt's leadership, with McKenna seconding. According to the correspondent of the *Age*, Evatt had persuaded Clarey in Melbourne earlier in the month to take this step. It was an important step towards unity, but at the same time tended to neutralise the efforts of the Kennelly group to get rid of Evatt, the correspondent said.

Before a vote could be taken, however, Evatt announced to Caucus that he would resign and stand anew for the Leadership. This was typical of Evatt's sudden gambles, and it paid off handsomely. With the Ward supporters still not ready to move, and Calwell both identified to some extent with the losing side and quite unable to organise, Evatt was returned by a handsome majority. He received 52 votes, against 22 for Calwell and 5 for Tom Burke, his only opponents. A further advantage for Evatt of his gamble was that the vote was by a show of hands; his opponents claimed he would have done less well at a secret ballot. The outcome, however, meant that Evatt would now be much harder to remove.

Tactically beaten, the Ward group now backed a 'spill'. E. G. Whitlam, the young Sydney barrister who would himself become Leader, moved that all Party offices, except those of Leader and Secretary, be vacated and re-contested. This led to an angry debate, in which Ward supporters singled Calwell, the Deputy Leader in the Senate, J. I. Armstrong, and the Whip, F. M. Daly, out for attack. These were the officers they hoped to replace, and there was no shortage of contenders for the vacancies.

Kennelly and his loyal supporter, Senator J. P. Toohey, urged caution, and postponement of the vote until the Federal Executive completed its investigations in New South Wales, and this course was adopted. Fraser, from Eden-Monaro, had complained in the debate that Ward was trying to introduce a 'reign of terror' in Caucus.

The 'spill' motion eventually came up for a vote on 4 May, after a compromise had slowed down events in New South Wales, and was defeated thirty-nine to thirty-three in a Division, after a thirty-five-all tie in a vote by show of hands. With Caucus almost equally divided, Evatt would be able to ride the tiger for some months yet.

Formation by the 'seven' of their own Party had produced an abusive press statement from Evatt, who said they should be known as 'the Santamaria Group'. He said they had come into existence solely because of the consistent actions of the Santamaria faction to control from outside all activities of the ALP. He followed up immediately, when the Coleman-Barry group crossed the floor, with a statement attacking the 'most wicked and treacherous manoeuvre in the history of the Australian Labor Movement'. Some Victorian members had been forced to betray their election pledges by the 'nauseating action of the Santamaria-McManus-Keon group', which had forced them to join the Bolte anti-Labor Party, Evatt said.

The 'seven' now were in an extremely difficult strategic position. Any move against the main Labor Party would be represented as 'betrayal' and aggravate the already practically irreparable damage. But to maintain silence or to support the main Party on all questions would deprive them of even a sporting chance at an election—a chance they were more likely to assume they had before the voting in the Victorian election a few weeks later.

Far from being all manipulated by Santamaria, the seven were in fact a fairly disparate group. Bryson and Cremean were orthodox Labor men; Cremean inclined cautiously to the right and Bryson rather more to the old left. Andrews was as orthodox, but closer to Santamaria and The Movement. Bourke was an individualist of intellectual bent who might have been more at home in the bigger and more comfortably diverse British Labour Party—and he was strongly opposed to the presumption of Santamaria and The Movement, though not to all their ideas. Keon had his own individualistic style of the far right on foreign affairs, while Mullens was influenced by both Keon and Santamaria. As a group, they were probably of above average ability, but the dominating intelligences were those of Keon and Bourke, the youngest members, not yet fully mature politically. Bourke was then forty-one, Keon just forty.

Some of these men believed they had taken a gamble which still might pay off, others that they had acted from conscience in refusing to accept an intolerable situation. No doubt something of both motivated most. At least, when they faced Parliament from the cross-benches on the afternoon of 20 April 1955, they were inwardly seething with anger, bewildered and bitterly hurt by their experiences of recent months.

Their strategy, which developed early, was to attack the ALP on a narrow front—on association with communists, Asian policy and the like—while remaining orthodox on other questions and voting as often as possible with Labor.

An important aspect of their psychology at this time was mystification and bewilderment at the events which had suddenly thrust them, in a year, from the threshold of Cabinet to the cross benches. There was, of course, the possibility that Evatt was insane, and this was considered; as was the theory of his innate political villainy. But another explanation often clutched at—on both Opposition and cross-benches—was that Evatt was under some hold by the Communist Party. It was often crudely assumed that the seven attacked Evatt for being a communist sympathiser himself, but except in moments of high anger and rhetoric this was hardly a serious suggestion. What was taken more seriously was a rumour that Evatt had once held a ticket in the Communist Party, in the 1920's, and that in some way this gave the communists a hold over him. Another rumour, which had gone the rounds of Caucus for eighteen months or so, was that the Party 'establishment' had collected £13,000 from the communists to help fight the 1951 referendum. This was also canvassed as a possible explanation of the supposed 'hold' over Evatt and had its appeal to men with a strong predisposition to anti-communism. In retrospect, Evatt's motives seem simpler, but the £13,000 story formed the basis of the first attack on Evatt from the cross-benches.

Once questions and other preliminaries were over on the first day, the Speaker, Sir Archie Cameron, announced that Bourke wished to debate as a matter of urgent public importance:

The subservience of the right honourable the Leader of the Opposition and his followers to the Communist Party, as evidenced by his acceptance of large sums of money from communist sources to the funds of the party led by him.

Eight members were required to support such a motion before it could be debated, and this required the support of at least one Liberal if the seven were to get their urgency motions before the House. As might be expected, such help was always forthcoming.

Speaking with obvious emotion and anger, Bourke said the 'followers' to whom the motion referred were 'not by any means the majority of the honourable members seated behind the right honourable gentleman'.

We all know that most of those honourable members do not support him. The followers to whom I refer are mostly outside this House. As a matter of fact, most of them are not members of the Australian Labor Party. . . .

We members of this Parliament are witnessing a very sad spectacle. We are witnessing the breaking up, the wrecking of the Australian Labor Party, a party with very great traditions, which even its opponents will admit has rendered yeoman service to the people of this country. Here we see something which nobody in this country can view with equanimity. We see the Labor Party being broken up as a result of the cold-blooded, deliberately worked out plot by the Right Hon. Member for Barton [Evatt], a man who has won an assured place in history for himself, who will go down in history as the man who wrecked the Australian Labor Party, and a man who has been the best friend the communists in this country have ever known.

Bourke said Evatt's motives had been that he wanted:

to make the remnant of the Labor Party which he will be leading soon a mere front organisation of the Communist Party so that it can give effect to Marxian socialism in internal affairs and follow a communist-line policy in the interests of red imperialism in external affairs. Anybody who studies the record—the honeycombing of the Department of External Affairs by avowed communists, the Right Hon. gentleman's remarkable actions since he became leader of the Labor Party, his appearances before the Royal Commission. . . .

Bourke said the communists would be able to step into the vacuum created by abolition of the Industrial Groups. He said there had been a pledge and obligation that the Labor Party would have nothing to do with the Communist Party in its referendum campaign, but the Communist Party had contributed £13,000 to the 'slush fund' of the Labor Party.

Mr Curtin: 'Judas!'
Mr Bourke: 'Some people talk about Judas. He sold his principles for a few pieces of silver, but others have sold their principles for a few pounds from the Communist Party.'

Bourke said that Beazley—'a man of unimpeachable honour, high ideals and strong principles'—had told him in the latter half of 1953, as he had told others, that Kennelly, then Federal Secretary, had related to him in considerable detail conversations between Kennelly and the Victorian Communist Party Secretary, Ted Hill. The story was that Hill, using on Kennelly's advice an assumed name so Mrs Kennelly would not know, had called at Kennelly's South Melbourne home. This had been at the instance of Evatt. 'Senator Kennelly argued and bargained with Mr Hill and spoke about who would be in Pentridge if this legislation went through,' Bourke said. Hill had promised to arrange a contribution of £13,000 from Communist sources to the ALP funds.

Evatt immediately responded, angrily, with a flat denial. It was 'absolutely and wickedly false' to suggest that the ALP under his leadership had got £13,000 from the Communist Party, he said. 'I do believe that whisperers and slanderers then in the Labor Party spread that rumour in the lobbies of this Parliament,' Evatt said. 'It was directed against Senator Kennelly in the first instance and primarily against him. He denied it to the world, and not in Parliament under privilege.' Evatt said that, he, Calwell and McKenna, as trustees of the Party trust fund, had issued a total denial on 13 November 1953.

Evatt said Keon, Mullens and Bourke had tried to sabotage the referendum and then asked to whom they were 'subservient'. 'I think we know. They are subservient to a totalitarian group,' he said. 'I have said it over and over again. They are completely subservient, or they would not make false charges of this character. Their methods are completely totalitarian. I have already referred to their attempt to wreck Labor in 1951. . . .'

And so the debate went on, with Evatt throwing in all of his 'sinister Santamaria' rhetoric, Keon, Mullens and Cremean elaborating in ever more colourful detail on the £13,000 story and the general infamy of Evatt. Calwell denied it, while Pollard and Ward flayed the 'seven' with all the vilifying oratory at their command. Here are two examples:

Mullens: There is evidence that the suppression of the Industrial Groups and of every worthwhile anti-communist force in this community is entirely his [Evatt's] work. The Communist Party of Australia has the screw on him and will have it on him for ever. What a cheerful destiny with which to confront our children! A potential Prime Minister who is under the influence of the communists. . . . More than 400 million Asiatics, with their claims of nationalism, are pressing down on us, and these men, who are so skilled in foreign affairs [Evatt and Burton] are willing to advocate that our last line of defence should be Darwin. In the meantime, the communist enemy would have dynamited the whole industrial structure of Australia. . . .

Ward: It is quite evident from the joy which this action of the betrayers of Labor, who now sit in the corner, has given to those whose particular cause they are serving in this debate, that they are out to damage and destroy Labor if they can possibly do so. It is not a recent decision of theirs to undermine Labor. The Hon. Member for Yarra [Mr Keon], who is designated as the deputy leader of this nondescript group, could not, judging by his type of speech, represent a more appropriate electorate, not on account of the electorate itself, but having regard to the tales that are told about the smelly Yarra which flows through it. . . .

The debate ended with a personal explanation from Beazley, who said he had a private conversation with Bourke about the affair and passed on a conversation he had had with a senator. But Beazley said he had never claimed to know for a fact that the money had been handed on to Evatt, and he had accepted Evatt's denial of this.

Debates of this kind, which were to occur almost weekly while Parliament sat, had such potential for division that little help from the Government parties would be needed. But that evening, 20 April, Menzies was able to throw one solid ideological issue into the arena, on which bitter division could flourish for weeks.

This was the long dormant question of whether Australian troops should be committed to fight in Malaya, then at the height of the protracted battle between British-led troops and jungle guerillas, mostly Chinese by race and led and dominated by communists. Pressure from Britain and the United States for Australia to commit troops in South-East Asia had been likely for some years. The end of the Korean War in 1953 and formation of SEATO in the spring of 1954 produced the situation where Menzies, during a trip to London, Europe and Washington, became subject to this pressure. On 1 April 1955, he announced that the small air representation Australia had in Malaya would be supplemented with further air units, naval representation and a battalion of infantry with supporting arms. He repeated the announcement to Parliament when it opened on 20 April, but did not make it clear until some weeks later that the Australian forces would be free to take part in both anti-insurgent operations and general defence.

Labor's position had been made clear at the Hobart Conference, and Evatt strongly attacked the commitment when he opened the debate on Menzies' statement on 27 April.

Evatt said Menzies had no positive plans for promoting peace in South-East Asia or elsewhere. His, Menzies', speech had been almost entirely negative. Menzies was hardly a supporter of the United Nations. The ALP believed the use of Australian troops in Malaya would gravely endanger Australia's relations with Malaya and her Asian neighbours. The guerilla operations in Malaya had been going on for years and the final settlement or agreement seemed certain to take the form of some amnesty and rehabilitation plan.

Evatt said Malaya was outside the scope of SEATO. The doctrine of fighting 4,000 miles away to avoid fighting nearer had some truth, but not with a nation of Australia's limited resources in peacetime. It was certain to be regarded as provocative. Would it be right for China to allocate armed units, by arrangement with Indonesia, to forestall possible military operations from Australia?

These may well have been Evatt's genuine, deeply felt views, though his record of politicking on foreign policy in previous years suggests such a conclusion should be tentative. But there is no doubt that views of this kind found much support throughout the Labor Movement, and would help to restore a belief in him as Leader. Also, according to a few references in the press about this time, Evatt appeared to believe that the next election would be fought on foreign policy, and that opposition to committal of troops in Asia would be a winning issue; certainly it would tend to force the Liberals and the breakaway Party together.

The emotional appeal of Evatt's policy in the Labor Movement lay, in the main, in a feeling that imperialism (for which some Australians of the inter-war generation seemed to feel somewhat guilty) and local capitalists and landlords had been exploiting Asian peoples. Any rebellion was to be welcomed and, very often, was assumed to have popular support. The idea of white troops fighting coloured, leftist rebels became abhorrent in these circumstances, and doubly so when it was assumed that such an action would inflame Asian opinion against Australia. There was a fear that, by taking arms against rebel movements, Australia could become bogged down in a war of the kind that eventually broke out in Vietnam. There was a common tendency to apply this theory indiscriminately, and to assume that all 'Asians', with the exception of a few landlords, were much the same.

In the particular circumstances of Malaya, vocal public opinion in Malaya and Asia generally was divided and difficult to follow. The Chinese and Indian left, particularly in Singapore, was opposed to commitment, though Malay leaders generally were not. However, the opposition seems to have been in part inspired by local political exigencies, and once Australian troops were commited only the far left of public opinion was opposed. Certainly, within a decade, when Britain was finding her commitments onerous, the overwhelming force of opinion in Malaya and Singapore was for other Commonwealth troops to be stationed there. Malaya became independent in 1957 and Singapore in 1959. There was pressure for independence earlier, and certainly in 1955, but British and much Malay feeling was that it should wait until after the emergency.

Labor speeches in the debate of 1955 on this and related issues tended to be highly emotional, with frequent references to the Asian landlords, the imperialists and the presumed hatred Australia would earn by committing troops. With the exception of Beazley, who had a right-wing approach in keeping with his Moral Rearmament attitudes, Labor speakers rarely attempted sophisticated or detailed analysis, or showed any feeling for the intricacies of diplomacy or international military strategy. The Liberals and the Country Party had no worries about imperialism or landlords, and most of their speakers revealed typical conservative attitudes, in which support for the West and status quo were natural. (In general, *Hansard* records an almost continual decline in the quality of debates on foreign affairs in the Australian Parliament from 1950 onwards.)

Joshua followed Evatt and showed that a new force had arrived in Australian politics. It was a competent speech, though mainly in strategic and military terms and indicating no great feel for the political problems. Keon, cataclysmic as ever, spoke on 3 May and said the Malay peninsula was the only place where a Chinese force coming to invade Australia could be stopped. He accused the 'followers of Evatt' of 'selling out the gateway of this country'.

Foreign affairs and the Industrial Groups were the only issues on which the two Labor parties showed themselves in debates to be divided. The breakaways, dubbed in the Press 'Joshua-Keon Labor', voted in nearly all divisions with 'Evatt Labor', even at times when it appeared to cut across their expressed policies. In domestic affairs, with few contentious issues raised, they were conventionally Labor in approach. Joshua, Keon, Mullens and Bourke dominated the debates.

Even the small area of division adopted provided the fuel for almost continual outbreaks of fire, however. Approximately once a week, the

Joshua-Keon group raised some issue which would embarrass the Opposition benches, and to which there rarely was an answer. Sometimes they used the device of moving that Parliament debate a question as a matter of urgency, and for less important questions they used the traditional Wednesday night free debate on the question that the House adjourn.

After its embarrassment by the first urgency motion, on the £13,000 story, the main ALP adopted a strategy of proposing rival urgency motions. Invariably, short, heated debates followed as to procedure and which motion should be chosen and these often had the effect of inflaming the Parliament before the main debate even started.

On these occasions, the House of Representatives is recalled as a chamber of high, tense drama. Eloquent invective, occasionally degenerating to personal insult, flashed across from cross-benches to Opposition benches, and back again. Inevitably, what had been left of worthwhile personal relations disappeared as the bitter months wore on. After the Victorian elections, the Joshua-Keon men realised that they had little chance of survival and this helped to maintain their rage against the main Party. The compromise in New South Wales in April had also cut off the prospects of early support from the last solidly Grouper state.

Suspensions from the Chamber were a regular occurrence when the Joshua-Keon Party attacked the Evatt Party, as interjections and insults flew both ways. Almost always, it was Keon or Mullens (or both) suspended on one side and Ward or Cameron on the other. Evatt, Ward, Cameron and Haylen dominated the replies from the Opposition benches; little was heard except on 'roads and bridges' questions from the 'anti-Evatt' Labor members.

As early as 27 April, Ward, Haylen, Keon and Mullens were all suspended in an adjournment debate. Keon had raised an allegation by Haylen, at a pre-election rally in Melbourne the previous weekend, that the Industrial Groups had obtained £7,000 from the United States Labor attaché, Herb Weiner. It was intended as an answer to the £13,000 allegation. The attacks by Keon and Mullens on this statement were of extraordinary intensity. Accusing Haylen of really being opposed to Evatt's foreign policy, Keon said, 'We hear these wicked smears, the only effect of which can be to poison the relations between this country and the United States of America, the country upon which the future of Australia largely rests.' This led to a fiery defence from Haylen, who colourfully attacked the Groups, and the entry of Evatt into the debate. Mullens said anti-Americanism was in the sub-stratum of Evatt's political philosophy. Evatt had 'spread a smear to the world' about 'our great friend and ally, our wartime helper . . . [Evatt] with his tender solicitude for Communist China. . . .' Menzies even took the unusual step of entering a minor adjournment debate to 'apologise on behalf of the Parliament for this gross insult [to the United States]'.

In fact, it had been for years a commonplace rumour that United States representatives would willingly provide financial aid for anything that smacked of vigorous anti-communism in Australia, unless perhaps it had lunatic fringe associations. The author knows personally of one approach from a United States official and has heard of others. It would be surprising if a United States representative had not at least approached the Groups with offers of finance.

The new ALP rulers in Victoria, with their disregard for the political wing, could be depended on to provide ammunition for the cross-benchers.

On 24 May Keon obtained a debate on an urgency motion to discuss: 'The renewed drive of the Communist Party to recapture control of key trade unions, following the attempted disbandment of and attacks upon Australian Labor Party Industrial Groups.'

Quoting published communist plans to renew a drive for the 'united front' with Labor, he said 'renewed hope, vigour and drive' had come from the communists because they could campaign in the name of the ALP in common cause with Evatt-supporting members of that Party. The ALP candidate for office in the Amalgamated Engineering Union had recently lost to an 'Evatt candidate' following a campaign 'repeating word for word all the catch-cries, smears and sectarian innuendos by which the Australian Communist Party was able once more to gain control of the Commonwealth Council of the union through a stooge'. The Communist Party had already submitted a team for elections due shortly in the Victorian branch of the Australian Railways Union, with 'Evatt supporters' as candidates. A unity ticket was also being prepared for the Ironworkers' Association to 'hand control of the steel industry back to the Australian Communist Party'.

Again, on 9 June, Bourke secured a debate on: 'The alliance between the Communist Party and the Evatt-Stout-Cain Labor Party, running a joint unity ticket for the election of the Victorian branch of the Australian Railways' Union to re-establish control of the railways industry by the Communist Party under the leadership of J. J. Brown.' Bourke revealed full details, complete with references to Evatt and the strike years in the railways, of a 'unity team' standing for the ARU elections in Victoria against the Neill-led Industrial Group candidates. He pointed out that one member of the unity team, V. Delmenico, a signalman from Castlemaine, was a member of the Victorian Central Executive of the 'Stout-Evatt Party'.

Both Calwell and Evatt were among speakers to these motions, but they could make little more than debating points in reply. Evatt's usual technique was to deny personal complicity in such questions, to denounce 'smearers' and then attack the 'Santamaria-Keon-McManus faction', 'semi-fascist outside organisation', etc. In the event, the Brown ticket won most of the ARU positions contested and Brown returned triumphant to the union offices as Assistant Secretary. The following year the position of secretary was open for election and he displaced Neill. Anti-Catholicism was a significant factor of this election, though inexperience and mistakes could also be attributed the Groupers, who had been in control only a year. A 'unity' team also entrenched itself in the Melbourne branch of the Waterside Workers' Federation that year and the same was true of most unions where there was a fine balance between Groupers and the anti-Grouper forces. The more entrenched Industrial Group control of the Ironworkers' and Clerks' unions rode the storm, however.

Parliament rose in mid-June for the winter recess until the Budget debate in mid-August. The fairly technical, domestic nature of the debate on the Budget and Estimates damped down controversy in the early weeks, but in this period the 'seven' became eight; they spread to another State and Chamber.

The Tasmanian Senator, Cole, had been suspended from the ALP by the Tasmanian Executive after his part in the boycott of the Hobart Conference. When the Senate resumed on 24 August, Cole announced that he would represent the Australian Labor Party (Anti-Communist) in the Senate. 'I join with the other members of this Parliament who refuse to accept the leadership of [Evatt] and the pro-communist foreign policies laid down by the unconstitutional rump conference held in Hobart earlier this year,' Cole said.

Senator O'Byrne: 'You'll become known as Senator Maria.'

Cole said the Tasmanian Executive had waited until after the Victorian election to suspend him. 'They were not game to come straight out and expel me,' he said. 'Instead they suspended me with the idea that I would remain quiet and not say or do anything until the next State Conference; otherwise I would be expelled automatically at the next State Conference. Since I am not easily intimidated, I would not accept that. Consequently, I will express my views in this Chamber. . . .'

The Government subsequently accorded Cole, to the rage of the ALP, the full status, with salary, offices, car and allowances, of a Party Leader. He employed his fellow boycotter, Morgan, as Secretary. Between them, they now had the base for organising the Anti-Communist Party in Tasmania. Cole had been well known as a footballer in his youth and his family was very well known in Northern Tasmania, and in the intimate atmosphere of Tasmanian politics this gave him eventually a second term in the Senate. However, though he and Morgan recruited a few sympathisers, and Victorians and Movement men worked assiduously, the new Party actually made little impact in Tasmania.

The defence question arose again when the Estimates were debated in late September, with Labor moving for a cut in defence spending. The ensuing debate was on predictable, heated ideological lines. A frequent innuendo in the speeches of the Anti-Communists was that many Labor members really did not support Evatt's 'pro-communist' foreign and defence policies; sometimes it was alleged that they had once expressed the opposite viewpoint. This was probably true to some extent, as there was something of a scramble towards conformity as the year drew on. But what Keon and Mullens, as well as the Labor left, did not seem to appreciate was that not everybody shared their black-and-white certainty of opinion on the issue. The speeches of most Labor members at this time, as at most times, suggested uncertainty and lack of ease as much as anything on questions of foreign policy.

Bourke caused a sudden sensation in his Budget speech on 8 September. He claimed that often Labor, more than the Liberals, had sided with big business, and illustrated his case with Evatt's promised tax concessions of the previous year. Then he said that as part of the 1954 legislation extending liquor trading hours in New South Wales restrictions on ownership of hotels by breweries had been eased.

'Why did [the Cahill Government] do so?' Bourke asked. 'The action was taken because, as I have said, the Labor Party in this country has sold its soul. It has sold out to the mammon of iniquity because the men who were responsible were well paid for what they did. It is a fact that Mr Cahill, the Premier of New South Wales, and three of his senior Ministers were paid a substantial sum of money, running into thousands, by the brewery interests of New South Wales, for that remarkable and disgraceful legislation. . . .'

This led to a fury of interjections from the Labor benches, denials, claims that the Liberals must have been in it and impassioned defence of the New South Wales Government by New South Wales members. The debate certainly did not make clear whether Bourke's charges were true, or whether any money that did change hands went to personal or political funds. The point was made that there were technical reasons for the legislation, which made it more innocuous than it might have seemed.

Part of the cross-bench anger against Cahill was for his part in the April compromise, which forestalled Federal Executive intervention in New South Wales. Under the original 'Cahill Plan', many Industrial Groupers would have been dropped from the Executive and from jobs, but it was not adopted. This plan had seemed a sell-out to the enraged 'seven', who depended on a split in New South Wales for delivery. On 18 May, both Keon and Bourke had referred to 'Jellyfish Joe Cahill'. Such remarks helped widen the gap between their group and the New South Wales 'anti-Evatt' group.

There was a spectacular scene on 29 September when the seventy-year-old coalfields member Roly James, red faced and shouting, moved across the Chamber and shook his fist at Keon, holding his walking stick aloft in the other hand. This incident came during the debate on the Defence Estimates, when Keon said the Opposition's foreign policy coincided with that of the Communist Party. Keon said a statement by Evatt that Australian troops were going to slaughter Asians in the interests of British imperialism should provide communist terrorists with an excuse to shoot Australian soldiers. James interjected, 'Why don't you get over to the other side?'

Mr Keon: If there were a 'comm.' side, I would suggest that you should cross over to it.
Mr James: I have never stooged for 'comms.' in my life.
Mr Keon: Then why don't you deal with your leader?
The Temporary Chairman: Order! Hon. members must contain themselves.
Mr James: I have been summonsed by 'comms.', you haven't been.
The Temporary Chairman: The Hon. Member for Hunter must resume his seat, or leave the Chamber.
  Mr James interjecting.
The Temporary Chairman: Order! If the Hon. Member for Hunter cannot contain himself, he had better leave the Chamber. The Chair has been fairly tolerant.

Mr Keon: I can understand the feelings of Hon. members who sit behind the Right Hon. Member for Barton. . . .

Incidents of this type, and the extravagance and venom of the inter-Labor debates, naturally attracted prominence in the press and in discussion. The spleen of the attacks on Evatt, with the persistent concentration on him, tended often to produce a reaction of sympathy among Labor supporters and the rank and file, further cementing the factionalism that raged throughout Australia. The Leader was sacrosanct among many of the rank and file, and the abuse against his person often made the attackers seem what Evatt said they were.

The new régime in Victoria provided ammunition again on 7 October, when it passed a resolution that the 1937 Federal Conference decision, which outlawed any form of united front with Communist Party members, did not apply to trade union elections. This was their reply to constant criticism of the 'unity tickets' which had appeared in several unions. Tripovich, who had been appointed Secretary when Lovegrove entered the State Parliament, told the press this decision gave unionists 'greater freedom and responsibility'. He said ALP members would still be banned from advocating the policy of the Communist Party, or for supporting affiliation of their union to the Communist Party. 'This is not a sell-out. We will still deal with people who become stooges of the communists,' he said. The decision had been made solely to prevent interference with the democratic rights of trade unionists.

It is impossible to know whether this decision was made as a result of a 'deal' with the communists, or as a short-term expedient to reducing Grouper strength in the unions. Its effect was to encourage the very united front that the communists were now seeking to develop and to give able, determined communist union leaders indirect access to the structure of the ALP.

The Anti-Communist Party naturally attacked it volubly, in the press and in Parliament.

With these discouraging trends developing in Victoria, continuing rancour and division wracked the Party in New South Wales and to a lesser extent in other states. The Anti-Communists had successfully established a small, if politically unknown, organisation in South Australia and Western Australia, based on handfuls of supporters.

The Liberals, in danger of defeat little more than a year before, now had the rosiest prospects of office continuing indefinitely. It was hardly surprising that during the spring there was persistent speculation in the press and in the lobbies that Menzies would call an early election.

There was also an old stand-by time bomb ticking away, in the form of the Petrov Affair. The final report of the Royal Commission on Espionage had been tabled in the Parliament on 14 September. The three Commissioners reported that the Soviet Union, from its Embassy, had operated for many years an effective spy system in Australia, and that this was only possible with the help of Australian communists. But, the Commissioners said, the Australian Security Service, formed in 1949, killed the effectiveness of the espionage. The Commissioners said no prosecution of anybody whose actions they had inquired into was warranted, but the Australian law was inadequate, especially in peacetime, to combat such espionage. They said they could not say whether the public servants involved knew that the recipients of their information were Soviet agents.

The Commissioners said they accepted as truth the evidence of the Petrovs, but only after submitting it to exhaustive testing. On a specific question, they found that Ian Milner, since about 1949 at the University of Prague, but in the immediate post-war years head of the United Nations Branch of the Department of External Affairs, had given secret information to Walter Seddon Clayton, who was involved in the Soviet spy ring.

The effect of this was most damaging to Evatt. He had been Minister for External Affairs at the time of the leakages, and when Milner was head of the UN Branch—a branch which would have been particularly important for him, because of his Presidency of the UN. Ironically, however, he was also Attorney-General when the Security Service was formed, and was instrumental in its formation. The report of the Commissioners, of course, was also a refutation of his whole appearance before the Commission, and of his charges.

The opportunity was not to be missed by the corner benches, and that night Joshua issued a press statement saying it was now surely impossible for Evatt to continue as Leader of the Opposition, or for his Party to put him forward as their candidate for Prime Minister. 'In effect, the Royal Commissioners found Dr Evatt to be a wicked defamer, making unsubstantiated allegations for political purposes,' Joshua said.

It is certainly true that supporters of the extreme left, and some Communists, held influential posts in External Affairs during Evatt's control of it. Even on the far right of the Labor Movement, however, this was not—except perhaps in moments of high passion—seriously thought to be the result of a Red Plot involving Evatt, but rather the result of his poor judgment of men and tendency to be naive about his admirers. Also, at that time, the Australian intelligentsia was so saturated with, albeit often hazy, far left attitudes that they were bound to be well represented in a department like External Affairs. There was also a good deal of 'jobs for the boys' freemasonry among the left, and no doubt the hard core of communists encouraged this feeling and took advantage of it.

The debate on the report was not held until 19 October. Evatt rose at a minute past 8 p.m. and spoke for almost two sensational hours.

The report of the Royal Commission on Espionage requires forthright analysis and plain speaking: What is the upshot of this Petrov Affair? Two foreigners, the Petrovs, and one foreign-born Australian spy, Bialoguski,[1] have made a lot of money. The form in which they appeared cost the taxpayers £140,000, plus unlimited security expenses. The nation has suffered heavy loss in trade and the breaking of diplomatic relations with a

---

[1] Dr Michael Bialoguski, a flamboyant, bearded Polish physician, was a security agent who helped induce Petrov to defect. He attracted considerable publicity.

great power. There has been the attempted smearing of many innocent Australians, grave inroads have been made into Australian freedoms by attacks on political non-comformity. . . . But after eighteen months of inquiry, at this great cost to the nation, no spies have been discovered. Not a single prosecution is recommended.

This was the standard left-wing attitude towards the Royal Commission, and unexceptionable in that sense. Evatt then continued in this vein, with the charge that it was now 'abundantly clear' that Menzies had known of Petrov's impending defection months before he 'made his melodramatic and coldly calculated announcement to the House'.

Evatt then said he would concentrate on major issues, such as the genuineness of the documents.

Determined to ascertain the truth of these grave matters, I took two steps, as follows. . . . First of all, I communicated with His Excellency the Foreign Minister of the Soviet Union. I pointed out that most of the Russian language documents in the Petrov case were said to be communications from the MVD, Moscow, to Petrov, MVD resident in Australia. I pointed out that the Soviet Government or its officers were undoubtedly in a position to reveal the truth as to the genuineness of the Petrov documents. I duly received a reply, sent on behalf of the Minister of Foreign Affairs of the Union of Soviet Socialist Republics, Mr Molotov.

[*Hansard* understates the ensuing uproar as 'Honourable members interjecting'.]

Dr Evatt: Honourable members may laugh, but they have to face some facts tonight. They will not put me off by their organised opposition. They have to listen to this because this is the truth of the affair. The letter to which I have referred informed me that the documents given to the Australian authorities by Petrov—'Can only be, as it had been made clear at that time and as it was confirmed later, falsifications fabricated on the instructions of persons interested in the deterioration of the Soviet-Australian relations and in discrediting their political opponents.' I attach grave importance to this letter, which shows clearly that the Soviet Government denies the authenticity of the Petrov documents. It seems to me that in these circumstances the matter cannot be left where is, and that, if possible, some form of international commission should be established by agreement with the Union of Soviet Socialist Republics to settle the dispute once and for all. The Soviet Union was not represented at the hearing. It will be in a position to prove clearly, definitely and unequivocally, that the letters are fabricated. . . .

Most of the rest of Evatt's speech was his standard arguments against the authenticity of the documents and some evidence, a partly political and partly legal oration. He emphasised matters such as the *News Weekly* scoop and the £5,000 payment and analysed a number of other incidents in the huge volume of the report, which may have indicated weaknesses.

The political foolishness of the 'Molotov letter' beggars belief. In Evatt's situation, it invited further innuendo of sympathy with communism and could not have in the real world advanced his political cause an inch. No country *ever* admits to spying: it is an unwritten international code that they do not. The suggestion that Molotov could ever admit that the letters were genuine was simply absurd. Perhaps it was Evatt's instinct as a lawyer, which often seemed to come suddenly and unwisely to the fore, that made him wish to make this grotesquely methodical addition to his case.

Also, by the spring of 1955 Evatt appeared to be again losing control of his complex personality, as he had been a year earlier, despite an apparent recovery at the height of the battle. He was by now completely obsessive about the Petrov affair, and there are innumerable stories of the lengthy, conspiratorial theories he would expound to often reluctant listeners in private conversations. His obsession about the 'Santamaria Movement' was by now almost as bad. Evatt was morbidly suspicious of people he believed to be 'CA' (Catholic Action) in the Party, the press, the government departments, among employees at Parliament House and elsewhere in his connections. He was wont to believe any story peddled to him, no matter how fantastic or how suspect the source, provided it fitted his conspiratorial vision of the Santamaria-Menzies-Petrov 'plot'. He came to believe that some of the most unlikely people were 'CA'—though in the high hysteria of 1955, he was not the only person to do so.

By 23 October, the Sunday, Evatt was apparently sensitive that he had made an appalling error, for at a fete at Hurstville Grove, in his electorate, he said:

The issue at the next Federal Election will not be to whom I wrote a letter. It will be won on the broken pledges and callous indifference by the Menzies Government in relation to the nation's social and economic problems. The Menzies Government will not get away with threats, implied or direct, of election stunts and sensational issues. The object of the Menzies Government is to blind people to economic and financial recession which is being brought about by its political administration. The people were deceived once. They will not be deceived twice. The people of Australia have only just heard the beginning of the Madame Ollier case. . . .

The same day, Archbishop Mannix told an Irish Foresters' Communion Breakfast in Melbourne, 'Politicians could ask Molotov if he approved of the bishops' statements on communism . . . and if he approved of the Industrial Groups and communists and Labor men placing their names on the same ticket.'

According to the *Age*, Menzies told the Cabinet on 25 October that he intended to hold an early election, on 10 December. But that night it was his turn to reply to Evatt, in the House, on the report of the Royal Commission.

All the mutual hatred and contempt between these two brilliant barristers flowed to the surface in the course of this reply. A deep, controlled rage ran through Menzies' speech:

I hope not to take up the time of the House until 10 p.m. [in fact, he almost did]. When a Royal Commission sits for months to investigate matters of national security, it is not common to have the tabling of the report followed by the making of charges relating to the very matters inquired into. But on this occasion the Leader of the Opposition has indulged himself in the luxury of once more becoming the advocate in this House of causes of which he was the professional advocate before the Royal Commission; professionally but unsuccessfully. In short, he is asking this Parliament, which has not heard the witnesses, to sit as a court of appeal from three judges who heard every word of the evidence, who read every word of all the documents, who listened to all the cross-examination and who, for some weeks, not two hours, listened to the right honourable gentleman himself. This is a state of affairs so astonishing that if it were not for the office held by him in this Parliament and his leadership of a great Party, I would invite the House and the people to treat the whole of his submissions as being either frivolous or offensive. . . .

The following extracts give some impression of the exchanges that developed as Menzies continued:

[Menzies] . . . he seemed to be appearing for himself, and to find it impossible to distinguish between his somewhat nominal functions as counsel for a couple of members of his staff, and his real function as the political exponent of points of view which, before the Royal Commission, made him the instant ally of Lockwood and Hill and all the other communists involved in the inquiry.
Dr Evatt: A typical Menzies smear!
Mr Menzies: I am familiar with that sort of allegation.
Dr Evatt: McCarthyism!
Mr Menzies: If the right honourable gentleman could get through ten minutes in this House without referring to McCarthy and smears, it would be a wonderful thing. However, as I propose to show with studied moderation, the right honourable gentleman, in this matter, has sought to smear every decent person associated with this inquiry . . . all I need to do is remind the House that when it made an interim report on these matters, the Royal Commission said—I do not want to worry honourable members, but this deserves to be heard and heard widely—
Dr Evatt: A great smear!
Mr Menzies: Every finding against the right honourable gentleman is a great smear. In this case the smearers are Mr Justice Owen, Mr Justice Philp and Mr Justice Ligertwood. Do let us have that in mind. . . .

On Evatt's request for an international commission of inquiry, Menzies said:

. . . the Right Honourable gentleman's passions, which he has with careful preparation exposed to the House, are against the Prime Minister of his own country and for the Foreign Secretary of the Soviet Union; against three Australian judges of impeccable reputation and for some nebulous and hypothetical international commission; against the Australian Security Service, headed by a distinguished and patriotic Australian, and for people like Sharkey and Clayton. The truth is, of course, that the one passion animating his mind here, as before the Royal Commission, is for himself. . . .

The following evening Menzies announced to the House that there would be an election on 10 December. This was almost eighteen months before an election was Constitutionally necessary and Menzies gave as reasons the need to get Senate and House of Representatives elections back into line, after the disruption caused by the 1951 Double Dissolution, the need to avoid clashes with four State elections due in 1956 and the need for the Government to have a 'clear mandate from the people to deal with the economic problems facing the country', notably bringing the balance of overseas payments and receipts back into balance by June 1956.

Parliament sat until 2 a.m. on 27 October, before rising for the election. To the last 'the seven' and the Opposition benches were tearing at each other. Almost the last clash of the night was a charge by Mullens that Calwell had collected money on behalf of the ALP from the Liquor Trades Defence League, while Mullens was employed by it prior to 1930, and an emphatic denial from Calwell, who claimed, 'I never got a penny from [J. J.] Liston in my life.'

Just as predictably, the *Age* of 30 October reported that there had been a highly confidential, and unsuccessful, move among Labor Parliamentarians, in the dying hours of the Parliament, to find a new Leader. Few doubted that the real reason Menzies called the election was the torment of the ALP, capped by the Molotov letter.

Unable to get a new Leader, Labor had to make the most of the one it had. The method it chose was to keep a close watch over Evatt in the formative days of the campaign, to see that excesses either on domestic promises and the means test, or on Petrov, were avoided.

The Federal Executive met in Canberra on 31 October. All four Federal Parliamentary Leaders—Evatt, Calwell, McKenna and Armstrong—went before it on 1 November to address the Executive on policy for the campaign. It was a step the *Sydney Morning Herald* described as 'unprecedented', as in the past the Federal Leader—the alternative Prime Minister —had alone addressed the Executive on policy. Caucus then met on 3 November at the direction of the Federal Executive to approve the policy. Press reports were in conflict on the reasons for these precautionary measures: Some said they were to prevent the Liberals and Anti-Communists from saying Evatt alone decided the policy—a defensive attitude that could easily arise in the ALP; and others more bluntly saying it was a way of controlling Evatt. Possibly both were true. The press reported that Caucus was divided over the foreign policy sections of Evatt's speech.

Evatt delivered his speech on 9 November, before an incessantly cheering crowd of 1,800 in the Rivoli Hall, Hurstville, Sydney.

He promised to raise aged and invalid pensions by 11 shillings a week, to increase widows' pensions and child endowment and to end the means test over a period, after an inquiry to find the best and fairest way. He said he would abolish income tax on all incomes of less than £250 a year and end sales tax on household equipment and furniture. Repatriation benefits would be increased by £6 million a year.

Evatt said he would finance the proposals by a Federal Land Tax on Unimproved Value of property of more than £10,000 value and would save £40 million by a cut in defence funds. There would be an excess profits tax on 'exorbitant' company profits, where a company had a taxable income of £25,000 a year or more. This, he estimated, would raise £50 million a year. Labor would review import controls, eliminate or curtail luxury imports and give preference to imports essential to Australian industry. Under a Labor Government, the Commonwealth Bank would enter hire purchase; and a Shipping Commission, on the lines of Trans-Australia Airways, would be established to provide Government competition for interstate ship-owners. The total proceeds of the petrol tax would be made available to the states and municipalities for spending on roads. A Labor Government would also, Evatt said, intervene before the Arbitration Court and direct it to restore the quarterly adjustments to the basic wage, abandoned as inflationary in 1953.

Evatt said a Labor Government would support the admittance of all countries, including Communist China, to the United Nations. It would withdraw Australian troops from Malaya. Labor's policy was 'welfare, not warfare', and it would struggle to give the world the era of international peace and effective disarmament for which the hearts of all men yearned. 'War is an evil and wicked thing,' Evatt said. 'The Menzies Government seems afraid lest peace break out.' Labor's policy was to establish firmer relations with Asian countries by practical assistance, especially in relation to health, education and development.

Evatt said the Menzies Government had squandered Australia's overseas reserves. 'We have begged and borrowed all round the world,' he said. 'Our credit has never been lower. Labor approaches this election in a fighting spirit, absolutely determined to curb monopoly power in Australia, to give all sections of the people a fair deal and to save for them what is left of the pound . . . the Liberal and Country parties have run the country for the benefit of monopolists and speculators. . . .'

Much of the policy he revealed was unexceptionally redistributist—tax the rich to help the poor—and 'left-liberal'—butter and peace instead of guns and war—in sympathy. The speech as a whole, however, was yet another example of Evatt's dreadful, but not uncommon, political style. Most of the economic ideas were flung at the public a month before they had to vote on them, without being subject to any prior public discussion. The excess profits tax was vague in conception, and supported only by continual reference to spectacular profits made in those years by General Motors-Holden's and to rises in company profits in a period of inflation. The spectacular promise on the means test of eighteen months before had disappeared, never to issue from Evatt's lips again, despite his 'stab in the back' protestations over it.

Evatt, and indeed much of the Party behind him, never seemed to grasp the way in which Australian society was changing in the 1950's. He—as far as his political statements could be assumed to be his real thoughts— was prepared to propose highly inflationary measures, but at the same time promise (shades of Menzies in 1949!) to 'save what is left of the pound'. He was prepared to propose heavy public spending, but to attack overseas borrowing. On foreign policy, he tended to be grandiose, to quite unrealistically identify himself with 'peace' and friendship to Asia, and his political opponents with an anti-Asian 'war' policy.

Much of this was perhaps similar to the Menzies campaign of 1949. But that campaign developed against a theme of 'freedom from socialist controls'; it held out a vision of a new society; it was developed over several months and only a few titbits were kept for the policy speech. Menzies chose his own time and place to make statements, balancing attacks against the Government with positive statements.

Evatt's style was to reply immediately to every attack, direct and indirect, made upon him. He crowded every thing into one policy speech—the 1955 one covered twenty-three closely typed pages—and made so many specific 'promises' that it was difficult for electors to remember them. Almost everything he said smacked of opportunist 'vote catching' of the crudest type. Most of the time he was on the defensive, acting like a Leader of the Opposition rather than aspiring Prime Minister.

In the campaign that followed, Evatt read from a standard set speech at most of his meetings, and some of the correspondents travelling with him, while marvelling at his energy and exuberance, complained that it was difficult to find anything new to report. The result was that much of the time Evatt was reported on the defensive, replying heatedly to 'smears' and the like from Menzies, Joshua and the Catholic Archbishop of Hobart, Dr Guildford Young.

Yet the correspondents also reported crowded, enthusiastic Evatt meetings and, except in Victoria, the outcome of the campaign was not the débâcle one might have expected. Many Australians, and certainly much of the Labor movement, by now felt sympathetic to the embattled, derided, courageous figure of 'the Doc' and embittered against the hostile Anti-Communists and the supercilious figure of Menzies. Evatt sometimes said privately during the split years—it is difficult to pinpoint just when— that 'for every Catholic vote I lose I'll get two Protestant ones'. This may have had its element of truth.

In his policy speech, Evatt largely avoided mention of the breakaways, being content to deny the 'slander' of communist association and to condemn as a 'shocking thing' that 'sometimes men from the sacred pulpit will come into this hue and cry and try to destroy me because I fight for freedoms'.

On 10 November, Evatt attacked the ABC for giving Joshua broadcasting time. In Adelaide, on 16 November, he told the press, 'I shall not be deterred by Menzies' adoption of the techniques of Goebbels, with which Menzies was no doubt familiar when shortly before World War II he publicly acclaimed . . . Hitler. . . . I care nothing for Mr Menzies' malevolent abuse of myself. . . .'

On 22 November, when both Evatt and Menzies were in Hobart, Archbishop Young issued a statement calling on Catholics and other citizens to oppose 'any revival of communist influence and power in the political, industrial and cultural life'. The Archbishop said he would be accused of entering politics but 'the same kind of thing was said, remember, by the Nazis'. Evatt replied: 'Most Australians will associate this statement with the extravagant praise given by the Prime Minister, Mr Menzies, to the political faction called the Keon group, nominally led by Mr Joshua. Most of these members were closely associated with an organisation controlled from outside the ALP. . . .'

Joshua opened the Anti-Communist campaign in Ballarat Town Hall on 10 November, concentrating on defence and promising a fairly conventional range of social service benefits. He attacked Labor's policies on Malaya and China as dangerous to Australian defence and promised tougher legislation against public servants who 'betrayed their trust'.

On 16 November he announced that Anti-Communist Labor would run Senate teams in Victoria, South Australia and Western Australia and also contest a couple of seats—one Hindmarsh, held by Clyde Cameron—in Adelaide. Mullens announced that he would leave his old seat of Gellibrand and run against Calwell in Melbourne as a gesture against 'fence sitters'.

There were brawls at two or three of the Anti-Communist meetings and at Islington Railway Workshops in Adelaide on 24 November angry workers tore the microphone from Keon's hands when he quipped at 'Molotov Labor'. The exchanges were mostly confined to a war of words in the columns of the newspapers, however, and there was often a quality of anti-climax about the campaign.

Menzies, a superb exploiter of the situation, was able to appear by comparison a statesman of impeccable *gravitas*, standing loftily above the mêlée. His strategy was to make it an election on the personality of Evatt, and again on the irresponsibility of Labor. In his opening speech at Canterbury Town Hall, Melbourne, on 15 November he said a victory for Labor would 'land Australia in an international and internal financial crisis'. Evatt had made it clear, he said, that in any issue between communists and the responsible civil authorities of Australia, Evatt would side with the communists. He avoided promises, instead talking in fatherly terms about Australia's impending balance-of-payments crisis and the need for responsible government to meet it. He avoided answering Labor charges that he would put up taxes. (In the event, he raised a number of indirect taxes in the mid-term 'little horror budget' of March 1956.)

Evatt was the first to mention the Molotov affair, asking in Brisbane on 9 November: 'What's the difference between asking a question of Molotov and asking it of Petrov?' Menzies avoided making it an election issue, and instead he and Fadden relied on the occasional half-joking or casual mention of it, as did Keon.

Shortly before polling day, the Liberals inserted full-page newspaper advertisements on the theme: 'Evatt has wrecked the Labor Party. Don't let him wreck Australia.'

The result of the election was a landslide towards the Liberals, though not by the margin that might have been expected. All seven Anti-Communists lost their seats and only four new Victorian Labor men were elected to replace them: R. W. Holt in Darebin instead of Andrews; the doctrinaire left wing economic historian from Melbourne University, J. F. Cairns, replaced Keon in Yarra; H. J. McIvor, an unsuccessful contestant for the Gellibrand pre-selection in 1948, replaced Mullens there; and G. M. Bryant replaced Bryson in Wills.

After a protracted count, the Chifley Minister for Air, Arthur Drakeford, lost Marybyrnong to a Liberal. In other states, seats held for Labor by narrow margins in previous years were mostly lost. Tom Burke was defeated in Perth and disappeared from politics, as did Nelson Lemmon, defeated in St George, across the railway line from Evatt's Barton in Sydney. Both had been regarded as good ministerial material. Phillip (J. Fitzgerald) and Hume (A. Fuller) in New South Wales were lost to Labor, as were Sturt in South Australia and Swan in Western Australia.

It seemed for a while that Evatt himself might disappear from politics, following an apparently personal vote against him in Barton, where there had been a campaign against him from the pulpit. The count dragged on for nearly a fortnight, with a majority for Evatt of 226 after distribution of preferences from the independent, Trembath, compared with more than 4,000 in 1954.

The political break-up of the new House, compared to that of 1955, was:

Old House

	Labor	Liberal	Country Party	Anti-Communists
New South Wales	25	15	7	–
Victoria	8	15	3	7
Queensland	5	8	5	–
South Australia	6	4	–	–
Western Australia	4	2	2	–
Tasmania	3	2	–	–
Total	51	46	17	7

New House (elected after re-distribution in 1955)

	Labor	Liberal	Country Party
New South Wales	21	17	8
Victoria	10	20	3
Queensland	5	8	5
South Australia	6	5	–
Western Australia	3	4	2
Tasmania	2	3	–
Total	47	57	18

Percentages of the vote received by the parties were:

	House of Representatives	Senate
New South Wales		
Liberal	38·64 per cent	48·47 per cent
Country Party	8·62 per cent	combined with Lib.
Labor	49·56 per cent	43·82 per cent

	House of Representatives	Senate
Victoria		
Liberal	41·37 per cent	45·52 per cent
Country Party	5·48 per cent	combined with Lib.
Labor	37·12 per cent	34·98 per cent
Anti-Communist Lab.	15·77 per cent	17·77 per cent
Queensland		
Liberal	31·86 per cent	54·38 per cent
Country Party	20·95 per cent	combined with Lib.
Labor	42·06 per cent	41·47 per cent
South Australia		
Liberal	46·17 per cent	46·79 per cent
Labor	48·81 per cent	43·53 per cent
Anti-Communist Lab.	2·63 per cent	8·67 per cent
Western Australia		
Liberal	41·22 per cent	44·49 per cent
Labor	51·90 per cent	39·35 per cent
Country Party	–	9·50 per cent
Anti-Communist Lab.	–	3·44 per cent
Tasmania		
Liberal	49·13 per cent	44·35 per cent
Labor	45·76 per cent	38·24 per cent
Anti-Communist Lab.	3·86 per cent	10·97 per cent

Nationally, the Liberals received 39·73 per cent of the House of Representatives vote and 48·67 per cent of the Senate vote; the Country Party, 7·90 per cent of the House of Representatives vote; Labor, 44·63 and 40·61 per cent respectively; Anti-Communist Labor, 5·17 and 6·10 per cent respectively (without candidates in New South Wales or Queensland); and the Communists, 1·16 and 3·64 per cent respectively.

On 11 December, Evatt issued a statement pointing to the 'massive aggregate vote for Labor throughout Australia', which was greater than that of the Liberal and Country Parties. In the same spirit as his post-election statement the previous year, he spoke of 'manipulation of electoral boundaries', the 'self-satisfaction expressed by Mr Menzies' and the dangers of the 'open cheque mandate' to Menzies. 'The key to his success was the consistent activities of the Keon clique . . . every action was designed to give aid and comfort to Labor's traditional enemies. Acting as auxiliaries of Mr Menzies, the whole seven of this discredited faction have been completely eliminated by the Victorian electors. . . .'

In fact, the 'elimination' of Keon and Bourke was in doubt until 23 December. Bourke, unexpectedly, polled ahead of the official Labor candidate, Thompson, in the re-drawn and more Liberal Fawkner, but lost to the Liberal, Peter Howson, by 1,700 votes after Thompson's preferences flowed 'up the card' to Howson. Keon, who perhaps lost some of the personal anti-machine vote he normally got in Richmond because of his campaign as Deputy Leader in other states and electorates, was beaten in Yarra by Cairns, by 791 votes.

The Anti-Communists, partly in reaction to the 'unity ticket' tolerance of the Victorian ALP, had directed all their preferences to the Liberals, while official Labor in Victoria decided most preferences on the basis of voting convenience.

In the Senate, after another prolonged count, McManus was elected as fifth Senator for Victoria, by a narrow margin. This meant he would join Cole, who was in the middle of his six-year term, to make two members of the Anti-Communist Labor Party in Canberra in 1956.

An attitude of 'policies before votes' now began to strengthen in the decimated ALP. Cairns, the first member of the Melbourne University staff to be elected to the Parliament, expressed something of the new attitude at the declaration of the Yarra poll on 23 December. He said:

The purpose of Labor is not to make Governments, but to make better social conditions. . . . I believe Labor will long be prepared to remain in opposition rather than give up its policy by identifying itself with the parties of big business and other conservative organisations. I believe Labor, true to its ideals as the Party of change and progress, will be able to withstand years of opposition better than some of its political opponents will be able to withstand years of effort with little or no hope of electing candidates.

Chapter Eighteen
The Split in
New South Wales

The split in the Party in New South Wales had become so intense by the autumn of 1955 that some form of Federal intervention may have been necessary anyway, irrespective of the larger national issues involved.

The Combined ALP Unions Steering Committee, formed in January, had become the focus of the 'pro-Evatt' faction, with about twenty-two unions supporting it, and Dougherty, Platt, Campbell, Ormonde and Williams the leaders. This force coalesced with the 'pro-Evatt' Federal Parliamentarians, the 'out', or 'left' section of the State Parliamentary Party, anti-Grouper branch members and much of the old corrupt City of Sydney machine, formerly so influential on the City Council.

On the other side were ranged the State Executive, unions supporting the Trades and Labor Council, with or without an Industrial Group background, pro-Grouper and Movement branch members and the 'anti-Evatt' Federal Parliamentarians. The 'in' or 'right' wing of the State Parliamentary Party was broadly pro-Grouper, but at a distance and with many reservations. An election was due early in 1956 and pre-selection ballots for this had recently been concluded. It was a situation which dictated caution on the part of the State Parliamentary Party.

State Caucus met on 23 March and appointed the Premier, J. J. Cahill, the Deputy Premier, R. J. Heffron, and Caucus Chairman, F. O'Neill as a delegation to attend the State Executive meeting due the next day—the first after Hobart—and ask for a Special State Conference as soon as possible, to deal with the disunity within the Party. Such a Conference would have been a way of circumventing Federal intervention, or at least making it more difficult.

The *Sydney Morning Herald* quoted Cahill as telling the Caucus that most members of Caucus had been sorry to see the Ferguson Executive defeated in 1952, but succeeding Executives had had the loyal support of the Parliamentary Party as the constitutionally-elected Executive. The Party had passed contentious legislation, such as that for compulsory unionism, at the Executive's request.

Cahill's 'play it cool' strategy had limited support in the hurly burly of the split, however. About 800 people attended a 'pro-Evatt' rally at Wollongong on 24 March, called by the Port Kembla branch of the Waterside Workers' Federation and local ALP branches. Hundreds stood outside the overflowing hall to hear over amplifiers Evatt's first address since Hobart.

Parliamentarians on the platform included Ashley, Whitlam, W. Davies, a local MP, and the South Coast Labor MLAS, R. F. X. Connor, H. Fowles and L. Kelly.

Evatt told the cheering hundreds it had been proved beyond doubt that an outside Movement controlled by B. A. Santamaria had influence and in some cases control in a number of trade unions and in 'various ranks of political Labor'. The Industrial Groups were now connected with The Movement. Evatt said he could have avoided the present fight in the Party 'but as trustee of the Party I took on a job of cleaning up and I am not going to down tools until that job is finished. The question is not between left and right, not between those who want to move up more or less quickly and those who don't. The issue is whether Labor will continue to belong to its real supporters or whether it will be placed under the control of people who do not belong to the Labor Movement at all.'

It was possibly the speech in which Evatt most copiously used the 'Santa scare' and the innuendo of The Movement's total and sinister control of his factional enemies. 'The Menzies-Fadden-Santamaria-Fascist cell' was trying to push the Labor Party 'even further to the right than the Liberal Party'. It was all blatant, intrinsically meaningless propaganda, of course; it was and remained one of the standard tricks of demagoguery in Australian Labor to accuse one's enemies of wishing to subvert the Party's principles, or force it 'to the right of the Liberals'—whatever that means.

Next evening, 25 March, Cahill and the Caucus delegation addressed the State Executive and it decided to advance the date of the 1955 Conference from June to 23 April. The purpose of the Conference was to 'take such steps as are considered necessary to restore unity'. The Federal Executive officers were to be asked to attend.

The response of the Dougherty-led 'rebels', reported in the *Sydney Morning Herald*, was to threaten to ask the Federal Executive to call a rival Conference in New South Wales, and describe it as the official one.

The rank and file entered the fight at the weekend, when a number of conferences and rallies were held in the regions, into which New South Wales was divided for Party administration, and at more local levels again. Most of these regional meetings were called in the face of an Executive ban on them, and they were the centre of many local storms. Two branch officials, G. Neate, Assistant Secretary of the Clovelly Branch and S. Cory, Secretary of the Coogee South Branch, were suspended on 31 March for defying the ban by organising zone meetings. Both branches were in the belt of Eastern suburbs where Movement activity had been very strong, and where many influential figures on both sides lived.

A normally scheduled and authorised Newcastle Regional Conference on 27 March carried a vote of confidence in Evatt and the Hobart decisions, by 83 votes to 51. The atmosphere was such that Colbourne, the Executive representative, was refused permission to preside by the Chairman of Newcastle State Electoral Assembly, Alderman C. Jones. The Jones brothers, Charles and Sam, had been dominant in Newcastle Labor affairs for many years and had fought bitterly with the Industrial Group force there, an obvious alternative source of power. The most influential Grouper in Newcastle was F. P. Rooney, who had been a fitter and turner and upholsterer— as well as prominent in The Movement—in Newcastle prior to becoming Northern Organiser for the ALP in September 1952.

Reece had announced in Hobart on 28 March that the Federal Executive would 'consider Party affairs in New South Wales as soon as practicable'. In the ensuing tension, it became the main aim of the Steering Committee to 'line up' State Parliamentarians behind one or the other factions, both to gain wider support for themselves and to put opponents in the position of openly opposing the Federal Executive. On 30 March, the Committee announced that it was sending registered letters to all MLAs, asking them to declare themselves for or against the Federal Executive. This was a direct challenge to the Cahill strategy, of keeping the Parliamentarians officially neutral, thus containing the split in its ranks between supporters of both factions.

The Steering Committee backed the organisation of more illegal zone rallies for the following weekend, and about 1,000 ALP members attended rallies in different parts of Sydney on 3 April. Haylen, D. Curtin, J. Fitzgerald, C. Morgan, Whitlam and Ashley were Federal Parliamentarians attending, while Ward, E. J. Harrison and D. E. Costa sent apologies. Evatt's brother Clive, a flamboyant barrister and MLA, who had recently resigned from Cabinet after frequent rows with Cahill, was also prominent at the rallies; he was by now a leader of the Parliamentary 'outs'. The Press reported bitter scenes outside the rally at the Rivoli Hall, Hurstville, where pro-Groupers took the numbers of cars outside the rallies to shouts of 'pimps' and 'informers'.

Behind the public front of Cahill's 'wait and see' policy, intense negotiations were going on to try to prevent in New South Wales the sort of confrontation which had proved so disastrous in Melbourne. The old anti-Grouper majority on the Federal Executive was by now splitting into what might—in the political slang of half a generation later—be termed 'dove' and 'hawk' factions. Kennelly was the most influential 'dove', Evatt and Dougherty the leading 'hawks'.

After Hobart, Kennelly began private talks in Sydney with R. R. Downing, representing the State Cabinet. Reginald Robert Downing, born in Tumut in 1904, had been a union official before going to the Bar and, eventually, becoming Minister for Justice in the State Government and Leader of the Government in the Legislative Council. He was the minister closest to the Trades Hall and also, in personal viewpoint, closest to Kennelly. He had opposed the influence of Santamaria and was among those who influenced Cahill and the Church in Sydney to oppose Santamaria also. He was by instinct and training a negotiator and seeker of compromise.

The New South Wales State Executive now also began to divide into 'hawk' and 'dove' factions. Colbourne and Shortell were the leading doves, Kane and Short the hawks. The Trades and Labor Council was emerging as a dove force, with the State Cabinet, both keen to maintain the comfortable 'establishment' of New South Wales. Hawks tended to be those, such as Short, to some extent dependent on the Group structure and ALP label to maintain hard-won union office from bitterly active communist opponents; the dwindling handful of Santamaria supporters; and men such as Kane and Rooney, who were the subject of personal vendettas by 'pro-Evatt' leaders.

The first step in achieving a compromise was acceptance of the Hobart decisions and Federal authority, and this the State Executive voted to do—with a 'dove' majority of two—on 5 April. It voted to 'co-operate with the Federal Executive to bring about unity in the Party', to accept the Hobart decisions and to call off the 23 April Special Conference.

Part of the background to the mood for compromise now building up in Sydney was the vivid recollection of the splits of the 1930's, repaired only sixteen years before, and the realisation that men could be on different sides in one power struggle and on the same side in another, years later. Kane, the Lang man, and Colbourne, Chifley's closest colleague, were indeed living examples of this at the beginning of 1955. There was also a growing recognition that the tide of history was flowing against the communists in union elections and that the Group structure was becoming a marginal asset in this fight. Also Santamaria with all his persuasive gifts was physicallly distant hundreds of miles, with little influence in the Church and imparting little of his feeling of urgency about communism in foreign policy.

A split in Sydney on the Melbourne lines would also have been a tremendous boost for the Victorian breakaways and indeed it was at the centre of their strategy that such a split should take place. This knowledge was obviously an additional reason for Kennelly and his supporters to pursue a compromise.

The day of the Sydney decision to compromise, the Federal Executive had met in Melbourne and decided that its officers should meet in Sydney on 17 April to review the position in New South Wales. Talks with the New South Wales branch would begin the next day. This had also been the meeting where the Federal Executive decided to give Evatt another 'life' by authorising his membership of the Party, in the dispute over his membership ticket. The two New South Wales delegates, Colbourne and Blackburn, had flown back to Sydney to report immediately to their State Executive on the Melbourne proceedings.

While the doves were now cooing loudly, the hawks were flying strongly. At a rally at Lithgow on 7 April, Evatt praised the State Executive decision—but kept the tension up with the usual tirade against Santamaria, fascism, McCarthyism and the like. In the unions, the sudden turn of events had presented the communists with an undreamed of chance to recover their power. While in Melbourne there was a new ALP executive sympathetic to their overtures for industrial 'co-operation', in Sydney it had to take place on an individual basis. On 5 April, Alan Reid reported in the *Daily Telegraph* on an offer by the former Communist leader of the Ironworkers, Ernest Thornton, to A. Cameron, the New South Wales Secretary of the union who, while strongly anti-communist, was opposed to The Movement and some aspects of the Industrial Group approach. Reid reported that Thornton had offered, over a drink in the Newcastle Hotel in George Street, to provide the organisation for Cameron to run against Short as National Secretary. Cameron refused, and informed Short. Reid said this was typical of communist attempts to ride back to influence, through the 'united front' and 'unity ticket' technique, on the back of the anti-Grouper hysteria.

Over the fortnight between the 5 April decision to compromise and the arrival of the Federal officers, a 'Cahill plan' for unity emerged. The basis of this was that the minority of fifteen hawks on the Executive would be replaced by fifteen 'pro-Evatt' representatives, Colbourne would stay on as Secretary, while a Government job would be found for Kane.

The opening of the Federal talks was eventually set for 20 April— ironically, the day on which the Cain Government fell in Victoria, when 'the seven' breakaways first sat in Canberra and when Evatt retained his leadership so dramatically. This was a background that obviously dictated caution.

Meanwhile, the right wing hawks—often referred to then as 'die-hard Industrial Groupers'—began organising strongly against the winding up of the Industrial Group organisation, the necessary outcome of the decision to accept Hobart. At a meeting on 19 April, they demanded the right to give evidence at any inquiry, and on 21 April they decided to form a new anti-communist industrial organisation to succeed the Groups.

It was through their pressure and organising that enough votes were changed for the State Executive to refuse a blank cheque to its delegates to the unity talks with the Federal officers and to oppose the removal of members of the Executive. The delegates were thus compelled to report back on any compromise to a suspicious Executive, and the 'Cahill Plan' was dead.

After several days of discussions, and despite forecasts of a deadlock, the unity talks between the Federal officers and representatives of the two factions reached a compromise decision. The delegates were Downing, representing Cabinet; Shortell and F. Bowen, a Vice-President and Furnishing Trades union official, representing the State Executive; Campbell, Dougherty and Williams, representing the 'rebels'; and Chamberlain, Toohey, Colbourne and Schmella as the Federal officers. The decisions reached were as follows:

Firstly, that a Special Conference was to be held as early as practicable, under the authority of the Federal Executive and under the 1953 New South Wales rules, to elect a new State Executive. The change back to 1953 rules was a significant concession by the Groupers. In 1953, they had backed a resolution to double branch representation at the Conference. Group supporters were conceded to dominate the branch structure and the effect of the change would be to deprive the Groupers of as many as 100 votes at Conference.

Secondly, that the Federal Executive was to hear charges by Dougherty against Kane and Rooney of 'offences against the best interests of the

Labor Party'. Kane and Rooney would be given the fullest opportunity to defend themselves. Also, the Federal Executive would be requested to ensure that the incoming State Executive take no action to disturb the position of State Members of Parliament, selection ballots for whose endorsement had already been held.

The Federal Executive was also to ensure that no present Federal MP should be prejudiced as a consequence of election of a new State Executive. Finally, suspensions arising out of the dispute were to be lifted.

Next evening, 27 April, the State Executive accepted the provision for a Special Conference, but rejected the proposition that Kane and Rooney should be charged before the Federal Executive. Instead, it decided, they should be charged before the State Executive, the appropriate disciplinary body for offences committed within a state, with Federal officers as observers.

The mysterious Dougherty charges against Kane and Rooney—which never, at any stage, took on precise shape—lay around for months as a political football in the dispute. They were generally supposed to relate to allegations by Dougherty and Platt that Kane and Rooney had both been employees on The Movement's payroll before going on the ALP payroll in 1952. The 'rebel' unions made this charge to the Federal Executive in November 1954 and Dougherty made it again at the 1955 AWU Convention. Kane and Rooney strongly denied the charge and gave full details of of their pre-ALP employment in letters to the State Executive, subsequently published in *Labor Nails the Rebels' Lies*, a pamphlet based on the New South Wales Executive's replies to the rebels before the Federal Executive. Kane said he was self-employed as an owner-driver in the transport industry from 1937 to 1952 and from 1948 also had a half interest in a mobile crane. He said Platt, Dougherty and Oliver had been in attendance when the Executive unanimously appointed him Acting Organising Secretary in December 1952. Rooney said he had been working as a contract re-upholsterer.

The propositions on pre-selections, framed so as not to bind the State Executive, reflected a further issue intensifying the factionalism in New South Wales. It had been a major concern of the State Parliamentarians that their precious pre-selections and re-endorsements for the forthcoming State election not be upset by a hostile State Executive, under intense pressure from ambitious would-be parliamentarians. The 'unity conference' went some of the way on this. The problem of Federal Parliamentarians was much more difficult. The pre-selection ballots were still due; the Federal re-distribution had weakened some Labor divisions and abolished others; and there were some powerful eyes on vulnerable seats. There was strong pressure in the 'pro-Evatt' faction for spoils to go to the victors, in the form of safe Labor seats. Some of the New South Wales MPs were of notably small talent, and this aggravated the pressure to 'roll' them.

The unity talks resumed again on 28 April and referred to the Federal Executive the question of which body should hear the charges against Kane and Rooney.

Next day, Federal Executive met in Canberra and agreed to the Special Conference. It decided that the charges against Kane and Rooney should go before the Special Conference. Chamberlain, Toohey and Schmella were appointed delegates to a committee which would prepare for the Conference, the New South Wales members being Bowen, Colbourne, Williams and Campbell. Toohey was chosen as over-all supervisor ahead of Schmella, the reason, according to the *Sydney Morning Herald* of 30 April, being that Schmella was too subject to Dougherty's influence.

The Committee met in Sydney on 23 May, and eventually the date for the Conference was fixed as 13 and 14 August.

Both sides were now claiming that they had 'the numbers' to win—and in the ensuing weeks set about intensively organising to make sure they had. Most less involved observers forecast that, with the change of rules, the rival strengths at Conference would be extremely close. The outcome seemed about as difficult to predict as that of a well matched football game or horse race.

The 'pro-Evatt' faction, to improve its strength, was now cooperating with the far left and got two successful coups from that direction. In April, the communists had regained control of the political committee of the Amalgamated Engineering Union, and later the communist-influenced Australian Council of the Railways Union had temporarily take over the New South Wales branch on a technicality. This meant changes in the disposition of two of the biggest delegations to Conference. Several left-wing unions affiliated on a larger and more realistic membership than previously; this meant that their affiliation fees rose—but also the size of their delegations.

The behind-the-scenes influence of the State Cabinet and parliamentarians, which was considerable, particularly with branch representatives, went mainly to support the Groupers. The Government had no wish to see the AWU rampant again in control of the state machine. The Trades and Labor Council also gave its backing mainly to the Groupers, while control of the ALP office provided an immense strategic advantage. Control of the office often allowed the opportunity to select proxy delegates for some apathetic country State Electorate Assemblies and a few unions. The Movement, though by now disintegrating in most of New South Wales, provided useful organisation for influence in the branches.

Generally, the 'pro-Evatt' faction worked more in the open, through the press statements and 'leaks' and flamboyant rallies, designed to frighten opponents, influence the undecided and give the impression of winning strength to attract the weak and the opportunists. In command, the Groupers worked more quietly and used the formal channels of the Party.

What were the issues dividing them? The struggle was essentially a fairly blatant one for power between 'ins' and 'outs', arising out of obscure feuds of minor intrinsic importance. But burning feeling against The Movement, with the hysteria fanned at every opportunity, and against the brasher and more intense aspects of the Grouper faction, were a tremendous secondary drive behind the 'pro-Evatt' force. Though about half the 'pro-Evatt' leaders were Catholics, inflamed religious feeling was of great importance. The Groupers still tended to see themselves as more honest, progressive and realistic than their opponents and—in sharp contrast to their opponents—regarded The Movement as of minor importance and the whole issue a crude, sectarian red herring.

The Groupers had held their main mass rally on 22 May and it was a fervent affair, with Dougherty and the 'Dougherty faction' coming in for the bitterest attacks. On the issue of Kane and Rooney's alleged employment with The Movement, Kane said Dougherty 'works on the principle of Dr Goebbels—if you tell a lie big enough, often enough, someone will eventually believe it'. He said J. D. Keenahan, Campbell's assistant Secretary, was 'elected on Mr Big's ticket to the Bankstown Council'—a reference to the then developing scandal over allegations that the millionaire contractor R. E. Fitzpatrick controlled Bankstown Council. (Keenahan later said he had been elected on an orthodox ALP ticket.) Rooney threatened to charge Dougherty before the State Executive, with a long list of offences, for attacks on various arms of the ALP. R. Day of the Rubber Workers' Union, the Chairman of the Industrial Groups Committee in New South Wales, said that as a Protestant he refuted any inference that the Groups were dominated by The Movement. Short said Chamberlain's statements showed that he did not realise the extent of communist influence in the country.

The meeting appointed a Combined Labor Unions Committee as a rival pressure group to the Steering Committee, claiming the allegiance of twenty-two unions with a total of 400,000 members.

Apart from the hardly precedented factional bitterness in the Labor Movement, the winter of 1955 had seen an unusually large number of industrial strikes. Partly from issues arising from suspension of the quarterly adjustments to the basic wage in 1953, June and July saw strikes by gas, tram, fire brigade, sanitation and newspaper employees. The Bankstown Council allegations and a new series of allegations about undue political influence by fruit barrow operators in the city streets added more turmoil to Labor as the Special Conference approached.

Lloyd Ross, writing in the *Sydney Morning Herald* of 19 June, described the more ideological issues as many saw them.

Individuals excluded from positions of power seize upon issues which may lead them to power . . . sectarian feelings are colouring judgments. Everything, true or false, is thrown into the argument. And so on. I am convinced that Labor is suffering from failure to adapt its aims and methods to the needs of contemporary Australian democracy . . . Labor, out of office, tends to fall back upon slogans, doctrines and words . . . there is a repetition of words such as 'socialism', 'basic Labor principles', 'militant lead'. . . . Left politicians like Clyde Cameron suffer from the sickness of words. They list an industry they would like to nationalise, without stopping to consider any of the problems involved. . . . They call this opponent a 'boss's stooge' and praise that supporter as a 'militant'. . . .

Words were certainly in evidence at the 'pro-Evatt' rally, with 2,500 packing into the Sydney Town Hall on 7 August and hundreds more turned away. Seventeen Federal and thirteen State Parliamentarians were on the platform with the main speakers, Evatt, Dougherty and Ward. The

State Cabinet had boycotted the rally as 'factional', however, and most State Parliamentarians and the TLC representatives were absent. A surprise apology was received from A. S. Luchetti, MP for Macquarie, previously considered 'anti-Evatt'. Several members of the outgoing Central Executive also sat on the platform; there were moderates, and three had changed sides.

There were loud cheers at the frequent invocation of the name 'Chifley' and loud boos at Evatt's one mention of Santamaria. The Chifley legend was stoutly defended and the Victorian Parliamentary 'rats' and their destruction of the Cain Government roundly condemned.

Evatt made the usual references to outsiders not believing in the Labor Movement having got control of the Industrial Groups, McCarthyism, the Chifley Legend and the like. Ormonde—going against the view of many with experience—said 'anybody with any knowledge of the trade union movement' would know court-controlled ballots were not the way to beat communists in the unions. The Labor Party would get nowhere by selling its principles, he said.

'I cannot understand why any Labor man finds difficulty in attending a Labor rally which is supporting the decisions of his own Federal Conference,' said Ward, in an apparent taunt at the absent Cabinet. 'This business of waiting to see what the Conference decides isn't the sort of leadership you want in New South Wales . . . we are only losing a few Liberals.'

There was a more ominous note in Dougherty's speech, and perhaps a hint of the next AWU target. Gair, the Premier of Queensland, had led the breakaway move at Hobart, he reminded the audience. 'Have a look at Gair. I say Gair should be sacked now. Now let us have a look at Short [boos]. . . .'

It was a memorable—or, perhaps more accurately, forgettable—weekend on 13 to 15 August 1955. Passions and hates were high, careers and influence at stake. Nearly 650 delegates were credentialled and only an unpredictable slither of a margin divided the factions.

The equal, unpredictable character of the voting showed early with elections to minor offices. A key issue came early in the afternoon, with the Kane and Rooney affair.

Dougherty sought suspension of Standing Orders for a motion that Kane and Rooney be suspended. This led to a complicated procedural battle, with Dougherty eventually getting the 'numbers' to move the motion to suspend standing orders. But when this motion came before Conference, it was lost by 320 votes to 303.

Delegates voted during the day for the key position of President and when the numbers went up in the evening it was a victory now for the 'pro-Evatt' faction. Campbell was President, defeating the Grouper choice, Ross, by 329 votes to 295.

It was a short-lived and pyrrhic victory, however, because the votes for most of the other Executive positions went solidly to the Grouper choices. The Conference was all but a rout for Dougherty and the 'pro-Evatt' faction.

Shortell and Blackburn were chosen Vice-Presidents, with 323 and 315 votes respectively, ahead of Oliver (313) and Ormonde (307). Colbourne and Campbell became the delegates to Federal Executive and another 'mixed grill', Blackburn, Mulvihill, Oliver, Platt, Campbell and Colbourne, were chosen as Federal Conference delegates. Colbourne retained the Secretaryship against Williams—who was secretary of the Steering Committee—by 328 votes to 300.

The newspapers attributed the success of Campbell and the Federal Conference blend to a small swinging group, comprising some unions centred mainly on the printing trades, and country delegates influenced by State Parliamentarians. It was approaching the sort of broad Executive Cahill and Downing had been working for. A further point is that Campbell was a more moderate, responsible and gentlemanly man than some of his colleagues; there was a feeling that he should be prised away from Dougherty, Platt and Ormonde to both broaden the control of the Party and weaken the AWU faction.

The body of the Executive, however, was almost the mixture as before, with the whole Grouper ticket of thirty-two elected, though the composition of the ticket had been slightly widened, notably by the addition of H. A. (Alan) Manning, one of the editorial board of *Voice*, the moderate left monthly magazine. *Voice* was something of a *bête noire* and constant object of irritation to Santamaria and some of the young Movement ideologues, for its opposition to Dulles' policy in Asia. After a row in 1952, Manning had cultivated good personal relations with Kane. The result—with consequences that could hardly be foreseen—was that the tweedy, pipe-smoking farmer-intellectual from Coonabarabran district went onto the Executive as the Grouper-backed representative of Castlereagh electorate.

The delegates rose as a body to cheer Cahill and Evatt when they arrived together on the Sunday night to speak—though, as the *Sydney Morning Herald* commentator pointed out, half were probably cheering Evatt and the other half Cahill. With his usual urbane smoothness, Cahill—now nick-named 'the old smoothie' for his work in sorting out the split—spoke on his Government's record.

With the outcome of the Conference now clear, Evatt was—once again—in a tight spot. His enemies would now control his home state and his support from the Federal Executive was as tenuous as ever. His address to the Conference was shorn of the ranting about Santamaria and subversion that had characterised him for so long, so much so that some observers were quoted as wondering whether 'Doc' was contemplating another somersault. But it was a good, forthright speech, in which Evatt supported his policy on Malaya and China and attacked security service excesses, as well as calling for Party unity. It was perhaps the best speech he had made for months.

On the surface, the Conference may have seemed to be ending with a spirit of compromise and a desire for unity. But the 'pro-Evatt' faction leaders were quoted as saying that there were too many informal votes. One put it down to indistinct printing on the 'pro-Evatt' ticket. Ormonde said that 'in the interests of the Labor Movement, the Party officers should not declare this ballot until this lop-sided decision is investigated'. Dougherty commented bitterly to the press: '. . . it may prove to be an indigestible stew. We will continue to do the utmost in our power to remove the Groups from control of Labor in New South Wales. They have been removed in Victoria.'

About the time of the Special Conference, the first speculation was appearing in the press that there might be a Federal election towards the end of the year, or early in 1956. This climate dictated prompt action in pre-selecting Labor candidates.

The Grouper victory, by such a narrow margin, at the Special Conference ended any 'pro-Evatt' supporters' hopes of using a favourable State Executive to get pre-selection for coveted Labor strongholds against pro-Group Parliamentarians. A number of possible attempts by sitting members against each other had been discussed, but only two of these actually occurred in the pre-selection ballots, which took place on 24 September.

One was the contest for the Eastern Suburbs seat of Kingsford-Smith, in which the 'pro-Evatt' Dan Curtin defeated the right winger Gordon Anderson by 351 votes to 262. The other was for Dalley, in the inner Balmain district of Sydney, where the Grouper W. P. O'Connor defeated the 'pro-Evatt' Arthur Greenup, 581 to 447. Curtin's seat of Watson and Greenup's of Martin had both been eliminated in the redistribution. Although it had been strongly rumoured that Haylen would oppose the prominent pro-Grouper, F. M. Daly, in Grayndler, this contest did not take place and Haylen retained his weakened—from the Labor viewpoint—division of Parkes. Nelson Lemmon also retained the marginal St George seat—where he was defeated by a Liberal in the 1955 election—and Evatt his almost equally marginal Barton.

A ballot of all branch members in the State was held the same day to pre-select a Labor Senate team. This developed into an intense struggle between a 'pro-Evatt' ticket, led by W. P. Ashley, with H. E. Jensen, later Lord Mayor, and W. Bodkin a former Mayor of Newtown, and a Grouper ticket, led by the Deputy Leader in the Senate, J. I. Armstrong.

Press reports the following week said the 'pro-Evatt' ticket had been polling well ahead, but that Executive officers were considering action against the ticket. It had been headed with the words, 'Official Labor Senate Ticket—How to Vote for Support of Federal Policy and Leadership'.

On 30 September the State Executive instructed officers to discontinue the Senate count, pending an inquiry into this and other irregularities. Colbourne told the newspapers there had been sixty-three objections and protests over the ballot.

The Executive decided a fortnight later to order a fresh ballot for the Senate pre-selection, but shortly afterwards Menzies announced the December election date. This made for difficulties in organising a state-wide ballot in time and on 28 October, amid bitter protests, the Executive selected the Senate team itself. It placed Armstrong at the head of the ticket and Ashley as number two with Grouper Executive member Lindsay North, of the Textile Workers' Union, as number three.

Jensen and Bodkin protested to the Federal Executive, which started meeting in Canberra on 31 October. The vote on this showed the Federal Executive to be now equally divided between AWU-led 'hawks' and the 'doves' of the old Kennelly school. The Executive divided six to six on a 'hawk' proposal that the New South Wales Executive should be instructed to complete the discontinued 24 September ballot; this would have been a head-on challenge six weeks before the election. Then a 'dove' motion merely chastising the New South Wales action was also defeated by a six to six tie. The result was that no action was taken at all.

This incident kept the factional fever high, but was not as significant in the long term as yet a new allegation about an internal how-to-vote card. This was the affair of the 'bodgie' ticket, the last straw that finally split the ALP in New South Wales.

A former Newcastle Regional Chairman of the Industrial Groups, D. Sullivan, had signed an affidavit saying that anti-Evatt leaders had been responsible for distributing a false how-to-vote card at the August Conference. This resembled the 'pro-Evatt' ticket in every way, except that the number 25, in the order of preferential places for the seventy candidates, appeared twice, widely separated. The result would be that anybody who followed it would vote informal. 'Pro-Evatt' supporters were claiming that seventeen votes were informal for having followed this ticket, and that this affected the result in such a narrowly divided contest.

Writing in the *Daily Telegraph* of 4 November, Alan Reid said this ticket had been typed for duplicating in Dougherty's office, the headquarters of the 'pro-Evatt' faction. He said experts had inspected the machine on which the genuine 'pro-Evatt' ticket was typed and had said the faked card was almost certainly typed on the same machine. 'It suggests that, just as Dougherty has had informants on the other side, his enemies have near him not only an informant but someone able to use the AWU typewriter,' he said. Another explanation, of course, could have been that the 'pro-Evatt' faction knew a great deal about the ticket all the time.

The Federal Executive postponed this pregnant affair until after the elections. And thus the shattering, hysterical, embittered year of 1955 ended, for internal Labor purposes, with the feuding still to reach a crisis in New South Wales and the Party rent in other states as well.

By mid-January of 1956, there was speculation in the press that the Federal officers were about to visit Sydney to consider the new charges against the New South Wales Executive of the Party. Both sides began to organise for the conflict, but a state election was due and the internal dispute was passed over until the autumn.

The affair of the 'bodgie ticket' and the coming new intervention was discussed briefly at the Executive meeting of 20 January, however. Kane read a statement to the meeting saying: 'I am forced to say there has been organised against me a most wicked conspiracy to destroy me—and one of the chief supporters is Dr Evatt.' He clashed at the meeting with Ward, who had been elected to the Executive as one of the two Federal Parliamentary Labor Party representatives. Ward said the Federal leaders of the Party were men who 'could not be unfair to anybody'. According to the *Sydney Morning Herald* of 21 January, he was shocked to hear Kane say they could be biased.

During the election campaign in February, Federal issues intruded remarkably little, with the Labor Government defending its record and the Liberals, under the relatively new—and short-lived—leadership of P. H. Morton attacking it for various alleged weaknesses.

The result was a heavy swing against Labor, with the result in doubt for a week. In the big victory of early 1953, when memories of the 1952 credit squeeze from Canberra were still fresh, Labor had won a majority of twenty seats in the Legislative Assembly and was generally supported by two independents as well. The reverse of 3 March 1956 cut this majority to five, obtained only after close, prolonged counts in several seats. The Steering Committee and the Parliamentary 'outs' suggested that it was a vote against the stewardship of the Grouper Executive.

On 7 April the omnipresent Alan Reid reported in the *Daily Telegraph* that the Federal Executive would be arriving in Sydney shortly to implement, with an eleven to one majority, a 'Chamberlain peace with honour project' in New South Wales. The New South Wales Executive was to be sacked, but it was hoped that only a minority of irreconcilable Groupers would be lost to the Party. The promoters of this plan would like to see the end of this faction anyway, he said. Evatt's role behind the scenes was uncertain, but he had told the supporters of the plan he would back them. Reid said the only danger would be a counter-manoeuvre by Cahill.

The Federal officers met in Sydney from 16 to 18 April to prepare for the intervention, with intensive manoeuvring and lobbying behind the scenes.

The State Executive met on 17 April and decided its tactical position, with, according to the press, a thirty to six majority in favour. This position was that the charges were state matters and should be heard by the incoming Executive after the Conference listed for the first weekend in June. It used the precedent of the previous April, when the Federal Executive had referred the charges against Kane and Rooney to the State body.

Earlier, Kane had put his personal position. He would not give evidence before the Federal Executive or officers unless: he was notified of the charges against him; he was given time to prepare his defence; his own shorthand writers were present; the press was admitted to the hearing.

The same day, the New South Wales Labor Council wrote to the Federal Executive defending its State ALP and saying an intervention would cause an open split. The Grouper unions threatened to withdraw from the ACTU, thus opening the way to domination by the communist-orientated left.

The Steering Committee put a long memorandum before the officers, signed by Platt and Williams, once again listing their charges against the Executive. They said a hundred delegates at the August Conference had been 'under outside direction'; that The Movement had given branch delegates from the country 'the treatment'; members of the State Executive had shown a 'strange reluctance' to discontinue their activities in union ballots; The Movement had organised to defeat Labor at the Federal elections, but supported some Labor candidates. These charges were in addition to the 'bodgie ticket' affair.

By 20 April, the Federal Executive had decided on a full-scale investigation into the faction-ridden New South Wales Branch. It was to open at 9.30 a.m. on 23 April.

The members of the Federal Executive at this time were: Colbourne and Campbell from New South Wales; Stout and Davis from Victoria; H. Boland and Bukowski from Queensland; Chamberlain and Webb from Western Australia; Toohey (now a Senator) and J. Sexton from South Australia; and Duthie and H. Lacey from Tasmania. Colbourne was the lone Grouper. The others could be roughly divided into hawks and doves, with the hawks still the AWU officers, Campbell and Stout, and the doves those influenced by Kennelly. Chamberlain, as President, appears to have been aloof from these factions and Evatt's role was also unclear. Chamberlain at this time was developing the art of standing astride both factions and Evatt, thus strengthening his personal power. He was becoming as strong a Party President as Ferguson had been years before.

The 'inquiry' lasted fifteen days and was about as fruitful and as important to the outcome as that in Victoria eighteen months before. A string of witnesses proved that there was a faction fight going on in New South Wales, but little else.

The first witness was Con Wallace, proprietor of the Kings Cross 'Hasty Tasty' and other restaurants, prominent in City Council circles and among the supporters of the Steering Committee. He said a tall man, whom he did not know, had handed him the faked ticket at the August Conference. He claimed the Groupers had stacked the Toxteth, Newtown, Newtown East and Kingston Branches—hardly important, since branches had been stacked in this Glebe-Newtown section of West Sydney for generations.

The President of the Painters' Union, F. A. King, said he had found uncounted Senate ballot papers in a little yellow box. And so the parade of trivia went on, proving what everybody knew: there was a fight on.

The only substantial issue proved to be the alleged faked ticket. Apart from Wallace, the only witness for this was Sullivan, the Newcastle ex-Grouper, who expanded on two affidavits he had signed in October.

In the first of these affidavits, dated 10 October, Sullivan said he had been a spectator at the August Conference. He alleged Rooney had given him a bundle of the 'bodgie' tickets, closely resembling those of the Steering Committee. He said he had not distributed the tickets, but had thrown them in a city garbage bin. Rooney told him later that seventeen delegates had voted according to this ticket.

Two weeks later, Sullivan signed a second affidavit, in which he alleged Kane had urged him to distribute the tickets. He attached a copy of the ticket to this affidavit, but not the first one. The affidavits had been handed to the Federal Executive by Evatt, accompanied by letters from the MPs Ward and C. Griffiths. Griffiths represented Shortland, a Newcastle division.

Sullivan also alleged that two Group leaders had gone to Queensland and obtained large sums of money from a mines manager there, to help finance the Industrial Group campaign in the Miners' Federation.

Kane issued writs claiming £25,000 for libel from each of Ward, Griffiths and Sullivan, on 26 April. In a statement to the press at the luncheon break, he said he had refrained until then from taking legal action, in the hope that the Federal Executive would give a lead and reject the allegation.

Next day Toohey, the acting chairman, stopped Kane from cross-examining Sullivan. He said this was necessary because of the libel writs.

On Sunday 29 April, the Industrial Groups were resurrected in a new form, as 'The Industrial Labor Organisation'. After the meeting which formed it, the officers said the organisation had nothing to do with the ALP, but it was obviously a body intended to keep the Group organisation intact and provide for cooperation against the communists in union elections. The former President of the Groups, Robert Day (a Protestant and Rubber Workers' Union official), was elected President, and Ross and Short Vice-Presidents. Hurrell of the Ironworkers was elected Secretary, C. McGrane of the Postal Workers, Assistant Secretary and P. O'Toole of the Clerks, Treasurer. With three non-Catholics and three Movement men, it was not untypical of the Grouper complexion in Sydney.

The State Executive case before the inquiry started on 1 May. Shortell was to conduct the case for the Executive, but Chamberlain over-ruled him from the start when he tried to call Rooney. Chamberlain ruled that the Federal Executive had the right to determine who it would hear and when the inquiry would end. 'Everybody knows the situation in New South Wales is the same as it was in Victoria when the Federal Executive intervened,' he said. Shortell heatedly retorted that the position in New South Wales was quite different, with the State Government and Labor Council supporting the present Executive.

Chamberlain insisted that the Federal Executive would not call Rooney, because a letter Rooney had sent to the Executive was 'a piece of impertinence'. Rooney had written to the Executive saying he was under medical advice to stay home with a nervous complaint. But he said that, while challenging the Federal Executive's right to hear the question, he would give evidence against his doctor's orders. Chamberlain, according to the press, said, 'We have informed Mr Rooney that we have no desire that he attend against his doctor's orders. We have also no intention of allowing Mr Rooney to lay down the terms on which he would give evidence. He and Mr Kane are the only two who have challenged our authority.'

Chamberlain's cold, implacable authoritarian manner at the inquiries and conferences he presided over in the split years earned him admiration from those on his side, but a burning hatred from his opponents.

One of the key witnesses for the State Executive was the New South Wales branch returning officer, R. E. Savage, MLC, who stated that none of the 122 informal votes recorded at the August Conference had followed the pattern of the 'bodgie ticket'.

Kane and Rooney never got an opportunity to defend themselves against the 'bodgie ticket' allegation and the charges, other than this one, against them were never made specific.

On 2 May the inquiry received letters from both strongly protesting their complete innocence of the charge of promoting the faked tickets and protesting against the Federal Executive procedures.

The inquiry ended at 10.30 p.m. on 3 May, but of course the proceedings before it were window dressing, not serious politics. The real issues were being decided in the backrooms and by the tactics of the rival factions and sub-factions. Kennelly had been in Sydney in late April, and it was the 'old firm' of Kennelly and Downing, the shrewdest doves and negotiators of both sides, who began drawing the lines—at first dimly seen—of a fresh compromise.

On 2 May a previously silent Cahill had told the caucus of the State Parliamentary Labor Party that the Parliamentary Party would 'make up its mind without recriminations' when the inquiry ended. The *Sydney Morning Herald* reported that most members left the meeting with the impression that Cahill wanted to keep the Party united at all costs, but would prefer the pro-Grouper Executive intact. The press said Cahill would face the difficulty of six to ten 'rebels' in the Parliamentary Party who would back the Federal Executive in any action. The most prominent of these Parliamentary 'rebels' was generally conceded to be Clive Evatt. There were also thought to be about five members of the State Executive who would support the Federal Executive.

Cahill's brief hint of some line at last being taken by Caucus was followed by the bombshell of the 'Shortell Plan' on 3 May, as the inquiry was ending. This proposal, which Shortell put to Federal Executive, was that the present State Executive continue in office until the State Conference, which had now been postponed to 30 June. The two factions would in the meantime work out, with Federal assistance, a 'unity ticket' for the Conference to elect as the new Executive. Once the proposal was made, Cahill called a press conference and praised it as an 'excellent compromise'. The *Sydney Morning Herald* said Chamberlain and Toohey were 'dumbfounded' by this 'clever piece of strategy'.

Probably everybody concerned knew that the two factions would never agree on a compromise. Even if the Executive were evenly divided, Grouper control of the ALP office would give the Groupers a major tactical advantage in preparing for a triumphant return at the 1957 Conference. But more probably, the compromise would break down before the 1956 Conference, with the Groupers going ahead to win the day yet again, with the 'bodgie ticket' affair then becoming history and irrelevant.

The Federal Executive would be at a strategic disadvantage in rejecting this compromise, however. In the branches and among the electorate, should there be an election, the onus would be on it if there was a split. And

Cahill was now committed to taking the Parliamentary Party with the Groupers.

Evatt now was also backing away from the Stout-AWU hawks towards the Kennelly doves. He had been re-elected by a comfortable majority at the opening of the Parliamentary session, and thus was in less fear than for two years of losing his leadership. His relations with Kennelly were also better, and those with Dougherty that much worse. A big part of his motivation was a fear that Menzies would again call a snap election if there was a Labor split in New South Wales. Menzies would have a convenient excuse for this in the impending loss of control of the Senate; from 1 July, the Anti-Communist ALP senators McManus and Cole would hold the balance of power and it would not be hard for them to force Labor into defeating the Government on a suitable issue. McManus and Cole would certainly have a vested interest in aggravating any New South Wales split.

The method the Federal Executive chose was to fall back by strategic retreat to a stronger line. By a majority of ten votes to two, it referred the New South Wales position to a Special Federal Conference. The two opponents of this course were Stout, who wanted the New South Wales Executive sacked on the spot, and Colbourne, who opposed any intervention.

Federal Conference, Labor's supreme governing body, was a much stronger instrument against the Groupers than the Executive, with its questionable powers. It also had a strong anti-Grouper majority, thanks to the AWU. The Federal Executive, seeking another tactical advantage, also decided to hold the Conference in Melbourne. This would mean that interstate delegates, many bewildered and deeply impressed by the anti-Movement hysteria, would be meeting in a city where the Groupers were now a hated splinter party. In Sydney, they would have been subject to constant lobbying and perhaps realised the situation was less simple than they supposed.

Shortell put a different view on 11 June in Sydney in commenting on the decision to refer the New South Wales position to a Special Conference. 'Labor people in this state,' he said, 'will wonder how a Federal Conference that has not heard any of the evidence or had a chance of watching the demeanour of witnesses can possibly arrive at a decision which would have any of the elements of natural justice.'

The battle of tactics continued, with a tactical retreat by the New South Wales Executive on 11 May. It decided, in keeping with the Federal Executive order, to postpone its conference from 2 June to 30 June and to accept the authority of Federal Conference to determine policy and Federal Executive to implement it. But it insisted on the 'rights of the rank and file in Conference assembled in accordance with the rules of the New South Wales branch to elect its officers and Central Executive'. The resolution was carried by twenty-five votes to five.

During one of the heated scenes at this meeting, Kane had pointed a finger at Ward and said angrily: 'You tried to frame me. You tried to destroy me.'

The New South Wales Executive was now inspiring newspaper reports that it had £250,000 worth of assets legally its own and not those of the Federal bodies. They included radio station 2HD in Newcastle. The tenor of the reports was that, in a split, the Federally installed Executive would not get a penny or a fuse-wire of these assets.

As the climactic Melbourne meeting drew near, the dove forces on the Federal side appeared to be strengthening, while Grouper unity seemed intact. With Evatt edging towards Kennelly, and left elements thrown up by the AWU zig-zagging becoming stronger, the power of Dougherty was declining. The bridge from Kennelly to the State Government, and through it the Catholic Church, was making for growing unity of doves on all sides.

The hawk forces could now be distinguished as the left unions and Stout in Victoria, left unions brought into the ruling faction in Queensland by the AWU, and left Parliamentarians such as Ward and Cameron. These were calling for the strongest action against the Groupers, and for Labor to emerge as an outright socialist party. Chamberlain, who still appeared to be astride both camps, supported this policy of 'socialism or nothing' before the South Australian Conference in early June. On 9 June, the *Sydney Morning Herald* said Ward and Cameron were leaders of the faction saying that the New South Wales Executive must go; the Party must be purged of 'right wing' elements and become avowedly socialist; and the breach was the best thing that had ever happened to the Labor Movement. The paper named Calwell and McKenna as compromisers, with the role of Evatt and Chamberlain uncertain.

The arguments in favour of a compromise were obvious. The Party would probably be damaged, in its known sense, beyond repair in what was by far the strongest Labor State; the outgoing Executive would have legal title to the comparative wealth of the New South Wales Branch; and Evatt's chances of becoming Prime Minister in 1958, which seemed to improve in the recession of 1956, would be destroyed.

It is difficult to know what strength of conviction lay behind the ideas of the 'socialism at all costs' school. This was an idea, to some extent borrowed from the British Bevanites, which had been around vaguely for some years. In the years after 1956, Ward, Cameron and Chamberlain made no serious attempt to convert the ALP to this view in any positive sense; it seemed much more to be used as a weapon against opponents in the struggle. What must have been obvious was that any ALP seeking office in the conventional way would not entertain the idea of the bellicosely left wing Ward as Leader or probably even Deputy Leader, and would also look unkindly—if only from the viewpoint of electoral tactics—on an authoritarian leftist like Chamberlain exercising great power from the extra-parliamentary machine.

The Special Conference began in the Council Chamber of the Melbourne Trades Hall at 2.30 p.m. on Monday 11 June, the Federal Executive having met the previous evening to make arrangements. The

Conference was overwhelmingly anti-Grouper; Colbourne and Blackburn of the New South Wales delegation were the only remaining Groupers, while the others were approximately equally divided in allegiances between the emerging left, the AWU faction and the old Kennelly faction.

Chamberlain, as President, reported to the Conference, and according to the *Sydney Morning Herald* he said a 'grave state of affairs' existed in the New South Wales branch of the Party. He said the 'same basic problem' existed in New South Wales as in Victoria, but the position in New South Wales was 'more complicated'.

The record shows a complicated series of tactical manoeuvres ensuing, with some trying to get the issue immediately back to the Federal Executive and others opposing. The Conference adjourned after three hours and when it resumed at 7.30 p.m. a concensus had developed around this course. D. A. Dunstan from South Australia, later State Premier, moved:

That Conference views with grave concern the situation outlined in the report of the Federal President and the Federal Executive. That without prejudicing the issues, and mindful of the rights of appeal to Conference, this Conference refers the position in the New South Wales branch to the Federal Executive to make such findings and to take such action within its powers as it deems proper.

Kennelly, who was in the Victorian delegation, seconded the motion. Clyde Cameron, with Dr F. Dittmer from Queensland seconding, moved an amendment that the Federal Executive then report back to Conference. The amended motion was carried and Conference adjourned until 2.30 p.m. next day.

Shortell had come to Melbourne and set up a temporary Grouper headquarters at the Lygon Hotel, opposite the Trades Hall, the very heart of the hostile anti-Grouper territory. His stand was hopeless. The Federal Executive met all day on 12 June, except for one brief break to report on progress to a reconvened Conference, and finally decided the following recommendations:

The Federal Executive, in the exercise of all the powers it possesses, determines:
(a) That the State Executive of the New South Wales Branch of the Australian Labor Party has acted and is acting in a manner contrary to the Federal Constitution, platform and policy of the Australian Labor Party, as interpreted by the Federal Executive.
(b) That the present Executive of the New South Wales Branch of the Australian Labor Party is over-ruled.
(c) That such State Executive no longer exists.
(d) That the Federal Executive decides in accordance with the Federal Constitution, Platform and Policy of the Party to act in the stead of the State Executive until the Federal Executive as soon as possible sets up an organisation competent to carry out the Federal Constitution, Platform and Policy.

The record of the Conference continues. The President, Chamberlain, explained fully the deliberations and actions of the Federal Executive.

Moved Mr Oliver: 'That Conference notes the report given to us this morning by the President.' Seconded Mr Brebner. Carried.

Mr Shortell asked: 'Did the Executive make this decision on any specific charges against the New South Wales branch?'

Chairman replied.

11.30 a.m.: President Chamberlain introduced the Right Hon. Dr Evatt, Leader of the Labor Party.

Dr Evatt addressed the Conference at length.

Vote of thanks. . . . Conference closed 12.10 p.m.

On the instructions of the Federal Executive, Campbell and Colbourne had already flown back to Sydney to prepare for the takeover. (Shortell had then been admitted as an alternate delegate for New South Wales at the last session of Conference.) The Federal Executive followed shortly afterwards, and met again in Sydney on 15 June.

It appointed a Committee comprising Chamberlain, Toohey, Schmella, Colbourne and Campbell to submit a panel of names from which the Federal Executive might choose a new Executive for New South Wales.

The doomed New South Wales Executive sat until nearly midnight on 15 June, fairly equally divided between those prepared to accept the Federal intervention and those not, trying to avert a split. Those prepared to accept the intervention soon attracted the nick-name of the 'stay in and fight' group, while the others were the 'die hard Groupers'. Colbourne, Blackburn, Lindsay North, J. Bale (secretary of the Locomotive Enginemen's Union) and P. Hampson were named by the *Sydney Morning Herald* as leading compromisers.

The Executive split almost evenly on two tactical motions and then late at night Kane moved that the meeting adjourn until the Monday. This would have been a virtual defiance of the instruction to disband. Campbell, as President, refused to accept the motion and walked from the room when Kane moved dissent from his ruling. Colbourne followed him. Shortell took the chair, formally closed the meeting—and with it, the Grouper hegemony in New South Wales.

The great sectarian fight—as it had seemed to be developing a year earlier—had ended with a whimper, and in a shabby and degrading power struggle that was rapidly losing any ideological respectability it might have have had. Chamberlain and the other inquisitors had not, by this stage, even bothered to formulate specific charges against the New South Wales Branch, other than those of the 'serious situation' and 'best interests of the Party' type.

Throughout 1956 The Movement had been disintegrating in Sydney and most of the State and in June—ironically, within days of the sacking of the Executive—had been re-constituted, firmly under the control of Bishop Carroll. This was a half-way step to its final dissolution in 1958. But The Movement was never more than fringe politics in the affairs of the New South Wales ALP, however exotic it might have seemed on occasion. Some observers had the impression that by 1955-56, at least, there was a non-Catholic majority on the State Executive and certainly practising Catholics, let alone Movement members, were in a minority. Dedicated Santamaria-ite zealots and Catholic Social Corporatists who reached any importance in New South Wales Labor, even at the local level, were numbered in two rather than three figures.

The re-constituted Movement now gave its firm support to the 'stay in and fight' strategy and this was presented to appropriate Catholics as 'the Cardinal's wish'. It was, of course, in complete opposition to the break-away policy of Santamaria, who now had only a tiny following in the main population areas of New South Wales, though a few more in some country districts.

The 'stay in and fight' view was that one Party, however compromised, was better than two. In a split, the left section would have the name, the support of the Federal Leader and Executive, and at least half the Federal parliamentarians—and the state ones could not be relied on. It would tend to be regarded as the Protestant Party. In reality, as in Victoria, it would present a happy hunting ground for the left unions and for a resurgence of communist power. It would probably develop the flavour of the Marx-ist socialist party the Church traditionally abhorred. Yet all its advantages would probably put it electorally in front of a Party based on Catholics, and with Church blessing. On the other hand, if the Groupers maintained their cohesion, they would expect eventually to link up with other moder-ate elements. At the next Conference, or when the current mood of bitter-ness died down, they would return to strength in the normal life of the Party. Catholics would continue to have an influential role and the Church some political heft.

All revolutions seem to yield their reign of terror, and the shabby little revolution of the winter of 1956 yielded its own shabby little reign of terror.

The new New South Wales Central Executive, which met for the first time on 26 June, was essentially moderate and 'balanced', if somewhat lop-sided. The State Government had been influential in selecting it. There had been all-round agreement that the Victorian mistake of handing control to the left unions should be avoided. Colbourne and even, for a few days, Kane and Rooney, were kept on the payroll and the more tractable Groupers were retained as a substantial minority. The 'pro-Evatt' Group around Campbell, Dougherty and Ormonde controlled the Executive and also three key committees, the Disputes, Credentials and Organising committees. Campbell remained President, Ormonde and Oliver became Vice-Presidents. J. Fitzgerald, MP, L. Clay (Textile Workers), J. Anderson (Painters and Decorators), J. Coulthard (Tram and Bus), A. L. Drury (Electrical Trades), E. Bennett (Printing Trades) and A. Mulvihill (Railways) were prominent 'pro-Evatt' nominees. Early voting showed a 'pro-Evatt' majority of twenty to fifteen.

On the motion of Con Wallace, the caretaker Executive voted to meet again three days later to 'consider urgent business'. The press said this would be the sacking of Kane and Rooney.

Predictably, at the 29 June meeting Oliver successfully moved that Kane be given notice his period of office had expired. The background to this was that Kane had been appointed by the 1953 Conference, the first after he went on the ALP payroll, for three years. Kane contested this, saying that his appointment should not expire until the third Conference—marking the end of an ALP year—after his election. The Federal Executive direction was that there should not be a State Conference until 1957 and it would be the job of this Conference, Kane argued, to decide his future.

The Central Executive endorsed the motion that Kane be given notice at its next meeting on 13 June. He was given a month's pay.

Passionately, Kane addressed the Executive meeting for the last time. He defended his record, attacked his persecutors and said he would not compromise in fighting against rackets and malpractice in unions or against communist activities in them.

The next meeting was on 27 July, and the caretaker Executive voted eighteen to eleven to dismiss Rooney. It appointed Mulvihill, essentially a liberal young Catholic who had reacted strongly against some Movement attitudes, to Kane's old job of Assistant Secretary.

Kane and Rooney thus disappeared without the charges against them ever being pressed or specified. Press reports said they were regarded as the 'leaders of the Industrial Group Movement' in New South Wales. This is difficult to sustain, however. For most of the time there were a dozen or more men in Sydney who could have been described as the Group 'leaders', while Rooney was a hundred miles away in Newcastle for most of the period. Rooney had long been regarded as an enthusiast for The Movement, but Kane's character was more complex, though he was close to Santamaria then. For most of his career, he had had the knack of being a thorn in the side of established union leaders—for many years, for basically 'left' rather than 'right' reasons. His real sins may have been that he was competent, less inclined than Colbourne to compromise, and said what he thought. He had shown little inclination earlier in the fight to be 'bought off' with a Government job. But by the winter of 1956 there was a compelling political reason to get him out of the ALP office. The 'pro-Evatt' faction simply had to get their own man into the office to avert the danger of it being used as an organising point for a Grouper return to power in 1957. For the same reason, they needed a sympathetic country organiser.

The Disputes Committee met regularly through July and August, hearing an array of charges and arguments coming up from ALP branches throughout the state; the two years of faction fighting had seeped to every level of the ALP. The eventual expulsions were few, but the continual investigations and charges and countercharges kept the climate of the Party white hot.

Ironically, the first expulsion by the new Executive had been of Evatt's flamboyant and unpredictable brother, Clive, who had climaxed a long series of rows with Cahill by voting against the Government on 4 July over fare rises on public transport. He was expelled from the ALP on

13 July, on the recommendation of the State Caucus, by a vote of twenty-seven to eight.

The key expulsion came on 24 August, however, when by eighteen votes to fifteen the Executive expelled Alan Manning, the *Voice* man, from the ALP. Although impeccably anti-Movement, Manning had been infuriated and disgusted by the power politics of 1955-56. An articulate intellectual, he became a leader of the intransigent faction. He denounced the Federal intervention and suspension of the 1956 Conference in letters to the Editor of the *Sydney Morning Herald* in July and was expelled for these and for refusing to agree to stop public attacks. But a more serious offence may really have been his constant activity in addressing ALP branches throughout the Metropolitan area. He could hardly keep pace with the invitations. With a *Voice* man defending the old Executive so strongly and attacking the 'Evatt-Chamberlain dictatorship' so eloquently, the 'Santamaria' story started to sound thin. And on occasion, such attacks found their way into the newspapers, thus gaining wider attention.

Manning's expulsion had wide repercussions. He had been invited to address a number of branches over the coming weeks and his expulsion did not deter him. On 7 September a scuffle broke out at the Neutral Bay Branch when Manning tried to address it. The President and Secretary tried to leave the meeting, but furious Group supporters tried to stop them —to maintain the legality of the meeting—and police were called. The Executive, meeting that night, withdrew the charter of the branch, which had always been considered as unusually right-wing in flavour. The same evening it withdrew the charter of the Penshurst branch.

A week later, the Coogee branch split into two meetings in the same hall when Manning arrived to speak. This branch contained some influential Groupers and also 'pro-Evatt' leaders such as Ashley and Jensen. As a result of the Manning affair, the charter of this branch was also withdrawn, three members expelled and it was reconstituted by the Executive.

Federal Executive meetings were coming to be looked upon with apprehension and the one set down for Canberra in mid-September was no exception.

On 11 September, it passed a motion specifically banning 'unity tickets' between communists and ALP members in union elections. Chamberlain told the press the decision was unanimous, though the same week the Victorian Executive had insisted that such how-to-vote cards were acceptable 'in the spirit of the Hobart decisions'.

Next day, however, the Executive also—again unanimously, Chamberlain said—banned membership of the Industrial Labor Organisation to ALP members. This was the inter-union anti-communist organisation, with a structure resembling the Industrial Groups, established in Sydney on 29 April. On 29 July, it had appointed Kane as a paid full-time secretary-organiser.

Chamberlain said the Executive had 'fully considered' a New South Wales Executive report on the ILO and had found that the Organisation was in effect the same organisation as was previously known as (*sic*) the 'Industrial Group'; its reference in its stated objectives to its purpose being to assist in union elections made its existence 'an affront not only to the Labor Party but to organised trade unions'; its avowed intention to secure the election of certain private persons in trade union elections was 'comparable to the procedures of the former Industrial Group organisation'.

One might have been excused for imagining that the ILO was quite within the spirit of the Hobart decision on Industrial Groups, which merely said that ALP recognition was to be withdrawn. That resolution had said: '. . . it is emphasised that this decision of the Executive does not disband Industrial Groups. No authority is possessed by the Executive to so disband. . . . We are of the opinion that any form of industrial organisation designed to combat communist activity in the unions should be a matter for the sole determination of the members of the Union concerned.'

The reference to 'the Industrial Group' is also disconcerting. It occurred more than once in ALP decisions at this time. These references reinforce an impression gained by the author in conversations: that some Federal delegates, especially from smaller states with no significant Communist industrial activity, had only the vaguest understanding of the heresy they were hunting.

It is hardly possible to doubt that the real reason for the proscription was power politics. The new New South Wales Executive had no certainty of staying in power after the 1957 Conference. In some votes on the Executive the 'pro-Evatt' majority was already paper-thin and the Groupers were determined on a comeback. The obvious counter to the 'stay in and fight' strategy was to harass and seek to divide the Groupers.

In its way, it was a brilliant success. It was the last straw for Kane, with yet another career in politics being cut away. It had been difficult to accept the Hobart ban on the Groups, he said in a press statement, for those who had been carrying on the struggle against communism for ten years. 'This direction now to completely withdraw from the organised fight against communism is one that no clear-sighted Australian unionist can accept. We'll not be deterred by the decision of the Federal Executive or anybody who desires to assist the communists. My choice is now between carrying on the fight against communism or losing my membership of the Labor Party. My decision is to continue the fight against communism.'

The New South Wales Executive met again on 21 September and proscribed the second Grouper organisation, the Rank and File Rights Committee, formed after a pro-Grouper rally in May. It was ordered to disband by 15 October. At the same meeting, Jensen was selected by the Executive as its candidate for Lord Mayor of Sydney. The Group supporter, P. D. Hills (later State Leader) received only six votes, to eight for E. O'Dea, a former Lord Mayor and twenty-three for Jensen. This was in part a reaction against Hills holding two jobs, however; he had been elected MLA for Phillip in 1954.

The Rank and File Rights Committee was due to meet on 29 September, a Saturday, and in the days before the newspapers reported a split between those determined to defy the bans and those who wished to continue to 'stay in and fight'. 'Stay in and fight' won the day. Compared to the hundreds and even thousands at the great rallies, there were only forty or so people at the 29 September meeting. Kane, Manning and Rooney were among the few well-known figures there. Attendance was in effect walking out of the ALP and using the Rank and File Rights Committee as the basis for a breakaway party.

Kane and Manning had already, the previous night, worked out plans for a new party. Searching round for a name, they had tried to keep the name of the old party but also get in a reference to it being democratic— as opposed to the authoritarian power politics of the ALP. The name they arrived at was 'Democratic Labor Party'.

The Democratic Labor Party was thus formed out of the remnants of the Rank and File Rights Committee, at the Sydney Trades Hall, on 29 September 1956. Manning was its first President, Kane and Rooney respectively its first Secretary and Assistant Secretary-Organiser.

Manning told the Press he expected the DLP to take 3,000 to 4,000 members out of the ALP. He said he and Kane had spoken to about thirty ALP branches and had found 60 per cent of the members opposed to the present ALP executive. He had never met Santamaria or Keon—who had been reported organising in Sydney shortly before—and would get out if Santamaria came into the DLP.

'I was one of the early targets of Mr Santamaria's criticism,' he said. 'We would not consider becoming a branch of the Anti-Communist ALP. However, provided our objectives do not clash, we would consider an offer by the Anti-Communist Labor Party to cooperate with us in an election.'

Manning said the DLP would run candidates in the forthcoming City Council elections and in every seat in New South Wales in the next state and federal elections. Parliamentarians would be welcome and invited to join but 'we would not want many' of the State Parliamentarians who had been 'too spineless in their attitudes to the dictatorial State Executive'.

He said the first branches would be formed from the re-constituted Coogee, Neutral Bay and Penshurst ALP branches and there would be a full Conference early in 1957.

The ALP Executive, harshly, and Cahill, more kindly, predicted a bleak future for the breakaway party. Executive statements said the members of the new party had shown their real attitudes by forming it and hinted at secret Santamarian influence.

In fact, Movement and even Catholic influence in the DLP at that time was not great. The strong clerical support for the 'stay in and fight' strategy tended to prevent mass breakaways by Catholics and possibly something like half its first executive were not Catholics.

Among the members of the foundation executive were W. Slogrove and W. J. Beasley, the President and Secretary of the Rank and File Rights Committee, and four trade union members of the dismissed ALP Executive: Peter Carter (Painters and Decorators), W. Crane (Mining Mechanics), W. Allport (Timber Workers) and J. Kenna (Clothing Trades).

With Kane's driving energy spearheading the organisation, DLP branches were formed by the dozen over the next few weeks as ALP rank and file members voted with their feet against the events of the last few months. The entire Epping branch went over to the DLP on 11 October and large numbers went from other branches—sometimes more than half. The flow reflected a dozen issues of personality clashes, of influence by persuasive individuals, of an overwhelming disgust by the little people of the Party with cynical power politics at the top. It was not especially sectarian in character and was sometimes characterised as a 'revolt of the innocents'.

However, by then much larger events were shaking world politics, in Suez and in Hungary. And in Queensland, ominous rumblings were suggesting that an earthquake was about to shatter the ALP there.

Chapter Nineteen
The Split in Queensland

The Brisbane Trades Hall overlooks the city centre from a hill rising behind Edward Street. Dunstan House, the headquarters of the Australian Workers' Union and in the 1950's of the Queensland Central Executive of the Australian Labor Party, is in the low-lying heart of the city, in Elizabeth Street. This geographical divergence put in concrete form a feud that was almost as old as the organised Labor Movement in Queensland.

The traditional and intimate alliance between the Labor Party and the AWU in Queensland reached its peak during the premiership of William Forgan Smith, a dour and autocratic Scot, from 1932 to 1942. The AWU was then led by C. G. 'Clarrie' Fallon who, in addition to being State Secretary of the AWU, was also for much of the time State President of the ALP and even for a time Federal President and State Secretary. Though respected for his strength of character and radical ideals, Fallon was nevertheless the archetypal AWU 'boss' who liked things his own way. It was said that he liked to surround himself with physically huge organisers because they would not have enough brains to oppose him; another and more likely origin given for the Queensland AWU tradition of six-foot-six organisers was that men of this stamp could frighten the most recalcitrant cane-cutter or bush worker into paying his dues.

The reasons for the AWU-ALP alliance were simple and obvious: the AWU was the biggest union in Queensland, by far. It covered not only such traditional AWU fields as the shearers, cane-cutters, metalliferous miners and other bush workers but, more than in other states, competed for membership with other unions whose organisation was weak in the sprawling reaches of rural Queensland.

For most State and indeed Federal Parliamentarians, an alliance with the AWU was essential. For many years, the State had been organised into electoral divisions on the basis of geographically huge, lightly populated outback electorates—with their preponderance of bush workers and AWU members—returning disproportionately large numbers of State Members because of their small populations compared to city divisions. Pre-selection was on the basis of a plebiscite among members of affiliated unions, as in Victoria; this meant that the AWU officials, with their ability to organise in the back-blocks, had tremendous influence over pre-selections. And at election time, the local apparatus of the AWU, with its paid organisers and cars, was an invaluable aid to a Labor candidate. This alliance in the field was repeated at the Labor in Politics Convention, the supreme governing body of Queensland Labor, held every three years in a different city. About 60 per cent of delegates traditionally came from unions and 40 per cent from ALP local branches, but because of the expense many outback 'branch' representatives were in fact Parliamentarians or AWU organisers. The alliance between the AWU, the political wing and a small number of 'out' other unions was easily able to control the convention. The system under which affiliated unions voted their own representatives onto the Queensland Central Executive made control of this body, supreme between Conventions, more difficult, but the AWU and the political wing were still able to control it as long as they worked together.

The AWU greatly increased its hold over the ALP after the war, through the Industrial Groups. As these captured other unions from communist control, the new Grouper controllers tended to side with the AWU, which strongly supported the Groups. This more than made up for a tendency for the comparative strength of the AWU itself to wane, as Queensland slowly became more industrialised.

The alliance between the AWU, the Groups and the dominant Parliamentary faction thus came to form a powerful 'right' wing of the Party in Queensland after the Second World War. It was 'right' of course only in a limited sense, since the new Premier, E. J. Hanlon, and the AWU leaders rarely hesitated to attest the usual, if qualified, faith in rhetorical socialism.

The comparatively smaller, predominantly craft unions of the Trades Hall and the 'out' factions of Parliamentarians made up the so-called 'left' wing. The main Trades Hall unions considered themselves more intellectual, more militant and more correctly orthodox than the AWU faction. A climate of folksy quasi-Marxism permeated many and not a few were under communist control. For many years the Trades and Labour Council of Queensland had a communist secretary, first Michael Healy and later Alex Macdonald. This allowed the small local Communist Party considerable, though limited, leverage on Trades Hall ideology and strategy. Ideology apart, most of the Trades Hall unions were often engaged in competition for members and conditions with the AWU and the Trades Hall-AWU feud was in a sense bred into them. By the late 1940's, the Industrial Groups had become a convenient issue around which this deep-seated power struggle could fester.

Hanlon's Minister for Labor at this time was Vincent Clair Gair, born of a Scottish prison official father and an Irish mother at Rockhampton in 1902. Short, rotund, affable yet arrogant, devious and tenacious, Gair was the rising star of the post-war Hanlon Cabinet. He had a strong sense of Catholic anti-communism and supported the Groups warmly, yet had sufficent of the wheeler-quality to be a relative favourite—for an 'in' parliamentarian—with the Trades Hall in the difficult post-war years. He was remembered as an excellent Minister for Labor in an especially difficult time. Part of the price for this success was a degree of estrangement from the AWU leadership. Even then, the AWU leaders seemed to sense a declining role for their union in the second, more technical half of the century. Gair tended to be seen as a man less willing than an up-and-coming

Queensland parliamentarian ought to be to 'toe the line' of the AWU. But by 1950, when Gair became Deputy Premier and even 1952, when Hanlon died and Gair succeeded him, this difference was a faint cloud on the horizon.

The big issue of the 1947 Labor in Politics Convention, in Townsville, was the formation of the Industrial Groups. This was still an issue in Toowoomba in 1950, but it was passed in importance by a complicated faction fight, stemming from the State Parliamentary Party, in which the QCE had tried to remove the pre-selections of several parliamentarians, including the Speaker, J. H. (Johnno) Mann.

The Groups were a divisive issue again at Rockhampton in 1953, with eleven pro-Group and three anti-Group motions on the agenda. The right wing was easily able to control the Convention. Clem Lack wrote of this Convention in *Three Decades of Queensland Political History*:[1]

When the ALP Convention met at Rockhampton on 23 March, there was no sign of the internal stresses that in four years were to split the party in twain and destroy a Labor Government. The Party, under Premier Gair, had just achieved one of the most outstanding triumphs in the history of Queensland politics, winning an additional seven seats. It was high noon for the Labor Party in Queensland as in other states. . . . If any prophet had foretold that in less than four years the Labor Movement in Queensland would be disintegrating into warring fragments he would have been laughed to scorn. Labor in Queensland indeed seemed impregnable and immovable as a political force in the summer of 1953.

The political wing was firmly in the saddle at the Convention and the dominant figures were Messrs Gair and Bukowski [President of the AWU].

A motion by Dr F. C. Dittmer, MLA, then a strong supporter of the Premier, 'That it be the aim of the Labor Movement to obtain for the workers three weeks annual holidays in southern areas and four weeks in northern and western areas', was seconded and carried without discussion. Yet this was the main issue which ultimately brought about the downfall of the Gair Government.

Fifteen months later, Dougherty walked out of the New South Wales Central Executive meeting in Sydney and Labor in Queensland was never the same again.

The State President and dominating personality of the AWU in Queensland in the first half of the 1950's was Rochus Joseph John Bukowski, born at Mount Morgan in 1901. A boyhood contemporary of Gair in Rockhampton, Bukowski became an AWU organiser in 1935 at Ayr, Southern Districts Secretary, stationed in Brisbane in 1942, State President in 1951 and State Secretary in 1956 upon the death of H. Boland. Although not a practising Catholic, he was an intense anti-communist in the AWU tradition, with an almost physical hatred of communists, and he became Secretary of the Industrial Groups; in this role he worked closely with The Movement.

[1] Clem Lack (ed.), *Three Decades of Queensland Political History, 1929-1960*, Queensland Government Printer, Brisbane, 1962

The Groups were part of his power base as he rose to the top of the AWU, and with it, the ALP in Queensland. He was a huge, driving—almost driven—man, given to frantically hard work and hard play. He affected to despise 'rosary bead' practising Catholicism, yet was proud that his children were being brought up as Catholics. He was aggressively proud of the Polish name and Polish birth of his paternal grandparents. Many thought it part of his tragedy that he had the will to be an AWU 'boss' in the Fallon style, but possessed neither the emotional stability, the subtlety nor the time in history to do so. Men such as Dougherty and Bukowski seemed to have a strong sense that they were not attaining the same unquestioned power as Fallon, the man in whose shadow they lived.

Dougherty's walk-out in Sydney in the middle of 1954 and his subsequent support of the Evatt attack on the Groupers led to a Grouper initiative to back Bukowski against Dougherty for the Federal Secretaryship of the AWU. This collapsed and served only to intensify Dougherty's intransigence against the Groups. By the end of the year the whole East Coast AWU machine was behind Dougherty, after some deft manoeuvring, and Bukowski was 'on side'; perhaps his position was too vulnerable, since he was feuding with the North Queensland section of the AWU, for him to afford not to be. Anyway, by the AWU Conventions of January and February 1955 he was violently attacking his erstwhile allies of the Groups and Movement in the same melodramatic exposés as his colleagues.

The Federal intervention in Victoria in late 1954 and the Hobart Conference put Gair, who declined to change sides with the AWU, onto a collision course with the great union. He had rejected its invitations to do so and attracted the implacable hostility of Dougherty. This magnified intolerably the already existing cleavage between Gair and the AWU and with Bukowski personally in Queensland.

The feud deepened steadily throughout 1955 and 1956 and an unkind Providence produced many political events to aggravate it, if ever time seemed likely to be a healer.

The political wing had sufficient strength, even without the AWU, on the Queensland Central Executive, on 25 March to defeat a motion of no-confidence in the five Queensland delegates, led by Gair, who had boycotted the Hobart Conference. (The exception was the AWU State Secretary, Boland.) But subsequently a meeting of nineteen unions affiliated to the ALP, including the AWU, voted to censure them by thirty-one to twenty-three. The State Parliamentary Party, however, voted its confidence in the boycotters.

From this time, the previously feuding Trades Hall unions and the AWU worked increasingly closely together, with Bukowski leading the attack on the Gair Government. A winter of discontent was followed by a Queensland Central Executive motion on 23 September, recommending that the Parliamentary Party introduce the three weeks annual leave, as agreed to by the 1953 Convention. Cabinet decided, however, that the state finances would not support the introduction of three weeks leave at that time and on 2 November Caucus supported this stand by a unanimous vote.

While this issue was inflaming relations, on 7 October the State Industrial Court granted a rise of only five shillings a week to the Electrical Trades Union, which had sought a rise of £2.5s. a week. But on the same day, the Court gave very much bigger increases to some 'white collar' unions, involving an increase of £451.10s. a year for State Parliamentarians.

Some realignments of power brought control of the Queensland Central Executive to the Trades Hall-AWU faction by this time and it followed up the rejected 'recommendation' on annual leave a month later by 'instructing' Caucus to revoke its decision and introduce three weeks annual leave immediately. It threatened to reconsider nominations for the 1956 elections of Labor MLAS opposing the three weeks annual leave. Gair led the fight back against this in the Government and Caucus rejected the 'instruction' from the QCE by twenty-eight votes to twenty. The Gair Cabinet had to threaten to resign before even this narrow victory could be achieved in Caucus in the face of such a powerful threat. The stand was successful, however, and on 21 November the Executive carried a motion merely asking the Government to reconsider its decision. Gair, a member of the Executive, was present and clashed heatedly with several delegates.

Though the three weeks annual leave and other industrial issues were, in a sense, genuine, they had a greater element of symbolism. They were the sort of issues which from time to time created tension between the political and industrial wings of Labor, but which were most inflammable when cloaking much deeper power struggles.

Dougherty was making it clear in public statements at that time that he would use his great influence against Gair. He had attacked him at the 'pro-Evatt' rally in Sydney in August and a few weeks later virtually launched a 'Gair Must Go' slogan at an anti-Group rally with Ward in Brisbane.

It was unfortunate that these troubles came to Queensland at a time when approaches to industrial arbitration were changing. Until the middle fifties wage claims were based primarily on 'needs', relativities, automatic quarterly adjustments with the cost of living and an ad hoc approach to prosperity. The abolition of quarterly adjustments in 1953, after three years of intense inflation, ended this era. By the end of the decade, criteria such as productivity and 'work value' were to bring big gains in award wages. But in the years from 1953 to 1959, award wages tended to stagnate for want of suitable criteria, while the cost of living and, for most workers, additional 'over-award' margins, rose steadily. The situation was particularly difficult in Queensland, because there were many state awards. State wage-fixing authorities were traditionally more subject to 'political' influence in Labor-governed states than the Federal authorities, and in Queensland 'political influence' in almost everything was assumed after forty years of almost unbroken Labor government and AWU control of the machine.

This situation was seen at its most difficult in the great shearing strike of 1956. During the wool boom years of the Korean War, the Industrial Court had awarded a 'prosperity loading' on award wages for shearers, who formed one of the biggest sections of AWU membership. By 1955 wool prices were dropping and in November the Court reduced the award rate from £7.13.9 per hundred sheep to £6.18.6, following a claim by the United Graziers' Association for a 15 per cent reduction in the loading. The AWU had made a counter-claim for a 10 per cent increase in the rate. The Court's judgment was for a 10 per cent reduction, to take effect from 1 January 1956.

The shearers, claiming that the award was a minimum, not a compulsory, rate, and that many were paid above the award, refused to work at the new rate. On 17 February, the Court declared their ban to be an unauthorised strike and issued an order restraining the AWU from encouraging its members in the ban.

The ensuing dispute threw the AWU and the Trades Hall unions more closely together than ever. Without their support, the AWU would not have been able to fight the issue through. It was a momentously emotional one for the AWU and indeed the Labor Movement generally, for a shearers' strike in Queensland against reduced wages had led to the formation of the Movement in its modern form sixty-five years before.

On 27 February the Disputes Committee of the Trades and Labor Council declared wool shorn at the new rate 'black'. Many shearers, often from interstate, broke the union ban to shear at the new rate as the season opened in the North and the railways refused to carry the 'black' wool. Graziers started carrying it to Brisbane by road. In Brisbane, the Storemen and Packers', Transport Workers' and Waterside Workers' Unions refused to handle the wool and the April wool sales were cancelled. Several members of the Storemen and Packers' Union were dismissed.

The United Graziers' Association applied successfully to the Court in July for the clause in the award granting preference in employment to unionists to be struck out. There had been several brushes between the AWU and the Court.

The Gair Government was in an appalling dilemma. It was under pressure from the unions which controlled it to assist in an intensely emotional, bitterly fought dispute. Yet wool was vital to the Queensland and Australian economies. The Queensland Railways were losing £100,000 a month. Wool was piling up in stores and often on the sheep's overloaded back.

The climax came when the September sales had to be cancelled. The Government's attitude had been that it could not interfere in the jurisdiction of the Industrial Court. Now, ten months after the controversial award, it approached the Federal Government and both agreed to take whatever steps were necessary to ensure that the 'black' wool would be shipped. A special sale was scheduled for 1 to 4 October.

Dougherty declared in Sydney on 7 September that Gair would go down as 'the only Labor Premier in history who has openly consorted with an anti-Labor Prime Minister [Sir Arthur Fadden was Acting Prime Minister at the time] and asked an anti-Labor Federal Government to put troops in charge of the Brisbane wharves.' Both he and Bukowski accused Gair of disloyalty to the Labor Movement.

Gair replied that his government had a grave responsibility to see that the economy of the state and the welfare of its people were protected.

A meeting of union leaders on 23 September called on the Government to 'get on side' with the unions and on Parliamentarians to declare their support for the pastoral workers. Caucus replied by supporting Gair's stand, thirty-two to fifteen.

Gair convened the tenth conference between the parties and suggested as a basis for negotiation a rate of £7.9.6 per 100 sheep, but the AWU insisted on £7.13.3—a drop of only sixpence on the old loaded rate.

There were now 270,000 bales of wool, valued at £27 million, stored in Brisbane. The Government invoked emergency powers to order the Storemen and Packers back to work so the October sale could go on. They agreed to do so, at a secret ballot.

The Government then requested the Court to re-hear the original claim. It issued an interim award of £7.11s. per 100 sheep, to be challenged by either party within three months. The Graziers' Association challenged this unsuccessfully and the AWU accepted it. The dispute ended with the Court restoring the preference clause on 18 December, operative from 1 January 1957.

The 1956 Labor in Politics Convention opened in Mackay on 28 February in the militant atmosphere of the early shearing strike. The AWU and the Trades Hall, reversing most of previous history, acted together as a broad industrial wing. They controlled the Convention and captured every Committee. Besides Gair, the two leaders of the 'out' faction, the Deputy Premier and Minister for Transport, J. E. Duggan and Dr Felix Dittmer, were the only State Parliamentarians elected to the once politician-dominated QCE. These two were also elected as delegates to the ALP Federal Conference. Parliamentarians defeated included the Treasurer, E. J. Walsh, the Attorney-General, W. Power, and M. T. Brosnan, a member with Bukowski of the old Industrial Groups Committee.

Annual leave became the great symbolic issue of the Convention. J. P. Devereux of the Amalgamated Engineering Union—ironically, a former Grouper and State President of The Movement—moved that the Conciliation and Arbitration Act be amended to provide for three weeks annual leave, with four weeks for shift workers. This motion did not specify a date for the expanded leave to apply; but then V. T. Hefferan of the Shop Assistants' Union, moved an amendment that the Act be amended in 1956 and take effect from 1 January 1957.

The outnumbered political wing, while not opposing the principle vehemently opposed the move to direct them on timing. It introduced a completely new principle into relations between the industrial and political wings, they said.

Gair said that never before had a Convention presumed to direct a Labor Government on the timing of implementation of a policy decision. He said the move conflicted with the ALP Platform stipulation on 'constitutional utilisation' of governmental machinery. It would be fatal politically for the Government to accept a direction on timing, he said.

'Parliament would not be a supreme body if its members were subjected to outside coercion, intimidation or direction,' he said. 'You cannot have responsible government once the decisions of any party in Parliament become subject to review by an outside body other than the electorate.' Gair said Convention had left the timing of its decisions on a forty-hour week to Forgan Smith and Hanlon with confidence and he asked it to display the same confidence in his Government.

Jack Egerton (Boilermakers' Society), Secretary of the Metal Trades Federation, Vice-President of the Trades and Labor Council and a rising figure on the left (he later became full-time President of the Trades and Labor Council and of the ALP) put the militant view. Egerton said:

> I think there is much logic in what the Premier said, but the time for logic has disappeared. The Labor Party said that the time for logic was three years ago. . . . The Premier can have his Constitution and the Premier can have his Premiership and we will not presume to direct the Government. But we will presume—and only because it is forced upon us—to direct the Parliamentary representatives of the Australian Labor Party. There is no other body with a right to do so. . . . [The Parliamentarians] have got to learn that when they are attending Convention they are not the Premier, the Treasurer or any other member of the Cabinet, but members of the Party. . . . I believe that Cabinet misled the Labor Caucus and that they have to be shown that this is the governing body of the Labor Party and that this is where policy is made. If they do not carry out that policy, they can join some other party.

After a long debate, full of recrimination, with Duggan attempting a conciliatory approach, Hefferan's amendment on timing was lost. But Convention accepted a further amendment by G. G. Goding (AWU) providing as an addendum to the motion that the Premier include the three weeks annual leave in his policy speech for the election due in the autumn.

Cabinet held an emergency meeting that night, 29 February, and the press reported that Gair had threatened to resign as Premier. There was limited enthusiasm in Cabinet and—according to the press—in the industrial wing for a split and probable change of Government, however. Duggan probably summed up the feeling of many when according to the *Sunday Mail* of 4 March he said: 'If anyone wants to jump out of windows, they should be careful where they are going to fall. Personally I am not going to do any jumping!'

There were press reports of a compromise being reached, but next day Gair told Convention that Cabinet did not accept the resolution. He said the direction was contrary to the rule of constitutional government and a negation of the principle of responsible democratic government, namely, that the Government was responsible to the electors and only to the electors.

Convention appointed a committee of seven to meet the Premier and Deputy Premier to discuss the impasse. This reached an 'understanding', the precise terms of which were never made public.

Gair delivered his policy speech on 24 April, devoting most of his seventy-three-minute speech to an account of the Government's record. He did not mention the three weeks annual leave.

Despite the turmoil over this issue earlier, and the drawn-out shearers' strike, Labor was returned with a sweeping victory on 19 May. It held all its 1953 gains. A probable reason for its popularity was the 'little horror' Budget introduced by Menzies in the Federal Parliament a few weeks earlier; amongst other things, it increased the tax on beer. Other reasons probably included an unimpressive State Opposition and, according to some commentators, popular approval of Gair's 'standing up' to the industrial wing.

A sense of crisis returned by August, after the temporary closing of ranks for the election. The Governor did not mention three weeks annual leave in his speech opening the new Parliament on 21 July. At Caucus meetings in August, Gair said that Queensland was facing one of its worst financial years; 1956 was a year of minor recession and the Federal Government was paring spending in all sectors, including allocations to the states. Gair said every member of the Government would have to take his responsibility for unpopular decisions caused by the State's economic position. He called for a full attendance and told members they would have to obtain leave to be absent from Parliament.

The recession of mid-1956 strengthened Gair's economic arguments against extra annual leave. He insisted that a Labor Government could not give extra annual leave if it would mean dismissal of other State employees.

During the controversy, the predominantly right-wing 'white collar' and State Service unions had sought an extra week's leave for members already getting three weeks and the overall campaign had developed into one for an extra week's leave for all. Apart from the argument about shortage of State funds, Gair claimed that Queensland would not be able to attract the manufacturing industry it badly needed if it required longer annual leave than other states.

By September, the Queensland Central Executive was mounting its own counter-battle of tactics. It wrote to all Labor MLAS asking them whether they were prepared to vote for the introduction of three weeks leave in 1956, but the following day, 26 September, the Parliamentary Party again voted against introduction of the legislation, twenty-eight to nineteen. The Queensland Central Executive made various other moves to get its way, but in the face of Gair's determination, backed by uncountered economic argument, not to comply, it was powerless.

One other event with major implications for internal Labor politics in 1956 was the Lands Royal Commission. In 1955 and early 1956, the AWU paper *The Worker* had run a campaign alleging maladministration and hinting at scandal in the Lands Department. The Queensland Country Party Senator Ian Wood alleged in the Senate that some graziers had been forced to pay large sums of money to obtain renewals of their leases; and on 16 February Gair announced that the Government would appoint a Royal Commission of Inquiry. The Minister for Lands, T. A. Foley, was relieved of his portfolio at his own request. Bukowski was a witness before the Royal Commission. Foley denied that he had, as alleged, sought £1,000 from a grazier, F. M. Bell, for party funds in return for favourable consideration of a lease.

Gair announced on 22 April that Foley would be prosecuted on a criminal charge before a magistrate and the inquiry was suspended. On 1 May, Mr M. J. Hickey, SM, found Foley not guilty. Foley took part in the 19 May elections and retained his seat of Belyando. The Royal Commissioner, Mr Justice Townley, resumed the inquiry and on 14 June found that Foley had been guilty of 'corrupt conduct' in soliciting a donation of £1,000 to Labor Party funds in return for favourably considering a stud lease for Camboon holding, on the Dutton River, in December 1949.

Foley, whose portfolio had been restored after the magistrate's hearing, resigned from Cabinet again and Labor Caucus decided that Parliament should be asked to dismiss the suspended Chairman of the Lands Administration Board, V. R. Creighton. A strong campaign in support of Creighton developed among affiliated unions and Creighton applied to appear at the Bar of Parliament. The Queensland Central Executive expelled Foley and suspended H. R. Gardner, MLA for Rockhampton, who, during a bitter union faction fight in Rockhampton, had criticised the Executive for 'bulldozing' decisions. Both Foley and Gardner were Gair supporters in Caucus.

The Creighton affair came before Parliament on 2 August. Creighton was alleged to have formed a personal antagonism towards Foley, giving confidential information and making complaints about departmental affairs to Edgar Williams, an AWU official. The Minister for Public Lands, P. J. R. Hilton, said Creighton had used his privileged position to anonymously issue 'numerous false and scurrilous accusations'.

Creighton, before the Bar of the House, said there could be a time when loyalty was a cloak not merely for corruption, but for more serious dereliction of duty. 'Find me guilty of treachery to Her Majesty's ministers if you will,' he said, 'but neither that nor anything you may do will make me guilty of any breach of the higher loyalty which I at all times owed to the public of this state.' The motion to remove Creighton from office was carried on Party lines after a bitter debate lasting fourteen-and-a-half hours.

Three weeks annual leave was still a burning issue when the climactic year of 1957 opened. Apart from the issue involved, pride, principle and political advantage were—as it happened, irreversibly—aroused on both sides. For the AWU, half a century's domination of Queensland's politics was at stake. The idea of the industrial wing directing soft, self-seeking politicians to implement radical industrial measures was deeply ingrained in many of the militant left—as was the fear of being returned to its former relative impotence if the AWU and politicians got together again. Whatever Macdonald's personal inclinations as a responsible Trades Hall leader, the Communist Party had no love for Labor Governments and had a vital interest in maintaining a toehold in Queensland Labor as a shield for its foothold in Victoria; the communist 'line' at this time is believed to have been that Gair should be manoeuvred into resignation. For Gair and his Government, economics aside, the principle of reasonable freedom from machine dictation was vital; if it gave in on this, other demands could be expected and 'QCE dictation' was a longstanding allegation from the Opposition, to which the Parliamentary Party was sensitive.

Gair said in a Christmas message to the Brisbane *Courier-Mail* that the Government would not grant industrial benefits the State's economy could not afford. It did not propose to gamble with the security and welfare of Queensland wage earners.

Bukowski, now State President of the ALP and State Secretary of the AWU, replied with an attack on the Government. Labor had no need to gamble on any of its decisions, he said. Labor knew its own mind on all matters; only fools would run counter to Labor's wishes and only political inexperience would gamble on Labor not knowing what its wishes were. Bukowski advocated a means test for the Queensland free hospital system on incomes above £2,000 a year. He attacked the Government on its attitude to the liquor trade and accused Gair of being responsible for the failure of the Attorney-General and Minister for Labour and Industry to address the annual state delegate meeting of the AWU. It was now Government practice, he said, to open hotels, but the Premier and ministers would be better off acquainting themselves with the people of the State 'who put them where they are'.

In a further exchange, Gair said the AWU had failed to contribute to the 1956 election fund and Bukowski retorted that it had made available a a fleet of forty motor cars and the services of its organisers. He said the Premier had collected £12,000 from 'people unknown to the Labor Party'. This was a reference to the rather mysterious 'Premier's slush fund', to which private contributions to the ALP had gone for many years.

These exchanges illustrated the increasingly unpleasant turn that personal animosities were giving the issue. Gair's personal contempt, never well concealed, for Bukowski as a bully, was now obvious. Bukowski, who is remembered as having become rather rattled and distorted in judgment under the stress of the split years, retaliated with a burning hatred of Gair, who was capable of considerable arrogance and lack of tact in his personal relations.

On 28 February, the Queensland Central Executive issued an ultimatum to State Labor Parliamentarians on the three weeks leave issue. By fifty-two votes to eleven, it warned members that opposition to legislation for three weeks leave would be dealt with by the Executive 'in accordance with the Party's rules'.

On 27 March an increasingly nervous Caucus carried a motion by Gair's arch-opponent, Duggan, by twenty-nine votes to eighteen, that a conference on the issue be held with the Inner Executive of the QCE. A Parliamentary Committee comprising Gair, Duggan, the Treasurer, E. J. Walsh and two others was appointed and the Conference set for 5 April. The members of the Inner Executive were Gair, Duggan, Bukowski, Schmella, Egerton, Dittmer and Whiteside.

Meanwhile, two new disruptive issues had arisen for 1957. The first of these was the University of Queensland Act Amendment Bill, which made a number of uncontroversial changes to the Act controlling the

University and one highly controversial one—the provision of machinery to hear appeals by members of the University staff against appointments, punishments or dismissals. There was an outcry from the University Staff Association, which claimed the Government right to appoint an independent Chairman for the Appeals Board would undermine the independence of the University and make the Senate, in appointments, a rubber stamp. After an approach from University staff, the Inner Executive of the QCE recommended that the Government delay proclamation of the Bill. Although the Bill was passed shortly before the split, it was never proclaimed. The controversy surrounding it put the Government even further on the defensive.

The Motor Spirits Distribution Bill was much more serious in inflaming the atmosphere. This arose from the affair of 'dim sim petrol'. The Queensland Prices Commissioner had rejected an application from the oil companies for a rise in the price of petrol following the closure of the Suez Canal in late 1956, and in retaliation the oil companies threatened to stop sending standard grade petrol to Queensland.

Gair retaliated swiftly and on 27 February Cabinet approved proposals to force one-brand petrol stations to include an independent pump and to purchase fifty million gallons of standard petrol a year from an independent Taiwan Chinese company, the Chinese Petroleum Corporation. Gair said he hoped to have Chinese petrol in Queensland before the end of March. It would be 79 to 83 octane and would retail at 3s.6½d. a gallon or less, compared to the existing price of 3s.7d. for standard petrol. The purchase would be nearly half Queensland's annual consumption of 110 million gallons of standard and super grade petrol. Gair said the Chinese company obtained crude oil from the Middle East and refined in Formosa. The deal was negotiated through an international oil broker, R. G. Gaylor, President of Gaylor Petroluem Sales Corporation of Long Beach, California.

Gair said the Government had made the reasonable proposal to the oil companies that they make a fresh application to the Prices Commissioner for a review of their case. He told the companies that if there were difficulties about the formula for price determination, an independent arbitrator would be appointed. The companies had seen fit to reject this proposal and withhold supplies of standard grade petrol from Queensland.

On 29 February Gair announced that a public company 'to be controlled and operated by the people' would be formed in Queensland to handle the petrol from Formosa. He announced agreement between the Government and a Sydney oil consultant, O. L. Josephson. Josephson told the press the Government would provide seaboard storage facilities and rail and road tankers to distribute the petrol. The Government had indicated that precautions would be taken against the new company becoming 'part of the oil combine'. The new company would be known as National Petroleum Ltd.

The Minister for Labor and Industry, A. Jones, introduced the Motor Spirits Distribution Bill into the Parliament on 28 March. The Bill provided for licences for wholesale and retail distributors of petrol. Its effect was to prohibit retail trading in one brand of petrol only. Hotly opposed by the Liberal and Country parties as 'socialist', 'dictatorial', 'vindictive' and the like, the Bill passed all stages by 2 April.

At first, Bukowski had welcomed Gair's attack on the oil companies. But on 31 March Bukowski objected that the Central Executive had not been advised of the contents of the Petrol Bill and the University Bill and had not been given the opportunity to discuss them. Next day Gair replied that there was no necessity or obligation for the Government to do so. He challenged Bukowski to name the last Bill any minister had submitted to the Executive. He denied that the Executive normally received some notification of impending legislation and said he knew of no legislation dealt with by the Executive in 1956. Bukowski was 'wearing the wrong guernsey and playing offside' on the Petrol Bill issue.

Bukowski replied that the previous Premiers, Forgan Smith, Cooper and Hanlon, had discussed controversial legislation with the Inner Executive and obtained union reaction but the practice had not been followed in recent years. 'The Parliamentary Labor Party . . . is merely a small section of the Labor Party,' he said.

Duggan attacked the Petrol Bill when the Inner Executive discussed it on 3 April and the Inner Executive demanded its repeal. Ironically, Federal Labor Caucus on the same day had carried unanimously a motion congratulating the Gair Government on the Petrol Bill, following a personal message of congratulations from Evatt on 24 February. Again on the same day, the Trades and Labor Council supported the Petrol Bill but voted for withdrawal of the University Bill after hearing representatives of the Staff Association.

Duggan had strongly opposed both Bills in Cabinet and his attack on them in the Central Executive—he called the Petrol Bill 'the rottenest piece of legislation ever brought down in the State Parliament'—attracted much criticism as a breach of Cabinet solidarity. His attitude was that he was on the Executive as a Member of Parliament, not as Deputy Premier. He was also there on the industrial wing 'ticket'; his name had been omitted from the right wing ticket at Mackay the previous year.

John Edmund Duggan, born at Port Pirie, South Australia, in 1911, later came to Queensland and he entered the State Parliament from Toowoomba in 1935 when he was only twenty-four. He became Minister for Transport in 1947. Duggan was regarded as a gifted minister, who presided over the post-war restoration of the Queensland Railways from almost comic opera inefficiency. Despite an impoverished boyhood, he was a gentlemanly, cultivated man of high intelligence who gave the impression of being much better educated than he was—an unusual type in the rather folksy world of Queensland state politics. The gifted, fast-rising Duggan attracted considerable personal hostility in Caucus, much of it from the loyal mediocrities who constituted Gair's Caucus base. Rivalry with Gair intensified over the years and Duggan, even though elected Deputy Leader, became regarded as the leader of the 'out' faction. He was eventually joined by Dr (later Senator) Dittmer, a former Gair supporter who also clashed with the Premier. As in the other State Parliamentary

Parties, the Caucus 'out' faction tended to side with the 'left' in the machine for mutual comfort and support.

Many of the attitudes on the Petrol Bill were predictable enough, in view of the fierce power struggle and clash of personalities. There were many objectionable features to the Petrol Bill, even though the attack on 'monopolies' and 'cartels' brought much emotional support. It upset a pattern that had developed in the petrol reselling industry throughout Australia and it was strongly opposed by oil company employees, 12,000 of whom signed a petition against it. The reselling trade appeared divided. There was pressure from these sources on the Executive. Suspicions were raised about the bona fides of Josephson and other small oil entrepreneurs, about the ability of the oil companies to retaliate with supplies from across the border under Section 92 of the Australian Constitution and about the general wisdom of such hurried action with a vital commodity.

Yet much of the debate on the merits of the issue was obscured by a bad financial smell. There were insinuations of corruption on both sides, which were aired in the debate on the Bill in Parliament and again in the debate when Gair crossed the floor. There were stories of phone calls from oil executives to high political figures, of a revealing tape recording and of a mysterious £75,000 which would cause the legislation to be dropped. Josephson emphatically denied stories connecting him with part of this. Briefly, one story was that there was very big oil company money out for bribes to stop the Bill. The opposite one was that National Petroleum, once underway, could eventually be sold out to the major oil companies for an inflated and very profitable price.

The Queensland Central Executive retracted its hostility somewhat on 11 April, when the full Executive declared by thirty-two votes to twenty-seven its opposition to monopolies and cartels, but requested the Parliamentary Party to change some aspects of the legislation. It postponed discussion on annual leave and the University Act. The 'hawks' had had to moderate their approach to get the votes to defeat Gair on the full Executive.

Gair flew to Sydney on 14 April and there was speculation that he would talk there to the DLP. Instead, he told the press he did not think the Queensland Central Executive would expel him, as they would not risk breaking up a Labor Government. He had talks with the New South Wales Premier, Cahill, on state affairs, and with National Petroleum contacts, and he appeared on the 'Meet the Press' television programme to put his case in Sydney. He said on this programme that his Government would end the concessions to National Petroleum if the company lost its independence.

In the meantime the 5 April conference on annual leave had ended with yet further failure to agree and on 10 April Gair had said adamantly: 'I favour three weeks annual leave when Queensland can afford it—not when the Queensland Central Executive tells me to do it. Because of lack of money we have had to sack 2,000 men from Government employ. Three weeks leave would cost at least £400,000 a year—probably £1,250,000 when its implications are fully worked out. To introduce it we would have to sack more men. I won't do it. They are like children; you are fond of them but you have to say No when they want to take an expensive clock off the wall and throw it around like a four-year-old.'

Various compromises could have been considered, had the climate been less heated. Perhaps there could have been agreement on a suitable financial state to allow three weeks annual leave (which the Country Party-Liberal Government later introduced). Another proposal was that sections of the Public Service could be excluded in the early stages of the legislation. In the event, no such compromise made serious headway and Gair adamantly refused to publicly bow to pressure.

On 18 April the Queensland Central Executive carried by thirty-five votes to twenty-seven a motion declaring that the Premier no longer had the confidence of the Labor Movement. It called on him to attend a special meeting to show cause why he could not be expelled from the ALP. The motion was moved by Schmella and seconded by A. Summers (Meat Workers). The lengthy motion accused Gair of 'continued and openly expressed defiance of Convention' and the Executive. 'Further, this Executive is of the opinion that the Leader of the State Parliamentary Labor Party has acted in such a way as to bring discredit on the Party and confusion and embarrassment within the ranks of the Party itself,' the motion continued.

Goding, the new State President of the AWU and Williams, the Northern District Secretary, were among those who opposed the motion. An amendment that all members of the State Parliamentary Labor Party who had opposed introduction of three weeks annual leave should also be called upon to show cause was defeated.

The *dénouement* of two and a half years of internal strife was set for 24 April. The Premier, a tubby, jaunty, gutsy little figure in a bow tie and felt hat, entered the lift at Dunstan House in the late afternoon of that day and rode in the lift to the seventh floor to meet his executioners.

He had behind him a declaration from his Cabinet the day before, declaring its confidence in him and carrying the signed promise of each minister except Duggan to stick with him.

The document signed by the ministers read:

Resolution of Cabinet: The Premier having reported today on the meeting of the Queensland Central Executive of the Labor Party held on 18 April, and otherwise on the dispute between the Executive and the Government, Cabinet declares:

1 That it has complete confidence in the Premier and recognises the distinction with which he has led the party, and his outstanding work as head of the Executive Government.

2 That at no time, or on any matter, has the Premier done other than execute the decisions arrived at by Cabinet in accordance with the principle of Cabinet responsibility.

3 That therefore Cabinet regards as a matter of the utmost gravity the attempt being made to impose on the Premier responsibility for decisions to which we individually and jointly subscribe, and to which we adhere. And, we, the undersigned members of Cabinet wish it known that any punitive action by way of expulsion, suspension or otherwise, taken against the Premier will therefore be regarded as having been taken against each Minister individually.

Nine of then ten ministers signed two copies of the document. Duggan added his signature, but with the addendum, 'With the exception of the final paragraph, I agree'.

The issue then went to Caucus and after nearly six hours debate, the members voted twenty-six to twenty-one to give the Premier unqualified support, declaring that Gair had at all times scrupulously carried out the decisions of Caucus.

The support Gair obtained from his colleagues was reported to have astounded Bukowski and his other enemies, who had believed five ministers at most would back Gair in a showdown. But, as Bukowski had often pointed out, the Central Executive was the official ruling body of the Labor Party in Queensland.

The Gair affair had attracted publicity throughout Australia and far beyond; it even earned an editorial in the London *Times*. The weight of comment was overwhelmingly on the side of Gair, as the elected leader of a sovereign government refusing dictation by an outside machine. His position was also attracting attention from The Movement, the DLP and the Anti-Communist Labor Party, which began preliminary organisation in Queensland. They already had a core of support in some unions, most notably the Clerks' and State Service unions, and the allure of attracting a seemingly wronged Premier and Cabinet to the cause was obvious. In the Easter that intervened between the two momentous meetings of the Queensland Central Executive, the organisation and intrigue on all sides was as intense as the emotion.

Gair now faced six charges, laid by the judge and the jury:

1 Defiance of the decision of the Labor-in-Politics Convention at Mackay and on numerous occasions since—in Press statements, at meetings of the Parliamentary Labor Party Caucus, and at meetings of the Queensland Central Executive.
2 Refusal to accept decisions of the QCE interpreting Convention decisions.
3 Breach of the Pledge signed by all Members of the Party requiring them to uphold the policy and platform of the Party.
4 Discredit brought on the Party by such procedures as:
(a) Redcliffe Commission—designed to discredit one individual. (This was a reference to an inquiry into allegations of bribery in sewerage contracts at Redcliffe, near Brisbane, in 1955. The Speaker, J. H. Mann, was cleared of any implication.)
(b) Lands Commission—designed to discredit an Affiliated Union but only brought discredit on the Party and Minister.
(c) Club legislation initiated because of representations made by one individual (invasion of rights of privacy, and the principle that a person is entitled to choose his own company).
(d) University Bill initiated at the instigation of one individual and against all accepted authorities connected with the University of Queensland and all other Universities in British countries.
(e) Petrol Bill which contains some provisions of Fascist or Communist character, such as onus of proof on the accused and concentration of power in one man.
(f) Consistent false leadership by encouraging members of the Parliamentary Labor Party to refuse to accept decisions of the Labor-in-Politics Convention and the Queensland Central Executive.

(g) Soliciting and obtaining financial support from non-Labor sources and sources definitely unsympathetic to Labor and the rank and file interests of the Labor Party, without accounting to any individuals or any body such as the QCE.

5 Repudiating a personal Pledge given to a number of delegates at Convention and inferring that the report given by these delegates was untrue.

6 Organising and arranging the issue of a statement by Cabinet which is a direct challenge to the Queensland Central Executive and undoubtedly political blackmail of the most vicious type, by stating, in effect, that if the Leader could not run the party his way (without reference to the rank and file or its representatives) he would abandon the party and form or join another party opposed to Labor.

Note: Important Rules covering this matter are Rule 32 (r) which obliges the QCE to guard the interests of the Party generally, and Rule 32 (a) empowering the Executive to suspend or expel any member violating its Rules and Platform and Rule 32 (v) empowering the QCE to interpret its own rules and decisions of Convention, and to expel any member who refuses to abide by its interpretation or decision.

Gair had been a member of the ALP since 1919 and of the Parliament since 1932. His parents had been members of the Party since almost the turn of the century. Faced with the end of this tradition, he spoke emotionally, his eloquence sometimes disintegrating into choked groping for words.

There was no offence alleged against him, he told the Executive, which could be attributed solely and exclusively to any action of his. Therefore, it was really a trial of the Cabinet and Caucus. It was a trial of every individual member of both bodies. It was the trial of men who had given a lifetime of service to the Labor Movement and who had been privileged finally to represent it in Parliament. He said the history of the Party showed there had been differences between the Executive and the Parliamentary Party on many occasions. The indefensible publicity in the daily press exposing their differences, exaggerating their dissension, had fanned a difference into what could easily be a disaster.

Sworn by oath of office to administer in the interests of the peace and welfare of all citizens, the Parliamentarians found themselves torn between a tradition and a grave obligation. In such a moment of grave choice, they had no alternative in conscience. For a moment, tradition must be laid aside as it had so often been laid aside in times of national crisis, when the welfare of all must precede the welfare of some. . . .

Gair concluded:

I cannot help recalling at this moment of supreme crisis in this Party, other occasions on which Labor men—greater Labor men than I—have stood against the clamours and demands of those who lacked their vision.

Can I be blamed if I recall today the tragedy of 1929 when outside this same building I saw men cheering as Labor candidate after Labor candidate fell, and his defeat was posted in figures over the awning of the *Worker* building?

Can I be blamed if I recall only a few weeks later the same men appalled at the consequences of their own actions of a few short weeks earlier? . . .

I am glad this decision is for your making—not mine.

Bukowski ruled that Gair must now leave the room. Although an Executive delegate, he could not cast a vote as a delegate or make use of a proxy vote.

Schmella then moved that Gair be expelled from the ALP and E. T. Ashmore (Postal Workers) seconded the motion.

The historic motion read:

This Executive, after hearing Mr Gair state his case in showing cause why he should not be expelled from the Australian Labor Party, decides that he has not refuted the charge that he has defied Convention's decision on the matter of three weeks leave, and that he has not shown that he has not repudiated his personal pledge in the matter of three weeks leave, given to a number of delegates.

This Executive is satisfied that there was a pledge given the Convention delegates, and that Mr Gair has since repudiated that pledge.

This Executive declares that the Premier's policy as to why he has not carried out Labor-in-Politics Convention decisions in connection with three weeks leave, is entirely unsatisfactory. His continued refusal to accept ALP rules and platform render him unfit to be a member of the Labor Party. . . .

Mr Gair must accept responsibility for his leading role in this organised defiance of the recognised authority in the Party. . . . We therefore decide that the membership of Mr Gair be terminated forthwith; that is, that he be expelled from the Party and that the Parliamentary Labor Party be advised accordingly.

Five hours of debate followed and at 1.15 a.m. on 25 April the Queensland Central Executive voted by a reported thirty-five to thirty to expel Gair from the ALP.

It was significant that among those who opposed the expulsion were Goding, the AWU State President and Williams, the Northern District Secretary, a long-time internal opponent of Bukowski. Too late, the AWU front was cracking. W. F. Edmonds, MHR for Herbert, a former AWU official and considered a leading anti-Grouper in Canberra, also opposed the expulsion, as did Duggan and T. Bolger of the State Service Union. Evatt and other Southern leaders had also tried, too little and too late, to stop the Queensland split.

There were moves for a Federal Executive intervention, but on 26 April the Federal Executive voted by telegram ten to two not to intervene 'at present'. Only Campbell and Colbourne, from New South Wales, appeared to see the same urgency in the Queensland situation as in Victoria and New South Wales.

Gair called his Parliamentary supporters together on 26 April. Eight ministers were present and the Treasurer, Walsh, gave his support from Bundaberg. Twelve rank and file members of the Parliamentary Party and the two expelled MLAs, Foley and Gardner, were also present. An absent back-bencher also sent a message of support and the twenty-five men officially banded together that day as the Queensland Labor Party. The meeting appointed a committee of five to frame a constitution and rules.

On 4 May the Queensland Labor parliamentarians appointed T. Moores Minister for Transport to take the place of Duggan and elected office bearers. Gair announced that the Queensland Labor Party would not affiliate with the Democratic Labor Party.

Duggan resigned as Minister for Transport on 29 April and next day the Parliamentary Labor Party appointed him Leader and Dittmer Deputy Leader. Nicklin, the Leader of the Opposition, announced that the Opposition would not 'carry' the Gair Government and denied suggestions of a 'deal' by which Gair would be supported for some time in exchange for a revision of electoral boundaries and legislation for compulsory court-controlled ballots—a threat believed to terrify the AWU leadership, as court-controlled ballots would open the way to better organisation against them.

Parliament was then in recess and on 1 May the Opposition parties, at a joint meeting after separate Party meetings, asked the Administrator, Sir Alan Manfield, to call Parliament together not later than 11 June.

Expulsion of the Gair supporters from the ALP started on 4 May, with Walsh, Moores, the Minister for Health and Home Affairs, W. Moore, V. J. Cooper, the Government Whip, Brosnan, the Industrial Group Leader and the suspended Gardner going on that date.

According to press reports Evatt told the Federal Labor Caucus on 6 May that all members had a duty to support the Queensland Central Executive. It was Evatt's first comment on the Queensland split, which he appears to have at first tried to stop. Gair retorted angrily on 7 May that the whole Queensland break-up had been engineered by Evatt and his 'local quislings'.

Next day, Gair called on the Administrator, who summonsed Parliament to meet on 11 June.

The next weeks were bitter with public recrimination between the two Labor parties, with savage personal attacks between Duggan and Gair revealing the depth of their mutual personal antagonism. Senator Condon Byrne, a barrister who had once been private secretary to Gair, resigned from the ALP and joined the two anti-Communist ALP Senators, McManus and Cole, on the cross-benches in Canberra. Labor Party branches and regional bodies began to split throughout the state as the Queensland Labor Party spread from its Parliamentary nucleus.

Following the Parliamentary preliminaries on 11 June, Gair announced to the House that on 7 May Duggan had resigned as a member of the Executive Council and Minister for Transport and that Moores had been appointed to these posts. Duggan then announced that he had been elected Leader of the ALP.

The Speaker, Mann, appointed Duggan Leader of the Opposition on the basis that the ALP with twenty-four members (against twenty-five for the Queensland Labor Party) had the largest number of seats after the Government. The Country Party had sixteen members and the Liberals eight.

Nicklin challenged this ruling and in the ensuing debate Gair supported the proposition that Nicklin should be named Leader of the Opposition, on the grounds that the Country and Liberal parties were effectively one in Parliament. With QLP support, this motion was adopted by fifty votes to twenty-three. The two independents supported the motion and the ALP Speaker could not vote.

Gair next moved the motion to make way for an Appropriation Bill (Supply) and Duggan rose to oppose it, thus starting two days of perhaps the bitterest and angriest debate the jacaranda-shaded sandstone building beside the Brisbane River had ever known.

Duggan vehemently denied the suggestion that personal ambition to be Leader of the Party through Gair's fate had motivated his actions. Hostile interjections from the QLP and Opposition benches flew throughout his speech.

Gair asked why Duggan had not resigned if he thought Gair a 'little dictator'. Why had Duggan not got out of Cabinet if he objected so strongly to the Motor Spirits Distribution Bill? Gair asked. He said the Parliamentary Labor Party had been unanimous that the time was not opportune for three weeks annual leave but when 'Big boss Joe and others started to wield their whips we saw which way they went.'

Walsh spoke for nearly two hours in the Committee of Supply, at one stage the speech turning into a fierce argument with Duggan. Duggan, heatedly, retorted that he had been prepared to go to any length to preserve the unity of the Party. He said the affiliated unions did all they could to extricate Gair from a position brought on by himself. Government members, he said, had indulged in a campaign of character assassination.

For two days the QLP and ALP shouted, sneered, abused and impugned each other across the Chamber, with the Opposition remaining largely on the sidelines, dignified, shocked—and probably delighted. National issues such as Hobart, Evatt and communism were traversed, as were local issues like Foley, Bukowski, union ballots and even the transfer of police. Oil companies and their money were frequently mentioned. Walsh accused Bukowski of rigging ballots and of having been a member of the Communist Party in Mackay in 1942 (Bukowski heatedly denied this to the press). 'Rat', 'scab', 'traitor', 'gullible fools' and all the other verbal weapons of Labor splits were hurled back and forward across the Assembly.

On 12 June the motion to grant supply was defeated by forty-five votes to twenty-five. The ALP and the two Opposition parties voted together and the Gair Government had fallen.

Gair announced that in view of the adverse vote, he proposed calling on the Administrator to inform him that the House had refused Supply.

This was followed, on Liberal initiative, by a successful motion disallowing Proclamation of the Motor Spirits Distribution Act 1957, which was to have come into force on 1 August. The Liberal Leader, T. Hiley, said a Government under sentence of death should not use its administrative powers in extension. Duggan supported the motion, saying there were provisions in the Act that 'all decent, self-respecting people should repudiate'.

On 13 June, the Administrator issued a proclamation dissolving the Assembly. Gair announced on 25 June that elections would be held on 3 August.

The Queensland split had less sectarian bitterness than that in Victoria. There were many Catholics on both sides (including Gair, Bukowski and Duggan) and several Protestants in the QLP. In most dioceses, the Church remained neutral and The Movement, small in Queensland anyway, was hardly an issue. Nevertheless, the sectarian flavour of the whole National split had already affected Queensland and there were certainly elements of it present.

The campaign was predictably bitter and characterised by smearing between the two Labor parties. Duggan promised in his policy speech the immediate introduction of three weeks annual leave. The Liberal and Country Party leaders delivered a joint policy speech, promising good things in general but avoiding extravagant specific promises. Among other things, they promised compulsory court-controlled secret ballots in unions. Gair promised a continuation of his Government's developmental programme as well as the compulsory secret ballots and three weeks leave 'when the finances and general economy of the state are sufficiently buoyant to stand the strain'.

Evatt, Calwell, Ward and Cain from Victoria were among the Southern leaders who campaigned for the ALP and there were press reports that Evatt was less than welcome. Bukowski told the press the Queensland Central Executive had not asked Evatt to take part in the campaign, but the Trades Hall unions gave him an enthusiastic welcome. As it happened, Evatt suffered acute influenza and spent most of his time in Queensland confined to his Bundaberg hotel room.

Many seem to have felt deep down during the first half of 1957 that Labor could not really be defeated in Queensland. It had been there too long; the seats were too favourably distributed; the Liberals and the Country Party were too weak. All that had to happen was for the truculent Gair to go and be replaced by the more co-operative Duggan. On 3 August, this feeling was finally shown—though by now there was not much doubt that it would be—to have been quite misplaced.

The Country Party won eight seats to gain a total of twenty-four in the new Assembly and the Liberals added ten for a total of eighteen. The ALP obtained twenty seats and the QLP eleven, both Labor parties together thus being outnumbered by the combined opposition parties.

Duggan and Dittmer both lost their seats to Liberals. Although the QLP lost fourteen seats, seven of its ten Cabinet members, including Gair, were returned. Two months later Duggan stood again, in a by-election for the Division of Gregory; but the QLP split the once comfortable Labor vote sufficiently for the Country Party candidate to win.

Labor had governed in Queensland continuously for twenty-five years and, with the exception of the 1929-32 period, since 1915—since before most of the principal participants in the 1957 split could remember.

When the new Parliament met on 27 August, the first non-Labor Government for a quarter of a century sat on the Treasury benches. Nicklin was Premier and the Liberal Leader, Ken J. Morris, Deputy Premier in a coalition Cabinet. L. A. Wood, the Member for North Toowoomba, was Leader of the Opposition.[2] Gair led the shrunken QLP, with its eight former ministers, on the cross-benches.

A state-wide QLP apparatus had grown up, through intensive organisation by some very experienced politicians, before the election. Several of the more right-wing unions, including the Ironworkers', Clerks' and State Service unions, disaffiliated from the ALP and, while they did not formally affiliate, were regarded as QLP in 'complexion'. The inevitable ALP heresy hunt into QLP sympathy in its ranks followed during the spring, with the inevitable addition to the existing hatreds.

Thus, in three years, the once seemingly unbeatable Queensland branch of the ALP was totally riven by the last major act of the Australian Labor drama of the mid 1950's.

[2] Wood died on 29 March 1958 and Duggan succeeded him in both his seat and his office.

Despite the defeat of Labor at the 1955 Federal election, Evatt was re-elected Leader by a big margin when the new Caucus met on Monday, 13 February 1956 to elect its new office bearers. His only opponent was A. D. Fraser, and Evatt beat him by fifty-eight votes to twenty.

Fraser was reported as telling Caucus that he opposed Evatt as a protest against Evatt not giving his loyalty to the Caucus by not even telling the Caucus Executive beforehand of many of his actions. Although often discussed in the press as a potential Labor Leader in the years before, Fraser did not command sufficient popularity in a Parliamentary Party where many considered they also had the qualities to lead and where such attitudes reinforced a highly conservative view about changing leaders. Calwell, who saw himself as the legitimate successor to Evatt, was able to swing to Evatt votes that might otherwise have gone against him and Kennelly also was backing the Evatt-Calwell leadership team as a temporary stabilising force. Another important reason for Evatt's big vote was that state elections were due shortly in New South Wales, Queensland, Western Australia and South Australia. Labor governments were at stake in three of these and there was a fear of Evatt acting calamitously if he was defeated at that stage.

The same forces brought Calwell forty-two votes for the Deputy Leadership, against twenty for Ward and fourteen for Haylen, the last two splitting the more left wing section of the vote. It seemed that Ward had longer to wait. McKenna was not opposed as Leader in the Senate but Kennelly, commanding a wide anti-Grouper vote, defeated Armstrong for Deputy. He got forty-four votes against thirty-four for Armstrong, with Ashley—another defeat for the Ward left—and Toohey both being eliminated in earlier ballots.

Evatt flew to Sydney after the election to speak at the opening of the New South Wales election campaign and the balloting for Caucus Executive was not held until next day. Positions went solidly towards the uncontroversial. Armstrong and several Ward nominees were defeated, while Fraser was elected only ninth out of ten positions.

The Parliament that opened that week was widely looked on as one of the least talented ever, an anti-climax after the soaring, embittered debates of 1955. Many of Labor's most capable debaters were gone. Keon and Bourke on one side, Nelson Lemmon and Tom Burke on the other, had regularly been prominent in debates in previous years. The Grouper faction still in Caucus was temporarily discredited and did not work seriously. The new Liberal backbenchers who replaced the defeated Labor men were rarely as interesting or effective speakers, often men who would never have been elected but for Labor splitting.

Talent apart, the Caucus was dispirited and ill-led for most of the Parliament. After his feverish energy of 1955, Evatt had slackened and declined noticeably by the middle of 1956. He often seemed muddled in his behaviour and even more eccentric than usual. Breaking with previous tradition, he typically turned his back on the ministerial centre table in important debates and spoke direct to the Labor benches; cynics said this was because he was frightened of being stabbed in the back if he turned it.

Labor turned more than ever to slogans and rhetoric. The Party's understanding of the new industrial Australia opening before it had been open to question in the early 1950's. Now Labor was living in a social fairyland. All inflation was caused by high profits. 'Monopolies', particularly 'foreign' ones, were strangling the country. Unemployment was ever around the corner. 'Asians' would hate Australia forever, as white men and imperialists, if Australian troops were stationed in Malaya—despite significant demands from Malaya for them. Almost all Asian régimes not giving lip service to 'socialism' were dismissed indiscriminately as 'reactionary and oppressive' and not worth assistance, while praise was lavished on those claiming to be 'socialist', though the real picture was rarely as simple as that.

When the Suez affair broke out in October 1956, and Labor had a good case against Menzies' personal intervention, it often spoiled it with rubbish about 'oil monopolies' being responsible for everything. In his endless attacks on the Suez adventure, Evatt insisted on linking Britain and France with the Russians in Hungary, as equally reprehensible, and could not conceal what seemed to be burning jealousy at the prominence of Menzies.

It may have been apocryphal, but at the time of Melbourne Olympics there was a story among pressmen that Evatt was 'phoning through statements to newspapers from the Melbourne Cricket Ground. Even if this story was not true, it illustrated the energy with which he still persisted in making his frequent press statements, often roughed out in his own hand for distribution. He had no Press Secretary in his depleted staff.

The upsurge of the left in the wake of the split led to attempts to give Labor a more sophisticated, left wing ideology, but the energy only lasted a year or two. Burton, Evatt's old secretary and protégé, was the chief ideologist and issued two interesting pamphlets in 1956 and 1957 in which he tried to map out new ways: *Labor in Transition* and *The Light Glows Brighter*. The second of these, and much the worse, carried forewords by Chamberlain and Evatt. Burton often revealed an over-confident amateurishness in his writing and tended to think dogmatically in quasi-Marxist left wing clichés; but compared to the more typical Labor outpourings of the period the pamphlets had merit. In *Labor in Transition* he analysed with some perspicacity the changed position of Labor in an affluent, increasingly middle class society.

The Victorian Conference in the first weekend of June 1956 showed the left firmly in control where it was important. It, as Victorian conferences for a decade to come, was characterised by intense bitterness and tirades against the Groupers, the Anti-Communist ALP and the DLP. Much of this was promoted by the left to prevent reconciliation—which would destroy its power—but it was the moderate, Percy Clarey, who had often worked with the Groupers, who moved the motion in 1956 reinforcing an Executive decision after the 1955 election declaring the 94 expelled in the split out for life. The names read as the 'complete roll of infamy', he said. They had committed the unforgivable sin of wrecking a Labor Government.

The standard of competence in administration in Victoria had fallen sharply under the new rulers. It suffered a new setback in August 1957, when Cain died; then his successor, E. Shepherd, died a couple of years later. Kennelly soon broke with the new Executive, which came increasingly under the complete domination of the Stout-left union alliance. The successes of Communist-ALP unity tickets in the Railways, Tramways, Amalgamated Engineering and Waterside Workers' unions had given the Communists and far left sections working with them a magnificent foothold in the weakened and confused Victorian Branch.

With the defeat of Gair, the left unions were also well in control in Queensland. By late 1957, the AWU leaders were again bickering savagely with the ALP rulers in both New South Wales and Queensland. By December 1958, Bukowski had accused the Queensland Central Executive of being 'riddled with sectarianism, communist influence and inefficiency', and by 1 April 1959 he had been excluded from the ALP on a technicality. He died soon after. In New South Wales, however, the more moderate C. T. Oliver, the State AWU Secretary, became more prominent in the union's political role and within a year or two was working harmoniously with Colbourne and other Groupers against the expansionist left wing the split had thrown up.

South Australia and Tasmania were little changed by the split, but in Western Australia the parliamentary wing was weakened by both the 1955 Federal defeats and the defeat of the State Labor Government in 1959. As in other states, the socio-economic base of the AWU was also declining. At the same time, Chamberlain's national strength increased his power at home and he became an even stronger figure in the Western Australian Branch.

While hardly left wing in the sense of the new forces thrown up in Victoria and Queensland, Chamberlain was still sufficiently against the moderate, political tradition to work well with the new left and with the more old-fashioned left of South Australia. This base gave him tremendous personal dominance over the ALP in the post-split years. With Evatt dependent on him, he held perhaps unprecedented power as Federal President from 1955 to 1961.

The new complexion of the ALP was apparent at the 1957 Federal Conference, held in Brisbane in the second week of March. In every way it was Chamberlain's conference.

Chamberlain had begun to develop an ideology in writing in the preceding years and it reached its flowering in his Presidential address in Brisbane on 11 March 1957. This and his other writings, as collected in *A Selection of Talks and Articles on Australian Labor Party Principles*,[1] reveal a curiously authoritarian, negative and banal viewpoint. Chamberlain sees Labor surrounded by enemies, and many within, all determined to take away its principles and purity. Yet the nature of these principles and of the ideological threat to Labor is never made clear.

The following extracts from the 1957 Presidential speech are typical:

. . . I do not think there is any question that Hobart, in the pages of Labor history, will stand out like a beacon. A beacon that showed the path that must continue to be trodden by those who believe in the socialistic objective of Labor, and are convinced that the objective not only can be reached by constitutional means but must be reached if mankind is to attain its full stature.

We are beset on many sides by our enemies.

Not only do we continue to face the traditional enemy of conservatism, supported by a powerful daily press, we face too, the fanatical hostility of those who were defeated at Hobart; defeated insofar that they failed in their objective to win control of this Party on that occasion, but they have not laid down their arms.

Do not underrate this enemy. I do not refer to them because of any desire to hit back as a consequence of the personal campaign that has been consistently directed towards myself over the past two years. I refer to them quite objectively. I refer to them because the evidence is clear that they have not given up the struggle to control the policies of this Party. They are at this moment planning to retrieve the position they lost at Hobart. . . .

Some of these people have deliberately stepped outside the constitutional requirements of the Party, knowing full well the inevitable disciplinary steps that would be taken against them. They have offended quite deliberately as part of the plan, the plan which requires leaders in the breakaway parties, who, with the aid of the press, are presented as men of great principle, who have been rejected by the Labor Party.

But not all of them have left the Labor Party.

It is part of the plan to have many of them remain within. . . .

We must not depart from the course that was charted at Hobart.

The target must not be Parliamentary seats at any price, but Parliamentary seats to be occupied by members of this Party who will go fearlessly into the electorates of this country and expound the cause of Democratic Socialism.

If we are asked as to what we mean by 'Democratic Socialism', we should reply as simply this:

It means:

☐ Security in all its forms in the home.

☐ The breadwinner working usefully in the community and being remunerated at a level which will enable him to discharge the responsibilities of family life.

☐ His wife divorced from the drudgery of housekeeping as she can well be by the application of modern science.

[1] F. E. Chamberlain, *A Selection of Talks and Articles on Australian Labor Party Principles*, Western Australian Branch of the ALP, Perth, 1964

☐ Their children well equipped in our schools to play their part in the years to come in the maintenance and development of a human society based upon the principles underlying the freedoms of the Atlantic Charter. . . .

A powerful element in the community, with the aid of an influential press, will continue to endeavour to use the question of Communism to the detriment of Labor. These people are not afraid of Communism becoming a dominating force in the Australian community. What they are afraid of is that Labor will become really serious about its socialist objective. . . .

And it should never be forgotten that the Australian people in the exercise of their democratic franchise provided the opportunity of establishing that effective Opposition [in the Commonwealth Parliament] by the removal from public life of those people who, prior to Hobart, had by their organised obstructions set out to destroy everything that was worthwhile in the platform of this Party. . . .

Neither then, nor apparently since, did Chamberlain ever reveal precisely what he meant by 'Democratic Socialism' and the other abstractions he continually used. But the only reasonable deduction from careful reading of his speeches and writings is that he was supporting much the same sort of reformism as had always been the Labor tradition and was unlikely to be seriously contested, least of all from the right.

Chamberlain's speech introduced a theme of 'socialism' for the 1957 Conference and it was widely hailed in the press as a 'turning to the left'. But it was largely a pseudo left, of rhetoric and words, words and more words.

In fact, there were meaty left wing resolutions on the agenda from Victoria and Queensland, indicating the new pressures in the Party. Their fate was to be passed over and drowned in a sea of words and slogans.

Motions from Victoria had sought the achievement of 'socialisation by industrial action', with nationalised industries controlled by boards of workers and community representatives. The nationalised industries should elect a supreme economic council. Parliamentarians were to be required to be the propagandists for this abolition of capitalism. Queensland had asked for 'Prevention of the growth of monopolies' which the Queensland Central Executive said had developed to a dangerous stage, particularly with chain stores, the timber industry, the film industry and shipping.

In the event, resolutions adopted by the week-long Conference were more on the lines of writing the words 'democratic socialisation' into the platform, instructing a future Labor Government to end court-controlled ballots, changing the old policy of aid to 'education in all its forms' to aid direct to students (a Chamberlain favourite), attacking SEATO as 'fast becoming the instrument of bolstering reactionary régimes', renewing the policies on troops in Malaya and on recognition of China and also on banning unity tickets in union elections.

Evatt backed several dubious causes about this time. One was outright hostility to the first post-war Trade Treaty with Japan: on the grounds of a threat to Australian manufacturing. Another was support for a campaign for the proportion of British migrants to be raised from the desired 50 (it was falling below it in some years in the mid-fifties to 60 per cent. Much of this campaign was scarcely disguised racism, referring to the lack of skills of Mediterranean migrants, the right-tainted politics of many Eastern Europeans and an anti-Labor voting bias (and, one also suspects, though it was not often said openly, Catholicism). There was a slight excuse for this policy on economic grounds in the 1956 recession, when many un-skilled migrants were unemployed and a case could be made that the influx of unskilled workers difficult of assimilation had got out of hand. The whole campaign, however, was tinged with anti-Catholic, anti-foreign bigotry.

Evatt attacked the increasing inflow of non-British migrants in his ad-dress to the Brisbane Conference on 12 March and the Federal Executive also referred to it. It said the New Australian vote at the next election would be predominantly anti-Labor and also attacked many New Australian organisations as ultra-rightist. The result was a flurry of migrant and Liberal attacks on Labor in the press.

The split finally blew itself out inside the ALP by the second half of 1957, when it spread in a minor way to Western Australia and South Australia. In August, the veteran Catholic MPs Cyril Chambers, from South Australia, and Victor Johnson, from Western Australia, had publicly attacked Evatt's leadership and his 'sectarian campaign'. The result was a vote of confi-dence in Evatt by the Federal Executive and the subsequent suspension of both Chambers and Johnson by their State Branches. Both affairs aggra-vated a steady dribble into the Anti-Communist ALP, now the DLP. This had been going on for the past two years, partly a result of Grouper pro-vocation and partly of heresy hunting by the State Executives, particularly in Western Australia, where there had been several expulsions of Group supporters.

The breakaway parties merged into a National DLP in a series of steps during 1957.

They held a Conference in Sydney on 17 March, deciding in principle to form an Australian Democratic Labor Party. Delegates were present from all states except Queensland, where the QLP stayed apart, while co-operating closely, until 1962 when its State Parliamentary strength had practically disappeared. Among policies agreed on were support for SEATO, opposition to the recognition of Communist China, support for arbitration and court-controlled ballots and for the broad principle of economic decentralisation.

The Victorian Conference of the ALP (Anti-Communist) decided to affiliate at its annual Conference on 15 June, but with the qualification that it would retain in official documents its claim to be the true Labor Party in Victoria.

The first full conference of the nationally organised DLP was then held at the Hotel Kingston, Canberra, on 25 August. Joshua was elected the first Federal President, Manning and F. Moran, of South Australia, the Vice-Presidents and Kane, Federal Secretary.

The Party had spread rapidly in New South Wales in the preceding twelve months, assisted by frequent expulsions and suspensions from ALP branches. It called a number of public meetings to form other branches.

Following the August Conference, a part-time paid official was appointed in South Australia and a small membership stabilised, with the skeleton Anti-Communist ALP of late 1955 added to by a variety of newcomers. By late 1957, Western Australia, with a full-time secretary appointed, looked a major success story. By 1958 a phenomenal membership of 25,000 in Chamberlain's home state was claimed, but this receded to a much smaller number in a short time.

Victoria remained the great bastion of the DLP. The membership reached 12,000 by the late 1950's through intensive organisation, principally through the Catholic community. Extensive—and often also intensive—sympathy for the DLP in Catholic schools and youth organisations provided a base of young recruits, who were brought in in large numbers. The state-wide apparatus and enthusiasm of The Movement, with Santamaria's backing behind it, was invaluable. It was not surprising that DLP policies were soon, in important respects, resembling those of The Movement. Many of its leaders were hard-headed politicians of traditional Labor outlook and little inclination for ideology, but there was a compelling need for the Party to be both distinctive and have an appeal for the more zealous ideologues of the Catholic community if it was to survive, let alone prosper. The great fear of the early years was that, like other breakaways, it would fizzle out after a year or two: the fate ALP men were prone to forecast for it.

The Movement itself also changed its name and organisation in this period.

As early as 1954, division had been apparent between the dioceses of Melbourne and Sydney in attitudes towards The Movement. This continued until April 1956, though temporary unity had been obtained with the issue of the Pastoral on communism in April 1955. According to Duffy by 1958 about eight of the thirty-three bishops of Australia were supporting the 'Sydney line'—that The Movement should have a Federal basis, with the Bishop or Archbishop in each diocese having final control over it. Duffy listed, as well as Cardinal Gilroy and Bishop Carroll, Bishops Toohey (Maitland), McCabe (Wollongong) and Farrelly (Lismore) as supporters of the 'Sydney line'. About another fourteen, Duffy said, supported the stand of Archbishop Mannix: That laymen in an organisation such as The Movement could make their own decisions on industrial and political questions, with bishops ruling only on questions of faith and morals. The remaining eleven bishops were at this stage apparently uncommitted, Duffy said.[2]

The Episcopal Committee of the Catholic Social Studies Movement (i.e.,

[2] Paul Duffy, 'Catholic Judgments on the ALP Dispute', unpublished thesis, University of Melbourne Library, 1968

The Movement) met on 13 April 1956, and agreed that each bishop could reserve the right to veto decisions made by the lay bodies of The Movement.

Santamaria and his supporters viewed this decision as tantamount to breaking up The Movement, under Sydney pressure. The split in New South Wales Labor was then impending and they wanted the unfettered right to use The Movement to back the Grouper Party and help force such a degree of split that unity on Grouper terms would be sought. The 'Sydney line', on the other hand, was deeply committed, politically, to retaining Catholic influence in the broad ALP and preventing the growth of a rival Marxist Labor Party.

While this was the political division, backed by influential politicians in both Victoria and New South Wales, there were several other elements involved. Bishop Carroll appears to have deeply mistrusted Santamaria as using and perhaps exaggerating the communist issue to build up his own power; Santamaria was similarly hostile to Bishop Carroll. There was also traditional rivalry between the dioceses of Melbourne and Sydney, reputedly aggravated by the clashing personalities of Cardinal Gilroy and Archbishop Mannix over the years. A further element was that the Sydney diocese had a tradition of clerical authoritarianism and in the more liberal years of the 1960's remained one of the most conservative dioceses on earth on the issue of episcopal power. Archbishop Mannix, on the other hand, had always been sympathetic to lay initiative.

Supporters of the Sydney approach claimed that The Movement had been involving the authority and prestige of the episcopal office—even if indirectly—in questions outside the competence of the bishops. Firmer episcopal control would prevent this and would prevent one group of laymen using Church positions against others.

On 16 July Santamaria and his supporters resigned their positions in the Catholic Social Studies Movement and formed a new, more avowedly lay organisation, the Catholic Social Movement. In the old Movement, the degree of association with the official Catholic Action organisation and of control by the hierarchy had never been clearly established. In the new Catholic Social Movement the position was to be clear: there was no direct connection.

The letter of resignation, quoted by Duffy, said the Sydney Region could not be exonerated from responsibility for the collapse of the organised resistance to Communism.

The new organisation was given permission to establish in the following dioceses: Melbourne, Bendigo, Ballarat, Sale, Wagga, Armidale, Hobart, Brisbane, Toowoomba, Townsville, Rockhampton, Geraldton and New Norcia. The bishops of many of these dioceses were keen supporters of the National Catholic Rural Movement, and there was much personal admiration for Santamaria in the atmosphere of muscular Christianity of these provincial dioceses. In Hobart, however, Archbishop Young, though politically inclined to DLP ideas, was a Church liberal receptive to many trends. Archbishop Duhig, in Brisbane, had maintained for many years a policy of neutrality towards The Movement.

The resignations led to much bitterness and recrimination in the Church and the status of the new movement was still not clear. In October, a meeting of fifteen bishops, representing twelve of the twenty-five Australian dioceses, chose a delegation of three bishops to go to Rome and seek a judgment on the dispute. Eighteen other bishops, from thirteen dioceses, had refused to take part in the meeting.

In Rome, a commission of cardinals examined the dispute and gave their judgment in November 1957. They found that The Movement, as originally constituted, had juridical dependence on the body of the bishops. Because of this dependence, it could no longer engage in its former political and industrial activities. It was to assume a new profile, as a body for the formation of social and moral conscience for Catholics, with special attention to fighting communism. It was to be under the control of each bishop in the diocese and to leave organised action to unions and political parties. Action in these was to be as individuals, not involving the name or authority of the Church.

The judgment was something of a pyrrhic victory for both sides. The Sydney authorities (had they wished, which is doubtful) could no longer use their section of The Movement for organised political activity, while Santamaria's section was stripped of all claims to any official connection with the Church.

In December 1957 Santamaria's section underwent another change of name and status, becoming the National Civic Council. In this completely lay form it had the perfect right to organise its own support in Sydney, Adelaide, Perth and other dioceses where it was clerically unwelcome. In practice, such organisation was virtually impossible because of lack of an adequate base and episcopal hostility. Shortly after, the Sydney Movement was reorganised as the Paulian Society, the educative body suggested by Rome, and withdrew from all organised political and union work. And thus the historic, maligned and mysterious Movement passed into history.

What was its purpose and real nature? Even among those who were in it, the answers would range from black to white, but the *Bombay Examiner* incident, at the height of the controversy, threw a strange ray of light.

About the end of 1956, roneoed copies of articles by Santamaria in the *Examiner*, the official organ of the diocese of Bombay, of 18 and 25 June 1955, were circulated widely in the Labor Movement and Catholic Church. They appear to have originated from a talk by Santamaria to the National Convention of The Movement in 1952. Santamaria gave them, in modified form, in 1954 to Cardinal Gracias of Bombay, who had been visiting Australia. In the controversy which followed their circulation in Australia, Santamaria described them as a 'speculative thesis'. Many others, however, regarded them as evidence of Santamaria's designs for The Movement at its high noon.

Santamaria discussed the desirability of an organised Catholic political force to promote Catholic views in politics. He said that neither 'pressure group' activity nor Catholics acting as individuals were the best way of going about this. He suggested as the most desirable 'Action by Way of Permeation': a word that sounded sinister at the time, but in fact was

borrowed from the vocabulary and practice of the Edwardian Fabians in
Britain.

Santamaria said the permeation should be by way of an organisation
'united with the Hierarchy', who could check abuses. The three steps in
permeation were:

(a) The conscious training of individuals to participate in political and
industrial life.
(b) The development and maintenance of machinery to keep together in
association individuals possessing the same ideals so that their views will
make an effective impact and be of consequence.
(c) Continuous guidance by an authorised body entrusted with this work
by a competent authority to ensure that these individuals are guided in all
their actions by the moral law and the principles of Christianity.

He suggested that such an organisation should seek to displace:

(a) Individuals involved in graft or similar forms of dishonesty.
(b) Indivduals whose only purpose in acting in public life is their own
aggrandisement.
(c) Individuals who are ready to urge false and dangerous policies as a
means of keeping themselves or their party in office, or to preserve their
own supremacy within their party.
(d) Individuals who refuse to fight organised atheism or who, in fact,
objectively side with it or its supporters.
(e) Individuals who oppose the broad social policies laid down, for
instance in the Social Encyclicals.

While the ALP was indulging in its orgy of rhetorical pseudo-leftism and
highlighting its intention of 'socialisation', and the DLP was drifting into
Catholic Distributism, Australian society under the Liberals had never been
more prosperous.

There was a brief recession in the middle six months of 1956, after
Menzies' post-election 'little horror' tax-raising budget of February. This
was close to Labor's heart and eagerly seized upon, and for a time an
election had seemed a possibility, with the DLP opposing the Government's
Banking Bill in the Senate. Neither major party could afford an election
that winter, however, if only because it might mean more DLP senators.
By late spring, with the Melbourne Olympic Games near, the economy
had recovered. By 1957 Australia had entered a period of unprecedented
economic progress. Overseas capital poured into the country, the wages of
most people rose easily and well ahead of inflation. Takeovers and mergers
introduced the element of bigness required in a modern economy, in spite
of pious horror from the left.

The post-war flood of migrants was giving a new and by now welcomed
diversity to Australian society. The cities were sprawling out faster than
they ever had before. Primary production went steadily up, with mechanisation, while numbers on the land continued to decline. Most of the post-
war troubles of South-East Asia appeared to have been solved and with

independence for a divided Vietnam by 1956 and for Malaya by 1957 imperialism virtually disappeared from the region.

The Liberal and Country Party Government of Australia could have been subject to many criticisms in this period. Education, defence, social services and wages for those on awards without the benefit of over-award margins were lagging far behind the burgeoning general prosperity. In Sydney and Melbourne particularly, traffic and distance were becoming graver problems than ever. A Government less dogmatically confident of the market system would probably have tried to increase the Australian, and possibly publicly owned, equity in many of the new enterprises. It might have concerned itself more with the human problems of a society comprised increasingly of large self-generating corporations.

Even in America and Europe, these problems were then little perceived compared with a decade later. In Australia, while the Liberals identified themselves with progress, Labor identified itself with gloom and controls. It is difficult to imagine a supposedly pragmatic party—and this applied as much to the DLP—being more hopelessly out of touch with the real society. The response of both parties on domestic affairs, though from different standpoints, became destructive populism: mindless attacks on monopolies, profits and urbanisation.

The DLP, following The Movement line and also filling a vacuum, inevitably became the 'hawk' party of the cold war, while Labor became the Party of isolationism. It was, with qualifications, against migration on the scale that had been achieved; against significant trade with Japan; against any military involvement in Asia.

Labor thus came to the election year of 1958 still in an appalling position. Evatt, mistrusted and lacking credibility as a Prime Minister, was still its Leader. The DLP was functioning as a well organised Party in five states and it had an immensely powerful ally in Queensland. It now left little doubt that its second preferences would go to the Liberals. Migrant voters were coming on to the rolls in huge numbers, while Labor had grievously insulted them and was more open than ever to the 'communist-influenced' taunt that would deter many Eastern European workers. Its old Australian power base had been eroding throughout the decade, as people moved away from the older suburbs and climbed the social ladder of the affluent society. Its style of over-statement, 'calamity howling' and militant rhetoric produced an 'image' more than ever out of tune with the new Australia.

The first test of the new political climate came in May, with the Victorian elections. The DLP maintained the old anti-Communist Labor vote at about 14 per cent but its only remaining representative in the Legislative Assembly, Scully, was defeated; his vote was about 60 per cent that of the ALP candidate in Richmond, W. J. Towers. The ALP got about 37 per cent of the vote, approximately the same as the Liberals. The DLP preferences went straight to the Liberals, however, and the Bolte Government was returned easily. The result showed essentially no difference from that of the 'split' election three years before.

The Assembly result of 31 May was followed by a similar one for the Legislative Council elections on 21 June. With similar voting patterns, the DLP was eliminated from the Council and thus from the Parliament. Little, Bailey, Brennan and Sheehy were defeated, and Paul Jones had retired.

A by-election for the State Division of Kahibah (in Newcastle) the previous year had indicated a somewhat similar result likely in New South Wales. The DLP vote in Kahibah was about 14 per cent of the total. In New South Wales, however, the DLP had run into troubles of its own by 1958.

The climax of a number of internal troubles came on 3 January, when Manning announced to the press that he would resign the following day as State President of the DLP. 'I believe that I no longer represent the feeling of the majority of the Executive,' he said.

The split that Manning's resignation touched off was nearly as complicated as that which had produced the DLP little more than a year earlier. In New South Wales the DLP had attracted several different kinds of people. First were the Industrial Groupers, with union backgrounds, who had followed Kane; as most of The Movement had stayed in the ALP, they were not an especially Catholic group. Second were the Santamarian fringe and the more ardent Group supporters, mostly Catholics, from the ALP branches. Another group, of varying composition, had been produced by the protracted ALP power struggle. Yet a fourth group was made up predominantly of middle class people who were attracted to the DLP as a 'third party' which would avoid the socialism and trade union connections of the ALP, but also stand more for small business, public spending and avoidance of 'stop go' economics than the Liberals. There was a substantial demand for politics of this type in 1956 and 1957, when Australia was passing out of the second Government-imposed 'squeeze' and recession since the war and when takeovers and mergers were radically changing the business scene. This last group of DLP supporters included both Catholic and secular strands, with rather different motivations.

Early, Manning had become identified with the 'new National Party' approach and his personality had attracted many into the DLP. Kane and Rooney, on the other hand, were attracted to the Victorian and Queensland strategy of winning a big enough vote—of necessity fairly Catholic in composition—to keep Labor out of office and weak until it was forced to a 'deal' on DLP terms—mainly taking the DLP back in again, restarting the Industrial Groups and taking a more strongly pro-American, anti-Communist line in foreign affairs.

This was the background against which personal and, in a veiled, indirect way, religious antagonisms built up. In December 1957 Kane had organised a by-election for the state seat of Wagga (made vacant by the death of the Minister for Agriculture, E. Graham) on the basis of attracting Catholic support. Wagga was old Santamaria Catholic Rural Movement country, with a highly favourable Church atmosphere through Bishop Henschke. The DLP candidate got 12 per cent of the vote, a drop on the Kahibah by-election earlier in the year but still high by comparison with anything the DLP got in New South Wales subsequently.

Manning had been Western Traffic Manager for Butler Air Transport, a small apparently independent airline serving rural New South Wales, when he formed the DLP. The Managing Director of Butler Air Transport, C. Butler, and some other officials of the firm and a similar small provincial line, East-West Airlines, had joined the DLP. Both companies seemed the sort of small, independent, profit-sharing business that the DLP approved. They gave added strength to the Party.

Late in 1957 the national airline, Ansett-ANA, became involved in a takeover battle for Butler Air Transport, which had started moving into the Sydney-Melbourne trade to help finance new aircraft. Ansett-ANA claimed it was already financially interested in BAT, with the management's knowledge, and was justified in a full takeover. Manning resigned from BAT and joined Ansett-ANA as a Public Relations executive at the height of the acrimonious, publicised battle.

On 3 January, Kane told the press that a DLP officers' meeting had called on the Federal Government for 'sanctions' against Ansett-ANA to prevent the takeover of Butler Air Transport or East-West. Manning immediately announced his resignation as President. He said that, although invited, he had not been present at the officers' meeting 'because I don't mix political activities with business'. He said he would remain a Federal vice-president and a member of the Gordon branch.

On 5 January the newspapers reported fierce attacks by Kane and Manning on each other and also revealed that in the preceding fortnight four other key members had resigned. J. G. Aboud and D. Osborne had resigned from the Executive after the Wagga by-election. Butler and J. Bolton, of East-West Airlines, had resigned from the Party.

The *Sydney Morning Herald* reported on 6 January:

Asked to comment on a statement that there had never been any conflict with Mr Kane and himself, Mr Manning said: It is fantastic for Mr Kane to say that. There has been almost constant argument between us since last June. Mr Kane accused me of being a limelighter. He told members of the Executive I should be cut down to size. He tried to put somebody else in charge of the Party newspaper, *The Democrat*, which I was running.

Then came the Wagga by-election, when I was not consulted about the choice of candidate or the allocation of preferences. The DLP failed badly in Wagga. Yet at the following Executive meeting, votes of congratulation were passed on the running of the campaign. I told the Executive the Party had made a mistake in contesting the by-election on a sectarian issue.

Mr Kane's statement on Ansett-ANA inferred I had become involved in some anti-Labor activity and was obviously intended to force me to resign.

I made it clear when I got the job that I would be President in fact as well as in name or they would have to get someone else. Unfortunately the same element which destroyed the unity of the ALP—the diehard right-wing Industrial Groupers—is now dominating the DLP in New South Wales.

Kane replied to 'Mr Manning's latest spate of irresponsible allegations against me personally'. He said the Wagga candidate had been democratically chosen by the local branches. He said Manning was 'desperately trying to divert attention from the Butler-Ansett issue'. He said Manning had played a major role in having the DLP adopt its militant anti-monopoly policy, using the Butler organisation, by which he was then employed, as an example of an efficient, independent company that Australia could not afford to lose. 'Since he left Butler's and became an executive of Ansett, his personal interests have made it difficult for him to continue to support the anti-monopoly policies of the DLP. This is the real issue,' Kane said.

ALP spokesmen could not conceal their glee, heralding the break-up of the DLP. An obviously delighted Campbell (State ALP President) told the press Manning had proved himself to be 'one of the most unstable party leaders of all time'. Kane was 'the type of man no-one could work with for long without falling out with him'.

On 20 February Manning announced that he would not renew his membership. It was the day before the State Executive was due to meet and discipline him for the earlier statements; although he had beaten expulsion his membership was still cancelled. Three more resignations, of influential Manning supporters, followed on 27 February. These were of the Reverend Alan Laing, who was the Party's Federal Returning Officer, and two businessmen, Edward Dunn of Sydney and C. L. Morgan of Newcastle.

The three held a press conference at the Millions Club. Their statements had the general theme that the DLP had lost its early idealism, had become negative and that Kane was trying to run everything himself. They said there had been no reply to an earlier circular of complaints they had issued on these lines; among other things, it had said Kane was 'usurping the powers of the Executive'.

This split, over the crystallising issue of an airline takeover, destroyed the DLP as more than a minor splinter group in New South Wales. About the same time, many of those who had left the ALP but could not feel at home in the new organisation drifted away, often out of politics altogether. Manning and his supporters' resignations made it easier to dub the DLP a 'Santamaria Party' and its Protestant element dwindled. It developed into a predominantly middle class, Catholic, intensely anti-communist centre party, presided over by Kane and a tiny band of ex-ALP supporters. Despite its Catholic character, the Church frowned on it in all but two New South Wales dioceses, Wagga and Armidale, where the old Rural Movement sentiment provided a useful base. The Riverina, which had the additional advantage of much cultural orientation towards Victoria, provided a rural base to complement a thousand or so stalwarts in Sydney and a few more in Newcastle and the coal fields, where anti-Catholic sentiment was perhaps a little stronger than elsewhere.

The verbally militant ALP of 1957 was replaced by a studiedly moderate one in 1958, the election year. Evatt eschewed his abuse of 'clerical fascism' and praise for 'democratic socialism' of the previous year and became almost restrained in his attacks on the Government.

These centred around a peculiar economic situation that lasted for most of 1958. While most of the country had never been more prosperous, there were several areas of weakness. Unemployment stayed above the rather high level of 70,000 registered as seeking jobs and was most pronounced away from the metropolitan areas of Sydney, Melbourne and Adelaide. Farm incomes were not rising at the rate of the community as a whole. Company profits were also sluggish and Labor interpreted this as little business suffering at the hands of big. Social services were also declining behind general community levels.

The year 1958 was essentially a year of economic time-marking before the great boom of 1959-60. Labor became the Party of stimulus for the economy through improved social services and selective tax cuts. Whether this was wise in view of the regional nature of the unemployment and the boom that followed is open to question. But Labor—and Evatt—had a new style in 1958. It was at last seeking expert economic advice, though inevitably much of it was from a faction opposed to the Treasury economists and suspect to that degree. Evatt therefore sounded better informed and much more convincing on economic questions. In 1957 he had also acquired, for the first time since 1954, a full-time Press Officer in Cyril Wyndham, a young Englishman from Transport House who eventually became the first full-time Federal Secretary of the ALP. Evatt became less prone to rushing off ill-considered press statements. His public face became more attractive, though many who observed his behaviour in private found it strange and unpredictable.

With the DLP and QLP now national, the votes and second preferences of its potential supporters were of crucial importance to Labor. Evatt signalled a strategy for this situation in an interview on the Melbourne TV programme *Meet the Press* on 13 April. He said he would seriously consider stepping down from the Party Leadership if this would remove the main obstacle to the DLP giving Labor its preferences. He did not like the lie that the only reason he was remaining Leader was in the hope of becoming Prime Minister. Labor would be elected if the DLP behaved like a Labor Party and gave the ALP its second preferences.

Evatt opened Labor's campaign in the Assembly Hall, Sydney, on 15 October. The speech was praised in the Party and press as his best yet; as it happened, it was also his last policy speech. It was in line with his consistent theme of most of the year and he characterised it as a 'Family Policy designed to rehabilitate the Australian economy and restore the community's purchasing power'. He promised substantial increases in child endowment, doubling of the maternity allowance, free dental treatment for children under sixteen and marriage loans. Travelling expenses to work would be an allowable deduction from taxable income, sales tax on household necessities would be eliminated and the Commonwealth Trading Bank would introduce personal loans. There would be various measures to assist the farmer, including a subsidy on dairy exports.

Evatt said Labor was greatly aware of the need to avoid inflation, but it believed the economy needed a sharp stimulus. The money to finance the reforms would come from finance raised through revenue, but used by the

Menzies Government to finance works that should have been financed from loans.

For the first time, defence, foreign policy and New Guinea emerged as election issues. Evatt promised 'unwavering support to the principles of the UN Charter' and the 'recognition of all Governments which are proved to be in effective control, notwithstanding our opposition to their internal forms of government'. Australia should use any influence she had to secure the suspension of nuclear tests, the limitation of armaments and the holding of summit talks between the leaders of the great powers.

He opposed West New Guinea coming under the control of Indonesia and proposed Australian control of the whole island, preferably with UN support, if the Dutch withdrew. He suggested a three-way agreement between Australia, Holland and Indonesia over the future of West New Guinea. Labor would increase native representation in the Legislative Council of the Territory, he said.

Evatt said the more vigorous direction from a Labor Cabinet would lead to reform of the defence forces, which would save millions of pounds and at the same time give Australia more effective defence. He proposed the final winding up of National Service training.

He offered the unions Government support for equal pay for women, restoration of the automatic cost of living adjustments to the basic wage and relaxation of penal provisions in the arbitration system.

Trying to heal the 1957 breach with European immigrants, he said immigration would be considered in the light of the whole process of social and economic development. He said the New Australians were welcome to Australia and Labor would do its utmost to help them assimilate. 'They know that this assimilation must be based on their unreserved acceptance of our political democracy and our social and trade union standards, and on the adequate provision of employment, housing and essential services.'

Compared to the fantasies of 1954, the policy was a model of precision and of developed explanation of the links between its component parts. The *Sydney Morning Herald* editorial of 16 October described it as 'Dr Evatt's Formidable Challenge'.

Nevertheless, the policy was open to criticism on a number of grounds. Revenue had been used to finance works as a conscious, Treasury-evolved policy to manage public spending and thus control inflation. Evatt's proposal to end this system and greatly increase public spending, while more cogently and responsibly put, still begged the question of how much public spending Australia could afford without a renewal of serious inflation, reasonably under control by that time. Many of Evatt's other proposals also looked inflationary.

The defence proposals were, probably of necessity, vague. The foreign and New Guinea policies could be criticised as illustrating the naïve, moralising quality that often characterised Labor's (and perhaps, in a different way, the Liberal Government's) attitude to foreign policy. What if Indonesia did not agree (as was certainly proved a few years later) with Australia's desire to be big brother to the Pacific Islands? Who would foot the bill of developing the whole island? What was Labor's attitude to

Peking's adamant opposition to any 'two Chinas' policy as a condition of recognition? What would Labor do about SEATO? Such questions were hardly considered.

Cole launched the DLP campaign at an amazing rally of about 7,000 people at the new Olympic Pool in Melbourne on 20 October. The Party had gambled on hiring the huge amphitheatre and chartering supporter buses to bare its teeth, and this paid off handsomely.

The fervour of the speeches from the platform and of the reception they met from the huge crowd, often bitter to the point of frenzy, remained long in the memory of those who saw them. On 22 October, the *Sydney Morning Herald*'s political correspondent, Maxwell Newton (who was then also an unofficial economic advisor to Evatt), wrote incredulously of the emotional reception received by the 'dreaded incantation, Dr Evatt'. 'DLP Rally Gives Food for Thought', the article was headed.

Despite the bitterness evident against the ALP, the policy read by Cole was remarkably like that read by Evatt five days earlier. Cole also promised a range of moderate increases in social service payments, including marriage loans, and to abolish sales tax on essential household items. However, instead of the quarterly adjustments promised by Evatt, Cole proposed a wage policy based on the productivity index. And he promised to provide student endowments for children at private schools.

Differences emerged on foreign policy. Cole said Evatt and his 'political theorists had tried to drive a wedge forged in Moscow between Australia and the British' over Middle East policies. He said West New Guinea should be placed under UN Trusteeship. While the principles underlying the UN should be supported, he said, communist states were flouting the rule of law and the UN could make little effective contribution on a political level to the permanent establishment of world peace.

Cole said the DLP would promote decentralisation of activity over a wide field and 'halt the drift to bureaucratic socialism'.

In short, Cole promised ALP-style increased social services, modified Catholic Distributism and a militantly anti-communist, pro-Western foreign policy.

Menzies took the unusual course of not opening his campaign until 29 October, little more than three weeks before polling day and a fortnight later than his rival. Speaking in Canterbury Memorial Hall in Melbourne, he promised little, preferring to call for a vote of confidence in his nine-year record and emphasising the inflationary possibilities of the Evatt policy. 'As trustees, we can point to a great estate, in good repair, amazingly developed, sensibly managed, respected and trusted round the world,' he said.

Largely, the campaign developed, as far as the Menzies versus Evatt bout was concerned, into a fairly technical argument over safe against stimulatory economic policies. The battle for public good will between the 'images' of the two took place indirectly but inescapably in the background. The point might be made that the very (by comparison) reasonableness of the Labor proposals outlined the dilemma for an opposition, particularly a social democratic reformist opposition, in a modern, managed economy: how can you propose to manage the economy better than the experienced, non-aligned, economic technocrats advising the government—and on whom you would have to depend anyway?

To this extent it was a quiet, restrained campaign. But Evatt was, of course, fighting on two fronts and he was a bonny fighter.

Was it a masterstroke or another piece of Evatt madcap? He had made one bid for the DLP supporters or at least their second preferences with a social policy pleasing to Catholic sentiment. Now he made another, more sensational bid.

He was speaking in Preston Town Hall, Melbourne, on 21 October, the day after the DLP's formidable opening rally. Suddenly, in a break from his economic and social argument, he offered to resign from the Leadership after the election if the DLP would give Labor its second preferences. The loyal audience cheered and clapped and there were shouts of 'Good on you, Doc'.

First he appealed for the DLP preferences. He argued that there was much in common between the two policies, but that the DLP would never be able to implement its policy. He denied that either the ALP or he himself were pro-communist. And then he said:

Win or lose, I undertake to vacate the leadership of the Party after the election—and I will not seek re-election as Leader—if they [the DLP] give us their preferences and make a genuine effort to see that this preference policy is carried out.

Evatt seems to have consulted nobody on this remarkable offer, which would have meant the country was voting for an unknown Prime Minister and a Labor Party of quite uncertain character. But it did have its political point. It put the DLP leaders on the defensive; even if, as might be supposed, they rejected it, they would have the job ahead of convincing many previously loyal Labor supporters that they had good reasons for stopping the election of a Labor Government that would implement many of their own professed policies.

There were hurried telephone conversations among the DLP leaders next day and the press reported Cole's decision to reject it as a victory for the 'hard core' of the DLP determined to thrash the ALP until it agreed to a suitable merger. Reports said many leaders in Hobart and particularly Melbourne had been disposed to accept it, in the belief that other issues could be sorted out after the election.

Cole told a meeting in Hobart that night:

Dr Evatt's offer in itself does not touch on the vital issues between the two Labor forces, nor would his resignation affect them. These matters can only be determined by the ALP's governing body. Therefore I say to Dr Evatt that if his offer means that the ALP is prepared to abandon its decisions made at Hobart conference in 1955—effectively ban unity tickets, reintroduce political endorsements for the fight against Communism in the unions and change its foreign policy—then I can assure Dr Evatt that his offer will receive every consideration by the DLP.

Evatt's predictable response was not to argue on this ground, but to appeal over the heads of the DLP leaders for the support of the DLP rank and file. He did this in a speech in Perth on 23 October.

Later in the campaign, apparently reacting to divided opinion inside the DLP, Cole offered to open negotiations with Evatt on the question, but again insisted on the policy differences he had mentioned earlier. Again he was ignored.

It is easy to exaggerate even the small ideological differences between ALP and DLP raised by the campaign. There was a general disposition on both sides to believe the emphases each played on foreign policy and some sections, particularly the young, believed in them fervently. But among many of the leaders and the great body of middle level opinion on both sides, there was neither the interest nor the expertise to make foreign policy a great issue, as distinct from a politically convenient one. Much the same might be said to apply to union elections, while the instinct towards moderate reformism was too deeply ingrained among such people to be much disturbed by the flowery words used to describe it.

At its most fundamental, the struggle between the ALP and DLP in 1958 was a power struggle with religious undertones, except for one point: There was genuine concern among the DLP leaders at the trend to the left in the unions since 1955 and the tendency for a subtle form of 'united front' activity to build up, quietly encouraging a neutralist tendency in foreign affairs.

The second memorable sensation of the campaign came in the closing days. The opposition of the Catholic 'establishment' in Victoria to the ALP since 1955 was vehement and often expressed from the pulpit, the schoolroom, the youth leadership dais and the diocesan press. Rightly or wrongly, the ALP believed it to be the major factor behind the big DLP vote. There was mounting fear as the campaign neared its end, reinforced by rumours, that Archbishop Mannix would issue a statement in support of the DLP.

The situation in Sydney, Adelaide and many other dioceses was very different, but the bishops had not sought to publicise their differences and the secular (not to mention Catholic) press had been cooperative, in Victoria to the point of pusillanimity. The result was that in the 1958 campaign there was a split of tremendous potential public interest, and perhaps political importance, evident in the Church.

The Labor leaders, mainly Evatt, Calwell and McKenna, decided to gamble on themselves publicising these differences in a bid to rescue what they could of the Catholic vote. Between 19 and 21 October, advertisements began appearing in the newspapers, featuring views attributed to Cardinal Gilroy. 'Every DLP Voter Should Examine His Conscience on the Question of his No. 2 Vote,' they said. The basic text was a statement in the Cardinal's Lenten Pastoral of 1957 that 'All citizens are free in conscience to join or support any of the political parties represented in public life except the Communist Party'.

When a comment was sought, the Cardinal replied that he regretted such use of his name but 'I am interested in the soul. I do not wish to

become involved in political matters which are the concern of the individual. I wish well to the followers of all parties except the Communist
Party. I wish well to the Liberals, Country Party, DLP and ALP—everyone
except the communists.'

The result was a statement from Mannix on the afternoon of 20
November:

Amid the turmoil of the election, one thing seems clear. Every communist
and every communist sympathiser in Australia wants a victory for the
Evatt Party. This is alarming. It should be a significant warning for every
Catholic and for every decent Australian.

Hitherto, I have not deemed it necessary to sound a note of warning.
The communists have been falsely suggesting that Cardinal Gilroy stands
for comparatively neutral benevolence. Of course, the Cardinal ignored
their malevolent misuse of his name. But now that the Evatt Party, forgetting all about sectarianism, is trying to shelter under his name in nation-
wide advertisements and in pamphlets distributed outside Catholic churches
to congregations on Sundays, I deem it timely to recall the official attitude
of the Cardinal and all the Catholic Bishops of Australia. . . . [Mannix
went on to refer in some detail to the 1955 bishops' Pastoral.]

Mannix's statement brought a spate of statements from other bishops
and clergymen. Archbishop Duhig was characteristically neutral, though a
keen reading could indicate a slight bias against the ALP. In Adelaide,
Archbishop Beovich stated a position similar to that of the Cardinal, but
more strongly stated. The Sydney Catholic spokesman, Dr Leslie Rumble,
told the press that Dr Mannix's statement expressed only a personal view.

There were also statements from several well known Protestant, particularly Methodist, churchmen who had earned a reputation over the last few
years for a militant, conspiratorial view of what Rome and the ALP split
were all about. The DLP and the political role of some bishops was 'a
menace no less, and indeed more powerful than communism', said the
Reverend Dr George Wheen of Canberra.

The economic debate, the offers to resign, the clerical intervention—all had
the effect of a mountain labouring to produce a mouse. The majority of
political pundits, who had forecast a significant swing to Labor, were
proved wrong. The Australian public as a whole, more prosperous and
apathetic than ever before, had hardly budged in their allegiances since
1955.

The Liberals won, on aggregate, two seats, and Labor lost two. The DLP
won no new places in the Senate, though Cole was re-elected and Byrne,
styled the QLP Federal Leader, was defeated. McManus still had three
years of his six-year term to run. The Liberals and the Country Party
picked up two new positions in the Senate from Victoria, thus regaining
control of the Upper House.

In New South Wales, where the size of the DLP vote created most interest, the DLP attracted a mere 5·59 per cent of the vote for the House of
Representatives and 4·86 per cent of the Senate vote. Its vote in Victoria,
at the other extreme, held fairly well, at 14·75 per cent for the House and

12·54 per cent for the Senate. Observers, however, noted a tendency for it to go down in old Labor districts and rise in the new sprawls of suburbia. The DLP vote ranged between these extremes in other states, except for 16·98 per cent in the Senate election in Tasmania, where Cole, once a well known North Coast footballer, was reputed to have a personal following as well as being placed first on the ballot paper (it compared with 7·88 per cent in the House election). The following two tables show how Australia voted:

House of Representatives Election:

	No. Votes	% Total Valid Votes						
State	Liberal		Country Party		ALP		DLP-QLP	
New South Wales	685,614	(35·89)	183,187	(9·59)	900,483	(47·14)	106,805	(5·59)
Victoria	531,404	(37·81)	103,735	(7·38)	555,470	(39·52)	207,247	(14·75)
Queensland	224,449	(31·07)	140,093	(19·39)	270,676	(37·47)	80,035	(11·08)
South Australia	205,810	(44·91)	–		217,727	(47·52)	27,703	(6·04)
Western Australia	138,467	(41·64)	38,305	(11·52)	116,302	(34·98)	34,944	(10·51)
Tasmania	73,436	(44·53)	–		77,232	(46·83)	12,989	(7·88)
Australia	1,859,180	(37·23)	465,320	(9·32)	2,137,890	(42·81)	469,723	(9·41)

	Australian National		Communist		Independents		Informal*	
New South Wales	–		14,170	(0·74)	19,822	(1·04)	55,041	(2·80)
Victoria	–		3,021	(0·21)	4,512	(0·32)	35,114	(2·44)
Queensland	3,577	(0·49)	3,581	(0·49)	–		22,532	(3·02)
South Australia	–		3,265	(0·71)	3,708	(0·81)	15,619	(3·29)
Western Australia	–		1,051	(0·32)	3,424	(1·03)	12,305	(3·57)
Tasmania	–		1,249	(0·76)	–		7,005	(4·07)
Australia	3,577	(0·07)	26,337	(0·53)	31,466	(0·63)	147,616	(2·87)

* Per cent of total vote cast

Senate Election (First Preference Votes Cast):

	No. Votes	% Total Valid Votes				
State	Lib-CP		ALP		DLP-QLP	
New South Wales	752,362	(43·73)	761,767	(44·28)	83,636	(4·86)
Victoria	570,567	(43·95)	549,481	(42·33)	162,799	(12·54)
Queensland	325,224	(47·03)	282,284	(40·82)	73,037	(10·56)
South Australia	195,929	(44·82)	205,380	(46·98)	23,310	(5·33)
Western Australia	178,981	(57·30)	111,499	(35·69)	19,713	(6·31)
Tasmania	61,130	(40·05)	62,616	(41·02)	25,922	(16·98)*
Australia	2,084,193	(45·19)	1,973,027	(42·78)	388,417	(8·42)

	Communist		Others		Informal**	
New South Wales	101,516	(5·90)*	21,213	(1·22)	224,828	(12·46)
Victoria	11,525	(0·89)	3,715	(0·29)	142,416	
Queensland	6,508	(0·94)	4,459	(0·64)	54,431	(7·17)
South Australia	12,536	(2·87)*	–		36,677	(7·74)
Western Australia	2,178	(0·69)	–		32,427	(9·40)
Tasmania	–		2,972	(1·95)	19,271	(11·21)
Australia	134,263	(2·91)	12,511	(0·27)	529,050	(10·29)

* No. 1 on ballot paper
** Per cent of total vote cast
Lib-CP and Labor won 3 seats each in New South Wales and Victoria, where there were six vacancies, because of mid-term deaths etc. Lib-CP won 3 to Labor 2 in Queensland, and in Western Australia, where the Country Party candidates were grouped separately. Labor won 3 to Lib-CP 2 in South Australia and Tasmania

Evatt provided the by now usual diversion after the campaign, blaming a 'Menzies-Mannix axis' for Labor's defeat.

'In spite of Archbishop Mannix's slander of Thursday last, directed against the ALP, the electorate have shown steady and most impressive support for the Labor Party,' Evatt's post-election statement of 23 October said. Having regard to the Gallup Poll's indication during the campaign of a swing to Labor, Mannix's statement was—and he quoted Calwell's earlier reply—a 'deliberately timed bomb' to weaken Labor, he added. He quoted freely from Calwell and McKenna, pointing out that both were 'devout, practising Catholics', went on to mention Mannix's 'patronage of the Santamaria Movement' and then said it had been freely rumoured in Sydney some days before that such a statement would be forthcoming 'on the lines of the Zinoviev letter'. He said the 'bomb move' was largely inspired by the 'desperate political situation of Mr Menzies and the Liberal Party in the face of an unfavourable Gallup Poll. The publication of Dr Mannix's letter can fairly be regarded as an illustration of the Menzies-Mannix axis in operation.' He contrasted this with the attitude of the 'kindly, gentle and charitable Cardinal Gilroy'.

A public attack from Mannix's episcopal supporters followed immediately. The statement was released by the Vicar-General of St Patrick's Cathedral in Melbourne, in the form of messages of support to Dr Mannix from Archbishop Young of Hobart and the Bishops of Ballarat, Sandhurst and Sale (Victoria), Wagga and Armidale (New South Wales), Toowoomba and Rockhampton (Queensland) and Geraldton (Western Australia).

The bishops referred to Evatt's 'impertinence' and accused him of setting himself up as 'an improper judge of Catholic conscience'. 'People are getting tired of cries of "conspiracy" whenever someone in this free democracy says or does something that is not pleasing to Dr Evatt,' said Archbishop Young. The three Suffragan bishops of Victoria said Evatt himself had 'intruded the religious question' by the use of Cardinal Gilroy's name.

'I stand up to defend Labor's rights against its detractors, whoever they may be,' Evatt said in a long reply, pointing out that the bishops had blamed only him and not Calwell or McKenna.

Chapter Twenty-one
The Revolution
and its Children

The split had now run its course, changing the shape of Australian politics. Time was at last running out for Evatt and Calwell's hour was approaching. Evatt stood again for the Leadership when the new Caucus met in 1959 and this time had to withstand the long-awaited challenge from Ward. With Calwell waiting in the wings, Evatt defeated Ward by forty-six votes to thirty-two and the dream of a left wing, 'radical' Labor Party was thwarted for a time.

The Party now set out to find what was unofficially called a 'soft landing place' for Evatt. An opportunity arose the following summer, when the Chief Justiceship of New South Wales became vacant. The Party, still in Government in Sydney, organised to get the job for Evatt. He resigned from Parliament to take it in February 1960, twenty stormy years after he first entered the House of Representatives and after several weeks of semi-public argument in the New South Wales Government.

Even the final years were not to be dignified or free of tragedy. Evatt's mental condition had deteriorated markedly, if unevenly, throughout the second half of the decade. Many of the New South Wales Labor men who organised the job for him as a dignified exit from politics, had grave misgivings afterwards. There were many stories of his strange behaviour on the Bench. In 1962 he took leave of absence for a trip abroad, but collapsed while the ship to Europe was still on the Australian coast. His mind had broken down completely. He withdrew from public life and was an invalid until his death in the spring of 1965.

Under Calwell's leadership, the new divisions working in the Party became sharply apparent on the Federal bodies, now as bitterly factional as a decade before. The Victorian and Queensland branches, working with Chamberlain and partly with the South Australian branch, constituted a 'left' wing; New South Wales and Tasmania the nucleus of a 'right' which often attracted some support from South and Western Australia. The ideological differences were most pronounced on foreign policy, the left wing tending towards neutralism and opposition to the American alliance, on specific issues rather than as an overall policy. Its style was more intolerant and authoritarian than the old right. Victoria remained a pressure group for 'unity tickets' with the communists in union elections. These continued to flourish there, despite majority Federal disapproval, and the DLP vigorously publicised each example.

The 'right' was centred on New South Wales, where the AWU-Colbourne alliance—sometimes nicknamed 'the grippers [Masons] and Groupers'—continued to provide a traditionalist, anti-communist base. The New South Wales machine was less strident than in the Grouper days, though it gained little in tolerance and lost much of the idealism and modernising zeal of 1952-54. A substantial left wing had developed from the left wing unions encouraged in the split years and built upon by men leaving the Communist Party from the Hungarian invasion of 1956 onwards. Much of the right's efforts went into fighting off the challenge from this quarter and the rather uninspired approach of the right helped gather support for the left.

Calwell's leadership style was to seek compromises between the two factions nationally, a strategy to which his personal charm lent itself. It paid off in keeping reasonable unity in the Party in the early 1960's, but left deeper issues to intensify unchecked.

There was early success for the Calwell strategy in the election of 1961. The heated boom of 1960 had, with Government action coming too late, turned into a short-lived but severe recession in 1961-62. Economic growth stopped, unemployment was substantial and several spectacularly large companies that had evolved in the boom years crashed ignominiously. Labor again emerged as the party of economic expansion in the election towards the end of the year. To the amazement of most Parliamentarians and the public, it came within a few votes in one Queensland seat of winning a majority, despite a continuing large vote for the DLP. The weak spot was Victoria, where the DLP vote remained high and the ALP vote correspondingly low. Had there been no 'Victorian problem', Arthur Calwell would have been Prime Minister of Australia.

The Government's thin majority of only one seat in the House of Representatives led to a feeling of optimism in Labor ranks and a determination not to 'rock the boat' before the next election. Menzies, sensing a better climate, called a premature election in 1963, after only two years. This showed the Labor optimism to have been misguided, for the voting pattern fell back to about that of 1955 and 1958.

This meant that Labor was once again in a dilemma. Unless the Victorian problem was solved, and the influence of the new left broken, Labor could expect to be out of power indefinitely.

A new moderate-right force developed in Victoria in 1964, thrown up by both the electoral reverse of late 1963 and the death in office in March of Stout, aged seventy-eight. Jordan was elected to the Secretaryship of the Trades Hall Council by a small majority, after months of bitter fighting with the left unions. The unions supporting him—now including the AWU under the ageing Davis—allied themselves with moderate branch members, but the new force commanded only about a third of the votes at Victorian ALP conferences.

At the same time Calwell, who had been sixty-three when he was elected Leader, was declining and losing credibility as an alternative Prime Minister. He had relied on creating an impression of vigour, which disguised his generally old-fashioned approach, in the early years of Leadership; but even in 1963 this 'image' had been breaking down.

To an impartial judge, it must have seemed that it was now time for Whitlam, who had defeated Ward for the Deputy Leadership in 1960 and emerged as an enemy of the unity ticket, machine-minded left, to take the stage.

The years from 1964 to 1967 were, however, marred by an undignified bout of further faction fighting. Calwell stubbornly refused to step down and to the amazement and dismay of his friends joined the Victorian Central Executive in 1964. This body turned even further to the left after 1965, spurred on by a new generation of the far left, including a 'pro-Peking' Party that split off in 1963, and Calwell remained its presumably willing prisoner. He had gone full circle from a generation and a half before, when he was thought typical of the moderate Catholic right. The fight of Whitlam and his supporters from the right and 'moderate' sections of the Party against the Victorian Executive, Calwell, Chamberlain and the left generally spiralled, without real success, in an intensity that threatened a new split.

Calwell finally stepped down in 1967, a discredited man of seventy, after leading the Party to a devastating defeat; it lost 11 seats in 1966. The issue of immediate withdrawal from the Vietnam War was paramount. Whitlam at last succeeded him, but refused to work with the far left. He was faced with the choice of leading a united party destined never to win office—and therefore unlikely to stay united—or fighting the left to recreate an electorally successful left of centre party dominated by its Parliamentarians. He chose to fight and by the end of the decade, as the twentieth anniversary of the defeat of Chifley's Government neared, Labor's position seemed more intractable than ever before.

Calwell had ignored the questions of modernisation, of a more expert, less emotional approach to policy-making, of building up a corps of expert advisers, of freeing the Party from its dependence on the internal politics of capital city trades hall. Whitlam made this a central question of his leadership, but, as fifteen years earlier, the main effect was once again to touch off power struggles and for modernisation to become smothered in deeper factional issues.

However, Menzies' retirement in January 1966 led to increasing internal difficulties for the Liberals, under Holt and then John Gorton from 1968. Labor under Whitlam did well at the 1969 Federal elections and there seemed a chance that the weakness of its opponents could help unite Labor outside Victoria and offer a chance of eventual victory.

Calwell had forecast early in his Leadership that the DLP would 'wither on the vine'. This was not to be, for the organisation and vote of the DLP, despite weak support in the smaller states, showed as much staying power as that of the ALP. A decade and a half after the split, it was still waiting, fairly intact, for 'reunification'. But it was not without its troubles.

The role of The Movement and Santamaria in founding the DLP and guiding its early years determined much of its continuing character. This, and its inability to elect more than an occasional Senator to Parliament, caused a steady falling away of many of the politicians most notable at its birth.

As early as the 1959 Victorian DLP Conference, Keon and Bourke had roundly condemned Santamaria's influence on the Party from the floor—to angry shouts of protest from the massed supporters. Keon later told the press—it was reported on 8 June 1959:

I told the Conference on Friday that the DLP could not win an election because many Australians regarded it as a church party. I said that Mr Santamaria's attempts to gain control of it and influence it were responsible for that label being tacked onto it. I said Mr Santamaria had no right to usurp the role of spokesman for the DLP, which he did so often in TV interviews, or attempt to use his supporters to turn the DLP into a specifically Catholic Party, for which there is no place in Australia.

Bourke said the DLP was being branded as a Santamaria or Church party. 'His [Santamaria's] organisation straddles our shoulders, stopping us from making progress,' he said. '. . . if Mr Santamaria gets control of this Party, I am certainly going to get out of it. We should be completely independent and not operated from behind the scenes.'

Many well known names fell away from the DLP in the succeeding year or years, but sufficient remained and sufficient new blood was recruited to keep it astonishingly effective. The 'Santamaria' and 'centre party' issues recurred from time to time, but never ruinously. A more pressing problem was maintaining an effective organisation in South Australia, Tasmania and Western Australia, where the DLP had to work from a small original base and small total population. In 1962, the QLP joined the DLP, Walsh and another of its parliamentarians resigning as a result, but remaining in the State Parliament until 1969 as independents.

By the middle of the 1960's both the DLP and National Civic Council had become essentially pressure groups for a strong, militant Australian defence and for generally what became known as 'hawkish' policies in Asian affairs involving communists. Their distinctive, decentralist economic policies and other domestic questions tended to become relatively unimportant. It is probable that many of the DLP leaders never really believed in their party's domestic policies.

McManus was elected a Senator from Victoria from 1955 to 1961, when he went out on the anti-government wave, and again from 1964 to 1970. Cole finally lost his Senate seat in 1964 and died in 1969 while planning to recontest it in 1970. However, in 1964 Gair had been elected a DLP Senator from Queensland and was appointed his party's Federal Parliamentary Leader. An out-of-turn Senate election in 1967 (a result of the early election in 1963) saw declining public enthusiasm for the Government—now with Harold Holt as Prime Minister—little proportionate enthusiasm for Labor, and a significant breakthrough for the DLP. It elected second Senators from Victoria (J. A. Little) and Queensland (Condon Byrne) for six-year terms. Such victories helped the DLP retain vigour in its years-long fight to force the ALP to eschew the left unions, turn to the right in foreign policy and bring the breakaways of the mid-fifties and their successors back into its ranks.

The National Civic Council maintained a base of union influence in Victoria, created a new one in Tasmania in the 1960's and also had significant influence in Queensland. Its power in the Melbourne Trades Hall grew rapidly after Jordan's death in 1969 as a four-way power struggle between 'pro-Peking' communists and ultra leftists, orthodox communists and leftists, moderates and the NCC intensified.

The spirit of hatred that had disfigured the Labor Movement for a generation continued to fester and the tendency to see the world as alive with plots against Labor hardly abated.

The issues of 1955 seemed to be becoming a permanent part of Australian public life. The result was to weaken overall public interest in politics, to make Liberal rule virtually unchallengeable Federally and in Victoria and perhaps some other states, and for the ALP to remain in a state of perpetual struggle. By the late 1960's, as the magnitude of Whitlam's task became clear, many wondered if the ALP had entered a chronic stage of decay that would in time destroy it, unless the Federal Government destroyed itself from within first.

The great Labor split of 1954-57 was so all-embracing in its sweep that it is almost too tempting to draw morals from it. Religious bigotry, industrial wing Messianism, communist penetration, bad political judgment, bad leadership, demagoguery and authoritarianism, woolliness and laziness, lack of personal courage—these do not exhaust the list of causes.

The central figure must remain Evatt, the gifted but tragically inappropriate intellectual at a time when Labor needed intellectual distinction at its head. Evatt's failings were enormous: his egocentricity, his naïveté, his lack of feeling for economics in an age dominated by economics, his sheer lack of judgment and his disastrous errors, under pressure, over the means test, the Petrov inquiry and then in touching off the split. Yet he had a quality of human tenderness and lovable eccentricity that tinged even the harshest judgments of him with affection. The decline of his mental stability in the 1950's was not only his own terrifying tragedy but a tragedy for his Party and his country.

In assessing Evatt, account must also be taken of the immensity of his task. As Calwell's career and the early years at least of Whitlam were to show, leading Australian Labor was a task almost beyond human resources. In many European countries, the union movements split into warring camps. In Australia, it was always a desperate struggle to keep them united at least in organisation. Leadership of the ALP meant not only keeping a trade union base working in harmony, but keeping it in harmony with the often conflicting interests of the political wing—themselves complex enough —and then meshing this with the interests of six states as well as the nation. This had to be done in an atmosphere essentially demanding emotion, cunning and understanding of vested interests, more than calm, reasonable discussion.

The frequency of elections meant a continual job of patching over troubles, rather than seeking out causes. Constitutionally, Federal elections had to be held every three years, but the Government had the right—which Menzies used three times—to call early elections. These in turn produced Senate elections in 'off' years which could not be ignored, for control of the Senate is vital for energetic government. As well, there were triennial elections in six States and never-ending union and municipal elections. All these affected vital interests.

The split of the mid-fifties in some ways resembled the First World War. The incident that touched it off was comparatively minor, many of the issues involved were in themselves too old or new to cause a conflagration, but once started it proved impossible to stop. As with the First World War, the tendency in the first years afterwards was to ignore the enormous complexities in favour of emotional over-simplifications produced by war-time propaganda. These tended to deepen the damage done.

Thus on one side the story was widely believed that the ALP had narrowly escaped an at least semi-fascist, clericalist plot to turn it into an organ for introducing the corporate state, or at best subsistence farming on the grand scale, into Australia; while a less lurid story, accepted by many intellectuals, was that the split was part of Evatt's wish to make the ALP more 'socialist'. This was often accompanied by theories about the changing socio-economic status of Catholics in Australia, making them more 'conservative'.

A *Dictionary of Politics* published in Britain in 1957 could say in its entry on Evatt: 'In an attempt to make the Australian Labor Party adopt a policy of Socialism rather than social welfare he antagonised the Catholic right wing of the Party which opposes, in particular, his toleration of communists.'

An article in the (Anglican) *Australian Churchman* of 2 May 1955 said: '. . . the Groups, having been perfected as a highly efficient machine for working within the unions against the communists, were turned inwards to be used against the radicals within the Labor Party. Moreover, far-reaching policy changes were attempted.' It went on to say that Catholic views tended to become less radical with changing economic circumstances but 'instead of changing their allegiances they attempted to change the Labor Party's basic policy'.

'All these things aroused great opposition among the Labor Party Centre and Left,' the article continued. 'For some years there had been a running fight between the non-communist, Labor-controlled Melbourne Trades Hall Council and the 'old' Victorian ALP Central Executive, on which the Roman Catholic Right Wing had an approximate seventeen to eight majority. But the troops really began to mobilise when the Group machinery started to move in on the powerful Australian Workers' Union, a union with a 100 per cent non-communist record, but whose principles of rural development conflict in some essentials with Roman Catholic rural policy on the development of peasant proprietors. . . . Further events have led to the formation of a breakaway Labor Party in Victoria comprising almost exclusively the conservative wing of Roman Catholics—of twenty-five State and Federal Parliamentarians who went with the breakaways at the time of the split, only two are not Roman Catholics.' The article concluded the issue was not basically sectarian, however, because many 'Catholic radicals' had adhered to the 'new' Victorian ALP Executive. 'We are seeing in Australia a phenomenon fairly common on the European Continent— Catholic anti-clericalism. There are many devout Roman Catholics who disapprove of the direct intervention of the Church in political life, and who believe that the Church can give effective guidance without concerning itself with direct participation.'

From another direction, Niall Brennan could write in his biography of Archbishop Mannix as late as 1964:

[Evatt] had made some desultory attempts to woo the Catholic vote; but it was clear that a man of his outlook would go further with the left wing secularists than with the Catholics. . . .

Federal elections followed shortly after [Evatt's Petrov appearance] [sic] and Labor was again defeated. It was close; Labor had a majority of votes but no seats. The general opinion was that Evatt's association at various levels with left wing activities, but most of all his excited espousal of a left wing cause in the Petrov inquiry—to the point of discourtesy involving his removal—made him a poor bet for Prime Minister. . . . Evatt's motives in what followed do not matter. It was astonishingly reminiscent of 1917. . . .

This was a unique explanation. The tendency on the DLP side was much more to blame communist manipulation and conspiracies, sectarianism and at least naïveté or cynicism and at worst communist sympathies on the part of Evatt. For many years, DLP sympathisers would hardly admit that The Movement had even existed, let alone try to explain what it was all about.

Attempts to create coherent ideological explanations for the split, as a cleavage over fundamental ideas of left of centre politics, were all too widely accepted and discouraged assessment of the more intractable and complex questions of organisation involved.

Perhaps a more appropriate quotation is from Evatt himself, in the tranquil industry of his High Court and literary period. It was about a Labor split and the actions of Labor leaders nearly forty years before his own tragedy. In his conclusion to *Australian Labor Leader*, his biography of W. A. Holman published in 1940, Evatt wrote:

In 1916, when the Labor Executive expelled Holman and [Prime Minister W. M.] Hughes, it entered upon a long era of powerlessness and futile opposition. It should have foreseen some of the disastrous consequences of life-long expulsion. But the two leaders should also have foreseen the consequences to Labor and to Australia. In truth there was an intermingling of passion and sentiment, of jealousy and resentment. The spirit of disinterestedness was absent.

Appendix

FEDERAL EXECUTIVE REPORT, 1 AUGUST 1954 TO MARCH 1955

SECTION 1

The resignation of Senator P. J. Kennelly was considered at the July 1954 meeting of the Federal Executive and it was resolved that the resignation be accepted and that the Executive place on record, on its own behalf and on behalf of the Labor Movement, appreciation of the vigorous and energetic manner in which Senator Kennelly had carried out the duties of Federal Secretary over a period of years.

Mr Jack Schmella, secretary of the Queensland Central Executive of the Australian Labor Party, was appointed Acting Secretary in Senator Kennelly's place.

The next meeting of the Executive was a Special Meeting held at the Hotel Kingston, Canberra, commencing on Wednesday, 27 October 1954, at 3 p.m. It was attended by the following delegates:

New South Wales: W. R. Colbourne, C. Anderson.

Victoria: D. Lovegrove, J. P. Horan.

Queensland: Hon. E. J. Walsh, MLA, J. Schmella (Acting Secretary).

South Australia: Senator J. P. Toohey, J. F. Walsh, MHA.

Western Australia: F. E. Chamberlain, H. Webb, MHR.

Tasmania: Hon. E. E. Reece, MHA, G. Duthie, MHR.

The purpose of the meeting was to consider correspondence and statements made by Dr Evatt, Messrs Mullens, MHR, Keon, MHR, Bourke, MHR, R. Holt, MLA, W. Divers, secretary, Municipal Employees' Union, Victoria, and the New South Wales State Executive.

Personal appearances were also made by Dr Evatt, Messrs Mullins, Keon, and Bourke. Allegations and counter allegations were made by individuals and the Executive discussed the whole matter in some detail up till 10.30 p.m. on Thursday, 28 October. The Executive decided unanimously as follows:

That this Executive is of the opinion that the references to the Central Executive of the Victorian Branch of the Party as contained in the written submissions of Dr Evatt, W. T. Divers, and R. W. Holt constitute grave charges against that body which affect the well-being of the Labor Movement; as a consequence of this opinion we agree that the fullest investigation of the Victorian Branch be undertaken by this Executive sitting in

Melbourne on a date to be fixed when the aforementioned persons and any other or others agreed upon by this Executive shall be called before it.
The following resolution was carried:

That the Federal Executive of the Australian Labor Party views with concern the general lack of discipline which is having an adverse effect on the Labor Movement generally throughout Australia. We therefore call upon the Federal Parliamentary Labor Party, the State Branches, affiliated bodies, and all members to refrain from any public comment or action related to the present dispute.

It may be seen that the members of the Federal Executive were much concerned at the general trend of events in the Movement throughout Australia.

It was decided that to further consider the matters in question the next meeting of the Executive would be held in Melbourne on Tuesday, 9 November.

Later it became necessary to alter this date, and the Federal Executive resumed at the ACTU Board Room, Melbourne, on Wednesday, 10 November 1954, when the following were present as delegates:

New South Wales: Messrs Colbourne and Kane.

Victoria: Messrs Lovegrove and Horan.

South Australia: Messrs Toohey and Walsh.

Western Australia: Messrs Chamberlain and Webb.

Tasmania: Messrs Duthie and Reece.

Queensland: Messrs Gair and Schmella.

On Friday evening, 12 November, this meeting was adjourned until Monday, 29 November, when it continued at the ACTU Building Melbourne.

During the two meetings held in Melbourne the following persons attended before the Executive:

Rt Hon. Dr H. V. Evatt, MP, Leader of the Federal Parliamentary Labor Party.

Mr S. M. Keon, MHR, Federal Parliament.

Mr J. Mullins, MHR, Federal Parliament.

Mr W. Bourke, MHR, Federal Parliament.

Mr R. Holt, MLA, Victorian Parliament.

Mr F. Scully, MLA, Honorary Minister.

Mr M. J. Gladman, MLA, Victorian Assistant Minister Lands.

Mr J. V. Stout, Secretary, Melbourne Trades Hall Council.

Mr W. T. Divers, Secretary, Municipal Employees' Union (Vic. Branch).

Mr A. McNolty, Secretary, Sheet Metal Workers' Union (Vic. Branch).

Mr D. McSween, Secretary, Clothing Trades Union (Vic. Branch).

Mr R. Parry, Secretary, Tanners and Leatherdressers' Union (Vic. Branch).

Mr H. O. Davis, Secretary, Australian Workers' Union (Vic. Branch).

Hon. P. L. Coleman, MLC, Minister for Transport, Victoria.

Hon. John Cain, MLA, Premier of Victoria.

Hon. W. Galvin, MLA, Deputy Premier of Vicoria.

Senator the Hon. P. J. Kennelly, Federal Parliament.

Mr R. R. Broadby, Secretary, ACTU.

Mr R. J. Corcoran, Secretary, Dandenong Branch ALP, Victoria.

Mr J. F. Cairns, Member Toorak Branch ALP.

Mr F. McManus, Assistant Secretary, Victorian Central Executive.

Mr D. Devlin, Member Victorian Executive.

Mr L. D'Arcy, MLA, Victorian Parliament.

Hon. J. Little, MLC, Victorian Executive.

It should be pointed out here that the Executive, realising the importance of its deliberations and any decisions it might make, examined carefully and thoroughly all statements and information made available, and, as a result the following report, findings, and decisions were adopted by a majority vote of the Executive.

As a result of the decision of the Federal Executive the Acting Federal Secretary proceeded to Victoria on 8 February 1955, and began arrangements for holding the Special Victorian Conference on Saturday and Sunday, 26 and 27 February.

Mr F. E. Chamberlain, the Senior Vice-president, was also in Melbourne on ACTU business and took part in the preliminary arrangements and discussions.

Mr Reece, the Federal President, was unable to be present as he was engaged in the election campaign in Tasmania.

An advertisement was inserted in all metropolitan daily papers on Monday, 14 February, calling for nominations for delegates from State Electorates. The usual form of Pledge was included in the nomination form.

On 16 February Mr D. F. Woodhouse, member of the Victorian Executive, served Messrs Schmella, Lovegrove, and Horan with Notice of Motion for an Interlocutory Injunction to restrain members of the Federal Executive from convening the Special Conference, and at the direction of the Acting Federal President the Acting Federal Secretary consulted Mr A. P. Brodney, of Maurice Blackburn & Coy., solicitors, ACTU Building, Melbourne, who are recognised as the official legal advisers to the Victorian Branch of the Labor Party. Mr Brodney briefed Mr R. M. Eggleston, QC, to act for the Federal Executive.

This case came on for hearing on 21 February, and continued for three days. Mr Horan appeared on the first day and advised the Court that he did not object to an injunction being granted. Messrs Lovegrove and Schmella appeared each day in the Court.

On 25 February judgment was delivered refusing the application for an injunction.

On 26 February morning newspapers reported that on the previous evening the Victorian Central Executive had declared that the Special Conference was not binding on any branch or affiliated union and morning papers carried an advertisement by the Acting Secretary of the ALP, Mr McManus, repudiating the Acting Federal Secretary's advertisement of 21 February.

The manner in which delegates were selected is the subject of a separate report prepared by Mr Lovegrove on behalf of the Credentials Committee. Mr Lovegrove acted as secretary of the Credentials Committee.

Mr J. M. Tripovich was also co-opted to assist the Credentials Committee because of his special knowledge of country electorates in Victoria, he having been employed as Country Organiser for some years prior to tendering his resignation as from Monday, 14 February.

Other particulars as to the preparation and organisation in connection with the Special Conference are covered in the report of the Credentials Committee attached hereto, but suffice it to say that every possible precaution was taken to ensure that only supporters of the Labor Party in good standing should be admitted.

Fifty-three (53) Unions were represented by 215 delegates and thirty-one EEC's by 34 delegates, and of the total of 249 delegates 15 were non-members of the ALP.

Attached herewith is a copy of a Statutory Declaration that was signed by persons not members of the ALP, and it can confidently be stated that not one person was admitted where there was the slightest reason to think that he or she was not a Labor Party supporter and in good standing as such.

Full particulars are given as to Unions and State Electorate Councils represented in the report attached hereto, and it should be pointed out that numerous nominations were rejected because the necessary information was not forthcoming which would show that they were fully entitled to be present.

Ballots resulted in the election of the following officers to the Victorian Central Executive:

State President: J. V. Stout.

Vice-presidents: R. Cameron, A. McNolty.

Treasurer: D. R. McSween.

Federal Executive Delegates: D. Lovegrove, J. V. Stout.

Federal Conference Delegates: J. P. Brebner, H. O. Davis, J. V. Stout, W. Divers, P. J. Kennelly, D. Lovegrove.

State Executive: John Cain, P. J. Clarey, R. Broadby, L. W. Galvin, H. O. Davis, R. Balcombe, P. J. Kennelly, A. E. Monk, V. G. Delmenico, W. Divers, J. Petrie, R. W. Holt, F. Carey, L. Higgins, J. P. Brebner, F. Courtenay, W. Butler, T. Coe.

The Executive would like to express its appreciation to all those who assisted the Federal Secretary and other members of the Federal Executive in carrying out the duties involved. It can readily be imagined that there was a considerable amount of work involved, spread over a period of three weeks which involved working at night time and on week-ends as well.

Messrs Chamberlain, Lovegrove, and Tripovich were particularly helpful and the Federated Municipal Employees' Federal Office was made available by courtesy of Mr T. Winter, of Sydney, Federal Secretary.

Union officials too numerous to mention also gave valued assistance.

It is to be hoped that the present differences of opinion which have had such a damaging effect on the Party in Victoria will be dispersed in the near future.

The Tory press made a Roman holiday of the differences of opinion in the Party and appeared to do everything possible to create dissension and ill-feeling. It should be mentioned that, with the exception of a few anonymous telephone calls, there was no animosity displayed by anybody towards the Executive officers in carrying out their duties. On the other hand there was an atmosphere of courtesy, and it is felt that there is no reason whatever why all supporters of the Party in Victoria should not get together in furthering the interests of our great Party and in implementing its enlightened policy.

Reference was made during the Conference proceedings to the vital importance of showing tolerance towards the viewpoint of others, and it is essential in a Party such as ours that the necessity for tolerance and goodwill amongst members should always be kept in mind. Healthy differences of opinion are beneficial and helpful, but it must always be kept in mind that the policy and platform of the Party leave no room for ambiguity in essentials.

Once again the hope is expressed that Labor's industrial and political position in Victoria will rapidly become stabilised and united.

In accordance with the Federal Executive instruction the Acting Secretary visited the Northern Territory and held meetings at all branches. This is the subject of a separate report.

Enclosed herewith is the financial statement from July 1954 to 31 December 1954. It may be seen that the financial position is far from good. As a matter of fact there is not sufficient cash on hand to pay amounts owing. This is due to the fact that three Special Meetings were held in the latter part of the year and unexpected expenses were incurred in connection with the Victorian position.

If a full-time secretary and office is to be maintained dues from the various State Branches would have to be quadrupled because, as may be seen from the financial statement, receipts for the year were just a little over £1200. This Conference will have to give serious consideration to this matter.

Every endeavour has been made to keep expenses down to a minimum, but the income is far from sufficient to meet any unusual expenditure under the present circumstances.

> E. E. Reece, MHA,
> *President.*
> Jack Schmellla,
> *Acting Secretary.*

Section 2

Report, findings and decisions of the Federal Executive, Australian Labor Party, in respect to submissions, allegations and charges made by a number of persons affecting the general welfare of the Labor Party.

At 3 p.m. on 27 October 1954, the Federal Executive met at the Kingston Hotel, Canberra, to commence a Special Meeting as a consequence of a number of press statements by members of the Party, including the Federal Parliamentary Leader, the Rt Hon. Dr H. V. Evatt, MHR, which in the opinion of the Executive, affected the general welfare of the Labor Movement as referred to in Rule 9 (i) of the Federal Executive Rules.

The Executive met subsequently in Melbourne on 10 November 1954, and again on 29 November 1954.

The submissions made to the Executive by a number of persons, all members of the Party, not only involved individuals, but contained charges against the Central Executive of the Victorian Branch of the Party.

The following persons attended before the Executive in the course of its investigations:

Rt Hon. Dr H. V. Evatt, MP, Leader of the Federal Parliamentary Labor Party.

Mr S. M. Keon, MHR, Federal Parliament.

Mr J. Mullins, MHR, Federal Parliament.

Mr W. Bourke, MHR, Federal Parliament.

Mr R. Holt, MLA, Victorian Parliament.

Mr F. Scully, MLA, Honorary Minister.

Mr M. J. Gladman, MLA, Victorian Assistant Minister for Lands.

Mr J. V. Stout, Secretary, Melbourne Trades Hall Council.

Mr W. T. Divers, Secretary, Municipal Employees' Union (Victorian Branch).

Mr A. McNolty, Secretary, Sheet Metal Workers' Union (Victorian Branch).

Mr D. McSween, Secretary, Clothing Trades Union (Victorian Branch).

Mr R. Parry, Secretary, Tanners and Leatherdressers' Union (Victorian Branch).

Mr H. O. Davis, Secretary, Australian Workers' Union (Victorian Branch).

Hon. P. L. Coleman, MLC, Minister for Transport, Victoria.

Hon. John Cain, MLA, Premier of Victoria.

Hon. W. Galvin, MLA, Deputy Premier of Victoria.

Senator the Hon. P. J. Kennelly, Federal Parliament.

Mr R. R. Broadby, Secretary, ACTU.

Mr R. J. Corcoran, Secretary, Dandenong Branch, ALP, Victoria.

Mr J. F. Cairns, Member Toorak Branch, ALP.

Mr F. McManus, Assistant Secretary, Victorian Central Executive.

Mr D. Devlin, Member of Victorian Executive.

Mr L. D'Arcy, MLA, Victorian Parliament.

Hon. J. Little, MLC, Member Victorian Executive.

The Executive investigation may be placed under four main headings:

1 Disunity and lack of discipline in the Federal Parliamentary Labor Party.

2 Charges and counter charges involving individual members of the Party.

3 That, in effect, the Central Executive of the Party in Victoria is dominated and/or influenced by an outside body referred to as the 'Movement' to detriment of the Labor Party's basic principles.

4 That industrial group organisation has developed away from its original purpose, and is being used as a vehicle to further the political aims of an outside body referred to as the 'Movement'.

It is proposed to deal with them in that order.

1 There can be no doubt as to the alarming disunity and lack of discipline in the ranks of the Federal Parliamentary Labor Party, and many factors have played a part in creating this condition.

It is not intended to critically examine all those factors. Sufficient for the purpose of the Executive is to say that it is accepted as a fact.

Having regard for the fact that the Federal Executive is the administrative authority to carry out decisions of the Federal Conference and to interpret the Constitution and Federal Platform vide rule 9 (a) of the Executive Rules, it has become imperative for the Executive to exercise that authority for the purpose of issuing a directive to the Federal Parliamentary Labor Party to ensure that members will conduct themselves in accordance with the basic requirements of membership of this Party.

This directive is issued in the following terms:

(a) That the Executive of the Federal Parliamentary Labor Party shall accept the responsibility of reporting to the appropriate State Executive the behaviour of any member of the Federal Parliamentary Labor Party which, in the opinion of the Executive, warrants disciplinary action.

(b) The Executive of the Federal Parliamentary Labor Party shall at the same time notify the President of the Federal Executive of its action under (a).

The matter shall be placed before the Federal Executive, who shall, if it be deemed necessary, call for a report from the State Executive concerned.

(c) In the event of a majority of the Federal Executive deciding that the State Executive concerned has not taken disciplinary action in keeping with the offence alleged by the Executive of the Federal Parliamentary Labor Party, the Federal Executive shall take whatever action it deems fit under the provisions of rule 9 (h) of the Federal Executive Rules.

(d) Provided that this directive is not to be construed as in any way amending or disturbing any existing rules of State Branches.

2 In regard to the matters falling under this heading which involved Dr Evatt, Messrs Keon, Mullins, and Bourke, the Executive, after a full examination, have reached the following conclusions:

(a) That the charges preferred against Dr Evatt are not sustained.

(b) In the case of the allegations affecting Messrs Keon, Mullins, and Bourke, it must be noted that no specific charges were made against them by Dr Evatt before the Executive.

It should be further noted that the handling of the controversy by the daily press was largely responsible for the widely held belief that charges against them would be laid before the Executive by Dr Evatt. As a consequence of these circumstances we are now compelled to find that whilst the conduct of the three members named has on occasions been in conflict with the welfare of the Labor Movement the fact that responsible bodies concerned, including the Federal Executive, failed to take action against them at the time does to a material extent condone such conduct, and as a consequence it is not intended to press these matters further other than to direct their attention to the Executive directive under (1) of this Report.

3 The Executive's examination of this—the most vital question before it—involved voluminous submissions from a number of persons in varying forms of allegations, some of them being extraneous to the question.

In addition, the Executive sought the assistance of a number of people in its deliberations, notably the Premier of Victoria, Mr Cain, his Deputy, Mr Galvin, and the Secretary of the ACTU, Mr Broadby. We feel that the information and balanced objective views presented by these gentlemen materially assisted in the formulation of our conclusions.

They are set out hereunder:

(a) That a Special Conference of the Victorian Branch of the ALP is directed to be held on a date to be named, and on the following conditions laid down by the Federal Executive.

(b) That with the exception of the Secretary and Assistant Secretary and Woman Organiser, all offices and members of the Central Executive, as referred to in Rule 5 of the Central Executive Rules, shall be declared vacant as from 9 a.m. on the date fixed for the Special Conference referred to under (a) hereof.

(c) That the Federal President or other officer of the Federal Executive shall preside over the Special Conference.

(d) That credentials for the Conference shall be addressed to and be in the hands of the Acting Federal Secretary at the ACTU Office, Melbourne, three days prior to the opening of the Conference.

(e) A Credentials Committee consisting of two members of the Federal Executive and the State Secretary of the Victorian Branch, Mr Lovegrove, shall be appointed by the Federal Executive.

(f) That members of the Federal Executive shall, if possible, be in attendance for the purpose of facilitating the business of the Conference.

(g) That the business of the Conference shall consist of considering and determining the following matters:

1 The election of officers and members of the Central Executive as provided under Rule 5 of the Central Executive rules, with the exception of the Secretary and Assistant Secretary, and Woman Organiser.

2 The election of six (6) delegates to represent Victoria at the then next Federal Conference of the ALP.

3 Election of two representatives to the Federal Executive.

Provided that all existing members of the Central Executive and delegates to the Federal Conference and Federal Executive shall be deemed to be eligible for nomination and re-election.

(h) Representation at the Conference shall be in accordance with Rules 3 (a) and (b) and Rule 12 of the Central Executive rules, but the proviso of Rule 22 that delegates so appointed must be financial members of the ALP for the last two years shall not be observed for the purpose of the Special Conference and shall be deemed to be suspended pending further consideration by the Federal Executive, and that Rule 21 shall be adjusted accordingly.

(i) Persons who are expelled or suspended from Party membership shall not be eligible to nominate as delegates to Special Conference.

(j) That portion of Rule 26 of the Central Executive rules referring to '25 per cent of the Central Executive shall be resident in the country', shall not be applicable to the election of officers and members as referred to in (g) (1) hereof. That portion shall be deemed to be suspended pending further consideration by the Federal Executive.

(k) That all affiliated unions seeking representation at this Special Conference shall conduct new elections in respect to its delegates within the framework of its rules, and subject to the conditions herein laid down, provided that any person who may have already been elected as a delegate shall be deemed to be eligible for nomination and re-election, provided that any union whose rules will not permit such election in time for the Special Conference shall be exempt from the provisions of this paragraph.

(l) Any union which has become disaffiliated with the Party during the last 12 months shall, upon application to reaffiliate, be admitted, subject to payment of arrears of affiliation dues, and shall then be deemed eligible for representation upon the Special Conference.

(m) Members appointed to the Central Executive as a result of the ballot conducted at the Special Conference referred to herein shall remain in office until the ordinary Annual Conference in 1956.

4 (a) That the Constitution covering ALP Industrial Groups as referred to on pages 101 and 102 of the current Constitution and Rules of the Victorian Branch shall be deemed to be non-existent after 31 December 1954.

(b) That it be agreed that this Executive shall submit a recommendation to the next Federal Conference in respect to the overall question of Industrial Groups organisation in Australia, having particular regard for its original purpose of combating Communism in the unions, and that pending a determination by Conference there shall be no recognition of this type of organisation by the Victorian Branch after 31 December 1954.

Date of Special Victorian Conference: That the Special Conference in Victoria commence at 10 a.m. on Saturday, 26 February 1955, and continue on Sunday, 27 February.

Personnel of Credential Committee: Mr J. Schmella, Acting Federal Secretary, and Mr F. E. Chamberlain, Vice-president, appointed as Credential Committee with Mr D. Lovegrove, Secretary of the Victorian Branch.

Date of Federal Conference: That Federal Conference now commence in Hobart on Monday, 14 March 1955.

Press Statements: That the Federal Executive of the Australian Labor Party views with concern the general lack of discipline which is having an adverse effect on the Labor Movement generally throughout Australia. We therefore call upon the Federal Parliamentary Labor Party, the State Branches, affiliated bodies and all members to refrain from any public comment or action related to the present dispute.

Section 3

Report of Convention and Credentials of Delegates to Special Conference of the Australian Labor Party—Victoria.
Convened by Direction of the Federal Executive—ALP.
At the Trades Hall—Melbourne, 26 and 27 February 1955.

1 Convention of Special Conference.
(a) On 8 December 1954, a circular to convene Special Conference was issued to affiliated unions by the State Secretary of the ALP, Victoria.

(Append 1)

(b) A notice for State Electoral Councils was published in the January issue of the official paper 'Labor' issued 19 December 1954, to a meeting of union and branch ALP representatives, and issued on 20 and 21 December to all affiliated unions and ALP branches. (January issue of 'Labor' was published prior to Christmas.) This issue of 'Labor' also contained the Federal Executive's decision concerning Victoria.

(Append 2)

2 Deferment of Special Conference by Victorian CE.
On 17 January 1955, a circular was issued to affiliated unions and ALP branches by the Victorian Executive advising:
(i) A motion adopted by the meeting of 19 December.
(ii) A motion adopted by the Central Executive on 22 December.
(iii) A motion deferring Special Conference, adopted by the Victorian Central Executive on 14 January.

(Append 3)

3 Convention of Annual Conference by Victorian CE.
(a) On 8 February, the Victorian Central Executive issued a circular to affiliated unions and ALP branches convening the Annual Conference of the ALP, Victoria, on 8 April 1955.

(Append 4)

(b) On 14 February the Victorian Central Executive issued a circular to affiliated unions and ALP branches advising, inter alia, that credentialling of delegates to the Special Conference on 26 February must be deferred until further notice, and delegates must be credentialled to the Annual Conference convened by the Central Executive for 8 April.

(Append 5)

4 Convention of Special Conference by Acting Federal Secretary.
(a) On 14 February the Acting Federal Secretary issued a circular to affiliated unions advising the Special Conference would be held on 26 and 27 February; requesting credentials by the 23rd; requesting particulars of Party membership or otherwise of all delegates; and advising decision of Federal Executive with reference to the Special Conference.

(Append 6a)

(b) On 14 February the Acting Federal Secretary advertised in the morning newspapers for nominations for State Electoral Council Delegates to the State Conference. Nominations to close with the Acting Federal

Secretary, Box 70, Trades Hall, Melbourne, at 11 a.m. on Saturday, 19 February. (Append 6b)

5 Legal Action Against Federal Executive ALP.

On 16 February Mr D. F. Woodhouse, a member of the Victorian Central Executive, served three members of the Federal Executive with notice of motion for an interlocutory injunction to restrain members of the Federal Executive from convening the Special Conference.

6. State Electoral Council Ballots Requested by Acting Federal Secretary.

On 21 February the Acting Federal Secretary advertised in the morning papers for State Electoral Councils, where necessary, to meet and elect delegates to Special Conference on or before 24 February.

(Append 7)

7 Supreme Court Proceedings.

On 21, 22, and 23 February the Victorian Supreme Court heard the case, and on 25 February handed down judgment.

8 State Electorate Council Ballot Repudiated by Victorian Central Executive.

On 26 February a morning newspaper reported that on the previous evening the Victorian Central Executive had declared that the Special Conference was not binding on any branch or affiliated union, and morning newspapers carried an advertisement by the Acting State Secretary of the ALP, Victoria, repudiating the method of selecting SEC delegates in the Acting Federal Secretary's advertisement of 21 February.

(Append 8)

9 Credentialling of Special Conference.

At 10 a.m. on 26 February the Credentials Committee of the Federal Executive comprising Messrs J. Schmella, Acting Federal Secretary, F. E. Chamberlain, Acting Federal President, D. Lovegrove, member of the Federal Executive, and J. M. Tripovich, co-opted to Credentials Committee, began to accept credentials on the following basis:

(a) Unions.

According to the Federal Executive decisions and according to the advice in a circular sent to affiliated unions by the Acting Federal Secretary.

This circular was made necessary by the refusal of the Victorian Central Executive to make records available to the Credentials Committee.

(Append 9)

(b) State Electorate Councils.

According to the Federal Executive decisions, with the following additional measures made necessary by the situation created by the Victorian Central Executive, as outlined in Clauses 2, 3, 5, 7, and 8 of this report.

The first two additional measures are related in Clause 4 (b) (Append 6b) and Clause 6. (Append 7)

The third measure was the use of Statutory Declarations where necessary for delegates to establish:

(a) Membership of ALP. (Append 10a)
(b) Authenticity of selection. (Append 10b)
(c) Non-membership of any political party or group opposed to the ALP. (Append 10c)

10 Representation at Special Conference.

Representation at Special Conference was as follows:

Fifty-three unions had 215 delegates.

Thirty-one SEC's had 34 delegates.

Total, 249 delegates.

Of the 249 delegates, 15 were non-members of the ALP from union delegations.

One hundred and forty-nine (149) delegates had attended the 1954 Annual Conference of the ALP, Victoria, and therefore had more than two years' membership of the ALP. Many other delegates had more than two years' membership but had not attended the 1954 Conference.

Seventy-six unions and 66 State Electorate Councils were eligible to be represented at Special Conference in terms of the Federal Executive's decision.

(a) Unions Represented.

Fifty-three unions represented were as follows:

Australian Workers' Union	Hairdressers
Bakers' Operatives	Liquor Trades
Bakers' Operatives (Bendigo)	Locomotive Enginemen
Blind Workers	Marine Stewards
Boilermakers (Melb. Banch)	Meat Industry Employees
Bootmakers	Timber Workers
Brick, Tile, and Pottery	Tramway Employees
Brushmakers	Tramway Employees (Geelong)
Cigarmakers	Transport Workers
Clothing Trades	Victorian Printers' Operatives
Cold Storage	Miscellaneous Workers
Coopers	Municipal Employees
Electrical Trades	Papermill Employees
Engine-drivers	Plasterers
Theatrical Employees	Plumbers
Tobacco Workers	Postal Technicians
Tramway Employees (Ballarat)	Posterhangers
Tramway Employees (Bendigo)	Printing Industry Employees
Engineers (Amalgamated)	Rubber Workers
Fibrous Plasterers	Sheet Metal and Agricultural
Fire Brigade Employees	Implement Makers
Flour Millers	Storemen and Packers
Food Preservers	Tanners and Leatherdressers
Fuel and Fodder	Textile Workers
Furnishing Trades	Vehicle Builders
Gas Workers	Waterside Workers
Glass Workers	Waterside Workers (Geelong)

(b) State Electorate Councils Represented.

Thirty-one State Electorate Councils represented were as follows:

Balwyn	Evelyn	Murray Valley
Ballarat South	Lowan	Portland
Dandenong	Mentone	Scoresby
Kara Kara	Mornington	Ballarat North
Malvern	Polwarth	Hampden
Moorabbin	Sandringham	Melbourne
Oakleigh	Brighton	Mildura
Rodney	Brunswick East	Northcote
Swanhill	Flemington	Prahran
Box Hill	Midlands	St Kilda
Benalla		

11 Credentials Rejected by the Credentials Committee.

The Credentials Committee rejected credentials from the Waterside Workers' Union, but Special Conference accepted the credentials after hearing correspondence and one of the credentialled delegates.

12 Nominations Rejected by the Credentials Committee.

The Credentials Committee rejected 113 nominations from 32 State Electorate Councils.

Conclusion.

This report is, to the best of our knowledge, an accurate account of credentialling of delegates to the Special Conference of the ALP Victoria convened by the Federal Executive ALP on 26 and 27 February at the Trades Hall, Melbourne.

> D. Lovegrove,
> *Member Federal Executive*
> *Credentials Committee.*
> J. M. Tripovich,
> *Co-opted Member Federal*
> *Executive Credentials*
> *Committee.*

The text of this report was obtained from the Parliamentary Library, Canberra, and is an extract from the official record of the 1955 Federal Conference.

Bibliography

H. S. Albinski, *Australian Policies and Attitudes Towards China*, Princeton University Press, 1965

Edward Barbor, *They Went Their Way*, Traralgon Journal and Record, 1960

Hillaire Belloc, *The Servile State*, numerous editions since 1912

Niall Brennan, *Dr Mannix*, Rigby, Adelaide, 1964

John Burton, *The Alternative, The Light Glows Brighter, Labor in Transition*, Morgan's Publications, Sydney, 1954, 1956 and 1957 respectively

F. E. Chamberlain, *A Selection of Talks and Articles*, Western Australian Branch of the ALP, 1964

J. B. Chifley, *Things Worth Fighting For*, (ed. A. W. Stargardt), Melbourne University Press, 1952

V. Gordon Childe, *How Labor Governs*, Labor Publishing Co., London 1923 and Melbourne University Press, 1964

Colin Clark, *Australian Hopes and Fears*, Hollis and Carter, London, 1958; *Property and Economic Progress*, Catholic Social Guild, Oxford, 1945; *The Advance to Social Security*, Melbourne University Press and Oxford University Press, 1943

L. F. Crisp, *Ben Chifley: A Biography*, Longmans, Melbourne, 1960

Allan Dalziel, *Evatt The Enigma*, Lansdowne Press, Melbourne, 1967

Paul Duffy, 'Catholic Judgments on the origins and growth of ALP Dispute 1954-61', unpublished thesis in University of Melbourne Library, 1968

H. V. Evatt, *Australian Labor Leader*, Angus and Robertson, Sydney, 1940

George Healey, ALP *The Story of the Labor Party*, Jacaranda Press, Brisbane, 1955

Colin A. Hughes and B. D. Graham, *A Handbook of Australian Government and Politics*, Australian National University Press, Canberra, 1968

Race Mathews (ed.), *Socialist Songs*, Victorian Fabian Society, Melbourne, 1962

Henry Mayer, *Catholics and the Free Society*, Cheshire, Melbourne, 1960

Clem Lack (ed.), *Three Decades of Queensland Political History 1929-1960*, Queensland Government Printer, Brisbane, 1962

P. J. O'Farrell, *The Catholic Church in Australia*, Nelson, Melbourne, 1968

Louise Overacker, *Australian Parties in a Changing Society 1954-67*, Cheshire, Melbourne, 1968

D. W. Rawson, *Australia Votes—The 1958 Election*, Melbourne University Press, 1961

Hans Rogger and Eugen Weber (eds), *The European Right*, University of California Press, 1966

B. A. Santamaria, *The Price of Freedom*, Campion Press, Melbourne, 1964; *The Earth Our Mother*, Araluen Publishing Co., 1945

Tom Truman, *Catholic Action and Politics*, Georgian House, Melbourne, 1959

Leicester Webb, *Communism and Democracy in Australia*, Cheshire, Melbourne, 1954

Index